A *Gertrude Stein*
Companion

Gertrude Stein, 1963. Photograph by Carl Van Vechten, 1963, of a painting by
Richard Banks, 1963, of a photograph by Carl Van Vechten, 1934.

A *Gertrude Stein*
Companion
content with the example

EDITED BY Bruce Kellner

Greenwood Press

NEW YORK • WESTPORT, CONNECTICUT • LONDON

Library of Congress Cataloging-in-Publication Data

A Gertrude Stein companion : content with the example / edited by
  Bruce Kellner.
        p.   cm.
    Bibliography: p.
    Includes index.
    ISBN 0–313–25078–2 (lib. bdg. : alk. paper)
    1. Stein, Gertrude, 1874–1946.   2. Authors, American—20th
century—Biography.   I. Kellner, Bruce.
PS3537.T323Z6153   1988
818'.5209—dc19
[B]   88–3126

British Library Cataloguing in Publication Data is available.

Library of Congress Catalog Card Number: 88–3126
ISBN: 0–313–25078–2

First published in 1988

Greenwood Press, Inc.
88 Post Road West, Westport, Connecticut   06881

Printed in the United States of America

The paper used in this book complies with the
Permanent Paper Standard issued by the National
Information Standards Organization (Z39.48–1984).

10   9   8   7   6   5   4   3   2   1

Copyright Acknowledgments

The editor and publisher gratefully acknowledge permission to use the following:

''Reading the Hand Writing: The Manuscripts of Gertrude Stein,'' by Ulla Dydo, (c) 1987 Ulla
E. Dydo.

Excerpts from *The Flowers of Friendship: Letters Written to Gertrude Stein,* edited by Donald C.
Gallup, copyright Alfred A. Knopf, Inc.

Excerpts from *Everybody's Autobiography, The Geographical History of America, Lectures in
America, Selected Writings of Gertrude Stein* and *The Autobiography of Alice B. Toklas,*
copyright Random House, Inc.

Excerpts from ''Four in America'' (1947), ''Two'' (1951), ''Mrs Reynolds'' (1952), ''Bee Time
Vine'' (1953), ''As Fine as Melanctha'' (1954), ''Painted Lace'' (1955), ''Stanzas in
Meditation'' (1956), ''Alphabets and Birthdays'' (1957), ''A Novel of Thank You'' (1958),
copyright Yale University Press.

''Or as Gertrude Stein Says'' by Vassar Miller. Copyright (c) 1962 by Vassar Miller. Reprinted
from *My Bones Being Wiser* by permission of Wesleyan University Press.

A book naturally explains what has been the result of investigation. . . .

A book has been carefully prepared together. . . .

A book more than ever needed.

A book made to order and the only thing that was forgotten in ordering was what no one objects to. Can it easily be understood. It can and will. . . .

—Gertrude Stein,
Descriptions of Literature, 1924

How pleasantly I feel contented with that. Contented with the example, content with the example.

—Gertrude Stein
An Elucidation, 1923

CONTENTS

ILLUSTRATIONS

ACKNOWLEDGMENTS

I am grateful to my contributors for their valuable essays, poems, and biographical studies, and I am additionally grateful to earlier readers of Gertrude Stein's life and writings on whose work of wider range several of us relied. For over two years, the staff members of the Helen Ganser Library, at Millersville University where I teach, traced a remarkable number of obscure references on slender evidence, and they assisted me in many other ways as well—always with good humor and interest in the project. Other libraries deserve acknowledgment also: the Beinecke Rare Book and Manuscript Library at Yale University, which shelters Gertrude Stein's abundant archive; the Manuscript and Archives Division of the New York Public Library; the Bodleian Library at Oxford University; the Library of Congress.

For permission to quote from the published and unpublished writings of Gertrude Stein, I am grateful to Calman A. Levin, representing the Estate of Gertrude Stein, and to the Collection of American Literature in the Beinecke Library at Yale University; for permission to quote from material under their copyright, I am grateful to Alfred A. Knopf, Random House, Yale University Press, and Joella Swope. Shirley Anders's poem first appeared in *Michigan Quarterly Review*, October 1986; Lindley Williams Hubbell's poem in *Pagany*, April 1930; Vassar Miller's poem in *My Bones Being Wiser*, 1963; and Tom Smith's poem in *Virginia Quarterly Review*, spring 1959.

For permission to reproduce illustrations, I am grateful to Joseph Solomon, representing the Estate of Carl Van Vechten; Calman A. Levin, representing the Estate of Gertrude Stein; the Collection of American Literature in the Beinecke Rare Book and Manuscript Library at Yale University; the Santa Fe Opera; Diana Barton Franz; and Tom Hachtman. Other illustrations are reproduced by permission from an anonymous private collection.

For many favors of many kinds, I am indebted to many people: the late Arden Andreas, Donald Angus, Desmond Arthur, Lisa Browar, Edward Burns, Claudia Campbell, Ulla Dydo, Kathy Everett, Judy Forster, Donald Gallup, Ray Hacker, Mary Jean Irion, Steve Jones, Kate Kellner, Richard Kirby, Evelyn Lyons, the late George McCue, Cindy Maxon, Kathryn Moran, Priscilla Oppenheimer, Sue Rohrer, Richard Rutledge, Leo Shelley, Connie Simon, and Joseph Solomon. Many thanks to Thomas Pappas, of inestimable help in abstracting materials in preparation for the annotated bibliography. Thanks, too, to Marilyn Brownstein, Juanita Lewis, and Penny Sippel, my patient and tolerant editors. Thanks, finally, to Hans Kellner who compiled the preliminary bibliography, verified references, and proofread my work. For ten years he has assisted me loyally and carefully, and I am in his permanent debt.

And I want to acknowledge a now-forgotten but far-sighted library staff at Southwest High School in Kansas City, Missouri, that introduced me to *Selected Writings of Gertrude Stein* when I was sixteen, just three months after Gertrude Stein's death, over forty years ago; I want to acknowledge Carl Van Vechten, editor of that book, whose friendship and persistence taught me "How to Read Gertrude Stein," as he had titled his own first essay about her work; I want to acknowledge Alice Toklas, for her encouraging letters and for a memorable afternoon at 5 rue Christine, in 1962, that surely added to this book's already growing impetus.

ABBREVIATIONS

Many of these abbreviations for Gertrude Stein's published books were established by Richard Bridgman for his *Gertrude Stein in Pieces* (1970), and they would be difficult to improve upon. With only a few exceptions, all subsequent Stein scholarship has employed them. The following list, all detailed in Part I of this *Gertrude Stein Companion*, includes his abbreviations as well as one for ephemera and for works published after Bridgman's book.

ABT	*The Autobiography of Alice B. Toklas*
A&B	*Alphabets and Birthdays*
AFAM	*As Fine as Melanctha*
BFF	*Before the Flowers of Friendship Faded Friendship Faded*
B&W	*Brewsie and Willie*
BDRF	*Blood on the Dining-Room Floor*
BTV	*Bee Time Vine*
CAE	*Composition as Explanation*
EA	*Everybody's Autobiography*
EPH	ephemera
FIA	*Four in America*
FS3A	*Four Saints in Three Acts*
G&P	*Geography and Plays*
GHA	*The Geographical History of America*
GSFR	*The Gertrude Stein First Reader*
HTW	*How to Write*
HWW	*How Writing Is Written*
IDA	*Ida*
LCA	*Lucy Church Amiably*
LIA	*Lectures in America*

LO&P	Last Operas and Plays
MOA	The Making of Americans
MPG	Matisse Picasso and Gertrude Stein
MR	Mrs. Reynolds
NAR	Narration
NOTY	A Novel of Thank You
O&P	Operas and Plays
PF	Paris France
PGU	A Primer for the Gradual Understanding of Gertrude Stein
PIC	Picasso
PL	Painted Lace
P&P	Portraits and Prayers
QED	Fernhurst, Q.E.D., and Other Early Writings
RAB	Reflection on the Atomic Bomb
RAD	Gertrude Stein: Form and Intelligibility: The Radcliffe Themes
SIM	Stanzas in Meditation
SW	Selected Writings of Gertrude Stein, 1946, 1962
TB	Tender Buttons
TL	Three Lives
TWO	Two: Gertrude Stein and Her Brother
TWR	The World Is Round
UK	Useful Knowledge
WAM	What Are Masterpieces
WIHS	Wars I Have Seen
W&L	Writings and Lectures 1909–1945
YGS	The Yale Gertrude Stein

In preparing any substantial reference work, editors inevitably transform the published scholarship of others into "standard reference sources." This book calls so often on a number of such works that they have been assigned abbreviations in the spirit of those already widely in use and listed alphabetically with them below. Full publication information is included in the bibliography of works cited and consulted. Abbreviations and dates, or authors or editors with short titles and dates, accompany individual entries for further reference. Different editions of the same title are distinguished from each other by date.

AAUB	American Authors and Books, eds. W. J. Burke and Will D. Howe, 1972
ABTC	The Alice B. Toklas Cook Book, 1954

AWW	*American Women Writers*, ed. Linda Mainiero, 1979
BABT	Linda Simon, *The Biography of Alice B. Toklas*, 1977
CA	*Contemporary Authors*, 1967–1980
CB	*Current Biography*, 1940, 1945, 1951, 1954, 1980
CC	James R. Mellow, *Charmed Circle: Gertrude Stein & Company*, 1974, 1975
CHAL	*Cambridge History of American Literature*, 1945
DAB	*Dictionary of American Biography*, 1928–1937
DLB	*Dictionary of Literary Biography*, 1978–1986
EE	Mabel Dodge Luhan, *European Experiences*, 1935
FAP	*Four Americans in Paris*, 1970
FF	*The Flowers of Friendship: Letters Written to Gertrude Stein*, ed. Donald Gallup, 1953
GSB	Donald Sutherland, *Gertrude Stein: A Biography of Her Work*, 1951
GSBIB	Robert A. Wilson, *Gertrude Stein: A Bibliography of Her Work*, 1974
GSCP	*Gertrude Stein: A Composite Portrait*, ed. Linda Simon, 1974
GSCVV	*The Letters of Gertrude Stein and Carl Van Vechten 1913–1946*, ed. Edward Burns, 1986
GSP	Richard Bridgman, *Gertrude Stein in Pieces*, 1970
GSRG	*Gertrude Stein and Alice B. Toklas: A Reference Guide*, ed. Ray Lewis White, 1984
JS	Leo Stein, *Journey into the Self*, 1950
LVV	*Letters of Carl Van Vechten*, ed. Bruce Kellner, 1987
MS	Mabel Dodge Luhan, *Movers and Shakers*, 1936
NAW	*Notable American Women 1607–1950*, ed. Edward T. James et al.; *Notable American Women: The Modern Period*, Barbara Sicherman et al., 1971, 1980
OXCAL	James D. Hart, *Oxford Companion to American Literature*, 1965
NYT	*The New York Times*, 1913–1986
SAGS	*Sherwood Anderson/Gertrude Stein: Correspondence and Personal Essays*, ed. Ray Lewis White, 1972
SOA	*Staying on Alone: Letters of Alice B. Toklas*, ed. Edward Burns, 1973
TCA	*Twentieth Century Authors*, ed. Stanley Kunitz and Howard Haycraft, 1940, 1955
VT	Virgil Thomson, *Virgil Thomson*, 1966
WIR	Alice B. Toklas, *What Is Remembered*, 1963
WWA	*Who's Who in America*, 1930–1981
WWAA	*Who Was Who in American Art*, 1984
WWW	*Who Was Who in America*, 1943–1968

WWNA　　　*Who Was Who Among North American Authors*, 1976

YCAL　　　*Collection of American Literature*, Beinecke Rare Book and Manuscript
　　　　　　Library, Yale University

　　Sources are cited in the text, or they are cited in parentheses with page numbers.
Where more than one passage in sequence derives from a single source, page
references are cited only once after the source has been identified. Unabbreviated
sources are identified in the text by author; they are identified in references by
author, short title, and date; to clarify various editions of Gertrude Stein's books
as well as of sources, references include dates after abbreviations. The single
bibliography of Works Consulted and Cited is inclusive of all contributions and
sections.

INTRODUCTION Bruce Kellner

How to Read Gertrude Stein

How-to-do-it manuals usually claim to guarantee practical salvation in times of secular despair: how to tune up an engine, how to rewire a house, how to fill out an IRS form, how to write. Gertrude Stein wrote one too—at least she titled it *How to Write*†—but nobody paid much attention when it came out in 1931, at which time she may have been the best known unread writer in American literature. She was not then and she is not now easily accessible, and offering up a "how to read her" manual suggests a defense this *Gertrude Stein Companion* does not intend. It is, instead, designed to introduce the novice to her work and the somewhat conversant reader to a variety of sources for approaching it. The material devoted to her writing is not designed for the Stein specialist but as an impetus for the student who wishes to travel in that direction. Similarly, the biographical entries, covering the enormous range of fascinating people who played larger or smaller roles in Gertrude Stein's life, and the selection of brief passages from her published work, may also encourage the student's subsequent attention to one of the most arresting personalities and unique artists in the history of American letters.

This *Gertrude Stein Companion* offers various evidences of her achievement and, through others, some assistance in approaching her work.

Part I is an annotated library of Gertrude Stein's published writing. Alphabetically arranged, it offers content summaries, rather like dust jacket blurbs, but is designed to inform readers rather than persuade them to purchase. As Stein's work was frequently published long after she had written it, each entry indicates inclusive dates, thereby making it possible for readers to approach her work by chronology of composition rather than chronology of publication. Each entry accounts for first publication and reprint information as well. Throughout this *companion*, titles appearing in each entry for the first time are followed by a dagger [†].

Part II begins with three essays, each by a distinguished Stein scholar. Like this introduction, each essay might be titled "How to Read Gertrude Stein," although each offers a highly individual approach to the work. Marianne

DeKoven places Stein in literary tradition by assessing her wide range in variance from it. Ulla Dydo examines Stein's process of composition, simultaneously calculated and spontaneous from notebook to manuscript to typescript. Marjorie Perloff offers an uncommonly practical guide to a number of demanding styles in Stein's work. All three essays avoid the dangerous practice of categorizing Stein by genre, demonstrating instead that in every case her writing evolves and identifies its own genres. Part II concludes with a selection of poems motivated by the character and work of Gertrude Stein. Each is unique and, moreover, valuable as literary criticism, putting to splendid use Gertrude Stein's only tool, the language itself. Aside from Gertrude Stein's own work, the poems are the only material in this book not prepared exclusively for it. All were published relatively obscurely, or, until now, were generally unavailable. Like the essays they follow, they too might each be titled "How to Read Gertrude Stein."

Part III could serve as an annotated, alphabetical arrangement of all of Gertrude Stein's address books. Generally, this directory of her associates concentrates on its subjects during the period of her own life, deliberately truncating early and later events, activities, and accomplishments, although accounting for them in summary. On occasion, available information determined the amount of space allotted to subjects; however, their relative importance to Gertrude Stein was influential as well. Conversely, many subjects of whom full-length biographies are readily available have not been given untoward attention at the expense of lesser figures who were also important in Gertrude Stein's life. Nearly all of the people who appear in her work are included in one way or another. Most subjects are identified according to the names by which they were best known and generally recognized. Surnames are followed by given names (unfamiliar or unused names appearing in brackets, maiden or married or actual rather than pseudonymous), or by nicknames or stage names that were used exclusively, when appropriate; finally, again when appropriate, full names that differ from familiar ones follow in brackets. Thus: Atherton, Gertrude [Franklin Horn]; Balthus [Balthasar Klossowski de Rola]; Brooks, [Beatrice] Romaine [Goddard]; Toklas, Alice B[abette]. Subjects recognizable by different names through their varying times of association with Gertrude Stein—for example, May Bookstaver who became Mrs. Charles Knoblauch, or Mabel Ganson Evans Dodge Sterne Luhan—are cross-referenced in the index. Birth and death dates are as complete as extant records have allowed, within the limitations of the compilers' research. Subjects' works are included if they bear some relevance to Gertrude Stein and her circle. Each entry concludes with its sources, listed chronologically in order of publication. Published sources are offered in abbreviated form, including author or editor, short title, and date, or an abbreviation (from a list of abbreviations printed before these notes), and date. Following them, manuscript and oral sources are listed. Throughout this *Companion*, names appearing in each entry for the first time are followed by an asterisk [*], except the names of Gertrude Stein and Alice Toklas as they appear in virtually every entry.

Part IV, titled "Gertrude Stein's ABC," culls her observations on a variety of subjects, from "accuracy" to "zero," by way of "grammar," "knowledge," "roses," and "Gertrude Stein" herself.

Part V is an annotated bibliography of major Stein criticism, limited primarily, however, to full-length books.

Part VI is a list of Works Consulted or Cited. Since different contributors used different editions of the same work, original publications and reprints are both included, as applicable.

An index to a book organized on alphabetical principles is not, in the present instance, redundant, since many figures and titles are referred to regularly and frequently throughout in subject entries other than their own. Through the index, readers may trace ancillary information about subjects of interest to them; furthermore, not every person connected with Gertrude Stein warrants a separate entry, nor are any individual titles from collections given separate entries. The index indicates where many of them are discussed.

Throughout, in quotations from secondary sources, I have silently corrected errors in spelling, punctuation, and typography. I have not altered anything whatever in quotations from the writings of Gertrude Stein and Alice Toklas, although all titles—many of which appear variously capitalized in their own work—have been conventionally capitalized.

During the forty years since Gertrude Stein's death, about two dozen full-length critical studies of her work have been published, and her list of advocates and allies is distinguished; so we are well past the period when it was easy to ignore her out of bewilderment. Gertrude Stein can be bewildering, but she was no fraud, and the several nicknames she endured in the twenties and thirties— "The Mother Goose of Montparnasse," "The Mama of Dada," "The Enigma in the Woodpile"—were not funny then and they are not funny now, even though vines out of reach often bear sour grapes, and foxy academics continue to savage her out of print and in the classroom, not knowing otherwise "how to do it."

We are all more comfortable with what we can readily grasp, and we grow suspicious when it turns out not to be more of the same. "What's that?" we cried in horror as children, staring at our dinner plates; "what's that?" we hesitate to say now, staring at unidentified flying objects. So it is not surprising that "A repulsive monster, a wounded, tail-lashing serpent, dealing wild and furious blows as it stiffens into its death agony" refers not to some Steinian effrontery but to Beethoven's Second Symphony, according to one critic after its premiere in 1802 (Gilman 8). Sixty years later, Ibsen's *Ghosts* was denounced as "An open drain, a loathesome sore unbandaged, a dirty act done in public" (Block and Shedd 67). And in 1913—just a year before Gertrude Stein published *Tender Buttons*, a piece of dissociative rhetoric over half a century before the deconstructionists came along—Marcel Duchamp's* *Nude Descending a Staircase* was popularly described as "an explosion in a shingle factory" (*CC* 171). Times change: Beethoven's symphony is a tuneful favorite in concert halls; Ibsen's *Ghosts* has joined required reading lists in some high school classrooms; and we have seen enough multiple-exposure photographs to recognize Duchamp's *Nude Descending a Staircase* as a nude descending a staircase.

Of course there is an oversimplifying danger in lumping the arts together. "Lots of people are willing to admit that they don't understand painting or music," W. H. Auden observed, "but very few indeed who have been to school and learned to read advertisements will admit they don't understand English" (15). That may be why we are even more resistant to unknown lands when our travel there demands we follow maps in unknown tongues: James Joyce's Dublin in *Ulysses* for instance, although Gertrude Stein—who shared nothing whatever with Joyce nor with any of her contemporaries—takes us into territory uncharted and unchartered elsewhere, guaranteed to put us off our course. It is not avant-garde; that overworked epithet for anything new presupposes something of which it is in advance. Gertrude Stein is only and always in advance of herself:

> No one is ahead of his time, it is only that the particular variety of creating his time is the one that his contemporaries who also are creating their own time refuse to accept. . . . That is the reason why the creator of the new composition in the arts is an outlaw until he is a classic, there is hardly a moment in between. (*WAM* 27)

Now, forty years after her death, Gertrude Stein has become a "classic," by her own definition anyhow; much of her work is back in print, although her name was rarely mentioned in the college classroom forty or thirty or even twenty years ago. Now she has begun to turn up in American literature anthologies, and the Library of American Literature, that formidable, uniform edition coming out a few books at a time to represent our pensioners on Parnassus, in sturdy bindings and printed on paper guaranteed to last three hundred years, has scheduled a Stein volume.

This latter-day activity has not always served Gertrude Stein well. Anthology selections too often amount to one excerpt from *Three Lives*,† printed solus or with a chapter from *The Autobiography of Alice B. Toklas*† or a chorus from *Four Saints in Three Acts*† or a few selections from *Tender Buttons*. They may do more harm than good. *Three Lives* bears little resemblance to anything else she wrote, character studies of servant-class women in turn-of-the-century Baltimore; *The Autobiography of Alice B. Toklas*, dashed off in part perhaps as a stunt to make money, she wrote in deliberate imitation of Alice Toklas's own acerbic speech pattern; *Four Saints in Three Acts* emerged for success from the huge stack of her unpublished manuscripts only because Virgil Thomson* turned it into a quirky opera; and selections from *Tender Buttons* do not represent the niftily progressive structure of that exhibition of verbal cubism. Piecemeal her work loses its authority. Out of sequence it resists penetration. Smugly cataloged in the century's chronology of writers, she is not comfortable preceding or following others in the literary hierarchy, nor are they at ease so oddly partnered. Because so much of her work is private, trying to identify it by genre encourages expectations it will not fulfill; with or without pronouns, it was all first person singular, genuinely singular.

How, then, to read Gertrude Stein? Read Gertrude Stein chronologically if at all, and if serious about reading her at all, read all of her, all daunting nine thousand pages of her at a conservative estimate, and in the process be prepared for impatience and somnolence and defeat, perpetrated and even encouraged by her numbing persistence of what she called "the daily miracle" (*PF* 3), written for herself and strangers, she declared early on (*MOA* 289). She pursued her aims with such conviction—her successive discoveries about what language might do once beyond the borders of all known maps—that we are likely to despair as the world did when it was still flat: "Here There Be Dragons."

There is a reasonable route through her work, however, with remarkable views along the way, although the landscape is as foreign as Oz, and although at journey's end "there is no there there," as she said on returning to Oakland, California, where she had spent her youth (*ER* 289). The concluding vista is less than satisfactory. So is this answer; so is Gertrude Stein's own answer. Just before she died she said, "What is the question," and when none came she continued, "If there is no question then there is no answer" (*SOA* 276). That does not underestimate what she found in the forty years she meditated on language and identity and time, and in communicating to herself all she had learned on safari toward a "there" as strange as space.

For Gertrude Stein, an awareness of audience could only weaken the authenticity of art, the contradiction she saw between human nature and the human mind always a danger in the creative act: human nature was a longing for approval from those "strangers" she had early on tried to reject, and it could lead in literature only to an awareness of self; the human mind avoided that danger, though it could become its own audience, another danger, for in the moment of making, of writing—and that moment was measured by no clock but by sustained concentration—the self had to be excluded as well. "Audience has no connection with identity. Identity has no connection with a universe. A universe has no connection with human nature," she told readers after her American lecture tour in the mid-thirties (*GHA* 157). "I am not I any longer when I see" (*FIA* 119), she admonished herself, especially after fame came and stayed until her death, and for all the wrong reasons.

In the thirties, B. F. Skinner suggested that Gertrude Stein was engaged in a series of exercises in automatic writing, since she had experimented in such activity as an outgrowth of her work in psychology with Hugo Münsterberg* and William James* at Harvard. In the fifties, Donald Sutherland* declared— in the first serious study of her work—that it was purely intellectual, devoid of autobiography, fresh fodder for the new criticism. Both missed the mark. Gertrude Stein said writing was always an entirely conscious act for her, and her manuscripts and notebooks in the Beinecke Library at Yale University offer more than ample evidence of her working methods to convince Skinner that nothing was ever "automatic." Just as insistently she said the normal mind was far more intriguing than the abnormal one since it was, after all, normal: hers, ours. Similarly, Sutherland asked the wrong question or rather avoided the right answer, for all of Gertrude Stein's work is autobiographical; the life's work is the life, including everything from her college themes to her last will and testament. She was as much the indecisive Saint Therese in her *Four Saints in Three Acts* as she was the literary lion eager to be hunted when celebrity finally came, admonishing us to "Think of the Bible and Homer think of Shakespeare and think of me" (*GHA* 117), and she wasn't kidding. She was as much the authoritative lecturer in crew cut and common sense as she was the vulnerable spouse requiring perpetual encouragement, physical as well as emotional, sexual as well as intellectual, from Alice Toklas. It all spilled over into her writing as inevitably as the redundancies and the silences in her most hermetic metronomics. Reading Gertrude Stein's work is no excuse to explicate it through her private life, although the reverse may be possible. The life and the work are so inextricably bound that they are in effect interchangeable, and as life moves chronologically, so does her work move successively through its stumblings and stridings, asseverations and doubts, successes and failures. In Gertrude Stein's protean output, almost any title will demonstrate the writer in the writing, so long as it is not read in isolation, so long as we do not expect "more of the same" each time, and so long as we are willing to let her follow her own calendar—from a sentence like this:

> In some kinds of women resisting is not a feeling of themselves to themselves inside them (*MOA* 118),

to a sentence like this:

> If the red is rose and there is a gate surrounding it, if inside is let in and their places change then certainly something is upright (*TB* 13),

to a sentence like this:

> As to be all of it as to be a wife as a wife has a cow, a love story, all of it as to be all of it as a wife all of it as to be as a wife has a cow a love story, all of it as a wife has a cow as a wife has a cow a love story (*SW* 481),

to a sentence like this:

> I am I because my little dog knows me, but perhaps he does not and if he did I would not be I (*WAM* 75),

to sentences like this:

> We cannot retrace our steps, going forward may be the same as going backwards. . . . Life is strife, I was a martyr all my life not to what I won but to what was done. (*LO&P* 87–88)

Written chronologically, several years apart, those passages are obviously distinct from one another, but all are autobiographical, from the erotic one about a vaginal orgasm to the one that Richard Bridgman assessed, in *Gertrude Stein in Pieces*, as the "bleak sum of mother's wisdom" (345), and perhaps it makes little difference which is which.

For a number of reasons it has never been easy to read Gertrude Stein chronologically, not that those passages illuminate anything out of context. Then, about twenty years ago, Bridgman brought all the work—before then erratically and inconsistently arranged for publication—into chronological order to demonstrate that it was all of a piece "in pieces," aesthetically and autobiographically, thereby contradicting earlier readers and Gertrude Stein herself. Until then, neither she nor her editors had done her good service. After an initial publication, *Three Lives*, which she financed in 1909, and *Tender Buttons*, the little book of cubist pieces issued in 1914, four of seven substantial volumes—issued prior to *The Autobiography of Alice B. Toklas* twenty years later—were published out of chronological sequence; two of the others were full-length novels, and those four contained shorter and longer pieces deliberately wrenched out of chronology but not, apparently, for thematic organization. To read her out of sequence, or to read her publication by publication, disguises the preoccupying eroticism in much of her work, but more significantly it ignores a natural progression from one effort to another. If it could be done why do it, she often told herself, and having demonstrated to herself that it could be done she moved ahead. One would never know that from her unpublished writings, edited by her old friend Carl Van Vechten* and issued posthumously in eight handsome volumes by the Yale University Press: the first was made up of early word portraits dating to about 1910, but the second was a novel written in the early forties; the last one issued was a novel written mid-career; and four of the five others were grab bags covering from fifteen- to twenty-five-year periods, organized out of chronological sequence, sometimes identified by genres that do not always apply, sometimes just titled by quantity: "Short Pieces," "Shorter Pieces," "Shortest Pieces" (*AFAM* v). Published over an eight-year period as well as out of order, they were guaranteed to obfuscate the work and perhaps to protect Alice Toklas. Similarly, Van Vechten's *Selected Writings of Gertrude Stein*,† preceding the Yale edition by five years, was organized—or, rather, disorganized—by genre. His anthology is probably the best introduction to Gertrude Stein but it offers little assistance in "how to read Gertrude Stein."

She put tags on her work too, from time to time, but they do not help either. Her own how-to-do-it manual to which I referred earlier, *How to Write*, tells us that "A Sentence is not emotional a paragraph is" (23), but its nearly four hundred pages offer no practical instruction and little impractical pleasure. As genre, *Four Saints in Three Acts* is called "an opera to be sung," but it has twenty-seven saints and five acts, and Virgil Thomson decided which saint was saying what when he set it to music because Gertrude Stein had neglected to assign many of the speeches to individual characters. The pieces in *Tender Buttons* usually get called "poems," probably because of their brevity, but they follow no discernible form—traditional or organic—and most of them are printed margin to margin in short paragraphs, and one of them is three words long and another one is fifteen pages long. She wrote a mystery story called *Blood on the Dining-Room Floor*,† but we never find out who got murdered and we never find out whodunit. *Brewsie and Willie*,† her novel about GIs in Paris after World War II, she wrote largely in dialogue. *A Novel of Thank You*† has three hundred chapters and endless names but no characters who do anything or say anything. Nothing happens in her operas and plays, chapter numbers in her stories get repeated, words in a circle make a poem, and her attempts to explain herself are just as eccentric. Here is a passage from *An Elucidation*, her first foray at going public, but several syntactical games get played simultaneously and the explanation becomes itself a direct example—a superb one:

> To begin elucidating.
> If I say I stand and pray.
> If I say I stand and I stand and you understand and if I say I pray I pray to-day if you understand me to say I pray to-day you understand prayers and portraits.
> You understand portraits and prayers.
> You understand.
> You do understand.
> An introduction and an explanation and I completely introduce as you please.
> I completely introduce. Yes you do.
> Yes you do.
> Yes you do is the longest example and will come at the end.
> The longest example.
> Yes you do.
> Will come at the end. (*P&P* 249)

Clearly, then, genre won't do it; but chronology may let us trace those steps Gertrude Stein said she could not retrace. "My writing is clear as mud," she admitted, adding, "but mud settles and clear streams run on and disappear" (*EA* 123), a sensible observation, provided we remember that streams always run in one direction, forward, not from beginning to end but from source to sea.

The chronology itself is easy enough to chart, and in *A Gertrude Stein Companion*, "STEIN, GERTRUDE, 3 February 1874–27 July 1946 (writer)" would not be untoward among its biographical entries. She was born in Allegheny, Pennsylvania, into a prosperous, slipshod family: a vague mother, Amelia;* an erratic father, Daniel;* two brilliant older siblings, Michael* and Leo;* and a couple of dull-witted ones, Simon* and Bertha.* Their influence—or lack of it—on Gertrude Stein is spelled out in their biographical entries, true of others as well who came into her life, rather than in this account of her work's life, once it began. Gertrude and Leo were conceived only to replace two other children who had died, perhaps at birth since they do not seem to have been named. Gertrude and Leo were inseparable for thirty years, as youngsters in France and Austria, as teenagers in California, as students at Harvard, and as young adults sharing quarters in Baltimore, London, and finally Paris. She and her brother were apart only during the period she studied medicine at Johns Hopkins, on the strong recommendation of William James that she prepare for a career in psychology. Even then she spent her holidays with Leo, traveling around the continent. Gertrude Stein did not complete her medical degree, in part because of her distaste for obstetrics, and in part because of the breakup of a grim love affair. In 1903 she joined Leo at 27 rue de Fleurus and set about two careers that occupied and preoccupied her for the rest of her life.

First the minor one: She began to collect contemporary painting, influenced surely by Leo but shortly developing her own fresh eye and sound judgment, though her only explanation ever was that she liked to look at it. During the early years, the walls of 27 rue de Fleurus held a great deal of Cézanne and Picasso,* also Matisse,* Rouault, and Braque,* as well as the earlier Renoir, Toulouse-Lautrec, Van Gogh, Gauguin, Delacroix, Daumier, El Greco, and surely others whose work did not survive them. Later, when she and her brother had separated, Gertrude Stein concentrated on her intimate friends, Picasso and Juan Gris*; briefly during the twenties on the young neoromanticists; and in the thirties, probably his only collector, on Sir Francis Rose.* From the beginning, the pictures hung floor to ceiling, many of them unframed and most of them unremarked by the academies. Everybody went to look—first at 27 rue de Fleurus and then, when she moved in 1938, to 5 rue Christine—from Bernard Berenson,* the art-collecting Cone* sisters of Baltimore, and some of the painters themselves before World War I, to most of what Gertrude Stein labeled (though she did not invent the title) the Lost Generation of the twenties; to the GIs of the forties.

But Gertrude Stein's major occupation was writing, first a conventional, naturalistic novel titled *Q.E.D.*†—*quod erat demonstrandum*—amazing for its time and unpublished for half a century, a recounting of her bitter involvement in a lesbian triangular love affair she suffered while she was in medical school. Like her other major titles, *Q.E.D.* is sufficiently valuable in her development to warrant serious attention among the "Ex Libris" entries in this *Gertrude Stein Companion*. She wrote *Three Lives* after she had already begun some work on a far more ambitious project, *The Making of Americans*,† a nearly thousand-page novel in its printed form, detailing the history of two families—clearly her own forebears—during a decade's composition in which she began to probe connections between people, categories, behaviors, many of them irrelevant to the meandering plot, autobiographical meditations that included her confessions of frustrations and achievements, tense, dogged, repetitious, as inexorable as plaque. Gertrude Stein considered it her major achievement. During this period there were powerful influences at work on her writing: positively, the cubist abstractions of Picasso; negatively, the defection of Gertrude Stein's brother Leo. That remarkably perceptive eye was unable to follow Picasso forward to his startling *Demoiselles d'Avignon*, and perhaps it is significant that Picasso's famous portrait of Gertrude Stein marks the change. He had been working on a fairly realistic likeness for months, as realistic as the stories in *Three Lives*; then, after a hot Spanish summer and exposure to some powerful African artifacts, he painted out the face and replaced it with the brooding angularity so clearly foreshadowing his following work—and hers. Nor could Leo Stein tolerate those hundreds of pages of his sister's seeming nonsense. While *The Making of Americans* was still in progress, bewildering enough on its own, she had begun to write a series of word portraits of people she knew or encountered, and either just before or just afterward came stupefying locutions like this:

> If he heard all he heard and he did hear all he did hear, if he heard all he heard and he said all he said he would not hear what he had heard when he had said what he said and he had heard what he heard and he had said what he had said and he did say what he said and he heard what he said and he had said everything and he did say everything and he was feeling all the beginning of saying everything being existing. (*TWO* 84)

"Disillusionment in living is finding that no one can really ever be agreeing with you completely in anything," Gertrude Stein wrote in *The Making of Americans* (483), only to find the observation contradicted by the advent in her life—no other word is so appropriate as advent, something not only momentous but holy—of Alice B. Toklas.

The Stein-Toklas alliance, rooted in eternity, was so complete a literary and emotional symbiosis that the work is forged from both their lives, beginning with Gertrude Stein's portrait "Ada," in which Alice Toklas is "Ada" and Gertrude Stein is "some one," in an interchange of "living" and "loving" and "telling." It begins with a fairly straightforward recounting of Alice Toklas's early life, but it rhapsodizes in conclusion:

> Trembling was all living, living was all loving, some one was then the other one. Certainly this one was loving this Ada then. And certainly Ada all her living then was happier in living than any one else who ever could, who was, who is, who ever will be living. (*G&P* 16)

In the fall of 1910, Alice Toklas moved to 27 rue de Fleurus, apparently with Leo Stein's endorsement, although he and his sister were already estranged by that time. He moved permanently to Italy in 1912; he wrote once or twice, but she never replied.

Relationships rarely shift instantly, either in life or on the written page, but coincident with the latter part of *The Making of Americans* and her prolix word portraits, Gertrude Stein began "A Long Gay Book," anticipating a shift from her discursive garrulousness to the witty concision of *Tender Buttons*. Published in 1914, that book brought Gertrude Stein a notoriety among New York's avant-garde from which she was never able to recover. Nobody was going to be taken seriously who wrote of chicken, "Alas a dirty word, alas a dirty third alas a dirty third, alas a dirty bird" (*SW* 436), even though one of a hundred pieces in the book is hardly representative. Gertrude Stein was quite seriously engaged in a process of direct description, modified by her own vision. Earlier she had denied conventional tense progressions and narrative in favor of protracted sentences built of impersonal pronouns and repeated participles. In *Tender Buttons* she denied herself any recognizable syntax through which to stare at the private city that informed her senses. For the next twenty years her expression, simultaneously concentrated and spontaneous, was charged with the consequential and inconsequential events of her life with Alice Toklas.

What little of this work got into print made no attempt to censor or expurgate, although the bulk of it was not published until after Gertrude Stein's death. These verbal collages are not only punctuated with Alice Toklas's comments; often the compositions seem to be dialogues, and we read them rather the way we half-hear without understanding private conversations going on in the next room. For Gertrude Stein and Alice Toklas to have brought any of this material into print was as daring then as it is astonishing now; disguised or not, it says clearly enough that Alice Toklas is "a wife [who] has a cow [in] a love story" (*SW* 481). Gertrude Stein proposed marriage to Alice Toklas in 1908, detailed in a piece called "Didn't Nelly and Lilly Love You" in *As Fine as Melanctha*.† They had fallen in love at first sight the year before; courtship had followed, and the union endured not only until the husband died in 1946 but for the lonely twenty years the widow survived her. "Little Alice B. is the wife for me" (*BTV* 12), Gertrude Stein wrote in endless variations during their marriage, and after death had separated them, Alice Toklas wrote to a friend, "Gertrude's memory is all my life—just as she herself was before" (*SOA* 54).

In her first two decades as a writer, Gertrude Stein had broken with most literary conventions, denying narrative, logic, punctuation, forms or genres, even meaning in any traditional sense. What she substituted was a narrative of continuum, an order of conception rather than perception, and a private discourse through which to detail her passion. The remainder of her writing career did not abandon these matters but built on them, first in the late twenties and a growing preoccupation with the natural world in which the landscape itself took on a life. She and Alice Toklas had begun to spend their summers in the Rhône Valley, first at the hotel owned by the Pernollet family* in Belley, not far from the popular resort spa, Aix-les-Bains. It is an area so drenched in beauty that the pastoral scenes and bucolic atmosphere spilled over into Gertrude Stein's work, notably in the novel *Lucy Church Amiably*.† In 1929 they leased the manor house at Bilignin, a tiny hamlet near Belley, and spent their subsequent summers there, entertaining old friends like Picasso and Van Vechten, and more recent ones like Thornton Wilder* and Virgil Thomson. *Four Saints in Three Acts* seems to have been infused with some of the idyllic landscape, too, written in 1927 and set to music by Thomson but not performed until 1934.

In the Stein canon, *Four Saints in Three Acts* is surely its own freak as a staged success, for Gertrude Stein's dozens of what she called plays were always interior, lacking characters, plots, scenes, stage directions; for her, they were exercises in telling what happened without conflict, climax, or dénouement. She seldom attended the theater or opera once out of college and was largely indifferent to music. That *Four Saints in Three Acts* got produced at all seems to have been a commercial side effect of the success of Gertrude Stein's *The Autobiography of Alice B. Toklas*, published under her own name in 1933, a fairly straightforward recounting of three decades of the artistic and literary life in Paris, full of gossip and personalities, but told in Alice Toklas's own words and with Alice Toklas's deadpan wit and sometimes lethal observations. Readers wouldn't know what a good mimic Gertrude Stein was, until several years after her death when Alice Toklas wrote a cookbook in that same unique voice that surely helped make *The Autobiography of Alice B. Toklas* a success. Gertrude Stein never wrote anything like it again; she went on to some other memoirs, all in a cozy, conversational babble, but that was a voice solely and wholly belonging to Gertrude Stein, and it bore no resemblance to the slightly sour, slightly baleful voice in *The Autobiography of Alice B. Toklas*.

Perhaps the difference in their voices is the clearest indication of their unique relationship, offsetting and complimenting each other, expressing not only markedly different styles in expression but in attitude, self-possession, and emotional equilibrium. Here are two passages relating the same incident about a minor hardship during the early, difficult days of the Occupation. They are almost exactly the same length, but they could never be confused. Here is Gertrude Stein's version from *Wars I Have Seen*:†

Madame Roux had the habit of carrying off the dish water to give to a neighbor who was fattening a pig, and as there was very little milk with which to fatten pigs, dish water was considerable of a help, this was in the worst days '41–42, in '43 life began to be easier, well anyway Alice Toklas said to Madame Roux, no we will not give away our dish water, if the neighbor wants it she has in return to be willing to sell us a certain quantity of eggs. So Madame Roux went to the neighbor and told her she could have the family dish water only under the condition of our having the privilege of buying from her a certain quantity of eggs, well she wanted the dish water and we bought the eggs, but alas she killed the pig at Christmas, and everybody killed their pig at Christmas and so there was no need any longer of dish water to fatten the pigs and so our right to buy eggs was over, we had not had the idea of making the bargain for longer. (115–16)

Ten years later, *The Alice B. Toklas Cook Book* recounted the circumstance:

One sombre afternoon I saw the good Widow Roux who was our handyman going to the portals with a pail in either hand. What have you got there, I asked. Our dishwater for the Mother Vigne's pig, she answered. Listen, I said, you tell her if she isn't ready to sell us an egg a day you won't bring her any more dishwater for her pig. The Mother Vigne accepted the proposal and our diet was appreciably increased. It was manna from heaven. With reasonable calculation, if the Mother Vigne was now selling us one egg a day, in a short while when her hens began to lay normally again she would certainly be willing to sell us two a day. It was a comforting thought, but a few days before Christmas my hopes were shattered. The Mother Vigne's son told me that he was killing the pig for the holidays. As they would no longer have any need for the dishwater his mother wanted to say that she was not selling us an egg each day. It was a blow. Perhaps something else would turn up. (206)

Even this modest example suggests a good deal of the essential difference between the women, and if the voice in *The Autobiography of Alice B. Toklas* is not Gertrude Stein's perhaps the content is not either. Indeed, it may be that Gertrude Stein so effaced herself from the book that people began to read it. That might have given pause to a willing Sisyphus obliged to shift his chore after thirty years.

When the book succeeded, Gertrude Stein dried up and could not write for a time. Just the year before, she had completed her longest, most demanding excursion into abstraction, in *Stanzas in Meditation*,† eighty-three verse-like units relying almost entirely on nonvisual elements, a dense experiment with her only equipment—words in lines—stingy of image, aphorism, metaphor, humor, but also autobiographical. Whether to relax after its rigors or to try to make some money—she was nearly sixty then and she had never made one cent from her books, most of which she had privately financed into print—she turned out her friend's "autobiography." Opinions differ; another possibility sets the hermetic *Stanzas in Meditation* as penance for the easier appeal to readers through *The Autobiography of Alice B. Toklas*. Afterward, her work was about equally split between writing for an audience and writing for herself, and in each case the attendant problems of identity and awareness plagued her. "I am writing for myself and strangers," she had told herself in 1905 or so (*MOA* 289), and now suddenly the strangers were friends—or seemed to be.

When she came back to America for her lecture tour in the winter of 1934–1935, they asked for her autograph; radio comedians made jokes about her broken-record sentences; audiences adored her, responding perhaps too easily to her beautiful speaking voice (if phonographs tell the truth); and to some cranky, commonsense lectures about "Poetry and Grammar," "Portraits and Repetition," "How Writing Is Written," most of them published in *Lectures in America*† and *Narration*.† Gertrude Stein and Alice Toklas got treated like movie stars on the lecture tour: the Chicago police gave them a midnight ride in a patrol car from the homicide squad; the president of the University of Virginia presented them a gold key to Edgar Allan Poe's dorm room; the University of Chicago whipped up a seminar for her to teach; George Gershwin gave them a private piano recital; they dined with Charlie Chaplin in Hollywood, and they had tea with Mrs. Roosevelt at the White House. None of which sold many books; none of which eased the pain of Gertrude Stein's awareness that her work had been infected by popularity. "Writing" and "really writing" became separate activities, and it is easy enough to distinguish between the two in her subsequent work. *Paris France*† and *Everybody's Autobiography*† are friendly, rambling memoirs, warmly rewarding examples of her success as a unique prose stylist; conversely, *Ida*,† a novel about publicity, identity, and sexual schizophrenia, and *The Geographical History of America or the Relation of Human Nature to the Human Mind*† are difficult and sometimes impenetrable. Separate or not, "writing" and "really writing" were both as autobiographical as everything else.

Gertrude Stein and Alice Toklas returned home to France encrusted with honors, but subsequent books got relatively small printings. A thousand copies of *The Geographical History of America* were printed, but less than two hundred sold, and apparently the rest of the run was simply destroyed. Even *Wars I Have Seen*, her book about hiding out in the South of France during the Occupation, written in so accessible a style that it got serialized in *Collier's*, was no bestseller.

Celebrity came all over again with the end of the war. Gertrude Stein was the first American civilian to broadcast back to the United States, and with Alice Toklas the first to fly to Munich, Frankfurt, Nuremberg, Heidelberg, Cologne: "Off We All Went to See Germany," she wrote for *Life* in August 1945. When in the following months that GIs were stationed abroad during the Occupation— "Hundreds of our soldiers, scoffing and incredulous but urged on by their companions," according to Thornton Wilder—off they all went to Paris "to see the Eiffel Tower and Gertrude Stein" (*FIA* xxvii).

When she died, of cancer in 1946, she made front-page headlines, although she was still writing for herself, largely out of print and largely unread. The friends were still strangers, for whom she was good for a laugh, maybe: "Toasted susie is my ice-cream" (*SW* 486); "It takes a lot of time to be a genius, you have to sit around so much doing nothing" (*EA* 70); "Rose is a rose is a rose is a rose" (*G&P* 187)—a line here, a line there, out of context and out of continuity, and unlikely to convince anybody that Gertrude Stein was a major explorer whose discoveries we have only begun to apprehend. The final lines in her *Stanzas in Meditation*, that most demanding of her compositions, are clear enough:

I will be well welcome when I come.
Because I am coming.
Certainly I come having come. (151)

REFERENCES: *TB*, 1914; *G&P*, 1922; *MOA*, 1934; *HTW*, 1931; *P&P*, 1934; *GHA*, 1936; *EA*, 1937; *WAM*, 1940; *PF*, 1940; WIHS, 1945; *SW*, 1946; *FIA*, 1947; *LO&P*, 1949; *TWO*, 1951; *BTV*, 1953; *AFAM*, 1954; Lawrence Gilman, *Orchestral Music*, 1951; *ABTC*, 1954; *SIM*, 1956; W. H. Auden, *The Dyer's Hand*, 1962; Haskell M. Block and Robert G. Shedd, eds., *Masters of Modern Drama*, 1962; *GSP*, 1970; *SOA*, 1973; *CC*, 1974.

Ex Libris: The Published Writings of Gertrude Stein

Neither Gertrude Stein nor her editors did readers good service in printing her work out of chronological sequence. Collections that she arranged—*Geography and Plays* (1922), *Useful Knowledge* (1928), and *Portraits and Prayers* (1934)—only confuse the record of her sequential experiments and discoveries. Similarly, those collections issued posthumously—Carl Van Vechten's *Selected Writings of Gertrude Stein* (1946) and the Yale edition of eight volumes of her previously unpublished writings (1951–1958)—further deflect the reader from following the natural progression of the work. However, until such time as some enterprising editor and publisher issue Gertrude Stein's complete output in the order of its composition, readers will be obliged to rely on her present published shelf of books.

The following alphabetical catalog accounts for Gertrude Stein's major publications. It does not include individual titles printed privately and therefore generally unavailable. Those few employed for reference in this book have been collected under "Ephemera." Similarly, various publications including major selections of Gertrude Stein's correspondence are collected under "Letters." The entries in this catalog are not intended to serve as critical analyses. Descriptive rather than explicative, they account for the physical history and serve to introduce the reader to the content in summary.

Full critical assessments are readily located in Richard Bridgman's *Gertrude Stein in Pieces* (1970) in which the work is treated in a biographical chronology, and in Donald Sutherland's *Gertrude Stein: A Biography of Her Work* (1951) in which the work is treated sequentially but by type or genre. Several other studies have assessed individual works or groups of works through a wide variety of approaches. James R. Mellow's *Charmed Circle* (1974) places the books in Gertrude Stein's biography, and Robert A. Wilson's *Gertrude Stein: A Bibliography* (1975) documents the publishing history. Several other critical, biographical, and bibliographical studies of her work are less satisfactory, by turns casual, indifferent, devious, unreliable, and even silly. The reader is directed to the annotated bibliography of secondary sources in this book for individual assessments. Robert Bartlett Haas's *A Primer for the Gradual Understanding of Gertrude Stein* (1971) is a good introduction for the novice—in less than one hundred wisely selected pages of the more than nine thousand in the Stein oeuvre.

In this alphabetical catalog, each title is followed parenthetically by its date or dates of composition and its date of first publication. For a chronological dating of each of Gertrude Stein's compositions, the reader should consult the appendix in Bridgman's *Gertrude Stein in Pieces.* Based on the 1940 *Yale Catalogue* of Gertrude Stein's published and unpublished manuscripts, it is reasonably complete, although Jayne L. Walker, in *The Making of a Modernist* (1984), has dated more specifically and individually the early Stein portraits. Thus far, no one has accounted for the frequent overlapping of compositions; eventually, a specific dating month by month, to establish Gertrude Stein's working on more than one composition at a time, may serve as a further aid to explication. Meanwhile, the following content summaries are designed to introduce readers to her work as it is presently available.

AN ACQUAINTANCE WITH DESCRIPTION (1926: 1929)

In this fifty-two-page essay, Stein theorized about a growing preoccupation with the landscape in southern France's Rhône Valley. In her imaginative works of this period—notably *Four Saints in Three Acts*† and *Lucy Church Amiably*†— the narrative is controlled through the actual process of describing; the thesis of *An Acquaintance with Description* is that example precedes precept. Obvious illustrations give way to more complicated ones, all showing the descriptive process itself in process. Comparing one red berry with another, for instance, the eye plays itself false because identical berries are not the same; similarly, disarrangements may occur between two disparate objects sharing no more than the same color, or through sounds of words or their physical appearance on the printed page. The process even operates with that most abstract means of communication, numbers: "When three go, two go" (6), since the latter is contained in the former, absorbed by it but still present. Further, variations of numbers themselves, as in "three" and "third," acquaint us with description through their influence on each other. Both stem from the same root, suggesting that we must count to three before being able to distinguish a third in sequence. The process manifests itself even more clearly in physical objects, the difference between a hedge and a tree or between a child and a parent, for example, "letting it be not what it is like" (10). One reflects the other, or one anticipates the other, though without duplicating it. The mind's natural desire to discover similarities and to discern differences leads to these parallels and approximations, whether trees and hedges which are not related or children and parents who are. Another example pushes the process further: "Eagerly enough they looked to see the differences between a horse and two oxen and they looked eagerly enough to see the difference between poplars at a distance and walnut trees" (12). Here, example precedes precept by showing rather than telling. The horse, a single animal, is contained in the oxen, two animals, and simultaneously the example demonstrates how the eye can confuse one animal with the other, or, more specifically, with another one of two. One kind of tree, recognized because of the eye's familiarity with any tree, can be mistaken for another kind of tree "at a distance." Stein urges the process on to declare: "There can be no difference between a circus a mason and a mechanic between a horse and cooking a blacksmith and his brother and his places altogether and an electrician" (26). The deliberate omission of punctuation fuses the images, forcing an awareness that our process of describing anything is based on what we are capable of describing at the moment of description, since there is, Stein concludes, "a difference between times" (27) of perception. We recognize the one only because we recognize the other. Stein refers to this distinction as the difference between acquaintance *with* and acquaintance *in*. Our acquaintance *with* description demands a description *through* acquaintance before we are capable of describing.

An Acquaintance with Description was published by the Seizen Press in London, bound in white buckram and stamped in gold, in an edition of 225 copies on thick rag leaves. The book has never been reprinted and is generally unavailable through rare book collections. Among Stein's forays to explain herself, it is a valuable tool in assessing her work during the late twenties.

ALPHABETS AND BIRTHDAYS (1915–1940: 1957)

This seventh of the eight volumes of the Yale Edition of the Unpublished Writings of Gertrude Stein takes its title from a composition's subtitle. Stein wrote "To Do: A Book of Alphabets and Birthdays" in 1940, a collection of stories initially conceived for children as a follow-up to *The World Is Round*;† however, the material in "To Do" is hardly suitable for children, although here and there one or another of the little tales might be amusing to a patient youngster. Nearly every letter of the alphabet is given four stories, each about someone whose name begins with the letter, although there are exceptions: there is only one *C*, one of the *G*'s is a *J*, one of the *K* stories is a *C*, there are two *L*'s, two *Y*'s, and there is a fifth *I*. A few actual people turn up: Kate Buss,* Thornton Wilder,* Tillie Brown,* Wendell Wilcox,* George Platt Lynes,* Robert Bartlett Haas,* and in one of the longest stories Carl Van Vechten.* Many of the stories seem to be involved with identity, a subject that preoccupied Stein for several years, but many are merely fanciful and most of them too engaged in private verbal games to communicate readily with readers of any age. Negotiations for publication broke down after four publishers rejected it. In this eighth Yale volume, "To Do" is followed by "All Sunday," the earliest of the pieces, dating from 1915, and involved with the Stein-Toklas living arrangements. When the war threatened, the women went to Mallorca for the winter. As is the case with much of the writing of that period, "All Sunday" is rendered in the form of a dialogue in which two unidentified speakers are in conversation much of the time. As an example of this especial form, it is unique in concentrating on a specific period of time and place out of the women's familiar surroundings. Private, crochety, and dulled with an ennui borne of prolonged exile from a comfortable milieu, "All Sunday" is nevertheless a good example of a kind of dramatized autobiography Stein indulged in after 1913 and returned to intermittently during the next twenty years. "A Birthday Book," written in 1924 with the intention that Picasso* would illustrate it, contains 365 little poems, some of them only one line long, some few expanded into whole paragraphs, with an interlude about red Indians between May and June. None of the dates seems especially significant to Stein, not even her own birthday, although Alice Toklas's birthday on 30 April is allowed some buildup and attention. "Dahomy" is not about North Africa but named after the title page of the *cahier* in which Stein was writing at the time, an abstract exercise in which familiar people appear, although there seems to be little chronology in the events. "Birth and Marriage," "A Diary," and "History or Messages from History" are similarly hermetic, the latter less reliant on dialogue but all apparently laced with materials from the Stein-Toklas alliance.

Donald Gallup* supplied the introduction to *Alphabets and Birthdays*, placing them in the Stein canon and accounting for the attempts at publication of various pieces. The Yale University Press issued fifteen hundred copies, bound in green cloth and stamped in gold, in 1957. The book was reprinted by Books for Libraries in 1969, four hundred copies issued in a coarse and vulgar red buckram stamped in black. A second printing was bound in dark blue cloth stamped in gold.

AS FINE AS MELANCTHA (1914–1930: 1954)

Like several other volumes in the Yale Edition of unpublished work, *As Fine as Melanctha* is a collection of occasional pieces written over a period of many years. It is therefore an exercise in obscurity to anybody attempting to trace Gertrude Stein's development as a writer. The earliest selections are directly autobiographical, sometimes verbatim transcriptions of conversations between Stein and Alice Toklas but couched in familiar repetitions. "No" and "One Sentence," for example, might better serve the reader in sequence with selections written at about the same time—those printed in *Bee Time Vine*† from volume 3 of the Yale edition or delayed until the penultimate *Alphabets and Birthdays*.† It is not mandatory to read Stein chronologically, but many of the bewildering problems besetting the novice might be lessened through such an approach. In *As Fine as Melanctha*, titled after a piece written when an editor requested something "as fine as Melanctha"—it isn't—the earliest material is domestic, comfortable, occasionally erotic, dating from before or during the war. Most of the material from the twenties is of a more public nature, "Subject-cases: The Background of a Detective Story," for example, which seems to explore preparations for publication of *The Making of Americans*† by abbreviating it. One selection from the twenties is significantly autobiographical in accounting for Stein's proposal of marriage to Alice Toklas. "Didn't Nelly and Lilly Love

You'' repeats its title as a question throughout, as Stein sympathized with Toklas over the failure of early romances; as it progresses, the women declare their love and commitment. Their forty-year alliance is never far below the surface in Stein's work, sometimes blatantly, and pieces like "A Third" account for disruptions as well as serenity. Although arranged out of chronological order, the pieces in *As Fine as Melanctha* are dated, and the reader who reorganizes them can trace the Stein-Toklas relationship without overwhelming difficulty. One late piece in the book, "More Grammar for a Sentence," written in 1930, belongs with a group of meditations about the nature of rhetoric. It could have been included in *How to Write,*† or it might have replaced a selection in that volume. Similarly, "Title, Sub-title," which concludes *As Fine as Melanctha*, might have been added to *How to Write*, except for its concluding line, "For the moment the end of grammar" (388).

The introduction by Natalie Clifford Barney* is only a charming memoir and of little value in unraveling Stein's—and her editors'—seemingly deliberate obfuscation. Bound primly in gray cloth boards printed in gold, *As Fine as Melanctha* was published in an edition of fifteen hundred copies. It was reprinted in 1969 by Books for Libraries, four hundred copies issued in red buckram stamped in black. A second printing was bound in dark blue cloth stamped in gold.

THE AUTOBIOGRAPHY OF ALICE B. TOKLAS (1932: 1933)

Unlike Daniel Defoe's "Robinson Crusoe," Gertrude Stein's "Alice B. Toklas" is not entirely her own invention but an imitation of her companion's voice relating their joint biography. Not until publication of *The Alice B. Toklas Cook Book* twenty years later, and Toklas's own memoir *What Is Remembered* a decade after that, was it apparent how uncannily accurate Stein had been in capturing the waspish, acidulous voice of her friend. Aside from several factual corrections and one or two of opinion, noted in the manuscript while she typed it, Alice Toklas contributed little to the actual composition of her autobiography. On two grounds, it is an interesting work in the Stein oeuvre but for reasons that have little to do with each other. *The Autobiography of Alice B. Toklas* is so entirely uncharacteristic of Gertrude Stein's writing that it can serve only as a false, even detrimental, introduction. Conversely, it is an entertaining re-creation of the artistic life in Paris for the first quarter of the century, filled with vivid portraits of painters and writers, laced with good gossip. Early chapters document the years before Stein and Toklas met, although the narrator herself drops out of sight after page 5 for about a third of the book during which Gertrude Stein's own history is detailed. The remainder accounts for their meetings with various celebrated people, friendships and alliances, literary feuds, parties, their driving an ambulance during World War I, and much of modern art. Matisse* and Picasso* move comfortably among the pages; so do Ernest Hemingway* and Carl Van Vechten;* and there are briefer appearances of Ezra Pound,* F. Scott

Fitzgerald,* Louis Bromfield,* Sherwood Anderson,* James Joyce, Margaret Anderson,* and dozens of other people connected with twentieth-century arts and letters. Until 1933, Gertrude Stein's name had been fairly familiar more as a personality than as a writer, but with the serializing of *The Autobiography of Alice B. Toklas* in *The Atlantic Monthly* and its subsequent success in book form, she enjoyed a brief period of popularity. Alice Toklas's voice as a narrator allowed Gertrude Stein to make several claims, the most familiar of which became the bells that rang each time Alice Toklas encountered a genius; there were three of them: Alfred North Whitehead,* Pablo Picasso, and Gertrude Stein (5–6). Elsewhere, the book may be read with subsequent grains of literary salt, since it is highly selective in what it includes and what it leaves out, and even factually inaccurate on occasion.

First published in gray cloth by Harcourt Brace and in black cloth by the Literary Guild, both editions were stamped in silver with "Rose is a rose is a rose is a rose" printed as circular device on the cover, and neither edition printed Gertrude Stein's name on the binding or the dust jacket or the title page. Authorship was thereby declared only in the last sentence of the text, in which Alice Toklas tells the reader that Gertrude Stein had been threatening to write her autobiography for her: "And she has and this is it" (310). There were 5,400 copies in the first edition; it was followed by a British printing later in the same year and subsequently in many paperback versions and translated into several other languages, and it is currently in print.

BEE TIME VINE (1913–1927: 1953)

Volume 3 of the Yale Edition of the unpublished work of Gertrude Stein was titled after one of nearly one hundred "short poems," as the editors call these hermetic pieces, some of which are not very short and most of which are not really poems. They often look like poems because their word units, phrases, and sentences are broken up into single lines strung down the pages. Many of them deal with the Stein-Toklas domestic life and others are erotic love songs. Nearly all of them are couched in private allusions and intimate exchanges, sometimes in dialogue between the two women. Two longer selections, "A Sonatina Followed by Another" and "Lifting Belly," concentrate on the same subject matter, sometimes childishly as in "I am your honey honeysuckle you are my bee, I am your honey honey suckle you are my bee, I am your honey honey suckle you are my bee" (21), and sometimes with scabrous implication as in the literal application of the second of these titles to love-making. In his note to "Lifting Belly," Virgil Thomson* describes it as "a naturalistic recounting of the daily life" (63). In many of these pieces, Stein's verbal playfulness and her vulnerability and dependence on Toklas operate simultaneously; the result can be disconcerting, as in "A Lesson for Baby" and "In This Way, Kissing." Elsewhere, the pieces engage in straightforward wordplay and punning, "Yet Dish" ("Yiddish") and "Oval" ("Offal"). Still others are tied to

World War I: "Decorations," "The Work," and "Won" are clear enough to require no gloss. Others are simply abstractions, a sentence strung out word by word down the page as in "One or Two. I've Finished," the text of which is completely lacking in any tangible image:

> There
> Why
> There
> Why
> There
> Able
> Idle. (179–80)

Nine years later she incorporated "One or Two. I've Finished" in "An Elucidation" as an explanatory example (P&P 248). The most substantial selection in *Bee Time Vine* is "Patriarchal Poetry," an essay with illustrations of its subject, based on accruing insight through verbal accretion. Written in 1927 and probably influenced by the neoromantic movement in painting, "Patriarchal Poetry" uses emotion in place of recognizable subject and substitutes the interplay of grammar and compositional structure for narrative. Describing emotion rather than literal activity, the essay is romantic rather than classical, a vast tract marshy rather than manicured. The subject itself "makes no mistake makes no mistake in estimating the value to be placed upon the best and most arranged of considerations" (272), and it "should be defined as once leaving once leaving it here having been placed in that way at once letting this be with them after all" (281). Elsewhere, Stein simply plays with her title, as in "Patriarchal Poetry sentence sent once" (271) and

> Patriarchal Poetry at peace.
> Patriarchal Poetry a piece.
> Patriarchal Poetry in peace.
> Patriarchal Poetry in pieces.
> Patriarchal Poetry as peace to return to Patriarchal Poetry at peace.
>   (281)

Forty-odd pages of these ruminations, interrupted by stuttering repetitions, make "Patriarchal Poetry" one of Stein's most demanding efforts. On the other hand, as a central illustration of the subject, Stein offers "To the wife of my bosom" (272), "a sonnet" of absolute clarity that is as clear a love song as a selection from, say, the *Amoretti* of Edmund Spenser. Aside from this isolated example, however, *Bee Time Vine* is singularly lacking in memorable lines and passages. Perhaps its private nature precludes much public communication.

Virgil Thomson's introduction and introductory notes to the selections are more helpful than most of the prefatory material offered in the Yale edition.

This volume was bound in black cloth and stamped in gold, issued in an edition of two thousand copies. It was reprinted in 1969 by Books for Libraries, four hundred copies issued in a red buckram stamped in black. A second printing was bound in dark blue stamped in gold.

BEFORE THE FLOWERS OF FRIENDSHIP FADED FRIENDSHIP FADED (1930: 1931)

This poem of thirty stanzas—some of them prose paragraphs and some of them only a brief sentence or two—began as a translation of *Enfances*, a lengthy sexual meditation in verse by the French poet Georges Hugnet.* In progress it became even less a free paraphrase and more what Gertrude Stein considered a reflection on the poem. Some of Hugnet's themes are alluded to, but the work is largely Stein's independent production. When Hugnet complained about the disparity, she gave the work its present title. Little of her version suggests Hugnet's poem: Stein avoided his sexual images; she freely employed material that might and did turn up in other work of her own; and from time to time she commented on the difficulties in the chore of translating: "Look at me now and here I am" (xi); a kind of love song to Alice Toklas in the twenty-ninth stanza (ixxx); and the concluding observation,

> What is my name.
> That is the game
> Georges Hugnet
> By Gertrude Stein (xxx),

all indicate her preoccupations, even in so deliberate an act as literary translation.

Before the Flowers of Friendship Faded Friendship Faded first appeared in the literary quarterly *Pagany* (II, Winter 1931) as "Poem Pritten on the Pfances of Georges Hugnet," the French and English texts on facing pages. Under the title implying the split between poet and translator, Gertrude Stein and Alice Toklas published it in their privately issued Plain Edition—the second of five titles in that series—later the same year, in a printing of 120 numbered copies on handmade paper. Eighteen, numbered I–XVIII were signed by Stein, and two numbered 0 and 00 were for legal deposit.

BLOOD ON THE DINING-ROOM FLOOR (1933: 1948)

This "detective story" is no major work, but it is of chronological interest, having been written during the summer of 1933 when after the success of *The Autobiography of Alice B. Toklas*† Gertrude Stein was impeded by a writer's block of insurmountable size. Until then, her "daily miracle" had occurred without prompting, but various private and public demons intervened to disrupt the regularity of her output. She and Toklas had fallen out over the disclosure of an earlier love affair; the fact of a wide reading audience led her to distrust her motives for writing. *Blood on the Dining-Room Floor* was Stein's transitional piece, actually another internal monologue in which the circumstances of the moment are so enmeshed with the material about which she was writing that they are inseparable. She moves from the "she" of the Toklas *Autobiography* to the "everybody" in the detective story, and the process rather than the conclusion—of writing and of solving the crime—obsesses her anew. The guilty are never apprehended and there is no conclusion. Frequently she asks, "Lizzie do you understand," both a reference to Fall River's hatchet queen Lizzie Borden who "took a axe and gave her father forty whacks" and to a friend of Alice Toklas's who never understood anything. The plot of *Blood on the Dining-Room Floor* is alluded to in other works, "A Water-fall and a Piano" and *Everybody's Autobiography*,† for example, but the events are no clearer there. That summer, the Bilignin house had been renovated; Janet Scudder* and a friend had come to visit, plagued by car trouble en route; the telephone didn't work; and in the nearby village of Belley, Madame Pernollet* had been found dead in the court-yard of her inn, accident or suicide unestablished, although the incident occurred following the disclosure of her husband's infidelity. The body was removed hurriedly, and nobody talked about it. The "blood on the dining-room floor," emblematic or actual, became the dénouement for the incidents. Carl Van Vech-ten* once referred to the story as "hair-raising." It isn't.

Blood on the Dining-Room Floor first came into print, hand-set in Garamond faces on Ruysdael paper, bound in quarter cloth and marbleized boards by the Banyan Press, issued in a slipcase, for $6 a copy—by present-day standards about $50—in a numbered edition of 626 copies. Subsequently, it was reprinted by Creative Arts Book Company in 1982, with an introduction by John Herbert Gill, who titled it "a murder mystery." In 1986, the Virago Press series of fiction by women writers issued it in paperback.

A BOOK CONCLUDING WITH AS A WIFE HAS A COW A LOVE STORY (1923: 1926)

Most interesting as a bibliographical rarity, this thirty-page pamphlet contains four lithographs by Juan Gris:* one of a woman, one of a man, one an introductory emblem for the title selection, and an endpiece. They have nothing to do with the content. A series of brief sketches—the shortest is only four words and the longest no more than sixty—make elliptical references to the Stein-Toklas home life: keeping money and candy locked up and out of reach, relatives, orgasms, objects, sizes, and a number of people identified only by their first names. All of them are laced with Stein's usual verbal play, and they are titled with single words or brief phrases. "As a Wife Has a Cow a Love Story," introduced by Gris's charming red and black still life, was referred to by Carl Van Vechten* in his *Selected Writings*† of her work as "an excellent example of Gertrude

Stein's adverbial and participial style'' (480). Perhaps; but it is more pointedly a love song to Alice Toklas, as Gertrude Stein's wife, written near the conclusion of a decade-long preoccupation with their "daily island living," as she frequently referred to the alliance.

A Book Concluding with As a Wife Has a Cow a Love Story was printed on Arches paper in an edition of one hundred copies after which Gris's lithographic stones were defaced for two additional copies for legal deposit. For a deluxe edition, ten more copies were printed on vellum and all were signed by Stein and Gris. Daniel-Henry Kahnweiler* was the publisher. The pamphlet was reprinted in a facsimile edition in 1973 by the Something Else Press.

BREWSIE AND WILLIE (1945: 1946)

In his introduction to *Four in America*,† Thornton Wilder* reported of the American occupation troops in Europe: "Hundreds of our soldiers, scoffing and incredulous but urged on by their companions, came up to Paris 'to see the Eiffel Tower and Gertrude Stein' '' (xxvii). In *Brewsie and Willie*, Stein recorded their conversations, largely about their concerns over a postwar America, speaking of their dismay over life back home, of race relations, the single tax, pin-up girls, fraternization, capitalism, virginity, casually drifting from one subject to another and sometimes back again. Willie is the more active of the two leading characters, bullying, easily exasperated; Brewsie is more thoughtful, voicing genuine distress about the dangers of industrialism and the conveniences of a comfortable life that can too easily lead to indolence and complacency. Returning for the first time since *Three Lives*,† forty years before, to protracted dialogue to carry her narrative, Stein used a dozen other enlisted men and a couple of nurses to voice these ideas and exchanges. Also, for the first time in forty years, she avoided any sense of place or time through description, with the minor exceptions of an occasional reference to morning or afternoon, to the sun shining, to narrow streets, to a change of seasons. The conversations carried on among these young Americans might occur anywhere, and perhaps Stein deliberately avoided settings to allow for that. There is little distinction among the voices, nearly always passionate, serious, slangy, and in their own way as stylized as the voices in *Three Lives*. Gertrude Stein herself is referred to at one point in the conversations, and she added an epilogue addressed "To Americans" to her novel, urging a "spiritual pioneer fight" to avoid the dangers of an overindustrialized United States following wartime's prosperity (113–14).

Brewsie and Willie was published by Random House in an edition of six thousand copies, and its popularity required a second printing almost immediately. Both were bound in tan cloth printed in black and red. Ellen Violett and Lizabeth Blake adapted *Brewsie and Willie* as a one-act play in 1954; Dramatists Play Service published one thousand paperback copies in 1960.

COMPOSITION AS EXPLANATION (1926: 1926)

"Composition as Explanation" was Gertrude Stein's first public attempt to explain herself. (She had written "An Elucidation" three years earlier, but it was not published until 1927, in the April issue of *transition*.) Written as a lecture for the Oxford and Cambridge literary societies, "Composition as Explanation" is probably the most straightforward writing Stein had managed in twenty years. By turns quirky, repetitious, and familiarly recondite, it nevertheless attempted to trace her development and to clarify her aims. From her point of view, the writer who is ahead of his time need only wait until his readers catch up with him, because "the creator of the new composition in the arts is an outlaw until he is a classic. . . . For a very long time everybody refuses and then almost without a pause almost everybody accepts. In the history of the refused in the arts and literature the rapidity of the change is always startling" (7–8). The lecture accounts for Stein's various discoveries involving repetition, what she calls her "prolonged present" and "continuous present" tenses, and their application to her early work. In its first published version, "Composition as Explanation" is followed by an early portrait of a Spanish dancer, "Preciosilla," memorable if only for its inexplicable tag line, "Toasted susie is my ice-cream"; portraits of Jean Cocteau* and Edith Sitwell;* and one of her landscape plays, "A Saint in Seven," which she explained in her *Lectures in America*† "like a movement in and out with which anybody looking on can keep in time" (131). Stein had read these four selections to illustrate her lecture at both Cambridge and Oxford.

The Hogarth Press printed these materials as *Composition as Explanation* in 1926, in green paper boards printed in black. The lecture has been reprinted frequently, notably in *What Are Masterpieces*† in 1940 and in *Selected Writings of Gertrude Stein*† in 1946.

DIX PORTRAITS (1922–1929: 1930)

In this modest pamphlet, ten portraits are printed first in English and then— translated by Georges Hugnet* and Virgil Thomson*—in French, rather than being interpaged or interlineated. "Bernard Faÿ"* reflects something of Stein's preoccupation with grammar and verbal constructions on which she had been laboring in some of the pieces in *How to Write*,† and "Genia Berman"* seemingly contradicts one of her elementary precepts in that book by contending instead "a paragraph can do what a sentence can do" (47). "Kristians Tonny,"* "Guillaume Apollinaire,"* and "Erik Satie"* are extremely short, hermetic pieces, and the portraits of Hugnet, Thomson, and "Pavlik Tchelitchef"* although of middle length are equally obscure. The translations demonstrate the difficulties in getting Stein into another language, especially where word order and pattern are crucial, as in the third line of her "If I Told Him. A Completed Portrait of Picasso":

"Would he like it would Napoleon would Napoleon would would he like
it."

"L'aimerait-il est-ce Napoleon est-ce que Napoleon l'aimerait l'aimerait-
il."

Structurally, there is no way to follow the order of her repetitions nor to maintain
the rhythm they set up in a line or passage. Similarly, because of syllabification
and declension, the insistence is lost in this passage, representative of the problem:

One.	Un.
I land.	J'atterris.
Two.	Deux.
I land.	J'atterris.
Three.	Trois.
The land.	La terre.

Dix Portraits was published in Paris by Librairie Gallimard in stiff cream
wrappers printed in black, in an edition of five hundred copies, of which one
hundred were numbered and signed by Stein, Thomson, and Hugnet, ten on
vellum, twenty-five on VanGelder, and sixty-five on Arches. All ten portraits
were reprinted in *Portraits and Prayers*† in 1934.

EPHEMERA (1912–1946: 1912–1974)

Several minor items, largely of bibliographical rather than scholarly interest,
have been printed in small editions, often privately and sometimes obscurely,
from Gertrude Stein's "motor automatism" papers, written while she was a
college student, to copies of her will. This material is accounted for in detail in
Robert A. Wilson's *Gertrude Stein: A Bibliography* (1974). The earliest of these
may be the best known: three hundred copies of *Portrait of Mabel Dodge at the
Villa Curonia*, printed in 1912 in Italy; the rarest may be *A Christmas Greeting*,
of which four copies were printed privately in 1969, one of them then destroyed.
Many of these collectors' items were throw-aways or keepsakes, including brochures for art exhibitions, invitations, and advertisements. Five of them have
served as reference sources for this *Gertrude Stein Companion*. George Platt
Lynes* published two hundred copies of *Descriptions of Literature* as the second
of his As Stable pamphlets, a name Stein had given to his fledgling printing
enterprise. These one- and two-sentence assessments—ostensibly of sixty-five
books in Stein's library—were printed in green on both sides of a salmon-colored
French-fold leaf. They were reprinted in *Reflection on the Atomic Bomb*† in
1973. *Chicago Inscriptions* was Mrs. Charles B. Goodspeed's* Christmas card

in 1934. This sixteen-page pamphlet, stapled into a light-green wrapper, contained Gertrude Stein's inscriptions in copies of her own books belonging to Mrs. Goodspeed and her friends. About fifty copies were printed. The Valentine Gallery in New York issued *Recent Paintings by Francis Picabia* in November 1934, a folded single-leaf brochure in an envelope, containing Gertrude Stein's brief "Preface." The Arts Club of Chicago issued *Paintings by Elie Lascaux* in February 1936, a folded single-leaf brochure containing Gertrude Stein's untitled introduction. The Associated American Artists Galleries in New York issued *Francis Rose*, in April 1947, a folded single-leaf brochure for an exhibition of Rose's* paintings, reprinting Gertrude Stein's (here untitled) introduction written for a 1939 exhibition in London. These notes were also reprinted in *Reflection on the Atomic Bomb*. The Passedoit Gallery in New York issued *Riba-Rovira* in May 1955, a folded single-leaf brochure for an exhibition of Francesco Riba-Rovira's* paintings, with a translated excerpt from Gertrude Stein's essay in French from *Fontaine* magazine in May 1945.

EVERYBODY'S AUTOBIOGRAPHY (1936: 1937)

The success of *The Autobiography of Alice B. Toklas*,† coupled with the publicity from her American lecture tour that followed, brought to Gertrude Stein a painful awareness of the difference between "writing" and "really writing," as she often afterwards referred to the difference between the kind of work at which she had labored for thirty years and the kind of work customers were seemingly willing to pay for. Her sense of "identity" and her sense of "audience," words she often employed as well to distinguish the difference, manifested themselves in the first two books she wrote after fame came. (*Lectures in America*† and *Narration*,† published before them, were texts of her speeches and therefore designed for other purposes.) *The Geographical History of America or the Relation of Human Nature to the Human Mind*† is "really writing," as toughly demanding as any of her earlier work; *Everybody's Autobiography* is its "writing" counterpart. Conceived as a sequel to *The Autobiography of Alice B. Toklas*, it is itself markedly different from anything else Stein had written before, a manner to which she returned in her subsequent memoir, *Wars I Have Seen*,† and some elements of which spilled over into her fiction as well. *Everybody's Autobiography* is immediately accessible, deliberately written for a popular reading public, a garrulous account of her American lecture tour more or less sequentially rendered in the book's second half. The first half, told out of chronological sequence, is a free association of events and meditations on them about the period following publication of *The Autobiography of Alice B. Toklas*. It is of particular interest in offering information about Stein's early life and relations with her family and about her reaction to her homeland after her long sojourn in France, and its running theme marries its materials: "Identity always worries me and memory and eternity" (115). *Everybody's Autobiography* has perhaps a more permanent value, however, through its memorable aphorisms and quirky observations on subjects ranging from avarice to writing and from money to playing the piano. Indeed, no Stein volume that explains how to be a genius—"you have to sit around so much doing nothing, really doing nothing" (70)—is without considerable interest. It may be her most quotable book.

Everybody's Autobiography was published by Random House in an edition of three thousand copies, bound in tan linen and including several photographs by Carl Van Vechten.* Cooper Square Publishers printed about a thousand copies by offset in 1971, and Vintage Books issued a paperback edition in 1973.

FERNHURST, Q.E.D., AND OTHER EARLY WRITINGS (1903–1905: 1971)

This omnibus volume includes Gertrude Stein's three earliest works, discounting her college themes written at Radcliffe and published as an appendix to Rosalind S. Miller's 1949 critical study, *Gertrude Stein: Form and Intelligibility*. "Fernhurst" is an aborted roman à clef about a romantic triangle in which a man and woman vie for the affections of another woman, based on the lives of three academics: Alfred Hodder, Helen Carey Thomas, and Mary Gwinn; Stein herself, in the role of Hodder's wife, serves as a fourth character. Portions of the fragment turn up in *The Making of Americans*† a few years later. Similarly, "Q.E.D." is a novel about Gertrude Stein and two college friends, May Bookstaver* and Mabel Haynes,* locked in a nearly identical triangle, remarkable for its candor about lesbian relationships and, in the Stein canon, remarkable for its conventional narrative skill. "The Making of Americans"—five brief chapters in sequence about some Stein progenitors—constitutes the "other early writings" in the title of this volume. They are printed in reverse order. Stein's first attempt, "The Making of Americans," of which only a fragment survives, is about unsuitable marriages that Julia and Bertha Dehning are about to enter into: Julia will forsake her middle-class virtues to marry a glamorous philanderer whose family has "by nature a pretty talent in the arts" (153) and Bertha will embrace as gloomy a future when she marries "the handsomest and biggest man in the most imposing bourgeois family in their set" (172). Stein carried little of this forward into *The Making of Americans*. "Q.E.D." is a short naturalistic novel about three women locked in an emotional though not exclusively sexual vise. Its objective narration is unique in Stein's canon. Adele finds herself attracted to Helen Thomas who is Mabel Neathe's lover. Mabel supports Helen, an arrangement that Adele considers no more than prostitution. Although Adele is repelled by the idea of physical sexuality, she falls in love with Helen, and after several meetings they declare their feelings and spend a night together. Mabel asserts her prior claim. The novel then explores the trio's behavior as its members' disparate characters attempt to manipulate each other: Mabel "unillumined and unmoral" from "the drag of unidealised passion" (55); Helen, an "American version of the English handsome girl" (54), intelligent but passively so; Adele, naive and in "the disillusionment of recent failures" (61) "a hopeless coward"

(80) as she calls herself. As a study of character types with fixed traits, "Q.E.D." is a dramatization of some of Stein's work at Harvard under William James* and Hugo Münsterberg.* Adele is intellectual and Mabel is emotional; Adele is cerebral and Mabel is passionate; Adele is innocent and Mabel is experienced. Their combat for Helen leads to the novel's stalemate. Adele is bourgeois, with middle-class values and their controlling sense of sin, while Mabel is aristocratic, free of that taint. When Adele finally succumbs to Helen, she suffers no guilt, however, and the stalemate among the three women is magnified by Adele's own personal stalemate at the novel's conclusion. "Fernhurst" tells much the same story, disguising Helen Thomas as Philip Redfern, Mabel Neathe as Helen Thornton, and May Bookstaver's previous lover Mabel Weeks* as Nancy Talbot. Also similarly, but satisfactorily, "Fernhurst" concludes in no resolution.

Fernhurst, Q.E.D., and Other Early Writings was published by Liveright in 1971, 4,000 copies bound in black cloth, and 3,000 copies in paperback in 1973. Leon Katz supplied a detailed introduction, and the 1950 essay by Donald Gallup,* "The Making of *The Making of Americans*," about the printing history of *The Making of Americans*, was appended. "Q.E.D" was issued in an edition of 516 copies, hand-set and hand-printed by the Banyan Press in 1950, and then hand-sewn into tan cloth boards. This early version—slightly bowdlerized to disguise the identity of May Bookstaver—was reissued by the Banyan Press in 1984, titled *Things as They Are* after a line in the novel.

FOUR IN AMERICA (1931–1933: 1947)

Gertrude Stein's quartet of biographical meditations extends her preoccupation with personalities and behavioral patterns, considering Ulysses S. Grant as a religious leader, Wilbur Wright as a painter, Henry James as a general, and George Washington as a novelist. This fanciful proposal offers little information about Stein's four subjects, but it allows her ample space for a series of random observations about "What They Thought and Brought," as she subtitled her work. In "Grant," Stein begins by probing connections between people's names and their professions to suggest that had Grant not changed his name from Hiram to Ulysses he would have been a religious leader. This feeds into her contention that people living within a common time frame are alike, so the effect of religious belief on their thinking is similar. Snatches of war and religious songs, like "Tenting Tonight," invade periodically to keep the piece focused on the nineteenth century, its camp meetings and its religious fervor, all divided erratically into a series of volumes, chapters, books, and numbered out of chronological sequence. "Wilbur Wright" begins with another meditation on names but shortly becomes a discussion of the content and expression in American painting. There are occasional analogies drawn between flying and painting, and rather more frequently than usual, Stein's favorite imprecation—"When this you see remember me"—appears. By far the most satisfying of the essays is "Henry James," limned with cogent observations about writing. It begins with a meditation on the difference between Shakespeare's plays and Shakespeare's sonnets and the correlative difference between accident and coincidence. As an early variation on Stein's quandary over audience writing and private writing, "Henry James" probes what she later called a sense of "identity": "writing what you are writing" is one way, and "writing what you are going to be writing" is the other (122). The first aligns the writer with the writing, but the second suggests an awareness of readers. Henry James "being a general has selected both" (138), Stein concludes, since his work is "a combination of the two ways of writing" (137). Part of the fourth section, "George Washington," had been written at least two years before the others; it appeared in *Hound and Horn*, a literary quarterly, as "Scenery and George Washington. A Novel or a Play." It evokes the Rhône Valley in the south of France and Gertrude Stein's summer home that inspired a whole series of works during the late twenties, static, romantic, preoccupied with the landscape. The rest of "George Washington" is titled "or a history of the United States of America" and is less concerned with the subject as a novelist than with his actions themselves constituting a novel.

Published shortly after her death, *Four in America* is prefaced with an insightful essay by Thornton Wilder* which, among other matters, offers in detail Stein's verbal explanation of her celebrated "Rose is a rose is a rose is a rose." Bound in tan cloth stamped in brown, *Four in America* was published in an edition of three thousand copies by the Yale University Press. The book was reprinted by Books for Libraries in 1969, four hundred copies issued in blue cloth stamped in red and gold.

FOUR SAINTS IN THREE ACTS (1927: 1934)

The success—a succès d'estime, at least—of Virgil Thomson's* opera led to publication of Stein's libretto. Written at Thomson's request about a subject they had agreed upon, *Four Saints in Three Acts* has sixteen saints and four acts and recounts the daily lives of a group of Spanish saints, notably Saint Therese and Saint Ignatius Loyola. Others are fancifully named Saint Settlement, Saint Plan, and Saint Answers; still others have the names of actual saints, although in no case does Stein seem to have deliberately incorporated events drawn from either history or iconography. As is usually true in Stein texts, there is some autobiographical material along the way, ruminations about purpose and intention, forgetting and remembering who was who, getting the saints on and off the stage. There is no plot to *Four Saints in Three Acts*, although Maurice Grosser* fashioned a scenario for its staging, and subsequent productions have invented plots to carry the action forward. In part because of Thomson's persuasive music but in part because of their own verbal charm, some of Stein's arias are memorable: "Pigeons on the grass alas," for instance, which Thomson set as a vision of the holy ghost for Saint Ignatius, and a processional march that puns and plays with "across" and "a cross," "wed" and "dead," and disparity in their ages, "Between thirty-five and forty-five" (52–53).

   Four Saints in Three Acts was published in Thomson's abbreviation of it as a libretto by Random House, four thousand copies in black cloth printed in gold, with an introduction by Carl Van Vechten.* Van Vechten included this version in his volume of *Selected Writings of Gertrude Stein*† in 1946; the full text had appeared in *Operas and Plays*,† published by Stein and Toklas in 1932, and Van Vechten reprinted it in full in his *Last Operas and Plays*† in 1949, and so did John Malcolm Brinnin in his *Selected Operas and Plays*† in 1970. The vocal score, bound in pink boards, was issued in 1948 in an edition of one thousand copies; thirty additional copies were issued in decorative paper boards, slipcased.

THE GEOGRAPHICAL HISTORY OF AMERICA OR THE RELATION OF HUMAN NATURE TO THE HUMAN MIND (1935: 1936)

After the success of *The Autobiography of Alice B. Toklas*† and the American lecture tour, Gertrude Stein's writing—with some admitted spillover—fell into two distinct categories. She called the work designed deliberately for an audience "identity writing" or simply "writing"; "entity writing" or "really writing" remained private and meditative. *Everybody's Autobiography*† and *The Geographical History of America*, written successively, illustrate the two categories; indeed, they are in some respects responses to each other. *The Geographical History of America* links the categories themselves with human nature (identity) and human mind (self) in a meditative consideration of literature, geography, autobiography, and the metaphysics of the writing process. Through a protracted series of illustrations—for Stein's method is always to explicate by example rather than by explanation—she uses our sense of time, of awareness of audience, of the influence of money, and our loss of self under the sway of such persuasions. Stein's frequently quoted line, "I am I because my little dog knows me" (144), is no non sequitur: self-recognition can become distorted when it identifies outside itself, but "my little dog," possessed of no sense of human nature or human mind or human time, "entifies" rather than "identifies." The masterpieces of literature—Stein's motivating preoccupation in *The Geographical History of America*—deal with matters of human nature; but their authors, in the act of writing, are free of human nature's restraints and therefore create timeless work. Since she herself has done "the literary important literary thinking of this epoch" (224–25), her admonition is not surprising: "Think of the Bible and Homer think of Shakespeare and think of me" (117). In *The Geographical History of America*, Stein also included portraits of Thornton Wilder,* Joseph Alsop,* Bennett Cerf,* and a story about her white poodle Basket,* not in isolation but as illustrations of her major premise, that her preference for human mind over human nature manifests itself in literature's longevity.

The Geographical History of America was published by Random House, one thousand copies bound in black cloth with a white quartercloth spine. Thornton Wilder supplied an introduction for it. In 1973, Vintage Books issued a paperback edition of ten thousand copies with a new introduction by William H. Gass.

GEOGRAPHY AND PLAYS (1908–1920: 1922)

Gertude Stein subsidized publication of a selection of over four dozen short pieces, ranging in length from a few lines to several pages, written over a twelve-year period. Like half the volumes in the Yale edition of her unpublished writings—*Bee Time Vine,*† *As Fine as Melanctha,*† *Painted Lace,*† and *Alphabets and Birthdays*†—the order, printed out of chronological sequence either by accident or by design, discourages autobiographical interpretations. Nevertheless, *Geography and Plays*, despite its elliptical manner, often recounts the private lives of Gertrude Stein and Alice Toklas, and when unraveled is astonishingly candid about their erotic life together, particularly in "Pink Melon Joy." The "Geography" of the title refers to several selections about countries and nationalities, but in a variety of styles. "Italians," for example, recalls the portraiture of her early period, and "England," more fragmented, suggests her work closer to the time of publication. There are several portraits in the book, including "Ada," Stein's beautiful apostrophe to Alice Toklas and the beginnings of their relationship, in a lucid prose to which Toklas herself may have contributed. Stein's first portrait of Carl Van Vechten,* "One," appears here, as well as a story about "Miss Furr and Miss Skeene"—Maud Hunt Squire and Ethel Mars,* early visitors at 27 rue de Fleurus—whose "gay" life is recounted, perhaps the first use of that appelation in print to refer to a homosexual alliance. "Rose is a rose is a rose is a rose" makes its first appearance in *Geography and Plays*, in a long piece called "Sacred Emily" dating to 1913 (187). The plays of the title include Stein's earliest attempts at the genre, in which she tells what happened without telling "What Happened," as the first one is titled. At first glance, the plays seem unstageable, but read aloud their dialogue is obvious (sometimes exchanges between Stein and Toklas in private conversation) and time has proven them stageworthy in several scenarios, although the scenarios have not always followed plots suggested by the words themselves.

Geography and Plays was published by the Four Seas Company in four binding designs, as its sheets were bound in 2,500 copies over a period of eighteen years, first in 1922 in gray paper boards stamped in dark blue; then, without stamping, in light gray; dark gray; finally in gold-starred gray, always with cloth spines. Haskell House issued a reprint in gray cloth in 1967;

Something Else Press issued a reprint in 1968, 2,000 copies in blue cloth and 2,000 copies in paperback.

THE GERTRUDE STEIN FIRST READER AND THREE PLAYS (1941: 1946)

At the suggestion of Carl Van Vechten,* Gertrude Stein wrote a "primer" for children that was to be in the manner of the nineteenth-century *Eclectic Readers* of William Holmes McGuffey. With such a book, Van Vechten claimed in a letter to Stein, "the youth of America as they grow up will take in GS at the breast as they should and from then on they will want to read nothing but GS" (*GSCVV* 702–3). *The First Reader* consists of twenty "lessons." Some are in prose narrative and some in verse, most of which deal with subjects likely to enchant young readers, although some are disturbingly violent. A dog decides he is going to learn to read, and a "daily bird" distracts the story from its impetus; a little boy learns new words; a "wild boy" named Willie Caesar seems to be a variation on Humpty Dumpty; Benjamin Baby cogitates on the days of the week; a poem about wild flowers follows; Jimmie and Johnnie get confused with each other; food ripens according to the passing of time; the thirteenth of March is a dangerous day; the sun speaks of its ability to shine; talking and thinking influence each other; food, again, is subject matter for children's discussion; a poem about sheep and buttercups is among Stein's more lyrical flights; a story about a discouraged little girl named Jenny is as grim as any nineteenth-century moral tale; a farmer's wife interviews a lonesome soldier; a lesson in verbal rhyming babbles along; in a brief three-act play, a little boy and girl get caught up in a talking blackberry vine; Johnny and Emma have a scarey meal; a big bird leads many smaller ones in a "ballad"; a "wild pen" has an extraordinary life of its own; and, to conclude, the twentieth lesson is a series of admonitions to "Be very careful" of just about everything. For all their playfulness, the lessons are frequently foreboding, rather closer perhaps to their McGuffey model than to twentieth-century versions. To the lessons, Gertrude Stein appended three plays, "In a Garden," in which Philip Hall and Kit Racoon kill each other in a duel over Lucy Willow who is far more interested in being a queen than in the boys; "Three Sisters Who Are Not Sisters," a version of a "film" Stein wrote for *Operas and Plays*,† "Deux Soeurs Qui Ne Sont Pas Soeurs" in 1929, in which children act out several murders; and "Look and Long" in which identities shift, and a white poodle dances.

Gertrude Stein's "first reader" was first published in a French translation as *Petits Poèmes Pour un Livre de Lecture* in 1944, bound and printed on pulp paper, although ten copies were printed on vellum. An English edition appeared two years later, including the three plays, bound in white boards with a linen spine; the American edition—two thousand copies offset from the English edition—was issued by Houghton Mifflin in 1948, bound in green linen stamped in pink. Sir Francis Rose* contributed fanciful illustrations for the English language version. "In a Garden" was set to music by Meyer Kupferman and published by Mercury Music Corporation in 1951. Ann Sternberg arranged several of the lessons from *The First Reader* and "In a Garden" as a musical entertainment, *Gertrude Stein's First Reader*, in 1969; it ran successfully off-Broadway and was published by Chappell and Company in 1970. Ned Rorem used "Three Sisters Who Are Not Sisters" as the libretto for an opera, published by Boosey and Hawkes in 1974.

GERTRUDE STEIN ON PICASSO (1909–1938: 1970)

Published to coincide with the Museum of Modern Art's retrospective Picasso exhibition, this oversized, sumptuous volume contains everything Gertrude Stein wrote about Picasso,* aside from casual reminiscences in her autobiographies. It begins with *Picasso*,† her monograph about his life and work, followed by her two portraits of him, written nearly fifteen years apart. These three pieces stand as excellent, if general, introductions to Stein's major manners: the repetitive drone of 1909, the concision and verbal play of 1923, the garrulous gossipry of 1938. Also included are passages from Gertrude Stein's notebooks about Picasso, and an essay, "They Walk in Light," by the editors of the volume, Leon Katz and Edward Burns.

The Museum of Modern Art published seven thousand copies, bound in brown cloth and stamped in silver, fully illustrated.

GERTRUDE STEIN'S AMERICA

Gilbert A. Harrison edited this selection of passages from various sources, including *Useful Knowledge*,† *Wars I Have Seen*,† *The Autobiography of Alice B. Toklas*,† *Brewsie and Willie*,† *What Are Masterpieces*,† *Everybody's Autobiography*,† *Four in America*,† *Paris France*,† *Lectures in America*,† and *Narration*,† as well as a number of essays from periodicals as diverse as the avantgarde *transition* and the Army weekly *Yank*. In no case are any of the passages used in their original contexts, and they range in length from a few lines to several pages. Harrison's introduction and headnotes occupy nearly a quarter of the book's brief hundred pages. The Stein material is divided into sections titled "The Doughboys," "The GI's," "Landscape," "We and They," "Success," and "Language."

Gertrude Stein's America was published in 1965 by Robert B. Luce in an edition of five thousand copies. The book was bound appropriately in red paper boards with a white spine printed in blue.

HOW TO WRITE (1927–1931: 1931)

What Richard Bridgman observes of the last selection in this book, "Forensics," might be said of all of it: "For her, How to Write was How I Write" (*GSP*

199). *How to Write* is one of Gertrude Stein's most hermetic works, composed of long monologues, private puns, and obscure word patterns. Its discovery that "A Sentence is not emotional a paragraph is" (23) and claim that "grammar is useless because there is nothing to say" (62) are helpful theses through which to approach its nearly four hundred pages, one of them as dense as the next. "Saving the Sentence" is a brief preamble to the rest of book, an autobiographical fragment about a trip to Rome with Basket,* interspersed with a description of the landscape at Bilignin. "Sentences and Paragraphs" is equally brief, but it establishes one of Stein's major claims, that sentences take their life from each other, since sentences are controlled by grammar, but paragraphs emerge naturally in the accumulation of sentences based on sense rather than on some syntactical prosody. The next selection, "Arthur a Grammar," recognizes grammar's function but contends that a sufficient vocabulary can communicate meaning without it. Stein concedes that a "grammar of intermittence" (89) is necessary for "explanation" (60), but her primary concern is to rid language of any dependency. "I am a grammarian," she declares at the outset of the next selection, "A Grammarian" (105), another brief piece with autobiographical suggestions. She repeats the opening declaration several times, but qualifies it: "I am a grammarian in place," "It makes me smile to be a grammarian and I am" (107), "I am a grammarian and I do think well" (110). In between, Stein distinguishes the difference between duplication and repetition. "Sentences" is a long meditation composed of examples of that elementary unit as short as two words and as long as perhaps two hundred, giving attention not only to their ability to communicate meaning but to their elementary parts of speech, the noun which "makes it plain" and the verb which is its "pressure" (191). Sentences, she declares, are not made "of" nouns and verbs, however, but "with" them; a sentence by itself "is not anything" (192). The pieces in *How to Write* were composed over a five-year period; the earliest of them, "Regular Regularly in Narrative," from 1927, is sandwiched in the book. It seems to have little to do with what has preceded and, instead, tells stories, includes portraits of Harold Acton* and Elliot Paul,* and includes casual references to other people in her circle at the time: Virgil Thomson,* Bravig Imbs,* Glenway Wescott,* and several unidentified people. The next selection, "Finally George a Vocabulary of Thinking," connects people whom Stein knew named George with her sense of George as a name, their similarities and differences. After a fairly accessible opening section, the sentences grow increasingly prolix, longer indeed than those in *The Making of Americans*,† and run on for several pages, in one instance (343–46) to well over a thousand unpunctuated words. "Forensics" concludes *How to Write*. Written last, in 1931, it may be her first confrontation with literary masterpieces and reputation, for she equates forensics not with argumentation but with what she later called "identity writing" (for an audience) rather than "entity writing" (for the self), with success rather than integrity. She could smile about that dichotomy in her work: "At last I am writing a popular novel. Popular with whom" (391).

How to Write was the third of five titles published by Alice Toklas as the Plain Edition, 1,000 copies primly bound in gray paper boards, the text crowded in stingy type on small pages. Something Else Press reprinted *How to Write* in 1973, about 2,500 copies, of which about a third were issued in chartreuse cloth printed in red and green and the rest in paperback. Dover reprinted the book in 1975, and Sherrie Urie reprinted it in 1977, both in paperback.

HOW WRITING IS WRITTEN (1928–1945: 1974)

Volume 2 of the Black Sparrow Press edition of the previously uncollected writings of Gertude Stein is comprised entirely of works from the last eighteen years of her life, over three-fourths of the text written with specific audiences in mind, "identity" writing as she called it. The "entity" pieces include "Grant or Rutherford B. Hayes," in which periods divide units within sentences from each other to isolate words and phrases from their context; two short poems that play with words and numbers; and six stories, two of which, "Ida" and "The Autobiography of Rose," anticipate *Ida†* and *The World Is Round,†* and two of which, "A Water-fall and a Piano" and "Is Dead," are inconclusive mystery stories. The "identity" pieces are divided up into five distinct subjects, all fair examples of Gertrude Stein's later manner but none of them of singularity. "And Now," however, is a good introduction to her private turmoil when success temporarily dried up her creative juices. A series of essays about American cities, food, houses, education, crime, newspapers, and money are fanciful, self-indulgent, and altogether winning communications with a broad reading public. Four fragmentary memoirs are about her experiences during and after World War II. "The Winner Loses, A Picture of Occupied France" (appended to the English edition only of *Wars I Have Seen†*) is a straightforward and informative account of rural life in and around her summer home in Bilignin and preoccupations with gardening, writing, superstitions, and predictions—"the business of daily living" (132). "Broadcast at Voiron" is a transcription of part of a radio speech about the liberation; whether written out or delivered extempore is unclear since it appeared first and only in Eric Sevareid's *Not So Wild a Dream* (1946). *Life* magazine commissioned "Off We All Went to See Germany," based on a flying trip on a troop carrier that Gertrude Stein and Alice Toklas made to Frankfurt, Cologne, Coblenz, Salzburg, and Berchtesgaden, Heidelberg, Munich, Nuremberg, and Mannheim. "The New Hope in Our 'Sad Young Men' " compares the GI Generation with the Lost Generation of the twenties, concluding they will not be "sad young men" like their predecessors because that part of their life is already behind them. Two other essays conclude *How Writing Is Written*. "Why I Like Detective Stories," including her own, explains how she worked to rid them of detecting to establish some other emotional response in the reader. The title piece for this collection, "How Writing Is Written," is actually a transcript of an off-the-cuff talk to Choate School students, transcribed by a stenographer, though incompletely, and doctored by Dudley

Fitts, the Greek scholar. It has been often reprinted; its abundant and conventional punctuation as well as its forthright clarity suggests that Gertrude Stein had nothing to do with its printed version.

Robert Bartlett Haas* supplied helpful introductory notes in editing *How Writing Is Written*, as he had for *Reflection on the Atomic Bomb*,† the first volume in this series. Fifty copies were issued in blue paper boards printed in red, green, and purple with purple cloth spines, numbered; 750 copies were issued with green spines; 2,626 copies were issued in paperback, all by the Black Sparrow Press.

IDA (1937–1940: 1941)

A novel about the love life of an American demimondaine seems an unlikely undertaking for Gertude Stein. In *Ida* she offered a good example of a kind of narrative she had discussed as "permanently good reading" in *Narration*: "there is really no actual conclusion that anything is progressing that one thing is succeeding another thing, that anything in that sense in the sense of succeeding happening is a narrative of anything . . . " (19). This geographical amorous history—state by state and lover by lover—begins with the unwanted birth of Ida and her twin Ida-Ida who disappears after a single mention at the end of the first paragraph. Deserted by her parents almost immediately, Ida is then raised by a series of relatives, grows up in the company of her faithful dog Love, and writes letters to the twin she reinvents to enter in a beauty contest. When Ida-Ida wins, Ida changes her name to Winnie; Winnie leaves the scene again; Ida seems to absorb the twin's personality into her own. Stein is again toying with the discrepancy between identity and entity, it would seem, here in a deliberate dual-personality. This early section of the novel strings together a series of what Ida considers "funny things," incidents of a vaguely threatening sexual nature from a number of men. Subsequently, Ida travels through several states and liaisons with several army officers and a quartet of husbands before ending up in Washington, D.C., as a popular hostess. Her alliance with Andrew Hamilton begins here, followed by brief flings with Charles, Henry, Eugene, Gerald, and Woodward. As it is "handy to have Andy," she returns to him in the end (139), although there is no clear indication that Ida's adventures have come to an end. Along the novel's erratic route of these romances, Gertrude Stein spliced in observations about superstition and magic, a good deal of her familiar rhyming puns and wordplay, and a lengthy digression to account for most of the dogs in her life, or in Ida's life, or both: Prince, Lillieman, Dick, Mary Rose, Chocolate, Blanchette, Polybe, and Basket.* They are not so numerous as Ida's lovers: Mark from Kansas City; Frank who tries to teach her to swim and gets kicked for his trouble, "Jesus Christ my balls and he went under" (113); Frederick who is married to a younger or an older woman; Arthur who sleeps in a cardboard bed under a bridge. They come and go as quickly as the others. The novel concludes with Ida "resting but not resting enough" (154).

Ida was published by Random House in an edition of two thousand copies bound in gray cloth stamped in black and gold. There was a second edition of one thousand copies bound in pink cloth stamped in black from Cooper Square Publishers in 1971, and in 1972 Vintage Books published nearly seven thousand copies in paperback.

IN SAVOY (1944–1945: 1946)

Subtitled "A play of the Resistance in France," *In Savoy* is about a French family under the German occupation and the varying ways in which its members respond to that crisis. It is the most conventional of Gertrude Stein's plays, with a recognizable five-act structure and realistic if somewhat stylized dialogue. Act 1 covers the Armistice of 1940: Henry is a member of the Resistance; his younger brother Ferdinand is in love with Constance, an American woman living nearby; Henry's petulant wife Denise thinks men should act like her brother Achille, a dashing fighter-pilot. Although there is no indication of time having passed, the brief second act seems to take place about two years later at Constance's house: her maids are frightened and upset because Germans have returned to the area; Ferdinand arrives to tell Constance he has decided not to join the Resistance and that he has been ordered to Germany to work in a labor camp. Act 3 takes place a year later at a railroad station: Denise and her family have left to attend the funeral of a relative; Henry and Constance have a conversation with a German soldier who says he knows about the Resistance fighters in the area. Act 4 occurs shortly afterward, back at Constance's house: she has joined Henry in the resistance by hiding dynamite; Ferdinand returns from Germany where he has been secretly working for his laboring countrymen on the black market, but he returns immediately; Henry arrives to tell Constance that his father has been killed by the Germans. Act 5 marks the Liberation of 1944: Henry avenges his father's death by beating up German prisoners; Denise's brother Achille is going off to fight with the Americans against Japan; Ferdinand returns for the celebration but goes back to Germany to organize his countrymen there. In this form, *In Savoy* is less than a satisfactory piece of stagecraft. Retitled with a line from the play as *Yes Is for a Very Young Man*, with several additional scenes appended to act 2, in the form printed in *Last Operas and Plays*† and *Selected Operas and Plays*,† it has often been staged with some success.

In Savoy was published in blue paper wrappers printed in red and blue by the Pushkin Press in London. Gertrude Stein made a French translation, *En Savoie*, of this abbreviated version of the play, but it has never been published.

LAST OPERAS AND PLAYS (1920–1946: 1949)

Although Gertrude Stein's work defies classification by conventional genre, two of her own collections—*Geography and Plays*† and *Operas and Plays*†—indicate she thought of the drama as a form suitable for her own work, so this posthumous volume of largely unpublished material was not untoward in its title. The earliest piece, "An Exercise in Analysis," begins by announcing that she has "given up analysis" and paid her "debt to humanity," despite a response to remind her that there is "splendid profit" in the endeavor (119). Two other brief plays, "A Circular Play" and "Photograph," are similar to other pieces of the period, full of names, verbal horseplay, brief scenes and acts, and the suggestion of dialogue, probably with Alice Toklas. Many of the selections come from the period from which *Four Saints in Three Acts*† emerged, when the landscape around Bilignin was of such a strong influence on Stein's conscience and consciousness. These include some "historical" dramas, one of them about the Bilignin house itself, "A Manoir." Selections from "They Must. Be Wedded. To Their Wife." were set to music by Gerald Lord Berners* and staged as a ballet, *A Wedding Bouquet*,† in 1937. The text has little to do with the scenario invented for the ballet; instead, it seems to be another disguised exchange about the Stein-Toklas alliance as much as anything else. "A Play Called Not and Now" is based on a dinner party given for Gertrude Stein in California during her lecture tour; mystery novelist Dashiell Hammett, Picasso,* Charlie Chaplin, Lord Berners, novelists Anita Loos and Gertrude Atherton,* and actress Katharine Cornell* are among the guests, or, rather somebody "who looks like" each of them is among guests (422), and the piece itself is essentially a narrative rather than a play. Chaplin's wife, actress Paulette Goddard, and Hammett's companion, playwright Lillian Hellman, were both present at the dinner but are not in the cast of characters of "A Play Called Not and Now." "Short Sentences" has about 550 characters, each of whom had a single line. "Listen to Me" is a play about Sir Robert Abdy* and his wife Diana, called Sweet William and Lillian. *Last Operas and Plays* contains the first printing of one of Gertrude Stein's major works, "Doctor Faustus Lights the Lights," her own unique version of the familiar story. Faust is the inventor of the electric light and insecure about its value since it is artificial rather than natural, and he is therefore denied the darkness of hell. Marguerite—called Marguerite Ida and Helena Annabel— is also insecure, but about her double identity. When a viper stings her, she goes to Faust to be cured. In act 2, Marguerite Ida and Helena Annabel, now enthroned like a haloed saint with an artificial viper at her side, is almost seduced by a man from over the seas, but she perceives Mephisto behind him and resists. In act 3, Faust still feels alienated because of his artificial lights, created at the expense of his own soul, and wants to go to hell. Urged by Mephisto to "Kill anything" (116) to get there, he gets the viper to kill a boy and a dog (both of whom have appeared intermittently during the play) and takes credit himself. Mephisto transforms Faust into a young man so he can seduce Marguerite Ida and Helena Annabel into accompanying him, but she refuses, faints into the arms of the man from over seas, and Faust and Mephisto proceed to hell. Both Richard Bridgman and Allegra Stewart have treated this highly symbolic play in depth. *Last Operas and Plays* also includes the full text of *Four Saints in Three Acts* from *Operas and Plays* published only in France in the Plain Edition.

Yes Is for a Very Young Man, the revised and expanded version of *In Savoy*,†
is included as well, extending its second act to full length, although the frequency
of conventional punctuation and revisions to Stein's words in the stage directions
render it suspect. Also, *Last Operas and Plays* includes the full text of *The
Mother of Us All*,† heretofore available only in its libretto form for Virgil
Thomson's* opera.

Last Operas and Plays was published by Rinehart in orange-coated paper
boards printed in black and gold. Carl Van Vechten* edited the selection with
an introductory essay.

LECTURES IN AMERICA (1934: 1935)

Gertrude Stein prepared six lectures for her American tour during the 1934–
1935 winter. (Others, written later, were published as *Narration*).† Of the six,
three are helpful in reading her work, and the other three are at least interesting
as aspects of her attitudes toward the subjects themselves. She equated "What
Is English Literature" with knowledge marking centuries predicated on political
and historical readings. Defending her own position in a natural evolution of
words themselves to their conscious use, she faces her own demons, "god and
mammon" (54), serving "god" in her "entity" writing for herself, serving
"mammon" in her "identity" writing for an audience. Along the way she drops,
if not all, a great many celebrated names in English and American literature but
without any individualized assessment of their work. "Pictures" is one viewer's
coming to terms with art as a process from painting to painting, but Stein's
strongest defense—"I like to look at it" (59)—is not especially helpful either
to the novice or the critic. She quotes from her portraits of Cézanne, Picasso,*
Matisse,* and Gris,* and she considers the question of form as it applies to a
painter's ideas and a writer's ideas. The third lecture, entitled "Plays," is the
least satisfactory, in part because Stein herself was not particularly interested in
theater as a performing art, although she hoped to see her own works staged.
Beginning with her first play, "What Happened," she explains her attempt to
show what happened without showing it; then she moves on to those plays of
her middle period, strongly influenced by the landscape, in which nothing happens. In both instances, Stein contends, she thwarts a fundamental principle in
the genre: the audience's emotional involvement "is always either behind or
ahead of the play" and "is never going on at the same time as the action of the
play" (93), time for reflection and thought having been ruled out by the passage
of time itself. If her plays do not tell what happens or if they are "landscapes,"
they do not have to make acquaintance: "You may have to make acquaintance
with it, but it does not with you, it is there and so the play being written the
relation between you at any time is so exactly that that it is of no importance
unless you look at it" (122). "The Gradual Making of the Making of Americans"
explains at length, and with helpful examples, Gertrude Stein's heroic struggle
with repetition, resemblances, rhythms, and accretions of her exactitude in "the

difficulty of putting down the complete conception that I had of an individual, the complete rhythm of a personality that I had gradually acquired by listening seeing feeling and experience'' (147). The lecture is an admirable introduction not only to *The Making of Americans*† but to the portraits and verbal games that followed. ''Portraits and Repetition'' explores ''the rhythm of anybody's personality'' (174), contending that ''insistence'' rather than ''repetition'' is the essence of her emphasis in these works (167). The lecture most often reprinted is the final one, ''Poetry and Grammar,'' in which Stein is guaranteed to please many a student by playing fast and loose with the conventions of punctuation and parts of speech. Admitting to ''a long and complicated life'' with punctuation, she simply ignores most of it, allowing the period but not the ''servile'' and ''enfeebling'' comma and semicolon and colon, the latter only useful in making the writer feel ''adventurous'' (216–21). Nouns and adjectives aren't as interesting as verbs and adverbs; prepositions are irritating; articles might do what nouns do if nouns weren't names; conjunctions live by their work; pronouns are preferable to nouns because they don't take easily to adjectives; and interjections have ''nothing to do with anything not even with themselves. There so much for that'' (211–14). Oddly enough, it makes sufficient, strange sense to be taken seriously. Elsewhere in this final essay, she takes up the difference between poetry and prose, sentences and paragraphs, amply illustrated with examples from her writing.

Lectures in America was published by Random House, 2,330 copies bound in beige cloth printed in red and black, 1,070 copies remaindered in brown cloth stamped in red and black. Beacon Press issued the book in paperback in 1957.

LETTERS (1912–1946: 1936–1986)

Although many passages from many letters to a number of recipients have appeared in various biographical studies of Gertrude Stein, and some few in periodicals, little of her personal correspondence has been published. Mabel Dodge Luhan* included ten letters from Stein in *Movers and Shakers* in 1936, all written in late 1912 and early 1913, about mutual friends and Dodge's assessment of Stein's work for *Arts and Decoration* in February 1913 at the time of the 69th Armory Exhibition. Stein's three dozen letters to Sherwood Anderson* were collected and edited by Ray Lewis White with Anderson's letters to Stein and their various writings about each other's work in *Correspondence and Personal Essays* in 1972. Samuel M. Steward* published his letters from Stein and Toklas as *Dear Sammy* in 1977, about a hundred, less than half of them from Stein. In 1986 Edward Burns's edition of the full correspondence between Gertrude Stein and Carl Van Vechten* was published. About four hundred letters from each of them to the other are arranged chronologically in two substantial volumes, so fully annotated and meticulously indexed that all subsequent Stein scholars can only gratefully pillage from Burns's labors. The letters establish a detailed record of Stein's life and work between 1913 and

1946. No other letters have been published either as substantial selections or collections, although some further exchanges similar to Burns's are in preparation. In these unrepresentative published letters, Stein is a comfortable, eccentric gossip. She does not discuss at length her working methods nor her private life in any compromising detail. *The Flowers of Friendship* (1953), edited by Donald Gallup,* offers ample evidence of the remarkable range of her correspondence and of her correspondents. Such letters of hers as may have been preserved are likely to amplify her work when they have been addressed to a musical collaborator like Virgil Thomson* or to intellectual admirers like Thornton Wilder* and Wendell Wilcox;* they are unlikely to disclose further intimacies of her personal life.

LUCY CHURCH AMIABLY (1927: 1930)

Just as "narrative" serves as a better noun than "narration" to classify much of Gertrude Stein's work, so may *Lucy Church Amiably* be called "a descriptive" rather than "description." Donald Sutherland* called it "pastoral romance" (GSB 143); Gertrude Stein subtitled it "A Novel of Romantic beauty and nature and which Looks Like an Engraving." Written just after *Four Saints in Three Acts*,† the book shares many of the same themes and concerns as that opera libretto: saints, the religious life, the unmoving landscape; a seemingly plotless progress. In *Lucy Church Amiably*, however, the concentration is almost entirely on the landscape itself, in what the book's opening "advertisement" calls "a return to romantic nature." All other elements bow to this, as that "advertisement" announces in an unfamiliarly lyric voice: "Select your song she said and it was done and then she said and it was done with a nod and then she bent her head in the direction of the falling water. Amiably" ([7]). The action—such as it is—passes in and around the area where Gertrude Stein and Alice Toklas spent their summers for many years, near Aix-les-Bains in the Rhône Valley, in Belley, a tiny town, and the Russian-domed little church in nearby Lucey. These locales supply the settings against which a double-level story is told: Lucy Church, a peasant girl, prepares to marry a local farmer, Simon Therese; and Simon Therese, also a priest, prepares to marry the church itself. Other characters, John Mary, James Mary, and Simon Peter, are friends as well as religious attendants. Lucy Church herself, as a result, is "amiable and very much resuscitated" (51). Other characters come and go without contributing to the book's progress, some of them additional saints, some of them additional churches, some of them actual people. Alice Toklas, for example, puts in a brief appearance along with Annie Lyal and Adele Simonds, although only in a passing conjecture (150). From time to time, autobiographical incidents intrude to suggest that Lucy Church is not only peasant girl and building but the author. For instance, she rents "a valuable house for what it was worth," once she is able to take possession, but "at the time" it is "occupied by a lieutenant in the french navy who was not able to make other arrangements and as the owner of the house was unwilling to disturb one who in his way had been able to be devoted to the land which had given birth and pleasure to them both there inevitably was and would be delay in the enjoyment of the very pleasant situation which occupying the house so well adapted to the pleasures of agreeableness and delicacy would undoubtedly continue'' (130–31). Over two years before Stein and Toklas were able to take possession of the manor house in Bilignin, *Lucy Church Amiably* was projecting intentions. What predominates in the novel, however, is merely a descriptive account of the drenching beauty and somnolence of the landscape.

Gertrude Stein and Alice Toklas published *Lucy Church Amiably* as the first of five titles in their Plain Edition (1930–1933). Bound in bright blue paper boards printed in black, one thousand copies were issued. Something Else Press issued two thousand copies in blue paper boards and a white spine stamped in gold in 1969, and two thousand copies in paperback in 1972.

THE MAKING OF AMERICANS (1903–1911: 1925)

This long narrative is a novel only in the loosest sense of the genre, interrupted as it is by frequent authorial conversations with herself about its mounting perplexities and demands on the attention. Gertrude Stein observes, about a third of the way into the novel, that she is "writing for [her]self and strangers" (289), and about two hundred pages later that she is "despairing" (458), clearly at work on something destined to alienate her work from conventional literary expression. Written sporadically over a period of years, *The Making of Americans* was interrupted by Gertrude Stein's more accessible *Three Lives*† and a whole series of abstruse word portraits of individuals and groups of individuals; consequently, sections of *The Making of Americans* differ from each other both in plot development and manner, although all of its nearly one thousand pages may be charitably described as recondite. Gertrude Stein's initial intention was to trace the history of a family's progress and, through it, to define American character. Although *The Making of Americans*, in its completed form, does follow several people through a slight plot, its preoccupation lies in identifying individuals through their differences and similarities; in probing their "bottom nature," so that "slowly every one in continuous repetition, to their minutest variation, comes to be clearer to someone" (284). Through what she often called a "continuous present" or "prolonged present" tense, Gertrude Stein built up an accretion rather than a narration of a family's existence. The Maryland Dehnings and the California Hershlands, loosely based on her own progenitors, are "middle class . . . , sordid material unillusioned unaspiring and always monotonous for it is always there and to be always repeated" (34). Julia, George, and Hortense Dehning parallel Martha, Alfred, and David Hershland, connected by Julia's miserable marriage to Alfred. After a brief opening section, however, Gertrude Stein abandons the Dehnings to concentrate on the Hershlands, interspersing their lives with accounts of governesses and seamstresses in their employ, of neighbors, of several unnamed ancillary characters. The second section is devoted to Martha Hershland whose unhappy childhood is strongly reminiscent of Gertrude Stein's own, as she later reported it in *Everybody's Autobiography*.† After a disastrous marriage to Philip Redfern, Martha is reconciled with her dying father. The third section is devoted to the marriage of Alfred and Julia, although there is no sequential plot development in its 250 pages, most of which are devoted to Gertrude Stein's observations about the other Dehnings and Hershlands. The fourth section, about David Hershland, is even further alienated from plot and action, and other characters are reduced to "some one" and "no one." If, in part, Martha suggests Gertrude Stein and Alfred suggests her oldest brother Michael,* David surely suggests her brother Leo,* metaphorically at least, in wandering into failure and death in middle age. In the book's coda, titled "History of a Family's Progress," pronouns take over completely: "any one" and "every one" join "some one" and "no one" in this final, insistent hymn in protracted sentences of endless variation that "Family living is being existing" (920).

The Making of Americans was first published in monthly installments in *Transatlantic Review*, April through December 1924, accounting for about 150 pages of it in print before it was finally published in toto the following year by Robert McAlmon* in France. Five hundred copies were bound in tan paper wrappers printed in black, of which a few were bound in leather on special order. A limited edition of five copies was printed on Japanese vellum with wrappers lettered in gold. Boni published an American edition of one hundred copies in 1926, bound in beige figured cloth with a black spine printed in gold. Harcourt Brace published an abridged edition with a preface by Bernard Faÿ,* bound in orange cloth printed in red in 1934, and a paperback edition in 1966. The complete text was published by Something Else Press in 1966, two thousand copies bound in white cloth printed in black and brown, and three thousand copies in paperback, both in 1966. Peter Owen published an English edition of the full text, bound in blue cloth lettered in gold, in 1968. *The Making of Americans* was dramatized as a play and an opera libretto by Leon Katz, published by Something Else Press in 1973.

MATISSE PICASSO AND GERTRUDE STEIN WITH TWO
SHORTER STORIES (1909–1912: 1933)

Three "stories," as Gertrude Stein labels them in her subtitle, make up the contents of this work, overlapping in the three-year period of their composition. They are all transitional: the title piece, abbreviated to "G.M.P.," and "A Long Gay Book" actually demonstrate the shift in Gertrude Stein's writing from the psychological probing of personality and character analysis of *The Making of Americans*† and portraits collected in *Two*† to the lyrical good humor and verbal games that followed, beginning with *Tender Buttons*.† "Now I have it. Now I see. This is the way. Not that way. The other way is not the way," she declares (87). Shortly thereafter, her joy in the discovery of change is unalloyed: "I sing and I sing and the tunes I sing are what are tunes if they come and I sing. I sing I sing'' (107). These passages, ferreted from the bewildering text of ''A Long Gay Book'' by Richard Bridgman, may apply as well to the third piece in this book, ''Many Many Women,'' in which Gertrude Stein first treats homosexual alliances positively. It seems to have been completed during the composition of ''A Long Gay Book.'' Like the conclusion of *The Making of Americans* and many of the portraits, it employs no proper names but, instead, ''any one,'' ''some one,'' ''one,'' ''she'' and ''they'' who are ''living'' and ''loving,'' ''loving and marrying,'' ''loving and completing that thing and are not marrying'' (137). ''A Long Gay Book,'' the first begun of the three pieces in *Matisse Picasso and Gertrude Stein*, started as an extension of *The Making of Americans* by treating similar traits in two people, then in groups of three, four, five, and so on. By its conclusion in 1912, the prolix, repetitive sentences had given way to images and ideas as startling as they were economical: ''Suppose it did, suppose it did with a sheet and a shadow and a silver set of water, suppose it did'' (114); ''Leave smell well'' (115); ''A practice, no practice is careless, a loud practice, no practice is silent, a wild practice, no practice is perfect'' (113). As a combining variation on the other two pieces, ''G.M.P.'' continues for over half its length with a series of sentences controlled by ''he,'' ''they,'' and ''one'' that convey action through present participles. If the virtually impenetrable content begins with the artists themselves as avant-gardists, it seems to conclude with sufficiently solid examples of the avant-garde itself: ''A change into a result means that nothing is overthrown'' (268); ''Wag and a waggon, wide and wishing, window and charging'' (278).

Gertrude Stein and Alice Toklas published *Matisse Picasso and Gertrude Stein* as the fifth volume in their Plain Edition, of which 500 copies were bound in tan paper wrappers and issued in a matching slipcase, both stamped in black. Something Else Press published 1,500 copies bound in brown cloth stamped in gold and 2,500 paperback copies in 1972.

THE MOTHER OF US ALL (1946: 1947)

Gertrude Stein's final work was a libretto for another opera by Virgil Thomson,* a ''successor in homespun'' to *Four Saints in Three Acts*† as Carl Van Vechten* often referred to it. She might have taken her lead for its cast of characters from a line in *Lucy Church Amiably*:† ''Supposing everyone lived at the same time what would they say'' (21), since her version of Susan B. Anthony's fight for women's suffrage includes such historical personages as Daniel Webster, John Adams, Thaddeus Stevens, Anthony Comstock, Ulysses S. Grant, and Andrew Johnson from politics, and Lillian Russell from musical comedy, as well as some of her own friends and contemporaries like Donald Gallup,* Constance Fletcher,* Joseph Barry* as ''Jo the Loiterer,'' and one of her GI admirers as ''Chris the Citizen.'' Alice Toklas turns up thinly disguised as Anna Howard Shaw, Susan B. Anthony's suffragette-compatriot, and Susan B. Anthony herself often seems to speak for Gertrude Stein. "Virgil T." and "Gertrude S." serve as commentators. Although *The Mother of Us All* has its own discernible plot line and definable characters, Maurice Grosser* fashioned a scenario, as he had done of necessity for *Four Saints in Three Acts*. Susan B. Anthony and Daniel Webster engage in a series of debates that Gertrude Stein derived in part from their writings, notably Anthony's *History of Women's Suffrage* and Webster's celebrated reply to railroad executive Robert Young Hayne. The debates are interspersed with several scenes involving love and marriage, discussions of the relative value of men and women as individuals, the irony in Susan B. Anthony's having achieved suffrage for black men but not for women of either race, and her frustrating dreams about the double standard in American political life. In its epilogue, *The Mother of Us All* enshrines Susan B. Anthony—and perhaps Gertrude Stein too—as a statue to which the other women in the cast pay homage "not to what I won but to what was done" (156).

First published with Thomson's vocal score, the libretto for *The Mother of Us All* is severely truncated. Thomson dropped several short passages throughout, turned a long "Interlude (Susan B. A Short Story)" into a brief prologue, and dropped all of the second and fourth scenes in the second act as Gertrude Stein had structured it. The vocal score was published by Music Press, in an edition of one thousand copies bound in gray wrappers printed in yellow and black, and fifty-five signed and numbered copies bound in gray cloth printed in yellow and black. Gertrude Stein's full text was included in *Last Operas and Plays*† in 1949 and in *Selected Operas and Plays*† in 1970.

MRS. REYNOLDS AND FIVE EARLIER NOVELETTES (1940–1943: 1952)

Mrs. Reynolds is Gertrude Stein's longest sustained narrative since *The Making of Americans*† thirty years before, and far more coherent. It may be her most accessible "novel," employing a consistent past tense in recounting the incidents in the plot and their attendant descriptions. Several characters are always identifiable and engaged in an ongoing series of chronological events. The book is even broken up into conventional chapters, and they are numbered in order rather than in Gertrude Stein's familiarly playful patterns. Mr. and Mrs. Reynolds— they are given no first names, although some of their relatives are assigned first names—live in an unnamed country, but obviously in the south of France in a landscape similar to Gertrude Stein's own at Bilignin (the setting for several other works), through a daily routine of uninteresting, monotonous experiences, realistic but unlikely to involve the reader's emotions. The Reynolds's lives are paralleled, however, by the year-by-year growth and development of former native Angel Harper. As he advances, so does Mrs. Reynolds's unnamed terror. Angel Harper is Adolph Hitler who, annually on his birthday, reflects back on a series of odd events in his early youth: at nine his bedroom is a prison; at twelve he dresses in drag; at fourteen he is a sexual misfit. Mrs. Reynolds wishes for his death with neither rancor nor sympathy. She is a nervous and excitable person, influenced by her dreams and fortune-telling; by comparison, her husband is solid and stable. Both of them rely on sleep to restore their courage, but her nightly visions suggest future fears, and she does not rest easily until the conclusion of the novel when Angel Harper is "not fifty-five alive" (266). The novel is an attempt, Gertrude Stein declares in her brief epilogue, "to show the way anybody could feel these years" (267). At the outset, Mrs. Reynolds cries a good deal, but she only learns to sigh gradually since "sighing is extra" (1), as if accepting one's apprehensions requires patience. To some degree, *Mrs. Reynolds* is an unwritten novel for which the reader is obliged to supply some details, but as a narrative it does progress, if sometimes through a series of casual miracles. Joseph Lane, for instance, who seems to be Joseph Stalin, is the offspring of three people instead of two (53–54), and the daily difficulties of Mr. and Mrs. Reynolds are mild compared to the private demons that afflict Angel Harper. The epilogue concludes by contending that the novel is concerned with the "state of mind" rather than a "historical" progression of events (267), itself a helpful avenue into those events.

Mrs. Reynolds, with an introduction by Lloyd Frankenberg, is the second volume in the Yale University Press edition of Gertrude Stein's unpublished work; 2,500 copies were bound in gray cloth stamped in gold. The book was reprinted by Books for Libraries in 1969, 400 copies issued in red buckram stamped in black. A second printing was bound in dark blue stamped in gold.

NARRATION (1935: 1935)

Gertrude Stein's successful lecture at the University of Chicago in the fall of 1934 motivated an invitation to offer a seminar to a small group of students and to give four new lectures. Written during the busy tour itself, they are less accessible and satisfying than those published as *Lectures in America*.† The first of the *Narration* lectures distinguishes between English and American literature. Placing herself in a long and distinguished list—"Emerson, Hawthorne Walt Whitman Mark Twain Henry James myself Sherwood Anderson Thornton Wilder* and Dashiell Hammitt [*sic*]" (10), she contends that American literature functions through a mobility of language absent from the stability of language in English literature. Since "literature is as anybody can see if they read the writing as a nation makes it be" (5), American writers use alternative rhythms that result from the kind of wrestling with grammar and punctuation she advocates. The second lecture contends that conventional narrative is inappropriate in the modern world. Gertrude Stein modifies somewhat her earlier claims about the emotional life in paragraphs rather than in sentences, finding greater strength in the balance of the latter, with examples from popular road signs as well as from the Old Testament. Her earlier arguments in *Lectures in America* and *Four in America*† about the difference between poetry and prose are also reinforced. In the third lecture, Gertrude Stein takes up journalism and its attempt to render the news "as if the writing were being written as it is read, that is what they mean by hot off the press . . . '' (35). That immediacy, she contends, is only superficial and incomplete, unlike various literary genres she had already mastered. The fourth lecture takes up Gertrude Stein's familiar argument about the influence of a writer's readers, both the external audience and the audience of the self. Talking and lecturing, writing and letter writing, and listening individually and listening as an audience member all differ, she suggests, not only in intention but in creativity. These observations return her to her definition of literature: "the telling of anything but in telling that thing where is the audience. . . . Undoubtedly that audience has to be there for the purpose of recognition as the telling is proceeding to be written and that audience must be at one with the writing'' (60). She excludes the historian and the journalist but suggests that in the future they might be included too. Just at that time, Gertrude Stein was contributing a series of articles to the *New York Herald Tribune*, and her next book was *The Geographical History of America*.† Thornton Wilder contributed an introductory essay to *Narration*.

Narration was published by the University of Chicago Press, 872 copies bound in orange cloth stamped in black, and 120 numbered and signed copies bound in blue stamped in black and gold, issued in a slipcase. In 1969, the University of Chicago Press issued a "collector's edition," 3,000 copies bound in pink paper boards with a chartreuse spine stamped in black and silver.

A NOVEL OF THANK YOU (1925–1926: 1958)

The eighth and final volume of the Yale Edition of the Unpublished Writings of Gertrude Stein is titled after her first extended narrative in nearly fifteen years. Since 1912, she had been working in shorter forms, by her definition "poems," largely accounts in obscure dialogue between her and Alice Toklas of domestic and erotic adventures. By 1925, Gertrude Stein's interests had begun to embrace saints and landscapes, both to play a more important role in subsequent work; in *A Novel of Thank You*, she noted that "a historical novel is not a history of everyone" (146). Talking to herself frequently, much in the manner she employed in *The Making of Americans*,† she broods on the novel as a form which tells the truth and suggests that art itself is life. Her interest lies in the happenings of the plot rather than in rounding off an action with a satisfactory conclusion. Again, the narrative line grows out of autobiographical materials, a disagreement or upset in the placidity of the family life, then a return to friendship as they are "glad to see each other" (72) after their distress. Familiar names of people in the lives of Gertrude Stein and Alice Toklas abound, as well as others not so quickly identified as Mildred Aldrich,* Henry McBride,* Avery Hopwood,* Virgil Thomsom,* Neith Boyce, Ethel Mars,* Romaine Brooks,* the black entertainer Josephine Baker, even the owners and waitresses at the hotel owned by the Pernollet family* where the women had summered in Belley. *A Novel of Thank You* is divided into three parts, the first of 213 erratically numbered chapters, the second of three chapters, the brief third section unbroken and inconclusive. What story or autobiography it does trace is vague and rendered in Gertrude Stein's usual repetition by increment. For example, "this is now to be a very long history of their son and they were after a while their father" (148) is followed by a lengthy description about emotional interaction between brothers, in a manner reminiscent but not imitative of passages in *The Making of Americans*. In effect, the novel is a series of meditations on the nature of the genre itself as a form, as Gertrude Stein notes: "A Novel of Thank You means that at any time they are as much when it is widened by its being worn out worn and less worn then and everybody can say should it be what they came to do" (xiii). The volume concludes with "Three Moral Tales," slight, charming narratives bewildering but relatively easy to read; an odd "Story of Avignon" called "Prudence Caution and Foresight," each given its own orderly section about the family life of Leon; and "A Little Novel," a fragmentary narrative about fourteen people that simply stops after thirty-seven lines without a terminating mark of punctuation. At the conclusion of his rather unilluminating introduction, Carl Van Vechten* relinquished his stewardship as Gertrude Stein's literary executor to Donald Gallup.*

Like all of the earlier Yale volumes, *A Novel of Thank You* was handsomely bound, one thousand copies in bright green cloth stamped in gold. It was reprinted in 1969 by Books for Libraries, four hundred copies issued in red buckram stamped in black. A second printing was bound in dark blue stamped in gold.

OPERAS AND PLAYS (1913–1931: 1932)

Gertrude Stein and Alice Toklas published *Operas and Plays* as the fourth book in their Plain Edition, its contents commencing with *Four Saints in Three Acts*† in complete form rather than in the abbreviated version Virgil Thomson* arranged when he set it to music. Similarly, "They Must. Be Wedded. To Their Wife." is included in complete form rather than in the severely truncated version Gerald Lord Berners* used for his ballet *A Wedding Bouquet*.† The earliest piece in this collection dates to 1913, the only play from that initial period of Gertrude Stein's work with the genre not included in *Geography and Plays*.† Titled "Old and Old," it is more recognizable as a group of brief essays, punning and repeating to describe a visible, domestic milieu, although its final section seems to be about Alice Toklas. The next plays date to the early twenties, including "A Movie," actually a shorthand scenario about an American painter and his Breton girlfriend mixed up in some high jinks with the Secret Service; "Saints and Singing," written in acts, scenes (several with the same number in the same act), and interludes, but with unassigned dialogue; "Reread Another," which assigns dialogue sequentially to mountains, dirigibles, soldiers, pounds, bankers, ribbon makers, grocers, record breakers, sculptors, Negroes, authors, boys, girls, reunions, and pearls, almost always in quartets of these classifications, divided one group from the other by authorial asides; "Objects Lie on a Table," a kind of narrative-dialogue between teachers and a pupil who Richard Bridgman suggests may be Ernest Hemingway; and "A List," the most conventional play in this group because its dialogue is based on speeches in the play *Our Little Wife*, by Avery Hopwood.* He and Stein had thought to collaborate on a drama; instead, she wrote her own and assigned specific speakers, Martha, Maryas, Marius, and Mabel, even though sometimes two of them speak in unison in going through lists in a few words or in paragraphs of non-sequiturs. One other early piece deserves mention: "Capital Capitals," in which the four Provençal cities, Aix, Arles, Avignon, and Les Baux engage in conversation, as Virgil Thomson arranged it for four male soloists and piano. The rest of the material in *Operas and Plays* includes "A Lyrical Opera Made by Two," in which the two are Gertrude Stein as "a large medium sized pleasant handsome man" and "a fair sized dark charming medium sized lady." Both its narrative and its dialogue are charged with embarrassingly intimate suggestions of domestic and erotic life, including some preoccupation with scatology. "Deux Soeurs Qui Ne Sont Pas Soeurs," also featuring Gertrude Stein and Alice Toklas as well as their poodle Basket,* is a brief scenario in French suggesting a silent movie farce. Two plays, "Louis XI and Madame Giraud" and "Madame Recamier," may derive from history, although some of Gertrude Stein's contemporaries put in appearances too. The first of these begins promisingly: "The courtiers make witty remarks" (345), but the reader is then offered none; the second of these, Gertrude Stein says in *Everybody's Autobiography*,† she wrote "in words of one syllable. . . . and it makes a very good poem" (114), but neither claim proves true. "A Bouquet. Their Wills." begins with an unpunctuated, undiagrammable paragraph about making a bouquet, followed by a series of acts in each of which Gertrude Stein contemplates wills and beneficiaries following various family catastrophes. "The Five Georges" includes George Platt Lynes,* Georges Maratier,* Georges Hugnet* (deliberately misidentified) but called by last initials and in one case as "of England"; "At Present," a play in which "Nothing But Contemporaries [are] Allowed," includes most of the people Gertrude Stein had been seeing at the end of the twenties, even those like Avery Hopwood who had died; "Lynn and the College de France" and "Say It with Flowers" have specified settings and characters, but like the other selections in *Operas and Plays* they are not stageable in any conventional sense, representing instead Gertrude Stein's attempt in the dramatic form to tell what happens without showing or telling it, in static action that like landscape itself is merely "there," as she often explained her intention.

Operas and Plays was published in an edition of five hundred copies, bound in tan paper wrappers and issued in a matching slipcase, both stamped in black. Of the pieces not included in *Last Operas and Plays*† or published separately, only "Say It with Flowers" was printed in *Selected Operas and Plays*† in 1970. The book was reprinted in its entirety by Station Hill Press in 1987. Virgil

Thomson's musical setting of "Capital Capitals" was published in *New Music*, April 1947.

PAINTED LACE (1914–1927: 1955)

Volume 5 of the Yale Edition of the Unpublished Writings of Gertrude Stein is another of those collections, either by design or accident, guaranteed to obfuscate by printing materials out of chronological sequence. Various sections are titled "Events," "Voice Lessons and Calligraphy," " 'Eye Lessons,' " "Landscapes and Geography," and "Portraits and Figures," all of which are accurate enough but of little value to the reader who attempts to read Gertrude Stein's sequential experiments and achievements. Such an arrangement guarantees to cloud auto-biographical implications. The earliest of the pieces deal directly with the Stein-Toklas domestic life, although few of them are so frankly intimate as the material in *Bee Time Vine*.† Some, like the title piece, seem to be transcriptions of conversations between the two women, largely of private interests, peppered with references impossible to identify. As is usually true, the love songs are more embarrassing than erotic. In many selections Gertrude Stein was experimenting with words in isolation, stringing them down the page, each followed by a period; other pieces make this a helpful collection in tracing this manner in its transition from the cubist-like isolation of images following *Tender Buttons*† from 1912 to the preoccupying landscape writing of the twenties. Some few selections in *Painted Lace* are interesting for themselves, and taken in chronological sequence with work in other Yale volumes, they amplify Gertrude Stein's progression. "Independent Embroidery," for example, dating to 1915, again an account of "daily island living," as she often called it, actually blurs the line between Gertrude Stein's writing and Alice Toklas's needlework, an assessment of one becoming an assessment of the other, interrupted by vagaries of the world outside their self-imposed shelter. As is often the case, Gertrude Stein's recording of the actual conversation is nonselective, but here, as in "A New Happiness," also dating to the earliest period represented in the book, the placidity of a symbiotic collaboration is clear enough. *Painted Lace* is valuable for containing "The Reverie of the Zionist," one of the few times Gertrude Stein commented on her being Jewish; perhaps her earliest meditation on saints, later to become more preoccupying; and, from 1924, a transitional piece, "Elected Again," that explains succinctly why she moved away from verbal games and back to narrative. From the earliest material, private and hermetic, to the latest, "Meditations on Being about to Visit My Native Land," written in 1934, *Painted Lace* at least embraces representative work from various phases of her most demanding period. And it is now and again modified with hilarious moments, as in "Mr. Miranda and William," a dialogue disguised in the shape of a paragraph that reads like an exchange out of either Samuel Beckett or Abbott and Costello.

Daniel-Henry Kahnweiler* supplied the introduction for *Painted Lace*, largely a memoir about his personal connections with Gertrude Stein and his belief that her poetry was "very close to the painting of Picasso* and Juan Gris,* and, in another field, to the music of Schönberg" (xii). Bound in rust cloth and stamped in gold, *Painted Lace* was issued in an edition of one thousand copies. It was reprinted by Books for Libraries in 1969, four hundred copies issued in red buckram stamped in black. A second printing was bound in dark blue stamped in gold.

PARIS FRANCE (1939: 1940)

Paris France is Gertrude Stein's loving apostrophe to her adopted country, but it is less about the capital city than it is about the country's character, and less about the country itself than about her own apprehensions over the coming conflict. *Paris France* was published the day that Paris fell to the German invaders, contradicting Gertrude Stein's passionate self-deception that there would be no world war. Written in her gossipy, confidential manner, familiar from *Everybody's Autobiography*† two years before, the book roams and ruminates freely about French rural life based on "tradition and human nature" (8). Nothing is important but "daily living and the ground that gives it to them and defending themselves from the enemy" (8–9). Gertrude Stein makes no attempt to follow the chronology of the calendar nor of her emotions; instead, she discusses at random such comfortable topics as fashion, food, and farming. She introduces various French people she knows with vignettes from their lives to demonstrate the national character, and she comments freely on its similarities to and differences from the rest of Western civilization. More than once, she allies herself as a writer with the country's attitude toward war itself, for example: "I like words of one syllable and it works out very well in the French order for general mobilisation. The printed thing gives all the detail and then it says the army de terre, de mer et de l'air. That is very impressive when you read it in every village" (65). War can even have its advantages, making "a concentration of isolation" (65), which she and Alice Toklas must themselves have been feeling at the time. "Perhaps this war will make ages reasonable again," she ventures (66). In the middle of *Paris France*, Gertrude Stein inserted a story about Helen Button, a little girl from her village, whose encounters with a probable bomb, and with a cart hauling the dead, bring war frighteningly close: "The nights were black and the days were dark and there was no morning. Not in war-time" (84). Nevertheless, Gertrude Stein concludes her book on a positive note, dedicating it to France and England because they will "civilise the twentieth century and make it be a time when anybody can be free, free to be civilised and to be" (120).

   Paris France was first published by Batsford in England, bound in pink cloth printed in blue. The Charles Scribner's Sons edition of imported copies identically bound was followed by two subsequent bindings, the first of red cloth printed in blue and the second of blue cloth printed in black. Liveright issued a paperback edition of five thousand copies in 1970.

PICASSO (1938: 1938)

Gertrude Stein wrote this study of Pablo Picasso's* work in French, not without difficulty and not without sustained assistance from Alice Toklas over grammar and other matters of rhetorical mechanics, according to her letters to friends at the time. It was published shortly thereafter in English, probably translated by Alice Toklas. Both versions were illustrated with sixty-four pages of paintings, drawings, and photographs. Essentially a restatement of Gertrude Stein's earlier opinions of modern painting, *Picasso* further identified her with the artist himself, indicating her understanding of his work because she was attempting to express "the same thing in literature" (16). More a monograph than a full-length work— it is only fifty pages long—*Picasso* moves chronologically without chapters or other divisions, accounting for the artist's major shifts of focus and his influences, and it is written in Gertrude Stein's most accessible style. Shortly after her own silence had fallen upon her, following *The Autobiography of Alice B. Toklas*, † silence overtook Picasso, and she makes something of the irony of that coincidence, both of them having become infected with an awareness of audience. She recovered to engage in a kind of writing to which her public could respond, and he recovered to illustrate the century's "splendor," less reasonable but more "splendid," a word she uses incessantly. The twentieth century, she concludes, "sees the earth as no one has ever seen it, the earth has a splendor that it never has had, and as everything destroys itself in the twentieth century and nothing continues, so then the twentieth century has a splendor which is its own and Picasso is of this century . . . " (50).

Picasso was published as *Anciens et Moderns, Picasso* by Librairie Floury, in stiff white wrappers printed in black and blue. Batsford published the book in England at about the same time, bound in pink cloth printed in blue. The identical American edition was issued by Scribner's a few months later, in 1939. A subsequent English printing was bound in white cloth. Beacon Press published the book in paperback in 1959.

A PRIMER FOR THE GRADUAL UNDERSTANDING OF GERTRUDE STEIN (1895–1946: 1971)

At the time of Gertrude Stein's death, Robert Bartlett Haas* was working with her on an anthology of selections to illustrate her major periods and styles, although Carl Van Vechten's* *Selected Writings of Gertrude Stein*† seems to have thwarted the project. Haas's *Primer* is "A Little Anthology" of brief pieces and selections from longer ones, beginning with Gertrude Stein's undergraduate themes at Radcliffe College and progressing through her early portraits of Alice Toklas and Picasso;* visible, audible, and spatial description illustrated with poems and plays; the natural landscape; what Haas calls "literary music" illustrated with Sherwood Anderson's* portrait, with its private songs to Alice Toklas; her first attempt to explain herself, "An Elucidation"; and examples of her "identity" or audience writing as well as of her "entity" or private writing. In addition to this "little anthology," an excellent introduction for the literary swimmer willing to test the water in the Stein sea, the *Primer* includes a transcript of Gertrude Stein talking about her work a few months before her death. Although her memory is faulty and often factually inaccurate, her recounting of her career and its aims is lucid, witty, and comprehensive, even though her explications of specific pieces from *Tender Buttons*† are less than satisfactory. The *Primer* concludes with a family hagiography by Gertrude Stein's niece, Gertrude Stein Raffel, and an essay by Donald Sutherland* assessing Gertrude Stein's place in twentieth-century literary aesthetics.

A Primer for the Gradual Understanding of Gertrude Stein was published by Black Sparrow Press in an edition of 510 copies bound in tan paper boards printed in red and brown with a red cloth spine, and 1,469 matching copies (minus the cloth spine) in paperback. A limited edition of 60 copies, identical except for a metallic cloth spine, issued in a red box, was issued simultaneously.

PORTRAITS AND PRAYERS (1909–1931: 1934)

Like *Geography and Plays*† and *Useful Knowledge*† before it, and several volumes in the Yale edition of her unpublished writings to come, *Portraits and Prayers* is deliberately a grab bag of shorter and longer pieces printed out of chronological sequence. At least a decade earlier, Gertrude Stein had conceived of such a collection as *Portraits and Prayers*, mentioning it on more than one occasion in her letters to Carl Van Vechten.* It begins with her earliest (1909) portraits of Matisse* and Picasso,* first published by Alfred Stieglitz* in *Camera Work* in 1912, followed by her second portrait of Picasso, written fourteen years later. Other portraits—including those from *Dix Portraits*† as well as Jean Cocteau,* "Sitwell Edith Sitwell,"* one of her nephews, Max Jacob,* several artists, several of friends like Mildred Aldrich* and enemies like Ernest Hemingway,* even one of her dog Basket*—offer a wide variety of styles in this particular self-generated genre. "Portrait of Mabel Dodge at the Villa Curonia," first printed privately in 1912 and partly responsible for Gertrude Stein's early literary notoriety in New York, is included in *Portraits and Prayers*; it is an excellent example of a transitional piece between Gertrude Stein's shift from prolix narrative to startling image. *The Autobiography of Alice B. Toklas*† calls "The Life and Death of Juan Gris"* "the most moving thing Gertrude Stein has ever written" (260); surely it is one of the most accessible pieces in *Portraits and Prayers*, a lament for one of her closest friends and a celebration of his role in the development of cubism. A group of anonymous portraits draws the collection to a close, followed by "An Elucidation," Gertrude Stein's first attempt to explain herself. Written in 1923 and first published in *transition* magazine in April 1927, it makes none of the concessions to readers that *Composition as Explanation*† and *Lectures in America*† offer. As hermetic as the work it sets out to explain, it operates almost exclusively through examples of itself, direct elucidation playing several syntactical games simultaneously so that the explanation becomes itself a direct example:

> To begin elucidating.
> If I say I stand and pray.
> If I say I stand and I stand and you understand and if I say I pray I pray to-day if you understand me to say I pray to-day you understand prayers and portraits.
> You understand portraits and prayers.
> You understand.
> You do understand. (249)

Portraits and Prayers was published by Random House in an edition of eighteen hundred copies, bound in cloth imprinted with a photograph of Gertrude Stein by Carl Van Vechten, and with a maroon and orange cloth spine, in a clear cellophane wrapper printed with author and title in maroon. A second printing was bound in tan cloth.

THE RADCLIFFE THEMES (1894–1895: 1949)

Gertrude Stein's important work at Radcliffe—then called the Harvard Annex—was done under William James* and Hugo Münsterberg,* but she took a course in creative writing too, taught by the American poet William Vaughn Moody.* Her compositions indicate almost nothing of the writer Gertrude Stein was to become, although some of them suggest some of her life-long concerns, if expressed only crudely. Often, the compositions are compassionate, and they are always candid. Also, inevitably perhaps, they are filled with the usual errors in grammar and punctuation that plague undergraduate writing, as well as some peculiarities of Gertrude Stein's own. Several pieces are autobiographical, both about some experiences at Radcliffe, and in one instance a childhood memoir about her brother Leo* and herself on a hunting expedition, at the conclusion of which their family calls them "infant prodigies" (136). One of the compositions offers a picture of how Gertrude Stein viewed herself at the time, "a young girl rather stout, fair and with a singularly attractive face, attractive chiefly because puzzling. Her mouth was just saved from complete severity by a slight fulness of the lower lip, which seemed rather an after-thought of her Creator. . . . Her chin did its best to counteract this apology by hard lines of determination, but in spite of its best efforts, she remained distinctly lovable" (127–28). Nearly all of the compositions indicate rather more mature judgment than undergraduate writing ordinarily offers.

"The Radcliffe Manuscripts" were included as an edited appendix—with Moody's criticisms—by Rosalind S. Miller to her *Gertrude Stein: Form and Intelligibility*. It was published by the Exposition Press, bound in brown cloth printed in gold.

REFLECTION ON THE ATOMIC BOMB (1913–1946: 1973)

Volume 1 of the Black Sparrow Press edition of the previously uncollected writings of Gertrude Stein is comprised of works spanning nearly the whole of her career. They appeared originally in magazines, as introductory notes for art exhibitions, and in books by other writers, all "obscure or transient" ([7]), as Robert Bartlett Haas* observes in his brief preface. Introductory notes precede the entries, however, and are helpful in placing these fugitive pieces in Gertrude Stein's career. Although grouped by type, each section is arranged chronologically. The astonishing range of publications indicates how far afield Gertrude Stein had to go to get herself into print, from the humor magazine *Life* to the slick *Vanity Fair* to the dignified *Yale Review*. In the section titled "Direct Description," several pieces about the first world war are of biographical interest in placing Gertrude Stein and Alice Toklas in its frame. "Portraits and Appreciations" includes notes or essays on painters Francis Picabia,* Raoul Dufy, Élie Lascaux,* and her last discovery Sir Francis Rose;* reviews of books by Sherwood Anderson* and Alfred Kreymborg, and about Oscar Wilde; and friendly assessments of Jane Heap,* Alfred Stieglitz,* and Pierre Balmain.* All of them reflect Gertrude Stein's consistent attitude that Haas points out: "Nobody needs criticism, only appreciation" (42). The section titled "Nature and the Emotions" contains work from Gertrude Stein's lyrical landscape period of the twenties, both in prose and verse. Two plays, "Daniel Webster. Eighteen in America," which seems to be an extension of *Four in America*† and a forerunner to *The Mother of Us All,*† and "Lucretia Borgia," a brief forerunner of *Ida,*† comprise a section. Haas arranges another group from the twenties as "Literary Music," analytical but playful, including an amazing inventory of a library: sixty single-sentence "Descriptions of Literature" without naming a single title. In "Syntax and Elucidation," Haas includes Gertrude Stein's meditations on history, sentences, narration, the writer and the critic, and, finally, the title piece, "Reflection on the Atomic Bomb," in which she expresses disinterest and no fear of annihilation because "there is so much to be scared of so what is the use of bothering to be scared," and her interest instead in the living (161).

Reflection on the Atomic Bomb was published by Black Sparrow Press, 821 copies bound in light green paperboards printed in blue, purple, and red, with a blue spine, 50 copies with a purple spine, and 2,241 paperback copies.

SELECTED OPERAS AND PLAYS (1913–1946: 1970)

John Malcolm Brinnin's edition of Gertrude Stein's plays includes a selection spanning her entire career in the genre, from "Ladies Voices" and "What Happened," trying, she averred, to tell what happened without telling it, to her major works in dramatic form, *Four Saints in Three Acts,*† "Doctor Faustus Lights the Lights," "Yes Is for a Very Young Man," and *The Mother of Us All.*† Also, he includes several plays from earlier collections, *Geography and*

Plays,† *Operas and Plays*,† and *Last Operas and Plays*,† and two of her children's plays from *The Gertrude Stein First Reader*,† "Three Sisters Who Are Not Sisters" and "Look and Long." Brinnin's introduction musters the case for Gertrude Stein's plays as extensions of the cubist movement and "the surrounding reality" of the landscape, aligning her with Samuel Beckett, Harold Pinter, and Eugene Ionesco (xiii). As an introduction to her use of the dramatic medium, the selection is commendable; as a representation of her total output in the genre, it is lopsided, since it concentrates on those that have been set to music or otherwise staged, while the bulk of the plays remains on the printed page only.

Selected Operas and Plays was published by the Univerity of Pittsburgh Press, three thousand copies bound in gold cloth printed in black with a black cloth front half-cover. A paperback edition was subsequently issued.

SELECTED WRITINGS OF GERTRUDE STEIN (1905–1945: 1946)

Carl Van Vechten* edited this first selective anthology of Gertrude Stein's work, with her cooperation. His appreciative introduction and cursory headnotes preface a wide variety of materials, arranged out of chronological sequence. *The Autobiography of Alice B. Toklas*† opens the volume, followed by Stein's lecture on *The Making of Americans*† and Van Vechten's injudicious cutting from *The Making of Americans*, drawn largely from its early sections but indicating neither by ellipses nor by paragraph spacing where he had excised massive portions. "Melanctha" from *Three Lives*† and all of *Tender Buttons*† are included, followed by the lecture "Composition as Explanation." Portraits of Cézanne, Picasso,* Matisse,* Henry McBride,* and Mabel Dodge;* two stories, "As A Wife Has A Cow: A Love Story" and "Miss Furr and Miss Skeene"; two plays, "Ladies Voices" and "What Happened"; two poems, "Susie Asado" and "Preciosilla"; an impressionist essay in the manner of *Tender Buttons*, "A Sweet Tail (Gypsies)"; and the libretto version of *Four Saints in Three Acts* offer a good deal of variety. The selection concludes with "The Winner Loses," Gertrude Stein's gossipy but engaging memoir about life during the German occupation of France, and the final section of *Wars I Have Seen* about the liberation and the arrival of the American army. Gertrude Stein wrote a brief preamble, just a month before her death, to introduce the volume, confessing that she "always wanted to be historical, from almost a baby on," acknowledging Van Vechten's loyalty and expressing her pleasure in the selection: "all that are here are those that I wanted the most, thanks and thanks again" ([vii]). Arguably, this book remains the best general introduction to her work.

Selected Writings of Gertrude Stein was published by Random House, bound in tan cloth printed in gold on blue in an initial printing of 10,000 copies. The Modern Library issued 7,500 copies in its standard binding in 1962, with a new introduction by F. W. Dupee. Vintage Books issued its first paperback printing of 7,500 copies, in 1972.

STANZAS IN MEDITATION AND OTHER POEMS
(1929–1933: 1956)

The title piece in the sixth volume of the Yale Edition of the Unpublished Writings of Gertrude Stein takes up well over half of it. Donald Sutherland,* who wrote the preface, and, later, Ulla E. Dydo have rightly observed that "Stanzas in Meditation" marked a turning point between Gertrude Stein's experiments with writing and her more accessible work that began with *The Autobiography of Alice B. Toklas.*† If, as Gertrude Stein contended, writing was either "identity" or "entity," "audience" or "self," *The Autobiography of Alice B. Toklas* and "Stanzas in Meditation" may be each other's alter ego. Each is unique, the *Autobiography* because it is entirely alien to anything else Gertrude Stein ever wrote, and "Stanzas in Meditation" because of its length, its subject matter, and its "summit of innovation," the "last reach of her dialectic," as Sutherland put it in his preface to the work (v). "Stanzas in Meditation" is divided into five sections, the first and shortest of fifteen stanzas, the last and longest of eighty-three; the others are of about equal length. The stanzas themselves vary from one line to several pages, and in lines varying from single words to a few lines so long that they spill over to a second one. None of them is *about* anything, and with few exceptions they go out of their way to avoid sensory images; rarely are nouns visualized; occasional names are never in context of action; occasionally rhyme intrudes and familiar patterns of repetition, but not often enough to allow construction of any visceral response to the material. Language is reduced to itself, useful neither for information nor communication, although there are occasional imprecations to Alice Toklas: "Tell me darling tell me true / Am I all the world to you" (50). More often, "Stanzas in Meditation," referred to in *The Autobiography of Alice B. Toklas* as Gertrude Stein's "real achievement of the commonplace" (276), is an apology for compromising herself in writing for a popular audience, a "parallel autobiography," in Richard Bridgman's judgment (217). More often, the lack of specific reference and image allows ideas to function independently of preconceived or automatic responses from the reader, so that a sentence like "This which I think now is this" (99) takes sense from itself, isolated in its own aesthetic rectitude. Read out of sequence, dipped into casually like, say, Tennyson's *In Memoriam*, the "Stanzas in Meditation" yield more readily, and "What is strange is this" (125). Moreover, the sequence ends on a note to suggest that Gertrude Stein had suffered no loss of permanent integrity: "I will be well welcome when I come. / Because I am coming. / Certainly I come having come" (151). The remainder of the volume contains "Winning His Way. A Narrative Poem of Poetry," written about the same time and familiarly concerned with friendship, fame, and poetry, the text broken into units of one or two or three words, in the manner of "They Must. Be Wedded. To Their Wife."; and it concludes with a dozen shorter pieces. Many of them approximate conventional prosodies, with ballad stanzas and rhymes, but all in one way or another are scarred by references to some dissension in the Stein-Toklas alliance.

Stanzas in Meditation was published by Yale, fifteen hundred copies bound in green cloth printed in gold. It was reprinted in 1969 by Books for Libraries, four hundred copies issued in red buckram stamped in black. A second printing was bound in dark blue stamped in gold.

TENDER BUTTONS (1912: 1914)

The best known and most often reprinted of Gertrude Stein's hermetic writings, *Tender Buttons* is an outgrowth of the experiments that began to occur in the second halves of "A Long Gay Book" and "G.M.P.," both published in *Matisse Picasso and Gertrude Stein*† twenty years later. There are three sections to the work: "Objects," "Food," and "Rooms," and the "tender buttons" of the first two are, figuratively, gently precise images, as in the familiar saw, "to hit it on the button." Various critics have assessed the work as too obscure to give up its meaning; as having too much meaning to communicate; as an unconscious mandala; as an imaginative rendering of the Stein-Toklas household; as that rendering with slyly erotic references; as the visible world described; and as cubist visions. Gertrude Stein, in *Lectures in America*† said she was making poetry by avoiding nouns because "nouns must go in poetry as they had gone in prose if anything that is everything was to go on meaning something" (242); for her, language was "not imitation either of sounds or colors or emotions" but "an intellectual recreation" (238). In an interview just a few months before her death, she thought *Tender Buttons* was "interesting as there is as much failure as success in it. When this was printed I did not understand this creation" (*PGU* 29–30). Her explanations of random selections from *Tender Buttons* are not so enlightening as a novice might wish: "A little monkey goes like a donkey" illustrates "movement"; "A white hunter is nearly crazy" is "an abstraction of color"; a longer excerpt from "Sugar" is "rather fine, looking at it dispassionately"; other selections are excused as private but "definite associations" (*PGU* 24–28). Word clusters rather than images clusters serve to integrate "Objects"; "Food" describes a varied menu, although "the whole thing is not understood" (34); neither includes rare invented words that turned up infrequently in other works of this period, but the startling wrenchings in conventional use frequently give the impression of invention: "A shallow hole rose on red, a shallow hole in and in this makes ale less" (26); "Asparagus in a lean in a lean to hot" (51); "It was an extra leaker with a see spoon, it was an extra licker with a see spoon" (57). Some few are almost immediately accessible: "A Petticoat" is "A light white, a disgrace, an ink spot, a rosy charm" (22); some are merely funny: one of four "Chicken" entries reads "Alas a dirty word, alas a dirty third alas a dirty third, alas a dirty bird" (54); but most are more demanding, even impenetrable: "Rhubarb is susan not susan not seat in bunch toys not wild and laughable not in little places not in neglect and vegetable not in fold coal age not please'' (50). The third section, ''Rooms,'' is composed of paragraphs but without titles. ''Objects'' and ''Food'' may occupy space; ''Rooms'' defines the space itself, but the content of the second operates at much the same level of private discourse about private perceptions. Read chronologically, *Tender Buttons* offers a dense assessment by association of a personal milieu and what it houses, including the endearments, sometimes erotic, of its inhabitants. Dipped into, a piece here or there, *Tender Buttons* offers even a reluctant reader the same combination of outrage and delight he is likely to experience on discovering in ''Preciosilla,'' a poem written at about the same time, ''Toasted susie is my ice-cream'' (*SW* 486).

Tender Buttons was first published by Donald Evans's* Claire Marie Press, which he had founded to print his own work, one thousand copies bound in yellow paper boards with a green paper label. It was reprinted in *transition*, fall 1928; in *Selected Writings of Gertrude Stein*;† and in *Writings and Lectures 1911–1945*.† Haskell House issued a stapled offset paperback, circa 1965.

THREE LIVES (1903–1906: 1909)

First published at Gertrude Stein's own expense, *Three Lives* is, with *The Autobiography of Alice B. Toklas*,† her best-known work. Neither is characteristic. Written, she claimed, under the influence of Flaubert and Cézanne, the first story actually imitates Flaubert's ''Un Coeur Simple,'' and in an interview a few months before her death, Gertrude Stein claimed that Cézanne had motivated her through his discovery ''that in composition one thing was as important as another thing. Each part is as important as the whole,'' avoiding a central idea or subject in favor of the entirety of the work (*PGU* 15). ''The Good Anna'' is about a German servant whose own idiom in expression infects the narrative line with attenuated locutions. Anna drives herself to death through loyal devotion to her employers. ''The Gentle Lena,'' written next but placed third in the book, is a better sustained narrative, and it is among Gertrude Stein's most successful achievements as a brief piece of naturalism. Lena, another German servant, is coerced into a marriage by a greedy relative, only to find herself abandoned at the altar, then married when her fiancé's father insists that the contract be fulfilled. Lena dies in childbirth. The third of the *Three Lives* is ''Melanctha,'' in which the protagonist is a black woman in Baltimore in love with Jeff Campbell, a medical doctor, locked in a frustrating and frustrated triangle with Melanctha's friend Rose. The story is spun out in a series of lengthy conversations between Jeff and Melanctha about the nature of loving and sexual torment. Melanctha deliberately distorts memory, living only for the present at the expense of the past, torn between her primal feelings and her sense of morality. The argument is between her ''laugh then so hard'' and her ''real sweetness'' (138). The story experiments with sexual euphemisms and verbal substitutions, later to play a crucial role in Gertrude Stein's work, and the laborious protractions of these largely inarticulate people signal her subsequent development. No plot summary can suggest the power of Gertrude Stein's prose in these stories, simultaneously compelling and numbing in their effect, particularly so in "Melanctha." Twenty years later, in *Composition as Explanation,*† and ten years after that, in a whole series of lectures, Gertrude Stein referred to this as a "prolonged present," delaying her telling until it had been transformed into a "continuous present." The convoluted sentences in endless repetition and insistence identify her early work, transforming the dialogue or monologue into narrative, as her ensuing *The Making of Americans*† and many portraits published in *Two*† generously demonstrate. Representative passages from each of the *Three Lives* indicate the direction her narrative would take. From "The Good Anna": " 'I stayed with him just so long as I could stand it, but now he is moved away up town too far for poor people, and his wife, she holds her head up so and always is spending so much money just for show, and so he can't take right care of us poor people any more' " (69). From "The Gentle Lena": " 'I never see anybody like you Lena. Herman is very good to you, you always say so, and he don't treat you bad ever though you don't deserve to have anybody good to you, you so careless all the time, Lena, letting yourself go like you never had anybody tell you what was the right way you should know how to be looking. No, Lena, I don't see no reason you should let yourself go so and look so untidy Lena, so I am ashamed to see you sit there looking so ugly, Lena' " (272). From "Melanctha": " 'Tell me true, Dr. Campbell, how you feel about being always friends with me. I certainly do know, Dr. Campbell, you are a good man, and if you say you will be friends with me, you certainly never will go back on me, the way so many kinds of them do to every girl they ever get to like them. Tell me for true, Dr. Campbell, will you be friends with me' " (127).

Three Lives was published by the Grafton Press, bound in navy cloth printed in gold, in an edition of 1,000 copies, 300 of which were issued in England by John Lane, the Bodley Head, six years later. John Lane* reprinted the book in 1920, bound in blue printed in gold. John Rodker reprinted it in 1927, bound in blue-gray paper boards printed in black. Charles and Albert Boni published the book in America that same year, bound in white and teal cloth with a red spine printed in teal. The Modern Library first published the book in 1933, 5,000 copies in its standard bindings. New Directions began printing it in 1941, the 2,500 copies bound in red cloth printed in black and subsequent printings in blue paper boards. The Pushkin Press in England reprinted the Rodker edition in 1945, bound in red cloth printed in black. Random House began *Three Lives* in paperback in 1958 with a run of 10,000, and Vintage Books has kept it in paperback since. No other book in Gertrude Stein's bibliography has undergone such a varied printing history.

TWO: GERTRUDE STEIN AND HER BROTHER AND OTHER EARLY PORTRAITS (1908–1912: 1951)

Two is the first of eight volumes in the Yale Edition of the unpublished writings of Gertrude Stein. It bridges the gap between the second half of *The Making of*

Americans,† actually overlapping it, and *Tender Buttons*,† radically different efforts that are both immediately identifiable as kinds of experiments in language for which Stein is usually recognized. The title portrait is the longest one, a 142-page exorcism written during the period that she began to distance herself from her brother Leo Stein* and to identify herself with Alice Toklas. Unlike other portraits, in which the concentration is usually on one person or on one group identified in the title, "Two" has several characters, typically unnamed but untypically confused. The "two" are Gertrude and Leo Stein, but as the portrait develops, the title suggests their sister-in-law, Sarah Stein, and eventually only Gertrude Stein and Alice Toklas. As she discovered that "sound was coming out of her and she was knowing this thing" (5), Gertrude Stein became less dependent on her brother, who had grown to dismiss her writing as valueless. As his literal deafness increases in the portrait, it becomes synonymous with his deafness to his sister's work; as Alice Toklas's receptivity to the work increases, so is she able to become the alter ego that Leo Stein had represented. Gertrude Stein's participial locutions deflect an easy read, but the elementary circumstances are not difficult to follow. Other portraits in *Two* include "Jenny, Helen, Hannah, Paul and Peter," identified in manuscript as "Laura, Miriam, Adele, Ben, and Joe" Oppenheimer, the family with whom Gertrude Stein often attended the opera during her student days at Radcliffe; and groups of unnamed people locked in various relationships or individuals, for example, painters Maurice Sterne,* André Derain,* Patrick Bruce,* and Arthur Frost,* sculptor David Edstrom,* writer Hutchins Hapgood,* and actress Julia Marlowe.* Sometimes the names are disguised, for example Leo Stein's mistress Nina Auzias* as "Elise Surville," and Isadora Duncan* as "Orta or One Dancing." In all of these pieces, Gertrude Stein probes character through relationships, spoken or unspoken, public or private, with others or with the self, rather than through plot, although a tenuous narrative always emerges. For instance, "Harriet Fear," who is Toklas's friend Harriet Levy,* is a woman whose portrait is drawn from her actually being afraid. She is "one extraordinary in being living" (343), but as "being afraid in being living is quite common, is in a way not very common, that is to say each one, that is to say very many are, for very considerable pieces of living when terrible things are happening, are not being afraid in being living and very many are sometime in their living quite completely afraid of being living" (344), she comes to "learn something" to enable her "being one going on being living and this one certainly was not then afraid in being living" (346). *Two* concludes with three group portraits, one a street scene, and the others at a department store in which the "one" person in earlier portraits becomes "some."

Yale University Press published two thousand copies of *Two*, bound in black cloth printed in red and blue. Janet Flanner supplied the foreword. The book was reprinted by Books for Libraries in 1969, four hundred copies issued in red buckram stamped in black. A second printing was bound in dark blue stamped in gold.

USEFUL KNOWLEDGE (1915–1926: 1928)

Like *Geography and Plays*† four years earlier, *Portraits and Prayers*† six years
later, this volume illustrates Gertrude Stein's deliberate breaking down of all
conventional genres. The selections span ten years, but they are not arranged
chronologically nor are they exclusively "short things she had written about
America," as *The Autobiography of Alice B. Toklas*† claimed (297). "Introducing" reads like a self-portrait, asking questions to lead to a clearer understanding through listening repeatedly. The first entry, "Farragut or A Husband's
Recompense," begins with Alice Toklas's year of birth, 1877, and seems to be
a conversation in the form of a catechism about early experiences, followed by
a contemporary exchange anticipating Gertrude Stein's 1922 recounting of her
proposal of marriage to Alice Toklas, "Didn't Nelly and Lilly Love You." This
is followed by a hymn to their domestic life together. Part 2 is titled "How
Farragut Reformed Her and How She Reformed Him"—Gertrude Stein frequently assigned herself the masculine pronoun—and concludes, apparently autobiographically, "We don't have to go on we wait until inspiration overtakes
us" (17). This longest selection in *Useful Knowledge* is succeeded by several
pieces about differences among various parts of the United States. Gertrude Stein
says she will give four or five examples of each, but they are sufficiently elliptical
to be useless, and at the conclusion she asks the reader to guess which state is
which, subsequently dismissing even that approach: "Supposing no one asked
a question, what would be the answer" (51), a passage anticipating her own
last words. "Among Negroes" is a joint portrait of musical comedy entertainers
then playing in Paris, Josephine Baker, Maude De Forest, and Ida Lewelyn, and
the then popular baritone Paul Robeson* and his wife Essie. "Business in Baltimore" has to do with Stein's relations there, and it ends with a liturgy in the
words, *yes, most, better*, and *best*, that goes on in variation for a page and a
half, an example of her verbal and visual horseplay. "Scenes from a Door" and
several "League" poems are nearly traditional in rhyme and line break. A few
other short pieces are followed by a series of portraits: of Pavel Tchelitchew's*
early lover, the pianist Allen Tanner; of Emily Chadbourne, who with her friend
Etta La Monte was an early visitor at 27 rue de Fleurus; of "Emmet Addis the
Doughboy," a lieutenant colonel in the U.S. Army who was the first husband
of Louise Hayden (later the wife of Redvers Taylor), an old friend of Alice
Toklas; of President Woodrow Wilson, written in 1920 at the time of the League
of Nations and Wilson's defeat; and of the often-reprinted portraits of Sherwood
Anderson* and a second one of Carl Van Vechten.* In "An Instant Answer or
One Hundred Prominent Men," Stein simply lists all one hundred of them with
descriptive epithets, often with hilarious or exasperating results, depending on
the reader's willingness to play her game for which only she knows all the rules.
The thirty-second, for instance, "is an irresistible pedestrian," the thirty-third
"is incapable of amnesty," the thirty-fourth "is second to none in value," the
thirty-ninth "is contented and alarmed," and the fortieth "is rapidly rained on."

The forty-sixth man enumerates all one hundred men, one by one by one by one; and between the sixtieth, who "actually rested," and the sixty-first, "who has had a very astonishing career," Gertrude Stein sandwiched in an extra to the list, a lieutenant colonel (Emmet Addis?) who "was found dead with a bullet in the back of his head and his handkerchief" (148–53). "American Biography" and "Lend a Hand or Four Religions," both dating from 1922, conclude the volume. The first of these is an essay on the genre in the loosest sense; the second, ostensibly a play, employs the form of the catechism again for much of its content. *Useful Knowledge* contains its fair share of memorable passages, at least two of which are of more than passing interest as touchstones for Gertrude Stein's whole career in letters: "Accuse me I accuse myself of earnestness of appreciation of reason and of learning. I do not vary in growth. I am not torn by age. How young am I" (104); "How can language alter. It does not it is an altar" (108).

Useful Knowledge was published by Payson and Clarke, bound in black cloth printed in red, and simultaneously published in England by John Lane, The Bodley Head, bound in black cloth printed in red and green. It is reprinted by Station Hill Press in 1988, with a new introduction by Edward Burns.

A VILLAGE. ARE YOU READY YET NOT YET (1923: 1928)

Most interesting as a bibliographical rarity, this twenty-page pamphlet contains seven lithographs by Elie Lascaux:* two drawings of village scenes from balconies; the other four—one for each village—are three-sided borders for Gertrude Stein's text. Dating to the same period as "Capital Capitals" later printed in *Operas and Plays*,† there is some mention of capitals here, although the four villages seem to be more bucolic than urban. Stein takes the villages up sequentially, then returns to them in more casual order. A couple of stories suggest themselves along the way. The incident, circa 1910, when A. B. Frost and Patrick Henry Bruce* had some conversation about Arthur Frost* (unmentioned here) and horses being led to water, is alluded to casually; then years later Stein spelled it out in *The Autobiography of Alice B. Toklas*.† A woman named Amelia has a furrier husband who has been a farmer. There is an "oration" involved with the subject of an earlier Stein play, "Counting Her Dresses," published in *Geography and Plays*.† Much of *A Village* seems to be another Stein-Toklas dialogue; the title page calls it "a play in four acts," but it is as remote from conventional dramaturgy as her other plays of this period.

A Village was printed on Arches paper in an edition of 102 copies, including 2 struck from Lascaux's defaced stones. For a deluxe edition, 10 additional copies were printed on vellum. Daniel-Henry Kahnweiler* was the publisher. The pamphlet has never been reprinted.

WARS I HAVE SEEN (1943–1944: 1945)

Originally titled in manuscript "All Wars Are Interesting," *Wars I Have Seen* is in part a journal that Gertrude Stein kept for a period of about a year and a half during the Occupation and first days of the liberation of France. It begins with a meditation on the nature of history and human life as correlative progressions through legend, mediaeval, pioneer, and modern periods of development, but shortly becomes a recounting of and running commentary on the life that she and Alice Toklas were obliged to live in Bilignin and, later, Culoz: their interaction with the local peasants and gentry, German troops passing through, bureaucracy, the black market, and the Maquis, or underground resistance movement. Some of Gertrude Stein's autobiographical background expands material introduced in *Everybody's Autobiography*,† and the narrative is interrupted by frequent ruminations in her "identity" manner, clearly designed with readers in mind. More often, however, it merely details the day-to-day survival. Coming immediately after *Mrs. Reynolds*,† in which the war is predicted regularly to be coming to a close, *Wars I Have Seen* reflects impatience, boredom, despair, some of which spills over into the sluggish narrative. Gertrude Stein longs for days "when vegetables grew not in the ground but in tins" (39), impatient with the constant gardening necessary for their survival. Companion's account of their trials, in *The Alice B. Toklas Cook Book*, is better: "In the beginning, like camels, we lived on our past," she begins (203), interrupting her remarkable recipes with incidents at least as memorable and surely more memorably rendered, than anything in *Wars I Have Seen*. The final section of the book makes up for its earlier garrulousness, detailing the excitement of the liberation and the arrival of American troops, officers and enlisted men she and Alice Toklas greeted with equal and unabashed enthusiasm and affection.

Wars I Have Seen was published by Random House, 9,700 copies bound in navy cloth printed in brown and gray; a second printing was bound in blue cloth printed in black and red. The English edition, printed a few months later, included "The Winner Loses" as an appendix, and "We Are Back in Paris," a brief afterword written apparently for this edition; "The Winner Loses" had appeared in *Atlantic Monthly* in November 1940, and Gertrude Stein incorporated "We Are Back in Paris" as part of "Raoul Dufy," written in 1946 and printed in *Harper's Bazaar*, December 1949. The English edition also had four photographs by Cecil Beaton,* and it was bound in blue printed in blue.

A WEDDING BOUQUET (1931: 1938)

Gerald Lord Berners* employed a drastically cut version of Gertrude Stein's play "They Must. Be Wedded. To Their Wife." as the libretto for his ballet, using less than six of its thirty-five pages as originally printed in *Operas and Plays*, † excising and rearranging passages, and repeating lines monotonously.

The result is something Gertrude Stein might have written but didn't. "Pretty soon. They will think. Of some one." occurs once in the original text; Berners repeats it thirty times, divided variously for some polyphonic choral work but nevertheless repeated thirty times. The play's dialogue, divided into brief units by the hundreds of punctuational periods Gertrude Stein was using at the time of composition, was rendered by a mixed chorus during the first performances, given by the Sadler's Wells Ballet; in subsequent revivals, a soloist has spoken the lines. In either instance, the text is declarative rather than lyric, anomalous rather than integrated, and Gertrude Stein's experiment with multiple speakers for single lines—apparent in other works of the period as well—is simply ignored. The scenario, devised by Berners and choreographer Frederick Ashton,* passes in a setting both French provincial from La Belle Époque and Edwardian English, and the tone is satiric: the country wedding of a rakish bridegroom and a bashful bride is disrupted by several former girlfriends, including a seduced and abandoned Julia who is herself pursued by an inebriated Josephine. Gertrude Stein's chihuahua Pépé* is among the cast of characters. Wisely, the title page indicates "words" by Gertrude Stein rather than "libretto," although Berners took liberties with the actual vocabulary from time to time as well.

A Wedding Bouquet, only nominally a work by Gertrude Stein, was published by J. & W. Chester in England, bound in pink wrappers printed in black.

WHAT ARE MASTERPIECES (1913–1936: 1940)

The full text of *Composition as Explanation*† as published in England in 1926— the title essay as well as "Preciosilla," "A Saint in Seven," "Sitwell Edith Sitwell," and "Jean Cocteau"—makes up the bulk of *What Are Masterpieces*; an essay and a lecture, separated by a puppet play, flesh out the book. "An American and France" begins, "America is my country and Paris is my home town and it is as it has come to be" (61). This chatty excursion explains the difference between adventure and romance and between history and romance, as well as the need for two civilizations and two occupations. For Americans, she suggests, England represents history and France represents romance, accounting for the two civilizations one needs. It is not very difficult to tell how Gertrude Stein defines her two occupations: "Writing and reading is to me synonymous with existing, but painting well looking at paintings is something that can occupy me and so relieve me from being existing" (69). "Identity a Poem" seems to be a dramatization of ideas Gertrude Stein had just finished meditating on in *The Geographical History of America*,† dividing human nature from the human mind through an awareness of identity: "I am I because my little dog knows me, but perhaps he does not and if he did I would not be I" (75), and, later, "I am I has really nothing to do with the little dog knowing me, he is my audience, but an audience never does prove to you that you are you" (78). The play is divided up into acts and scenes, with Gertrude Stein's customary repetitions and omissions, and those lines assigned are spoken by

"The dog," "Chorus," and "Tears." Gertrude Stein returned to Cambridge and Oxford during the 1935–1936 winter to lecture, on the invitation of Sir Robert Abdy.* "What Are Master-Pieces and Why Are There So Few of Them" was her work in lecture form, again concerned with the dangers of audience awareness and an artistic vision clouded by reputation: "The minute your memory functions while you are doing anything it may be very popular but actually it is dull. And that is what a master-piece is not, it may be unwelcome but it is never dull" (90). A masterpiece, she contends, "is an end in itself and in that respect it is opposed to the business of living which is relation and necessity," or at least that is what a masterpiece "talks about" (88). Isolation of self and, indeed, from self makes a masterpiece, uninfluenced, pure, inevitably difficult, though only temporarily: "If you do not remember while you are writing, it may seem confused to others but actually it is clear and eventually that clarity will be clear" (89). Beset as she often was by the influence of her readers on her work, Gertrude Stein's concerns in the lecture are not surprising.

What Are Masterpieces was published by the Conference Press, bound in blue cloth printed in red, with an introduction by Robert Bartlett Haas.* Gertrude Stein signed a limited edition of fifty copies. The book was published in an expanded version by Pitman, concluding with Gertrude Stein's replies to a questionnaire. Two thousand copies were issued in 1970, bound in blue cloth printed in silver, and three thousand paperback copies.

THE WORLD IS ROUND (1938: 1939)

On invitation from the publisher, Gertrude Stein wrote a book for children about a little girl named Rose, based on a neighborhood child in Bilignin. Rose sings a good deal and plays with her cousin Willie. He sings as well, and Rose cries a lot. They become involved with some wild animals, notably a lion named Billie. This shorter, first adventure in *The World Is Round* is less interesting than the second one, in which Rose carries a blue chair up a mountain. The journey is fraught with the perils of an epic for the nursery. There is a great deal of thinking about the trip, ruminating on the passing of time through the cycle of day and night, the deliberation of carrying rather than dragging the chair, and Rose's determination, her fear of the dark, and her bravery. Having survived the ordeals, she carves her name around a tree until it meets itself in the ring that "caressed completely caressed and addressed a noun," as Gertrude Stein explained her most famous line in *Lectures in America*† (231). In *The World Is Round*, the implication is that the line meets itself in a never-ending circle around the tree trunk, not as it initially appeared in "Sacred Emily" in 1913 and in several subsequent appearances: "Rose is a rose is a rose is a rose." Then bells ring, the mountain rises above a green grass meadow, and finally Rose reaches the top, sits down in her chair, and sings a number of songs. That night a searchlight from a neighboring mountaintop spots her, Willie at the controls. They turn out not to be cousins after all, get married, and live happily ever after. No summary of the charming plot conveys what is true of all successful children's stories, including this one: an ability to speak to readers of all ages. *The World Is Round* is yet another extension of Gertrude Stein's preoccupations with identity and with fear as well. Two years earlier she had written "The Autobiography of Rose" for Rose Lucy Renée Anne d'Aiguy, a little tale that first appeared in *Partisan Review*, winter 1939, in which fear and experience give way to happy satisfaction.

The World Is Round, on a staring pink paper, was printed in white and blue, with illustrations by Clement Hurd, bound in blue with "ROSE IS ROSE IS A ROSE IS A ROSE" in a large circle on the cover, published by William R. Scott in an edition of 2,975 copies. A limited edition of 350 copies, signed by the author and illustrator, was issued simultaneously, bound in white paper boards printed in gold, in a blue slipcase. Batsford published an edition in England a few months later, bound in red cloth printed in blue, with illustrations by Sir Francis Rose. Haskell House published an offset from the English edition, bound in tan cloth printed in black, in 1966. Scott Books published a new edition with the Hurd illustrations, bound in white cloth printed in pink and blue, in 1967. Camelot Books issued 7,500 copies of the Scott edition in 1972 and again in 1973. Arion Press published a newly designed edition in 1986.

WRITINGS AND LECTURES 1911–1945 (1909–1945: 1967)

Patricia Meyerowitz edited a substantial but unbalanced anthology for publication in England, with an introduction by Elizabeth Sprigge. The lectures include "Composition as Explanation," "What Are Master-pieces and Why Are There So Few of Them," and all of the *Lectures in America*† except "Pictures." The anthology reprints *Tender Buttons*† in its entirety; ten portraits ranging from "Matisse," written in 1909, to "Bernard Faÿ" written in 1929; two plays, "A List" and "Say It with Flowers," both from *Operas and Plays*† but misleading as representative of Gertrude Stein's seventy works in this genre; *Before the Flowers of Friendship Faded Friendship Faded*,† otherwise unavailable except in the Plain Edition of only one hundred copies; and among "later works" are the "Henry James" section of *Four in America*;† five short pieces about money written for the *Saturday Evening Post*; *Ida*† in its entirety; and five chapters plus the epilogue from *Brewsie and Willie*.† The selection claims to be "a collection of Gertrude Stein's most representative achievements," according to the jacket copy of the American paperback version.

Writings and Lectures 1911–1945 was published by Peter Owen in England, bound in green paper boards printed in gold. A paperback edition published by Penguin in 1971 retitles the anthology *Look at Me Now and Here I Am*, using the original title as a subtitle but with "1909" correctly substituted for "1911."

THE YALE GERTRUDE STEIN (1908–1936: 1980)

Richard Kostelanetz supplied the introduction for this anthology of selections from the Yale edition of the unpublished writings of Gertrude Stein. They are organized for variety rather than chronology, neither Gertrude Stein's own chronology nor the chronology of the eight books Yale issued between 1951 and 1958. From the first one, *Two: Gertrude Stein and Her Brother*,† only "Men" is included, representational of the early portraits, but brief and accessible. Three short novels are included from the second volume, *Mrs. Reynolds*:† "Hotel François Ier" and "Brim Beauvais," both from 1931 and both divided into brief units by hundreds of punctuational periods Gertrude Stein was using at that time, and "What Does She See When She Shuts Her Eyes" from 1936, about pulling weeds in Bilignin. The third volume, *Bee Time Vine*,† is represented by over half its full length, including several short lyrics, two autobiographical selections remarkable for their erotic candor, "A Sonatina Followed by Another" and "Lifting Belly," and the incantatory meditation on emotion and grammar, "Patriarchal Poetry," three long pieces from circa 1915, 1921, and 1927 respectively. *As Fine as Melanctha*,† volume 4, is represented only by "Subject-cases: The Background of a Detective Story" from 1923 and "More Grammar for a Sentence" from 1930, reflecting Gertrude Stein's preoccupations with those matters. Volume 5 is represented by the title piece *Painted Lace*† and a few scattered others, including her elliptical one-sentence endorsement for Mark Twain who did "a great American thing" in making "a dead man dead" (192). The sixth volume is also represented by its title piece, *Stanzas in Meditation*,† and it concludes Kostelanetz's anthology. The seventh volume, *Alphabets and Birthdays*,† is represented by "A Birthday Book" from 1924, offering a passage a day for each day of the year. The last volume, *A Novel of Thank You*,† is represented by two brief pieces, "A Little Novel," which opens Kostelanetz's anthology, and "Prudence Caution and Foresight: A Story of Avignon," both from the twenties. Many of these selections seem to have been arbitrary choices, as there are no headnotes nor introductory material to justify them, although Gertrude Stein's major achievements from her unpublished work are included. The 464 pages of *The Yale Gertrude Stein* make an admirable introduction to the 2,500 pages of the eight volumes; however, this book is not representative of Gertrude Stein's complete works and even may be misleading.

The Yale Gertrude Stein was published in paperback, white wrappers printed in blue and black, and in hardcover, bound in blue cloth stamped in silver.

Compositions as Explanations

HALF IN AND HALF OUT OF DOORS: GERTRUDE STEIN AND LITERARY TRADITION

Marianne DeKoven

As a major figure at the intersection of a number of literary traditions—American, modernist, feminine, avant-garde, postmodernist—Gertrude Stein is, like her own Saint Therese, "half in and half out of doors" (*FS3A* 21). Stein's major critics, beginning with Sherwood Anderson* and Thornton Wilder,* have made powerful arguments for Stein's seriousness, centrality, importance to twentieth-century and American literary traditions. Harold Bloom opens his introduction to the recent *Modern Critical Views* volume on Stein with a categorical superlative: "The greatest master of dissociative rhetoric in modern writing is Gertrude Stein" (1). The rest of his first paragraph finds her antecedents not just in William James,* the commonly acknowledged major influence, but also in Ralph Waldo Emerson and Walt Whitman, thereby placing her squarely in the major tradition, as it is currently constituted, of American literature and literary thought. In his subsequent discussion of *The Geographical History of America*,† certainly the central text in any consideration of Stein's relations to American literary tradition, Bloom sees Stein as a "belated" voice of the American Sublime, in the Whitmanian and Emersonian tradition of American literature as locus of abstraction, imagination, originality, freedom, wildness, exuberant affirmation. Bloom ends by naming the feature of Stein's writing that, perhaps more surely than any other, places her in the mainstream of American literature and literary thought: "here is an American writer who has made ghostlier the demarcations between the ordinary and the extraordinary" (6).

For unabashed arguments in favor of the "out-of-doors" view of Stein, we have to go back to earlier critical assessments, since it is no longer acceptable to savage so prominent a woman writer. Stein's current critics may be impatient with her vagaries, but they are never scornful or dismissive. That was not the case with Stein's contemporaries, and those mocking, scathing attacks in *transition* or by B. L. Reid remain a part of the critical discourse on Stein. What's more, even if those who are contemptuous of Stein no longer express their opinion in print, that does not mean that their number has decreased, nor that they hesitate to make their opinion known to colleagues and students.

While I am a staunch advocate of Stein's importance and centrality and am repelled by those ugly pieces of mockery, I want to claim again that the presence of both in the critical discourse on Stein is, as a whole, an accurate reflection of her double position. Stein's criticism is not an anticriticism; her writing is not an antiliterature. To say that would be to naturalize her, attempting again to make her comfortable at the center of some currently constituted oppositional tradition. She does not attack the idea of criticism or the idea of literature; she does not undertake a revision of those categories. She sees herself in her criticism as defining the generic nature of poetry or prose, drama or narrative, or as accounting for the history of English literature or the unique qualities of the American imagination; she sees herself in her literary work as writing "masterpieces" in the tradition of the Bible, Homer, and Shakespeare. Generally, she considers her work an embodiment of modernity; she thinks that she has done *the* literary thinking of the twentieth century. Of course, she is half right, but she is also half wrong. In spite of or along with those facts, it is also true that her work has a peculiar, intractable quirkiness. Richard Kostelanetz may identify *The Making of Americans* with Whitman's *Leaves of Grass*, Ezra Pound's *Cantos*, and William Faulkner's *Absalom, Absalom!* as another "colossal, uneven, digressive, excessive, eccentric masterpiece that every great American innovative artist seems to produce at least once" (*YGS* xvii), but Stein's is a quirkiness that no amount of earnest and reverent explication can entirely suppress. Richard Bridgman's profound and comprehensive account of the relationships between Stein's tormented psychic life and her experimental stylistic practice really amounts to a sustained treatment of the problem of that intractable quirkiness for the critic who wishes to come to terms with Stein's position in modern and American letters. But that position can be named only if we can think about what it means to be half in and half out of doors.

I would argue that Stein's oeuvre occupies, has always occupied, and in fact constitutes a middle ground between center and margin which, if I might shift discourse as I try to think about the Steinian half-in/half-out, deconstructs (puts into question, makes visible) the hierarchical-idealist duality of center and margin itself. That middle ground is invoked by feminist critics such as Christine Froula in "When Eve Reads Milton" as a genuine (nonseparatist, non–self-excluding and therefore non–self-defeating) antidote to patriarchal cultural hegemony. Stein's literary and critical work constitutes an unsynthesized dialectic of canonical and repressed, center and margin, speech and silence, authority and subversion. An exemplary text of that unsynthesized dialectic, the invention of that crucial middle ground, is *The Geographical History of America*.

The subtitle of that book is *The Relation of Human Nature to the Human Mind*, an Emersonian theme indeed, and a great deal of the book is in fact a serious, sustained idealist meditation on the difference between transcendence, or the human mind, and immanence, or human nature. Stein firmly advocates the human mind, and equally firmly places the American imagination in its camp: because our land is so large, so largely flat, and because so much of it, at least in 1935, was uninhabited, abstraction is the natural mode of the American imagination, and abstraction is a quality of the human mind.

I would like us to consider for a moment two things I have just done in the preceding summary. I have normalized both Stein's prose and her thought, and at the same time I have subverted that normalization by recuperating a certain amount of Stein's own defiance of serious thought's aura of responsibility. Stein enacts in *The Geographical History of America* both her desire to take her place within the Great American Tradition and at the same time her absolute refusal of its most elementary convention: the representation of a striving toward an ultimate profundity. Stein's thought is absolutely in earnest, and it is bent on achieving profundity, but her representation of her thought and its variegated paths makes us uneasy because it goes beyond playfulness or erratic individuality or stylistic aberration or any of the other ways we have of explaining to ourselves what Kostelanetz calls our characteristic works of digressive, excessive, eccentric American genius (*YGS* xvii).

In a characteristic and important passage on American geography and the human mind, Stein articulates a version of the theory of manifest destiny. That is certainly her content, her meaning. But I hope the following reading of that passage will make you feel that violence is done to Stein's writing by any such reformulation of her ideas.

> Some people like a big country and some people like a little one but it all depends it depends whether you can wander around a big one or a little one. Wandering around a country has something to do with the geographical history of that country and the way one piece of it is not separated from any other one. Can one say too often just as loving or tears in one's eyes that the straight lines on the map of the United States of America make wandering a mission and an everything and can it only be a big country that can be like that or even a little one. Anyway it has a great deal to do with the relation between human nature and the human mind and not remembering and not forgetting and not as much as much having tears in one's eyes. No no tears in one's eyes, whatever any one else can say. In wandering around a big country some people who live in a big country do not wander. What has wandering got to do with the human mind or religion. But really wandering has something to do with the human mind. A big or a little country. Wandering in a big or little country.
>
> The relation of nervousness to excitement and the death and the death of René Crevel. (92–93)

This passage is not hermetic, not even difficult to understand or to account for by means of standard literary-critical ideas, most notably that of writing as unedited recording of the process of thought. In his 1973 introduction to the book, William H. Gass gives the following explanation:

It is characteristic of her method here and elsewhere that every general thought find exact expression in the language of her own life; that every general thought in fact be the outcome of a repeated consideration of solidly concrete cases—both wholly particular and thoroughly personal—and further, that these occasions be examined, always, in the precise form of their original occurrence; in which, then, they continue to be contained as if they were parts of a sacred text that cannot be tampered with substantially. . . . (11–12)

Gass accounts admirably for Stein's characteristic repetitions and disjunctions, and, in a general way, for the eccentricity of her formulations. But what his account neglects, or perhaps chooses not to account for, is the nature of the "form of original occurrence" of Stein's thoughts, and the resulting effect of this "sacred text" *as writing*. Phrases such as "big country" and "little one," "wander around," "tears in one's eyes," "an everything," and "straight lines on the map" make me wonder whether this text is really written in the "language" of Stein's "own life"; whether we are seeing these thoughts in the "form" of their "original occurrence" or, rather, in a form that Stein reserves only to writing: *the* "sacred text" of "the human mind." To see *The Geographical History of America* as the unedited record of Stein's thought in the language and form in which it originally occurred is to see it essentially as the weird but interesting and sometimes brilliant babble of a slightly deranged and childish genius, and therefore the record of inner speech. Such a reading denies the privileged place Stein accords to writing, and also her sense of its radical difference from spoken language. She is not a precursor of Jacques Derrida in this, because she equates writing with her idealistic notion of the transcendent human mind:

> Whether or whether not the human mind could exist if there had been no human speech this I do not know but this I do know that the human mind is not the same thing as human speech. Has one anything to do with the other is writing a different thing, oh yes and this is so exciting so satisfying so tender that it makes everything everything writing has nothing to do with the human speech with human nature and therefore and therefore it has something to do with the human mind. (76–77)

A bit later she formulates the idea more succinctly: "What you say has nothing to do with what you write" (86). That statement is preceded by a sentence of characteristic Steinian linguistic play, involving a punning rhyme: "When you write well when you write anybody try to write and they will say that I am right" (86).

Stein employs rhyme sporadically throughout *The Geographical History of America*: "Because here is the pause they pause and the cause the cause is that they pause and they cannot pause," "what you say wants to make you say it another way" (55); "Some dogs eyes in the night give out a red ruby light" (79); "But which are they when once a day they do not eat and they do not go away" (95). Stein did not talk like that; more important, she did not think like that. She wrote like that. Her writing, even as it claims for itself not only a central but a preeminent position in modern literature, American literature, and world literature, is a violation, as I have argued in *A Different Language*, of the dominant modes of patriarchal writing. However, I would prefer to cast that argument in somewhat different terms here. Gratuitous rhymes within ostensibly serious prose, and the use of childish diction such as "big country and little one," "wander around," "an everything," and "straight lines on a map," make Stein's *writing*, but not her thought, irreducibly nonserious. Again, she insists simultaneously on the centrality of her work to literary tradition and on its refusal of assimilation to the conventions or tropes of patriarchal-symbolic authority. Stein's profoundest philosophical meditation is written in language which is calculatedly, deliberately, and disturbingly irresponsible, frivolous, even banal, qualities which all the important critical explanations and reformulations suppress. They must do so precisely because their aim is to assimilate Stein to one of the major established literary traditions. But Stein was in fact part of a phenomenon which we have only recently come to recognize: the reimagining, enabled by feminine cultural positioning, of all structures of dualism, including those of tradition and innovation, center and margin, canon and anticanon, self and other, sanity and craziness, symbolic and presymbolic, masculine and feminine. Stein not only calls all such boundaries into question; she creates a literary space which genuinely straddles them, bringing together the two terms of all our ultimately gendered cultural dialectics not in synthesis but in a conjunction which refuses to obliterate difference.

Even in her more conventional work, most notably the early *Three Lives*† (1903–1906), Stein was already challenging or destabilizing literary boundaries even as she helped to establish them, particularly the boundary dividing modernism from its literary forebears. We are accustomed to acknowledging Stein's subsequent radical departures from mainstream modernism, but we should make more of Stein's location in historical time: no one else was doing what she did *when she did it*, and it is only recently that a significant number of writers are going as far as she did in disrupting conventional uses of language. Even *Finnegans Wake* was decades after Stein's most radically experimental period; and Samuel Beckett, William Burroughs, the *nouveau roman*, postmodernism in general, divided from Stein by World War II, mark a different historical period entirely. Among her contemporaries were Guillaume Apollinaire* and Max Jacob,* the "cubist" writers, but even their work was never as radical as hers. She really was the only one in literature, as she says in *Picasso*† (16).

The juxtaposition of Stein's radical work with characteristic works of modernism reveals the extent to which modernist writing is still tied to the "nineteenth-century composition," as Stein would put it: not just "story" (her term again), or character-plot-and-theme, but oscillation between referential and nonreferential theories and uses of language. Stein emphatically and joyously leaves referentiality behind after 1911, while Faulkner's "radical" *The Sound and the Fury* of 1929 not only has story at its very core (and it has a core), but also relocates, after the Benjy section, its seemingly nonreferential uses of language within conventional reference. The same double structure can be found in James Joyce's *Ulysses*, with its conjunction of linguistic free play and rigid, if only halfheartedly enforced, schemata of correspondences.

The clearest way to demonstrate the distance between Stein and mainstream modernism would be to juxtapose something from the prewar *Tender Buttons*† period, "Susie Asado," written in 1913, for example, with Yeats or Pound of the same vintage.

> Sweet sweet sweet sweet sweet tea.
> Susie Asado.
> Sweet sweet sweet sweet sweet tea.
> Susie Asado.
> Susie Asado which is a told tray sure.
> A lean on the shoe this means slips slips hers.
> When the ancient light grey is clean it is yellow, it is a silver seller.
> This is a please this is a please there are the saids to jelly. These are the wets these say the sets to leave a crown to Incy.
> Incy is short for incubus.
> A pot. A pot is a beginning of a rare bit of trees. Trees tremble, the old vats are in bobbles, bobbles which shade and shove and render clean, render clean must.
> Drink pups.
> Drink pups drink pups lease a sash hold, see it shine and a bobolink has pins. It shows a nail.
> What is a nail. A nail is unison.
> Sweet sweet sweet sweet sweet tea. (*G&P* 13)

"Susie Asado" is contemporaneous with the Yeats poems that begin "Suddenly I saw the cold and rook-delighting heaven" or "Now as at all times I can see in the mind's eye" ("The Cold Heaven," 1912, and "The Magi," 1914), poetry which does not question either the stable position of the lyrical first person speaker or the discrete separation of poetic imagination from an often disappointing external reality, a reality to be redeemed precisely by that poetic imagination. At the same time, Pound was writing "You were praised, my books" ("Salutation the Second," 1913), and "I make a pact with you, Walt Whitman" ("A Pact," 1913), inserting himself firmly, if critically, within his own version of the Great Poetic Tradition.

But perhaps these contrasts come too easily. It works too well to make them a matter of apples and oranges, to say that Stein was already beyond or outside mainstream modernism by 1913, setting the limit of avant-garde linguistic experimentation or inventing *écriture féminine*. To make a fair comparison that would reveal both the limits of what we think of as modernist innovation and also how early Stein exceeded those limits, we might juxtapose *Three Lives*, particularly "Melanctha," with Joyce's *Portrait of the Artist as a Young Man*, so long considered a seminal work of modernist fiction. *Portrait of the Artist* makes a particularly apt reference point because Stein herself, toward the end of her career, saw Joyce as the *other* genius of twentieth-century literature; also, long after Stein went beyond modernism, Joyce became the most radical experimenter among the canonical modernists. Moreover, there are numerous similarities between the two works, some of which are that both are written from modernist "exile" about home; sexual desire outside various cultural laws, and the repression and guilt resulting from that desire, inform both narratives in complex, ambiguous ways; both texts disrupt conventional linear sequence; both exceed with radical innovation premodernist literary uses of language and modes of narrative.

No difficulty arises in discovering differences between these two works, especially those which pertain to modernist narrative. In *A Different Language* I have argued that *Three Lives* is modernist in its obtuse narration, detached, ironic tone, impressionist as well as spatial temporal structures, and disruptions of conventional diction and syntax. Stein even gave the book an epigraph from that modernist precursor so admired by T. S. Eliot,* Jules Laforgue: "Donc je suis un malheureux et ce / n'est ni ma faute ni celle de la vie." But clearly Stein is a modernist with a difference. "I'm a loser and it's nobody's fault" is not a promising assertion for a founding work of such a great literary movement. Joyce's much better known epigraph to *Portrait of the Artist as a Young Man*, on the other hand, has been used as a touchstone of modernism—see for example the introduction to Hugh Kenner's *A Homemade World*—"Et ignotas animum dimittit in artes": "and he turned his mind to unknown arts."

The contrast between these two epigraphs tells us a great deal. Stein uses the spare, unpretentious, self-effacing French of a little-known (albeit influential) poet, a Symbolist to be sure but a minor one. Joyce uses Latin, that signifier of orthodoxy, patrilineality and patriarchal authority taught to brothers but not to sisters, chronically envied and mocked by women writers, most notably George Eliot and Virginia Woolf. In fact, just before writing *Three Lives*, Stein had formulated the problem of gender equality using education in the classics as a controlling metaphor in her story "Fernhurst":

> I have seen college women years after graduation still embodying the type and accepting the standard of college girls—who were protected all their days from the struggles of the larger world and lived and died with the intellectual furniture obtained at their college—persisting to the end in their belief that their power was as a man's—and divested of superficial latin and cricket what was their standard but that of an ancient finishing school

with courses in classics and liberty replacing the accomplishments of a
lady. (*QED* 4)

Note the bitter, ironic conjunction of "classics and liberty," equally useless
when they are a "superficial" clutter of "intellectual furniture" rather than a
sign of genuine revision of gender relations in culture.

Stein's epigraph, unlike Joyce's, cites no chapter and verse, merely the name
Jules Laforgue; she doesn't even cite a particular poem. Who is the "je" who
speaks? Laforgue, a Laforguian mask, Stein, one of her narrators, one of her
heroine-victims? Joyce's Latin third person is a clear gesture of fixing—of distancing, locating, and identifying—while Stein's French first person is an ambiguous gesture, simultaneously establishing and refusing to establish a speaking
subject. French was the language she spoke, the language of the culture around
her, but very deliberately not the language in which she wrote. A French epigraph
spoken by a "je" rather than an "I" therefore pointedly announces a refusal of
both coherent subjectivity and of clearly defined narrative position.

Three Lives, one *Portrait*: the most obvious difference between Stein's book
and Joyce's. Again, at one level this is too easy a contrast; after all, Stein was
inspired in part by Gustave Flaubert's *Trois Contes*. But the dispersal of Stein's
book among three lives, as opposed to Joyce's obsessive focus on his one life,
one consciousness, to the exclusion of the possibility of significant narrative
entry into any other, is more than a neutral question of difference in fictional
genre. The dispersal in Stein's text is not merely among three lives, or even
among three lives narrated by three narrators. In fact, none of these stories *has*
a fixed narrator.

Like *Portrait of the Artist as a Young Man, Three Lives* encompasses shifts
in prose style. But Joyce's shifts are either carefully calculated mimetic reflections
of the progression in Stephen's stages of development or of soul, or equally
carefully calculated markers of the shifts in the narrator's distance from Stephen.
Stein's shifts make no such sense, other than the obvious chronological sense
of increasing stylistic radicalism according to date of composition, from "The
Good Anna" to "The Gentle Lena" to "Melanctha." Narrative position throughout *Three Lives* is unfixed, fluid, shifting in and out of characters' consciousnesses, sometimes narrating entirely from within the consciousness of the
character from whose point of view we are at that moment seeing the story,
sometimes hovering just above that point of view, sometimes entirely outside
it. Moreover, the detached narrative voice has various degrees of detachment.
These complicated shifts can occur within the course of a short passage or even
a single sentence. Here is a characteristic sequence, from "Melanctha":

> Melanctha sat there, by the fire, very quiet. The heat gave a pretty pink
> glow to her pale yellow and attractive face. Melanctha sat in a low chair,
> her hands, with their long, fluttering fingers, always ready to show her
> strong feeling, were lying quiet in her lap. Melanctha was very tired with

her waiting for Jeff Campbell. She sat there very quiet and just watching. Jeff was a robust, dark, healthy, cheery negro. His hands were firm and kindly and unimpassioned. He touched women always with his big hands, like a brother. He always had a warm broad glow, like southern sunshine. He never had anything mysterious in him. He was open, he was pleasant, he was cheery, and always he wanted, as Melanctha once had wanted, always now he too wanted really to understand. (*TL* 137)

The first half of that passage is narrated in relation to Melanctha, but notice how the narrative position moves from outside to inside her consciousness. In the first three sentences, the narrator shows us Melanctha from Jeff's point of view: the "pretty pink glow" on her "pale yellow and attractive face," the hands "with their long, fluttering fingers, always ready to show her strong feeling." The next sentence moves us suddenly to Melanctha's point of view: she "was very tired with her waiting for Jeff Campbell." That is Melanctha's language, her tone. "She sat there very quiet and just watching" next gives us a language common to the narrator, Melanctha, and Jeff: a genuinely multiple, shared, undifferentiable narrative voice. Then, suddenly, the narrator moves way outside and above the voices and consciousnesses of the characters: "Jeff was a robust, dark, healthy, cheery negro." From that sentence until the last half of the last sentence of the passage, we are in the seemingly neutral, nonjudgmental, almost clinical, but also racist, condescending, patronizing position of the most distant of the detached narrative voices. Then, in mid-sentence, the narrative position shifts again, and the passage ends first partly then entirely inside Jeff's consciousness: "and always he wanted, as Melanctha once had wanted, always now he too wanted really to understand."

This unfixed, shifting, multiple, fluid narrative position does, as Stein claimed in *The Autobiography of Alice B. Toklas*,† leave the nineteenth century entirely behind. To the extent that modernist narration did not do that, but was caught between what Stein called the nineteenth- and the twentieth-century compositions, or what we might call culture and representation as we still know them and as we figure them in feminist utopian aesthetics, Stein, in her one early originary modernist work, was already beyond modernism, deconstructing its boundaries as she constructed them, in what Derrida calls a "suspense between two ages of writing" (87); half in and half out of doors.

REFERENCES: *G&P*, 1922; *TL*, 1933; *FS3A*, 1934; *GHA*, 1936; *PIC*, 1938; *QED*, 1971; Marianne DeKoven, *A Different Language*, 1983; Jacques Derrida, *Of Grammatology*, 1974; *YGS*, 1980; Harold Bloom, ed., *Modern Critical Views: Gertrude Stein*, 1986.

READING THE HAND WRITING: THE MANUSCRIPTS OF GERTRUDE STEIN

Ulla Dydo

What makes Gertrude Stein more puzzling and disturbing than other modernists is her language. She refused the conventions of expression, for she considered them deadening to perception—mechanical formulas used by unthinking minds to limit rather than open thought. She attempted to work with a sense of language prior to codified syntax and usage in order to recover the sensation of life. As a result, her work sounds and looks unfamiliar and unidiomatic. She forces us to read and see anew with each new piece, sometimes appearing to write in a foreign language which yet turns out to be English. Her language constantly calls attention to itself—to what it is rather than to what it represents. Her word patterns, which do not match our constructive expectations and refuse to be pinned down, appear unstable. Like the glass bits in a kaleidoscope, they constantly move, combining and recombining steadily in new patterns. Since the forms of her work offer no familiar access to the world, they place in doubt the coherence of the world, the authority of language, and the possibility of representation.

Outside the words of her works, Stein gave no clues for reading. She kept no diary or journal. She added no prefaces or postscripts to her books. She rarely commented in letters. To Stein, a composition is complete when it is self-contained, making explanation superfluous and paraphrase extrinsic. The logic of her position is clear and consistent, and though her work changed dramatically over the years, her commitment to language did not. Yet precisely because her words point inward, to the piece, rather than outward, to the world, readers find entry to her work difficult and look for help.

Oddly enough, the most obvious source of information about how Stein wrote has hardly been explored: her manuscripts. Her printed books preserve what she wrote but are stripped of the process that gave them being. In the autograph manuscripts, however, that process is often preserved. It is a context filled with clues to her texts that asks to be ''read'' by scholars turned detectives.

In the Stein collection at Yale, autograph manuscript notebooks for individual pieces preserve most of the texts from which typescripts were prepared for submission and publication. In addition, the collection includes the voluminous early notebooks that she kept unsystematically between 1902 and 1913 on pads, loose leaves, scraps, and large and small student copybooks. They include personal observations, commentary upon ideas, descriptions, plans for books, quotations from reading, her typology of personality, identification of pseudonyms, advice to herself, responses to events. All these form the context for the various drafts of *The Making of Americans*† and other early works. Together, they represent the first stage of Stein's writing. In the second stage, many but not all the drafts were transferred, with or without revisions, into the individual manuscript books, where Stein also, however, composed directly, combining drafted sections that she copied over with new writing composed on the spot to continue or complete her pieces. The full text of each of her early works is preserved separately in one or more autograph manuscript books. There is also an almost complete collection of typescripts, which Alice Toklas prepared from all manuscripts after *Three Lives*† starting sometime between 1907 and 1909.

Unlike the Stein pieces, the early notebooks were private. They were never intended for publication and probably not even for inspection by friends. Alice Toklas, who had not read them although she knew of them, expressed distress in a letter to Carl Van Vechten* of 4 June 1947 after she heard that they had turned up at Yale among the papers Stein had hastily assembled for shipment in the spring of 1946. One reason was that they contained not only first drafts of Stein works, but raw personal comments, including detailed studies of friends and family members, whom the notes identified although the books usually did not. Precisely because they are so informative, however, not only about persons but also about the genesis of Stein's ideas, the steps in composition and the sequence of her works, the notebooks make possible an understanding of her early development that could not be achieved without them.

In the absence of notebooks for works after 1913, it was thought that Stein ceased taking notes and came to compose all her work directly in the manuscript books, as she had in part already done earlier. Leon Katz, who had access to the early notes and described them in detail, states categorically that Stein discontinued taking notes (10). Yet many of the manuscripts after 1913 show a hand so smooth, steady, and regular that one wonders whether it is possible to produce in first draft long and complex constructions of such finished fluency. The small emendations and changes visible in the manuscript notebooks begin to look like minor copying slips rectified rather than revisions—wrong starts for single words, erroneous endings corrected. Other changes are visibly revisions— longer crossed out passages with new sections scribbled above them, changed titles, and so on.

Stein was not interested in explaining how she worked, for that was her private affair. Only once, in a minor piece that is almost unknown, did she describe simply and clearly how she wrote. She spoke of a period of sterility following the success of *The Autobiography of Alice B. Toklas*† in 1933 and told of the difficult return from ''outside'' or ''audience'' writing for success to serious ''inside'' writing of literature:

> I write the way I used to write in Making of Americans, I wander around and I come home and I write, I write in one copy-book and I copy what I write into another copy-book and I write and I write. . . . I have come back to write the way I used to write and this is because now everything that is happening is once more happening inside, there is no use in the outside. . . . ("And Now," 1933, ms. draft)

No one has paid attention to these words, yet they acknowledge notebooks prior to the final texts. The absence of notebooks after 1913, then, means not that there were no notebooks but merely that they were not donated to Yale or that they were destroyed. The comment in "And Now" makes it impossible to consider the manuscripts after 1913 as the first and only versions of her texts and confirms the visual impression that they are too neat and perfected to represent the first writing.

Careful inspection of the Stein papers at Yale discloses over thirty of these small first copybooks, or *carnets*, that Stein identifies. They date from the twenties and early thirties and contain sections of various Stein works, along with other notations. They differ from the early notebooks in that they include almost no comments on ideas that are not drafts for pieces, and they focus more narrowly than the early notes on actual writing. At the same time, again unlike the early notes, they contain many jottings about daily life, including intimate details about Stein's relationship with Toklas, which was central for her capacity to write. It is not clear why these notebooks were included with the papers for the Yale collection. They do not constitute a continuous or complete series and can be no more than a small sample of the many she must have filled. However, the consistency of their matter and their manner, especially their nonverbal features, shows beyond doubt how Stein worked. Together, the small, preliminary notebooks, or *carnets*, and the larger manuscript books, or *cahiers*, allow us to enter Stein's mature creative process.

Apparently Stein bought *carnets* in large numbers to make sure they were always available. The booklets vary in size but are small enough to carry easily in a pocket or in the hand. They are scribbled full, often starting from both ends, and the pages are sometimes covered with writing in both directions, in an uneven hand, usually in pencil. Jottings must have been made under all sorts of difficult conditions, perhaps even in the dark, for they are often hard to read. In addition to text, the *carnets* contain letter drafts, shopping lists, guest lists, addresses and telephone numbers, doodles and small drawings, drafts of dedications for books, titles, calculations of income or expenditures, contents for proposed volumes, notes and poems to Alice Toklas, and book lists. If the entries are more carefully followed than this random list suggests, however, they begin to speak of the process of writing.

Stein commonly worked late into the night, when Toklas was asleep. The prospect of writing made her anxious, which prevented concentration. In both the *carnets* and the *cahiers* she devised ways to help herself focus. Often she began work in a *carnet* by pencilling little love notes, jingles, intimate addresses, and sometimes drawings to Toklas. These notes are written in a tiny, thin, "secret" hand to offset them from actual composition. None are literary; indeed, many are the kind of embarrassingly bad private verse full of sentimental diminutives that lovers keep to themselves and eventually destroy. The notes become a kind of correspondence between "Mr. and Mrs. Reciprocal," as Stein calls them in one *carnet*. A new *carnet* was frequently inscribed to Toklas, "To dedicate it all to wifie—" or "I have ordered fifty-two little books to write of my little Hebrew constantly." (Seven of these, which have distinctive covers, are preserved.) The ritual of dedicating a *carnet* to Toklas allayed anxiety, enabled Stein to know who she was, and allowed her to write. When something went wrong in her work, she might blame it on not having started with a word to Toklas. When she had finished work for the night, she went to sleep, leaving the *carnets* for Toklas to read or to copy marked sections the following morning. In the early notebooks, Toklas is one of many personalities studied and described as subject matter although she assumes growing personal importance. In the notebooks of the twenties, however, though Toklas is still often a subject of description, she is at the center of creative process as a person.

Toklas was a skilled reader of Stein's work. She also well understood Stein's need for validation and support. Occasionally she wrote answers to Stein's notes. Some pick up Stein's ideas, her banter or her humor, but others play in various styles with Toklas's own ideas. All are supportive. "A question mark is not admitted by us moderns," she comments after Stein questions whether she can make her happy. "Practice makes perfect / practice in appreciation makes perfect appreciation," Stein writes, and Toklas responds, "*Lu et apprové*" [*sic*]. The sentence, "Practice makes perfect," appears in "Natural Phenomena" (196), parts of which are drafted in this notebook. The sentence also refers to the draft of a review of Alfred Kreymborg's autobiography, *Troubadour*, that Stein was writing in appreciation of his inclusion of the "history of us" in his "history of himself." Stein sometimes asked Toklas to check facts: "When did he [Picasso]* leave rue Ravignan?" When, in the course of writing, concentration again became difficult, Stein regained her voice by writing another note to Toklas, or by composing verses for diversion on the small pages of the *carnets*:

> Mon petit blanc et
> mon petit toujours, mon
> petit blanc et mon
> J'espere et je l'aime. . . .

In this verse white (*blanc*) recalls blue (*petit blanc* echoes *petits bleus*, the notes mailed by pneumatic tube in Paris) and small (*petit*) recalls large (Basket, the white pet poodle, echoes Mont Blanc, the great mountain). The diminutives are to create endearment. Blue may also recall Alice Toklas, always in Stein's mind associated with blue. Slim and sentimental, the lines afford a glance into the transition from private life to writing.

Stein often begins literally with descriptions of what she sees, including Toklas. Very quickly these become elements of description, no longer elements of Toklas. By the time they are seen formally, they are elements of composition, and writing has begun. One notation, which started as a description of Toklas or another woman, ends up in "Arthur A Grammar": "She was photographed with trees" (*HTW* 79). This sentence is joined to an equivalent descriptive sentence, perhaps about the same snapshot and perhaps reflected also in a drawing of earrings in a *carnet* of the same period, "She was photographed with earrings" (*HTW* 79). In slightly different form, describing Alyse Gregory, the novelist and managing editor of the *Dial*, this sentence is also in the play *Paisieu* (*LO&P* 157). Joined in "Arthur" the two sentences have become a small grammatical paradigm—"she was photographed with": with what *was* she photographed? Stein has produced a humorous composition on the word *with*.

What look like dog-eared corners at the outside top and bottom of many *carnets* turn out to contain elaborate private signals from Stein to Toklas, showing her where to begin, how far to read or copy, or what to do with new writing. Toklas apparently folded corners with return signals when she left the carnets for Stein to pick up again. Doodles and simple drawings also appear in the *carnets* and occasionally in the *cahiers*. The doodles often play with repeated letters or calligraphic shapes, sometimes carefully distributed in the space of a page. Some of the drawings are representational though they lack detail—animals, flowers, earrings, human figures, and especially birds. Other drawings look abstract and sometimes suggest anatomical forms. The private ritual which the *carnets* document is astounding in its elaborate consistency.

In addition to the devices for starting work, many other notes show how Stein worked. Here, for example, she experiments with balanced expression and design, using the alliterating first and last names of friends, Bernard Faÿ,* the historian, and Christian Bérard,* the painter:

> Bernard or Berard
> balance believe balance
> with

This exercise is followed by the draft of a letter of appreciation to Laura Riding, where Stein praises the logo design done by Len Lye for the Seizin Press, which in 1929 published *An Acquaintance with Description*:† "They [the shapes of the logo] have real weight and balance in them in some strange way." The preoccupation with design, always important to Stein, leads from the names to the logo.

Many other personal scribbles—the kind anyone jots down on slips of paper or notepads—offer biographical information. Frequently jottings tell where Stein was—in Paris, in Belley, in Nice (where one *carnet* shows her writing concurrently the beginning of the second Picasso portrait and the end of "Are There Arithmetics" while in another she is working on a later section of the portrait and on "Geography"). The notebooks also permit dating. One *carnet* contains English addresses and other English notes as well as the beginnings of *An Acquaintance With Description* and of the portrait, "Edith Sitwell And Her Brothers The Sitwells And Also To Osbert Sitwell And To S. Sitwell." The *carnet* makes clear that both pieces were begun during the visit to England in June 1926. It also shows later sections of both pieces, interspersed with notes about the French countryside, to have been written after Stein's return to France. The last step in this sequence is in letters which document when Stein sent the finished family portrait to Edith Sitwell.*

There are also various lists, which always held special fascination for Stein. Reading lists appear to be culled from reviews, from suggestions of friends, and perhaps from advice of librarians at the American Library. Of course, a title of a book on a list does not necessarily mean that it was read. The book lists show Stein's special interest in popular biographies and personal as well as historical narratives. An interesting use of pronouns appears in shopping lists: seeing herself as husband and Toklas as wife, Stein also used the personal pronouns *he* and *she* not inflected and sometimes even capitalized, as names for herself and for Toklas. On her shopping lists appear "Material for she" and "Stockings for he." Such data are as important for understanding Stein's life as the drafts are for understanding Stein's work. In the *carnets*, work and life, text and context, are joined. In the *cahiers*, the work is largely but not completely decontextuated, the details of private life eliminated.

It is useful to establish the personal context of Stein's work that is visible in the *carnets* before looking at the drafts of text. The drafts also lead to the manuscript *cahiers*, for they were copied, sometimes with revisions, into the *cahiers*, where Stein often continued writing without prior draft. One *carnet* of the summer of 1928 is an instructive example. At one end appear the title and subtitle of Stein's play, *Paisieu / A Play / A Work of Pure Imagination in which no Reminiscences Intrude*. Stein's original spelling of the title, *Pasiue*[?], corrected in Alice's hand to read *Paisieu*, probably conflates *Pugieu*, a hamlet near Belley, and perhaps *Peyrieu*, another hamlet, with *pays*, country, and with *paix/ paisible*, peace/peaceful. After the title appears the author's name, "Gertrude," rhyming with *intrude*. (Stein liked writing her name. She signed even drafts of letters. Often she inscribed student *cahiers* that had on the covers spaces for name, subject, class or address, with her and sometimes Toklas's name and all sorts of hilarious wordplay.) The first twenty-five pages of the booklet show the beginning of the play. By page 26, perhaps at a different sitting, she changes from writing in horizontal direction to writing in vertical direction and produces another section of the same play, used later in the final text. This section is identified with the capital letter *P* for *Paisieu* and ends with the sentence, "Definition made a hand" (*LO&P* 160). The same sentence, copied over at the top of the following page, begins a section of "Arthur A Grammar" (*HTW* 80), identified with the letter *G* for *Grammar*. A sentence used in one piece becomes an occasion for a meditation upon writing in another piece, a common situation in the late twenties, when Stein wrote her language or grammar pieces along with other work. There follow in the *carnet* several letter drafts and further sections of both *Paisieu* and "Arthur A Grammar."

A review of Stein's transfer of the texts from the *carnets* into the manuscript *cahiers* leads to a startling discovery. The manuscript book of *Paisieu* opens with the title and the beginning of the play—in Alice Toklas's handwriting. After a few pages, the text continues in Stein's hand, only to change again later to Toklas's hand. The manuscript sections of *Paisieu* in the hand of Toklas are exactly those that Stein drafted in the *carnet*. Toklas copied them. Meanwhile, Stein herself copied the relevant sections of "Arthur A Grammar" into the manuscript *cahier* of that work. What happened next is a matter of conjecture. Either Stein composed directly in the manuscript *cahier* the next section of the play (the one written in her own hand in the *cahier*), or she drafted the next section first in another *carnet* not preserved, and eventually herself copied it into the *cahier*. (The presence in these passages of revisions, not merely corrections, suggests that Stein composed in the *cahier*.)

Richard Bridgman speaks of examining the manuscript books of "Ada" (1910) and *A Novel of Thank You* (1925–1926), which also show the hand of Alice Toklas. He concludes his comment on "Ada," the loving portrait of Alice Toklas, "given the manuscript in two hands; and given the conclusion that the two people are one, the evidence is persuasive that this was a collaboration of symbolic significance, sealing the relationship between the two women" (*GSP* 211). Bridgman interprets the presence of Toklas's hand as evidence of collaboration in composition. What confusion of writing and love! Surely union in love is central for the two women, but union in writing, especially in the manner of Stein, including the beginning of a new piece in the hand of Toklas? The very thought is preposterous, but it is indicative of the confusion about Gertrude Stein's art and her life, about what she says and what it means. Where Toklas's hand is visible in the manuscripts, even when no first drafts are preserved, it is because she copied, not because she composed. Although many questions remain about details of pieces for which no drafts and no notes are preserved, the *carnets* that survive make clear how Stein worked. Hundreds of these *carnets* must have been filled. The scribbled notes tell what she did, what she saw, what she thought, where she went, and how she worked, all interlocked in the service of composition. The details are not invented, and the process of writing is far more conscious than has been thought.

By the time the drafts were transferred into the *cahiers* the personal contexts visible in the *carnets* were left behind. What makes the *carnets* so valuable is that they preserve the contexts. In a way, they constitute Stein's unwitting introduction to her work. For her, once the *carnets* had served their purpose— after the text was copied into the *cahiers*, after the friends on the list had been invited for dinner, the drafted letters copied over, the groceries purchased, the car repaired, the addresses transferred—they became redundant. What remained, and what Stein intended to leave to Yale, was her writing, self-contained and disembodied movement, lifted from the context between the covers of the *carnets*. It is inconceivable that Stein should have considered giving the *carnets* to an archive. They speak of the process of composition and of living that was the source of her words but was not literature. What she wanted to preserve was her literature. Either the *carnets* must have been eliminated as she went along, or, if kept, they must have been destroyed at a later time. The inclusion among her papers of the few that survive must have been accidental, like the inclusion of the early notebooks. After Stein's death, Toklas burned papers at a friend's house. She gave no details about what she destroyed. But if further *carnets* had been kept, they might have been among the papers of which she disposed.

The manuscript *cahiers* share a few of the characteristics of the *carnets* but are also very different. Although they include some personal notes and verses to Toklas, they do not suggest the vast intimate context of the *carnets*. Yet they show far more than the words of Stein's pieces and tell stories of their own.

Although some of Stein's manuscript texts are written on loose leaves, scraps, and pads, most are in standard school copybooks such as could be bought in any French stationery shop. Some of these notebooks have simple, stylized line drawings and titles on the front covers (a dragon with the title ''Le Dauphin''; a sheaf of wheat entitled ''Le Bon Grain''; a bird, ''Avia''; ''La Science Guidant le Travail'' (Science Directing Work) with a female figure reading instructions on a scroll while a man performs physical labor). Others show on the front covers lively colored illustrations and on the back covers explanatory text on educational subjects. For example, the series *Mots Historiques* (Famous Words from History) includes stories of the circumstances under which famous utterances of French history were made (e.g., ''Madame, tout est perdu fors l'honneur,'' François I's note to his mother upon his defeat, telling her that all was lost but honor). The series *Les Phénomènes de la Nature*, which provided the title and starting point for Stein's ''Natural Phenomena,'' includes notebooks entitled ''Volcan,'' ''Foudre,'' ''La Marée,'' on volcanoes, lightning, tides.

When Stein began writing in a *cahier*, the stories on the covers sometimes helped her to get started. Here she writes in a notebook on Lamartine from the series *Les Educateurs de la Jeunesse* (Teachers of Youth): ''I wondered how I would begin / my Lamartine / with a song about my queen'' (''An Indian Boy,'' 1923). Lamartine and Toklas help Stein to start but do not become a part of her piece. Likewise, when she worries what to write about and decides that she will not write about a volcano, though the cover of the notebook on volcanoes tells us where she got the idea, it is clear without the *cahier* that volcanoes are not what she will write about. As Stein gathered her resources by concentrating on the immediate, details might enter her work from anything she could see, including the notebooks. Some of these details remain as casual triggers of words.

Others, however, determine central construction, making the texts difficult to understand unless the sources are traced. Wendy Steiner has shown some of the ways in which cover illustrations determine texts. For example, to understand the portrait of Ernest Hemingway,* the references on the covers must be understood (110–18). Stein apparently was not fully aware of how impenetrable some of her pieces became that relied on such details. The ways in which elements from the notebooks are selected, played with or absorbed into her work require further study.

Stein drew ideas not only from the *cahiers* but from everything that surrounded her. A few examples will illustrate her range. "A Bouquet" (1927?), incorporated in 1928 in the opera *A Bouquet. Their Wills*, is composed in a notebook from the series *La Parole du maître: Connaissances utiles* (The Master's Word: Useful Knowledge) and subtitled "L'Art de faire un bouquet," translated by Stein at the opening, "The art of making a bouquet." The picture shows a group of women busy with flowers on a garden terrace. The text describes the art of assembling bouquets, which requires taste, dexterity, talent, but mainly an artistic conception of the whole, like that of the painter or playwright. Stein treats this text as a set of directions, which she follows by writing a single, totally composed, totally abstract and balanced sentence—a bouquet of words. Her piece, not about flowers but about composition, literally exemplifies the principles outlined in the *cahier*. What could be simpler?

"A Diary" (1927) is written in a *cahier* from the series *Voyages autour du monde* (Travels around the World), subtitled "Un nuage de sauterelles en Algérie." The picture shows three tourists on horseback in Algeria, riding into a "cloud of grasshoppers." Stein originally included in her own title a translation of the French title, "A diary and a storm of grasshoppers on a trip" but then crossed out all but the essential "A Diary." In the spring of 1927, she was preoccupied with narrative and time. Whether that preoccupation led her to examine the diary form, whether the *cahier* with its hint of a travel diary gave her the idea, or whether she chose the Algerian *cahier* to fit an idea she already had, cannot be known. But her steps in the title are entirely clear.

Sometimes she used tiny details originating in the notebooks to compose. The lion in the *Third Historic Drama* (1930) comes from the *cahier* about a famous lion-hunter, which leads her to connect him with her own thoughts about being lionized. "Why is milk good" in Act 3 of *Say It with Flowers* (1931) comes from a notebook on nutrition. It is easy enough to identify such sources, but knowing where she got such details does not explain how she used them in her work, which requires reading from inside. The phrase "their origin and their history," which fits perfectly in the context of "Patriarchal Poetry" and also echoes the subtitle of *The Making of Americans: Being a History of a Family's Progress*, is a literal translation of *son origine et son histoire* from the title of a notebook in the series *Chants Patriotiques* (Patriotic Songs). Her wordplay with "patriarchal" and "patriotic" also derives from this title. The portrait, spelled "Lipschitz" (1926?), in part uses details of the *cahier* which shows a young soldier in World War I behind a battlement at a lookout post, watching with patient concentration for the enemy. The phrases "he was so tenderly then standing" and "[w]hen I knew him first he was looking looking through the glass" describe both the soldier depicted on the *cahier* and Jacques Lipchitz,* the sculptor for whom Stein had sat as a model and of whom she now writes her portrait. She uses the intense "looking" of the soldier to lead into the "looking at the looking" of the artist. "I look at him for him," derived from the *cahier*, may speak of herself as a model for Lipchitz or of her looking at him for her portrait of him. The fact that a verbal element originates in a notebook does not mean that it cannot be interpreted beyond its origin, but understanding its origin reveals context and prevents misreading. Even when the source of her verbal material can be discovered, the more important and difficult question is *how* and *how successfully* she composes the word ideas derived from her sources.

The manuscripts sometimes explain textual surprises. In "A French Rooster" (1930) appears, apparently out of context, the sentence "An erasure is our politeness" (*SIM* 214). A look at the manuscript explains what happened. At the end of the preceding sentence, Stein attempted to erase five words, but fully erased only one, crossing out the others. The sentence about erasure explains: the word was erased as a matter of politeness. Of course the five deleted words appear neither in the typed nor in the printed text.

Stein's technique of decontextuating in order to focus on essence can be documented by a study of her revisions, from *carnet* to *cahier*, within the *cahier* and to the typescript. Often the manuscripts retain, crossed out, the original nouns or names for which Stein substituted neutral pronouns in order to prevent attention from shifting to the references. "Business in Baltimore" (1925) is a relentless, bitter piece about the power of counting, associated with Baltimore, family, and money. Counting makes riches, and riches make weddings, which are not about people but about money. "Anything that begins with r makes read riches and this is as twice and once and once. . . . This is the way they make the day . . . this is the way they make the day, once a day and it is a reason for having heard of it." (*UK* 70; echoes of "The king was in his counting-house / counting out his money"?) Before substituting the last word, *it*, Stein had originally written *Pierpont Morgan*, the only proper name in this composition except Julian, Stein's six-year-old nephew, who opens the piece because he is learning the great Baltimore skill—counting. J. P. Morgan's name did not fit Stein's design, which used no names and only minimally referential words. She revised the phrase, "heard of Pierpont Morgan," first to "heard of *him*" and finally to "heard of *it*" since Pierpont Morgan stands for wealth, an *it*.

In "Regular Regularly in Narrative" (1927) Stein included a long portrait of Harold Acton.* One sentence begins, "Harold Acton can be finally withdrawn from Beatrice" (*HTW* 234). Is Harold Acton withdrawn from a girl he loved? In the manuscript remains the original identification, but crossed out, as indicated by the square brackets, and therefore not printed: "and so she might be Beatrice Beatrice [Cenci Cen] bent she she bent to bent to be bent to be he to be bent to be he to be bent to be Beatrice but to be he" (236).

Also in the manuscripts may be found revised titles and crossed-out subtitles that help to place works in context. Why is *Lucy Church Amiably*† subtitled "A Novel No. 2"? Why did Stein eliminate this subtitle from the final text? Which is novel No. 1? The title of the play *Say It with Flowers* is revised. Crossed out in the manuscript notebook, entitled "L'Alouette" (The Lark), in the series *Le Monde des Oiseaux* (The World of Birds), is an earlier title, which refers to the French title and illustration—a lark hovering above a field with flowers. Barely legible, Stein's original title appears to read, *The* [?] *World of Birds with Strange Flowers in It*. Does this title help the reader of the play? When was it created, when and why revised? Many questions are suggested, and some are answered by the manuscripts.

One more extraordinary aspect of the manuscripts demands attention: writing as a physical act in space. The title "Five Words in a Line," as usual, is literally true: in the *cahiers* approximately five handwritten words fitted on a line. Stein must suddenly have become aware of this fact and begun to play with it. She also frequently filled given spaces. For example, she sometimes drafted answers on the back of letters received. Since such letters were usually folded in half, in thirds, or both, she tended to fill each half or each third or sixth, as if it were a separate page, rather than to open the sheet and write from top to bottom. It is important to know whether the format of a notebook or even a scrap of paper determined the visual shape of words in composition. Some sections of "An Elucidation" (1923) are drafted in a tiny pad, which results in very short lines and small units—including the statement, "Small examples are preferable." By the time the pieces are typed or printed, the spatial quality of the handwritten work is gone. Yet to return to the manuscripts and follow the hand shaping words, lines, and pages in the *carnets* and the *cahiers* makes exhilarating contact with the act of composition.

Many manuscripts are filled to the last line of the last page of the last *cahier* of any one work. In such *cahiers* Stein did what painters do when they fill a canvas: she fitted a composition into a given space. For these works she cannot have completed a draft in a *carnet* and copied it since it is impossible to plan space from one notebook to another. Indeed, she often began or continued but hardly ever finished pieces in a *carnet*. Her artistic problem became to *complete* a composition within a set space, not simply to *stop* it. Sections of what became the teasing, grammatical portrait of Bernard Faÿ* appear first in the long "Sentences" (1928). Stein used sentences from this piece, with revisions, and transferred them into a new, illustrated *cahier* as the opening of the portrait "Bernard Faÿ" (late 1928). She continued composing directly in the *cahier* and finished the portrait at the bottom of the inside back cover. Completing works in a given space forced her to confront the problems of endings. Donald Sutherland, who never saw any of the manuscripts, was aware of Stein's use of pages as spatial units of writing (113–14).

Finishing pieces was a source of difficulty for Stein. She was reluctant to plan endings that suggested the premeditated or the mechanical. She did not organize content chronologically or logically toward a climax or conclusion. There is rarely a sharp end point in a Stein piece although her forms of rhetorical completion can be astounding. What was described at the outset as the instability and the constant shifting of her texts is visible in the verbal and mental "leaps" that they so often require. Stein's is a world—a space—of unending process, which does not unroll toward a conclusion but *goes on*, steadily and simultaneously, in many forms. The circles, on which she so often relies, complete pieces without the jolt of a stop. The discipline of a set space in the manuscript book offered a way to create endings with complete verbal flexibility. It is important to discover by what spatial or rhetorical means she completes the design of a work. The problem of endings returns once more to the questions asked earlier: only once we understand *how* Stein composed endings, does it become useful to ask *how effective* they are. The answer must always be rhetorical rather than representational.

What Stein meant to leave for posterity was her literature—self-contained, disembodied words in movement, without clues or keys to the world. As she said over and over, she wrote literature, not references. It is the construction, not the references, that creates her art and her meaning. The little *carnets* included with the larger manuscript *cahiers* preserve the links from life to literature. Together, the two provide a partial dictionary for some of the references. The inclusion of the private notes in the shipment of Stein's papers must have been an accident.

And yet, in spite of what Stein believed about the autonomy of her work, perhaps she also wanted to keep some slight tie to the referential world in which her literature had been made. Perhaps the accident which preserved a few *carnets* and included them with the papers sent for safekeeping was after all "carrying out an idea which was already existing."

REFERENCES: *UK*, 1928; *HTW*, 1931; *LO&P*, 1949; GSB, 1951; *SIM*, 1956; *GSP*, 1970; Wendy Steiner, *Exact Resemblance to Exact Resemblance*, 1979.

SIX STEIN STYLES IN SEARCH OF A READER

Marjorie Perloff

We usually think of Gertrude Stein's writings as falling into two broad categories: on the one hand, the public, accessible, "transparent," and more or less straight-forward mode of *The Autobiography of Alice B. Toklas*† or of such well-known essays as "Portraits and Repetition"; on the other, the opaque, private, exper-imental, "difficult" mode that ranges from *Tender Buttons*† (1914) to *Mrs. Reynolds*† (1941–1942), and beyond. Whether we take the distinction to be diachronic (see Marianne DeKoven, xiiiff.) or synchronic (see Ulla Dydo, 4ff.) is less important than that the "experimental" and the "straight" are placed in binary opposition. Obvious as this basic distinction may be, it doesn't get us very far. For is the device of repetition in, say, Stein's portrait of Matisse* in fact duplicated in a work like "Patriarchal Poetry"? And is the so-called plain style of *The Autobiography of Alice B. Toklas* equivalent to the plain style of *Wars I Have Seen*?† What, moreover, about chronology: does Stein's work chart some sort of progress from an early experimentalism to a mature directness or is it the other way around? Or neither, given the fact that *Stanzas in Meditation*,† one of Stein's most difficult and obscure works, dates precisely from the period in which she wrote "Alice's" autobiography?

My own view is that there are at least six basic variations on the famous Stein signature, which is to say, at least half a dozen permutations of the familiar model, "Very fine is my valentine. Very fine and very mine" (*P&P* 152), or "Toasted susie is my ice-cream" (*SW* 551). To examine the larger spectrum of Stein's styles may help us to dispel two still popular myths about her work. First, that her fabled "difficulty," like her rarer clarity, is all of a piece. And second, that her "easy" works avoid the stylization of her difficult ones and hence do not demand the same reading strategies. I want to suggest that, on the contrary, Stein's texts, whatever their date of composition or their hypothetical genre, must be read strenuously in keeping with her own notion that, whatever else a literary text may be, its central unit is always the sentence, that verbal unit which encompasses what Stein calls "Resemble assemble reply" (*HTW* 167).

Consider, for example, the status of description and narration in what is surely one of Stein's most transparent and seemingly innocent texts: *Paris France*,† the short memoir she wrote at Bilignin in the early months of World War II. Here is the opening:

> PARIS, FRANCE is exciting and peaceful.
> I was only four years old when I was first in Paris and talked french there and was photographed there and went to school there, and ate soup for early breakfast and had leg of mutton and spinach for lunch, I always liked spinach, and a black cat jumped on my mother's back. That was more exciting than peaceful. I do not mind cats but I do not like them to jump on my back. There are lots of cats in Paris and in France and they can do what they like, sit on the vegetables or among the groceries, stay in or go out. It is extraordinary that they fight so little among themselves considering how many cats there are. There are two things that french animals do not do, cats do not fight much and do not howl much and chickens do not get flustered running across the road, if they start to cross the road they keep on going which is what french people do too. (*PF* 1)

Generically, this account of French life recalls nothing so much as a fourth or fifth grade reader; indeed, Stein's simple declarative sentences probably do not contain a single word that a schoolgirl of her day would not have known. Nor do the sentences in this "reader" seem in any way remarkable, conveying as they do ordinary observations about what is perceived ("There are lots of cats in Paris") and remembered ("I always liked spinach"). The phrasal repetition for which Stein is best known, for that matter, is kept to a minimum, and even syntactic parallelism (for example, "talked french there and was photographed there and went to school there") is not especially prominent.

But the reference to "Paris, France" is redundant even for a grade-school child, and of course no primer written for children would contain the sentence, "PARIS, FRANCE is exciting and peaceful," the second adjective contradicting the first and making it all but impossible for Stein's reader to formulate an image of place. The semantic contradiction is reinforced by the syntactic one at the end of the first sentence, where the coordinating conjunction "and" joins a clause referring to a specific incident ("a black cat jumped on my mother's back") to the preceding "when" clause with its cataloging of habitual actions. Normal usage would require a period after "spinach," followed by a temporal marker like "One day."

Why then does Stein ignore the basic distinction between perfect and imperfect verb forms and draw the clause in question into the larger parataxis of her composition? Perhaps because even in as seemingly transparent a text as *Paris France*, Stein's urge is to minimize temporal distinctions, to present us with a spatial figure, a synchronicity, analogous to the flat or planar landscape of a Cézanne or Picasso.* As Lyn Hejinian observes, "one of the characteristics of

Stein's writing is that elements coexist with alternatives in the work; phrase or sentence A is not obliterated when it appears, slightly altered perhaps, as phrase or sentence B'' (137). Indeed Stein must, so to speak, draw the black cat out of her verbal hat so as to confirm the exciting/peaceful paradox of her opening sentence. "I do not mind cats but I do not like them to jump on my back. There are lots of cats in Paris and in France and they can do what they like." The two sentences are placed side by side without a linking adverb that might explain their relationship, but the positioning makes a sense of its own. Insofar as they jump, "french cats" (the lower case *f* designating that nationality is merely an attribute, rather like size or color) are exciting; insofar as they do as they like, they are peaceful. Indeed, we now learn, "french animals" in general are peaceful: "chickens do not get flustered running across the road." And from chickens it is only one step to human beings: "if they [chickens] start to cross the road they keep on going which is what french people do too."

End of paragraph. The "lesson" is as inexorable as that of any schoolbook. "PARIS, FRANCE is exciting and peaceful." How is it exciting and peaceful? Its animals and hence people are very lively and always in motion but "they keep on going" without getting "flustered." Stein's "argument," wholly devoid of logic or empirical evidence as it is, carries us along by the sheer force of its relational syntax. Accordingly, the text remains peculiarly impervious to explication. When Richard Bridgman suggests that Stein's optimistic portrait of a France, forty years into the twentieth century and hence ready to "settle down to middle age and a pleasant life and the enjoyment of ordinary living" (*PF* 119) is "pitifully unrealistic" (*GSP* 298), he is assuming that the mode of *Paris France* is essentially expository. But as Stein herself points out, hers is intentionally an external, and therefore an idealized, view of her adopted country:

> After all everybody, that is, everybody who writes is interested in living inside themselves in order to tell what is inside themselves. That is why writers have to have two countries, the one where they belong and the one in which they live really. The second one is romantic, it is separate from themselves, it is not real but it is really there. (*PF* 2)

Which is to say that the "France" of jumping cats and docile chickens is not "real" (indeed, one of the central ironies of the book is that Paris itself, the urban environment, is, so to speak, under erasure, the focus throughout being on country life), even as, within the synchronic field of the text itself, the exciting/peaceful realm called France is "really there."

The paradox, then, is that Stein practices what William James* called (with reference to *Three Lives*†) "a fine new kind of realism" (*FF* 50), even as she resolutely opposes mimesis, the notion that the verbal or visual construct can replicate the external world of nature. *Paris France* tells us precious little about French history or geography, but in its particular focus on, say, the village girl Helen Button and her dog William, or on the proper preparation of *quenelles*, it creates a verbal space we come to recognize as, so to speak, *Stein France*. In the same vein, the anecdotes about famous artists that fill the pages of *The Autobiography of Alice B. Toklas* are notable less for their informational content than for their attention to the principle that, as Stein put it about Cézanne, "in composition one thing was as important as another thing" (*PGU* 15).

The "transparent" style of *The Autobiography of Alice B. Toklas* is, of course, more complex than that of *Paris France*, given its fictional premise that Toklas rather than Stein tells the story. Like the later memoir, however, the *Autobiography* purports to tell its story quite literally, with a minimum of fuss. Here is "Alice Toklas's" account of the famous first night of Stravinsky's *Sacre du Printemps*:

> Nijinsky did not dance in the Sacre du Printemps but he created the dance of those who did dance.
>
> We arrived in the box and sat down in the three front chairs leaving one chair behind. Just in front of us in the seats below was Guillaume Apollinaire.* He was dressed in evening clothes and he was industriously kissing various important looking ladies' hands. He was the first one of his crowd to come out into the great world wearing evening clothes and kissing hands. We were very amused and very pleased to see him do it. It was the first time we had seen him doing it. After the war they all did these things but he was the only one to commence before the war.
>
> Just before the performance began the fourth chair in our box was occupied. We looked around and there was a tall well-built young man, he might have been a dutchman, a scandinavian or an american and he wore a soft evening shirt with the tiniest pleats all over the front of it. It was impressive, we had never even heard that they were wearing evening shirts like that. That evening when we got home Gertrude Stein did a portrait of the unknown called a Portrait of One.
>
> The performance began. No sooner had it commenced when the excitement began. The scene now so well known with its brilliantly coloured background now not at all extraordinary, outraged the Paris audience. No sooner did the music begin and the dancing than they began to hiss. The defenders began to applaud. We could hear nothing, as a matter of fact I never did hear any of the music of the Sacre du Printemps because it was the only time I ever saw it and one literally could not, throughout the whole performance, hear the sound of music. (*SW* 128–29)

Here the narrator seems to be doing nothing but recording, as faithfully as possible, what happened at the first night even as a child might report it. Nijinsky "did not dance . . . but he created the dance of those who did dance," "We . . . sat down in the three front chairs leaving one chair behind," and so on. No metaphor, no symbolism, no learned allusions, no background information about the Ballets Russes or Serge Diaghilev, no biographical sketch of Stravinsky, and, most important, no word as to Gertrude Stein's judgment on the music or the ballet. Instead, we are treated by the "naive" Alice Toklas to an account of Apollinaire's hand-kissing habits and a description of the pleated evening shirt worn by the unknown "tall well-built young man" who becomes the subject (dressed "In the best most silk and water much, in the best most silk") of Stein's portrait "One" (G&P 199–200).

Why the shift of focus from purported subject to ancillary detail? Like a cubist collage, Stein's composition creates its effect, not by representing the external event but by, so to speak, pasting up metonymically related items that, as in the case of *Paris France*, spatialize the narrative and make it what Stein calls a "continuous present" (*SW* 518). Thus Apollinaire's outrageous hand-kissing ritual ("He was the first one of his crowd to come out into the great world wearing evening clothes and kissing hands") ironically parallels Stravinsky's "rite of spring." "After the war," Toklas tells us, "they all did these things but he was the only one to commence before the war." The comic miniature version of the avant-garde ballet makes the latter accessible to us. We know that this is an important evening, an evening to remember—"the first time we had seen him doing it."

In the same vein, the never-before seen "soft evening shirt with the tiniest pleats all over the front of it," an evening shirt worn by a man who "might have been a dutchman, a scandinavian or an american," is a portent of things to come: "we had never even heard," says Toklas "that they were wearing evening shirts like that." The portrait Stein produces that night is appropriately called "One" because the evening shirt is a "first" even as Apollinaire's hand-kissing routine is a first. In this context, the actual performance of Stravinsky becomes a kind of anticlimax, even as a Picasso collage may place its "subject" in the corner and place primary emphasis on a calling card or a newspaper page.

The Autobiography of Alice B. Toklas neither describes the music nor the dancing, but the "anecdote," which is thus quite unlike the anecdotes found in the typical biography or autobiography, is all the more telling. What the reader comes to see is that (1) the first night of *Sacre du Printemps* is a watershed for the arts, prefiguring the watershed soon to be created by the war; (2) Stein herself is part of the magic circle of artists which includes Nijinsky, Apollinaire, and Stravinsky, in that the "well-built young man" (Carl Van Vechten)* becomes the occasion for her own artistic composition, the portrait "One"; and (3) the neutral and nonjudgmental voice of Alice Toklas, herself neither artist nor critic but a mere someone who is alternately "amused" and "astonished" by the furor in the theater, serves to highlight the brilliance of a Nijinsky, an Apollinaire—and of course of Gertrude Stein herself.

The compositional strategy of the *Autobiography* is thus one of metonymic deflection. Readers who know Stein's work primarily through James Mellow's biography or Marty Martin's play *Gertrude Stein Gertrude Stein Gertrude Stein*, or through the countless memoirs of Stein and Toklas in Paris, assume that Stein's own autobiography is "colorful," a series of juicy stories about the

French/American avant-garde. But in fact the style of the *Autobiography* is not especially imagistic, its descriptions less than concrete, the emphasis being on such pronoun-copula units as "He was," "We were," "We looked," "when we got home," "We could hear nothing." Nijinsky, for example, is defined as he who "created the dance of those who did dance." Period.

"The dance of those who did dance." Incremental repetition is not especially notable in the *Autobiography*, but such locutions as "We were very amused and very pleased to see him do it. It was the first time we had seen him doing it," recall those Stein texts, from *Three Lives* to *Lectures in America*,† in which repetition is the central device. I want next to consider the two poles of this more "difficult" Stein compositional mode, a mode that puts off many potential readers who equate excessive repetition with boredom. But once we understand the syntactic habits of the *Autobiography*, Stein's experiments in repetition will seem much less eccentric. Here, as my example of a third "style in search of a reader," is the opening of the short story "Miss Furr and Miss Skeene" (1908):

> Helen Furr had quite a pleasant home. Mrs. Furr was quite a pleasant woman. Mr. Furr was quite a pleasant man. Helen Furr had quite a pleasant voice a voice quite worth cultivating. She did not mind working. She worked to cultivate her voice. She did not find it gay living in the same place where she had always been living. She went to a place where some were cultivating something, voices and other things needing cultivating. She met Georgine Skeene there who was cultivating her voice which some thought was quite a pleasant one. Helen Furr and Georgine Skeene lived together then. Georgine Skeene liked travelling. Helen Furr did not care about travelling, she liked to stay in one place and be gay there. They were together then and travelled to another place and stayed there and were gay there. (*SW* 563)

The key to the repetition-permutation pattern in this rather unusual love story may be found in a comment Stein made in the "Transatlantic Interview 1946" on the subject of her own earlier *Tender Buttons*, specifically "A Piece of Coffee," which contains the sentence "Dirty is yellow" (12). Stein, who is not exactly someone given to frequent self-criticism, tells Robert Bartlett Haas,* "Dirty has an association and is a word I would not use now. I would not use words that have definite associations" (*PGU* 26). Which is to say that the best words, from Stein's perspective, are those whose meanings remain equivocal and hence able to take on slightly different shading at each reappearance.

Take "pleasant," as in "Helen Furr had quite a pleasant home." Unlike "dirty," "pleasant," and especially "quite a pleasant" provides us with what John Ashbery has called "an open field of narrative possibilities" (251). "Quite a pleasant" can connote anything from "very nice, very comfortable" to "barely tolerable." "Mrs. Furr was quite a pleasant woman. Mr. Furr was quite a pleasant man." Again, all we know is that Helen Furr was living with her parents, two people defined only by their indefinability. They are, one supposes, neither better nor worse than most parents—but then, even this supposition cannot be proven or disproven. In the fourth sentence, the phrase "quite a pleasant" is now transferred from persons to Helen Furr's voice, a transfer that makes that voice seem no more interesting than her "quite pleasant" home. "A pleasant voice a voice quite worth cultivating"—it is this bit of exposition that sets Stein's "plot" in motion. For it is Helen's decision to "cultivate her voice" that provides her with the motive she needs to leave home and to go to a place were "some were cultivating something, voices and other things needing cultivating."

In between these two references to "cultivating," the seventh sentence introduces the key word of the story: *gay*. At the time Stein wrote "Miss Furr and Miss Skeene," the designation of "gay" as "homosexual" was not yet so much as a known underground meaning, the word's dictionary definition—"happy," "merry," "good-humored," "blithe"—being the accepted one. Thus, its introduction in the sentence, "She did not find it gay living in the same place where she had always been living" strikes us at first as meaning no more than that Helen Furr is somehow bored at home. Not until "gay" begins to undergo its series of permutations, does its other meaning (inevitably prominent for the contemporary reader but surely latent in Stein's text) come into prominence.

"She did not find it gay living in the same place where she had always been living." How does the repetition of "living" work here? Why can't Stein simply say, "She did not find it gay living at home" or "in her pleasant home"? The locution "living in the same place where she had always been living" emphasizes the duration of Helen Furr's existence prior to her meeting with Georgine Skeene; it is the persistence of her prior "living" that will make the change that now occurs all the more important. In the same vein, the repetition of "cultivating" in "She went to a place where some were cultivating something, voices and other things needing cultivating," is wittily deflationary, its second appearance, modifying "voices and other things needing," suggesting that "cultivating" has less to do with "work" than with some sort of group "gay" activity.

Indeed Helen Furr's new association with a fellow-"cultivator" named Georgine Skeene (the punning names relate fur and skin, even as Georgine Skeene's rhyming name gives her an air of absurdity) suggests that "cultivating" is no more than an excuse for establishing a sexual relationship. But this relationship is already threatened by difference: "Georgine Skeene liked travelling. Helen Furr did not care about travelling, she liked to stay in one place and be gay there." This simple distinction casts doubt on the paragraph's final sentence, "They were together then and travelled to another place and stayed there and were gay there." For it is "travelling" that will produce the split between the two women.

Verbal and phrasal repetition, in this context, is neither ornamental nor, as for many poets, a form of intensification. Rather, repetition generates meaning. For even as the narrative seems to occur in a continuous present ("They stayed there and were gay there, not very gay there, just gay there" [*SW* 563]), the situation gradually and inevitably changes. By the end, Helen Furr is left alone but she has learned to be "regular in being gay" and "telling about little ways one could be learning to use in being gay, and later was telling them quite often, telling them again and again" (*SW* 568).

Who are "they," and what is Helen Furr telling them again and again? It is important that we not know. "Miss Furr and Miss Skeene" is curiously non-mimetic even as its "realism" is intense. The two women are given no motives; indeed, we know almost nothing about them. There is no explanation of their mutual attraction or of the activity in which they were engaging when they were "regularly" going "somewhere" with the "men who were dark and heavy" or with the men "who were not so dark" and those "who were not so heavy" (*SW* 565). The mystery of their being is thus left intact. To say that Stein's is a story of how a girl from a nice home comes out of the closet, has a brief fling with a less nice girl, and thus gains the experience to carry on with her "gay" life is to reduce Stein's enormously subtle work to a cartoon. The text itself remains impervious to such easy reading for it never allows us to make secure judgments about character and action. How "pleasant" is a pleasant home? What does being "regularly gay" entail? If we interpret "gay" as homosexual, what are Helen Furr and Georgine Skeene doing when they "sit regularly" with the dark and heavy men? And in the final standoff between Helen and Georgine, whose side are we on?

Repetition, variation, permutation, the miniscule transfer of a given word from one syntactic slot to another, one part of speech to another, creates a compositional field that remains in constant motion, that prevents closure from taking place. *Pleasant, gay, work, cultivate, regularly, somewhere*—these permutating counters make up a dense network of narrative possibilities without ever coalescing into a definable story line. But indeterminacy does not imply, as readers often assume, that Stein's story has no meaning. On the contrary, its meanings are multiple. Stein is describing a woman who moves out from the "quite a pleasant" home of her quite pleasant parents into a larger world where people are "cultivating" something. In the course of her "cultivation" and her "being gay" with another woman and "sitting" with men of all descriptions, Helen Furr learns to be "gay every day" and "learning other ways in being gay" that she can "tell" others about. By the end of this five-page story, Helen Furr is a different person. And it is the coming of this difference that "Miss Furr and Miss Skeene" charts.

Many of Stein's best-known texts—*The Making of Americans*,† "Melanctha," "Composition as Explanation," the first Picasso portrait—employ the mode of repetition used in "Miss Furr and Miss Skeene." But what of the many compositions that carry repetition to what seems to be a point of no return? Here, for example, is part 26 of Stein's improvisation on Georges Hugnet's* poem *Enfances*, which she called *Before the Flowers of Friendship Faded Friendship Faded*† (1931):

Little by little two go if two go three go if three go four go if four go they go. It is known as does he go he goes if they go they go and they know

they know best and most of whether he will go. He is to go. They will
not have vanilla and say so. To go Jenny go, Ivy go Gaby go any come
and go is go and come and go and leave to go. Who has to hold it while
they go who has to who has had it held and have them come to go. He
went and came and had to go. No one has had to say he had to go come
here to go go there to go go go to come to come to go to go and come
and go. (*W&L* 285)

Even as enthusiastic an advocate of Stein's "experimental writing" as Marianne
DeKoven refers to the poetic sequence in which this text appears as a "travesty"
(106). But if we think of Stein's series of permutations on a small corpus of
words and phrases as her verbal equivalent to the nonrepresentational landscape
of her painter-contemporaries, we begin to discern patterns not unlike the ex-
citing/peaceful clusters in *Paris France*.

"A sentence," as Stein puts it, "is an interval in which there is a finally
forward and back" (*HTW* 133). The "forward and back" in this case is the
buried phrase "to and fro." "Little by little two go"—the narrative begins
normally enough in the vein of a children's book, even as *Paris France* contains
sentences like "There are lots of cats in Paris and in France." Again, the logic
of "If two go three go if three go four go" sounds like a jingle in *Dr. Seuss* or
a nursery rhyme. But Stein never quite lets the "child's play" continue, so she
ends this first sentence with the twist "If four go they go."

Successive sentences provide us with further examples of this ambivalence
between instinct and knowledge, the perspective of the child ("To go Jenny go
Ivy go Gaby go"—a kind of jump-rope rhyme) and that of the grown-up ("It
is known"; "they know best and most of whether he will go"; "no one has
had to say"). Within this framework, embedded in the sound chiming of "come
and go" and "go go go," a single word stands out, rather like a white flag in
an otherwise black field—"They will not have vanilla and say so." "Vanilla"
is the only three-syllable word in the entire composition (for that matter, out of
144 words, there are only 6 that have two syllables, and 3 of those are proper
names); it is the only noun, and the only concrete image referring to a particular
sense impression.

What does it mean thus to embed *vanilla* in the field of *come/go, two/go, he/
they, who/no one, if/of*? Perhaps no more nor less than that the mind tries to
center its little verbal steps on something concrete and tangible, something one
might see or taste or touch. But "Who has to hold it?" No sooner does the noun
appear than it disappears again, obliterated by the march of "go go go." Like
a cubist collage, "vanilla" is the "pasted paper" that draws the eye only to
fade again as other relationships become apparent. And in this sense, Stein's
composition does have meaning: it suggests that the authority vested in "vanilla"
is rejected ("They will not have vanilla and say so") in the interest of the "two"
[who] "go," who "come to come" and "go to go."

An enigmatic text like this one demands, of course, a great deal from the reader; indeed, many readers will find the demand excessive. But, even at her most "repetitious," Stein is not just indulging, as some critics have supposed, in automatic writing. And, at their best, her enigma texts present us with a formidable challenge. I turn now to the most difficult of the Stein styles: first, the fragmented, nonreferential mode of *Tender Buttons* and then the "sound poetry" of texts such as "Lipschitz," "Jean Cocteau," and "Pink Melon Joy."

Like the great realists of the nineteenth century who were her precursors, Stein believed that the domain of literature is the real rather than the ideal, the ordinary rather than the unusual, the everyday rather than the fantastic. But, as Lyn Hejinian observes, "realism" can be an attitude toward language itself rather than only toward the objects to which language refers:

> Perhaps it was the discovery that language is an order of reality itself and not a mere mediating medium—that it is possible and even likely that one can have a confrontation with a phrase that is as significant as a confrontation with a tree, chair, cone, dog, bishop, piano, vineyard, door, or penny, etc.—which replaced [Stein's] commitment to a medical career with a commitment to a literary career. (129)

Which is not to say that references to tree, chair, cone, or dog aren't also obliquely present. In *Tender Buttons* (1914), Stein presents us with a series of objects, food items, body parts, and enclosures, naming each item only to set into motion a kind of riddle. "Cold Climate," we read, and then the single enigmatic sentence, "A season in yellow sold extra strings makes lying places" (*SW* 471). Does this mean that the title is pure nonsense, having nothing to do with the "description" that follows? Or can we relate the "cold climate" to the "season in yellow" (November? autumn? the time of fog?) and consider the possibilities raised by the suggestion that "extra strings" (for a blanket, a pillow, a lap robe) are sold at this time of year so as to make "lying places" more comfortable?

In such instances, language is certainly not "a mere mediating medium," but neither is it, as Stein's detractors often suggest, purely nonreferential. If what Hejinian calls the "confrontation with a [verbal] phrase" becomes as important as the confrontation with an event, it can only be because we have to be peculiarly attentive so as to uncover the connection between the two. Here is "A Waist":

> A star glide, a single frantic sullenness, a single financial grass greediness.
>
> Object that is in wood. Hold the pine, hold the dark, hold in the rush, make the bottom.
>
> A piece of crystal. A change, in a change that is remarkable there is no reason to say that there was a time.
>
> A woolen object gilded. A country climb is the best disgrace, a couple of practices any of them in order is so left. (*SW* 471–72)

Unlike my third and fourth examples, "A Waist" does not rely upon repetition as a form of defamiliarization. Neither is the characteristic sentence a simple declarative one. Rather, Stein here makes use of both synecdoche and pun, these figures being embedded in what tend to be short noun phrases and sentence fragments.

The first thing to notice is that "waist" has as its homonym "waste," and that both words generate what follows. "A star glide"—one immediately conjures up a dancer gliding into the room, a graceful person with a delicate tiny waist. But pinching the waist has its problems: "A single frantic sullenness" suggests that the waist has been laced too tightly, that it hurts. To force the dancer into this role is perhaps a "financial . . . greediness," the desire not to "waste" anything. "Grass" suggests envy on someone's part; it also recalls "glass" and hence takes us back phonemically to "glide" and to the image of a "single" graceful movement of the waist. The repetition of the phonemes / gl/, /gr/, and /l/ reenforce this image of fragility and gliding motion.

But in the second "stanza," Stein abruptly shifts to an entirely different image: "Object that is in wood." Perhaps the "waist" is now that of a carved wooden statuette or idol. Someone is carving a figure and "mak[ing] the bottom," but to talk of waists is, of course, also to talk of hips and bottoms. In the third paragraph, the object is explicitly defined as a "piece of crystal," and the image is that of the sort of little glass figurine one finds in display cases. The "change" that turns a bit of wood or glass into a sculpture is so great that "there is no reason to say that there was a time" (i.e., when it was not yet "made"). And now, in the fourth paragraph or "stanza," "glide" is metathesized to "glided," and the "object" has become woolen. Is the statuette dressed in wool? Or is Stein shifting from artwork to real life and to the benefit waists receive from "a country climb" or related "practices" occurring in some sort of "order"? What is "so left," then, is finally an image of tiny waists delicately moving, not wasting any motion, of an artist's carving, whether in glass or in wood, that creates a definite change.

Each item in *Tender Buttons* has a place on this larger continuum of change and transformation. Like *Paris France* which is exciting and peaceful, buttons can be tender, and a carafe that is a blind glass can be a spectacle. If, in her later work, Stein provides us with more connectives, the basic impulse, which is to "define" things as they really occur, not as if they are to be pigeonholed or seen from one angle only, is to force us to think about the subject, in this case, to come to terms with the word "waist."

In thus "confronting" a group of words as if it were an event in the external world, Stein also pays close attention to sound. Indeed, her corpus includes the first experiments with what we now call "sound poetry." Here is the opening of the 1926 portrait called "Jean Cocteau":

> Needs be needs be needs be near.
> Needs be needs be needs be.

> This is where they have their land astray.
> Two say.
> This is where they have their land astray
> Two say.
> Needs be needs be needs be
> Needs be needs be needs be near.
> Second time. (*P&P* 80)

No doubt, this is Gertrude Stein at her most "nonsensical," her most opaque. We know neither the subject nor the object of the locution "needs be," nor can we be sure whether the verb is indicative or conditional ("if need be"). Again, we can't pinpoint the meaning of the pun on "Two say" ("to say") or the effect of the rhyme "say"/"astray," any more than we can establish the reference in line 5 to "their land astray."

But read aloud, the poem has a particular rhythmic figure, specifically, the ballad rhythm of songs like "Skip to my Lou," with its refrain lines (three per stanza) like "I'll take another one, prettier than you," or "Fly's in the buttermilk, shoo fly shoo." Just so, the first line of "Jean Cocteau"—"Needs be needs be needs be near."—introduces what sounds like the kind of song children sing during circle games; indeed, the refrain "Second time" suggests that the physical movement (skipping? jumping? clapping?) associated with the incantation is to be repeated.

But just as *Paris France* is a parody schoolbook, so "Jean Cocteau" is a parody nursery rhyme or jump-rope song. For "needs be" is also a pun on "kneads bee" and the reference "This is where they have their land astray" refers to the world of grown-ups, not children. And, knowing that Stein admired the young Cocteau, who had praised her work but who never quite seemed to find the time to participate in her salon and become one of her *fidèles*, the "land astray" and "needs be" begin to make more sense. Stein regards her literary situation as one in which Cocteau "needs be near," since he regularly flatters and encourages her. But because their primarily epistolary friendship is more assumed than real, Cocteau never quite having time for Stein, she presents herself and the Frenchman ("Two say") as two fellow-artists whose "land" or common artistic property has gone "astray." Still, the need continues, and as she says in the line following that opening passage quoted above, "It may be nearer than two say." We may, that is to say, have more in common than even we think.

The singsong sound pattern of "Jean Cocteau" is so prominent that readers may well assume that this portrait has phonological value only. Wendy Steiner, for example, writes: "Relieved of specific reference, the words in this portrait have nothing more than their pale dictionary meanings, and even these are made ambiguous through the variations in context. Words thus are almost pure phonological quanta" (120). But the fact remains that there is something that "needs be," a land that has gone "astray," and, for the "second time," "Two [who] say." Indeed, once we have gotten the hang of finding the excited/peaceful configuration in *Paris France* or the metonymic account of the first night at Stravinsky's *Sacre du Printemps* in *The Autobiography of Alice B. Toklas*, we will find that even the most abstruse of Stein's sound poems or synecdochic riddles do refer, however obliquely, to the events of her extraverbal universe.

To recapitulate. Stein's oeuvre gives evidence of at least six different styles: (1) seemingly "straight" reportage (*Paris France*), (2) autobiographical narrative as ironized by presenting a fictional narrator who tells the story, as in *The Autobiography of Alice B. Toklas*, (3) narrative-as-permutation of phrasal repetitions, each reappearance of the word or phrase giving us a new view, as in "Miss Furr and Miss Skeene"; (4) "abstract" repetition of words and phonemes, as in *Before the Flowers of Friendship Faded Friendship Faded,* where the "action" is less a matter of incident than of verbal event; (5) the synecdochic riddling poetry of *Tender Buttons*, where a given title is the impetus for the creation of its cubist equivalent, and (6) sound poetry, as in "Jean Cocteau."

One might, of course, refine these distinctions; the mode of repetition in *Lectures in America*, for instance, falls somewhere in between the repetition-as-narrative of "Miss Furr and Miss Skeene" and the abstraction of *Before the Flowers of Friendship Faded Friendship Faded*. Or again, the fragments of *Stanzas in Meditation*† are at once similar to, and yet also recognizably different from, the concrete texts in *Tender Buttons*. Still, the six types I have isolated give us the basic parameters in which to read the Stein corpus. And in locating these styles on the Stein spectrum, I hope I have laid to rest the notion that Stein *either* writes "simply," so that anyone can understand her, or "obscurely," so that no one can. As she herself put it in "Arthur A Grammar," "Successions of words are so agreeable. It is about this" (*HTW* 39).

REFERENCES: *TB*, 1914; *G&P*, 1922; *HTW*, 1931; *P&P*, 1934; *PF*, 1940; *SW*, 1962; *W&L*, 1967; *PGU*, 1971; *FF*, 1953; John Ashbery, "The Impossible," *Poetry* 90; *GSP*, 1970; Wendy Steiner, *Exact Resemblance to Exact Resemblance*, 1978; Marianne DeKoven, *A Different Language*, 1983; Ulla Dydo, "Stanzas in Meditation," *Chicago Review* 35; Lyn Hejinian, "Two Stein Talks," *Tremblor* 3.

HOMMAGE À GERTRUDE

Shirley Anders

Old hulk, splay-hammed
and hunkered comfortably
while the tailor tacked
around you, calculating
your dimensions for another copy
of the same old skirt—

fitted while sitting, to assure you ease
in this most characteristic of your postures—

practical: by whose couture conceal
the lump God sunk your spirit in?
Better be plain, let body be matrix
for your crystal wit. Why drape a rock?
Skeletally delicate, your gravity would crack
to find *en fin* Stein adamant, modish.

ODE: WALKING IN SNOW

Tom Smith

I

This evening children in the street have run
out of their mittens making lovely men
of snow. From odds and ends of coal a stare
and grin that little hands leave guardian
exclude our praise surrendering to prayer.
Hello, Miss Stein. And when you left your chair
beside the fire, walking in the snow
you made discovery of prayer for fun
that once upon a time. Hello, hello,
Miss Stein, hello: the variations fall
into the snow as you repeat them all.

II

We often see a picture of Miss Stein:
The hills have gardens on them and the lawn
is growing up behind her back and she
of course is seated and surrounded on
all sides;—but truthfully we do not see
the gardens on the hills and truthfully
we do not see the grass. The rocker waits
to carry her away; meanwhile, serene
and distant as a snowfall, she excites
our love of solitude, for she is round
and full of private fun in repetend.

III

The children in the street know how to play,
know how to pack the falling snow away
behind the snowmen's eyes. The children take
the weather in their arms exceedingly
and roll it up; and that is how to make
an image, finding fun in every flake
of snow, heroic comedy, to pack
the formless drift of every happy day
into a bright and private globe of fact.
Comedienne of days, Miss Stein can show
us how to make a snowman out of snow.

The way to build a snowman is through prayer
in repetend. Miss Stein has written for
our eyes considerable snowfalls bold
to keep their secrecy of sense: the more
the story of a life is left untold
the more we give ourselves; in time we build
our snowmen and our saints. The greatest fun
I find on looking into Stein whose sure,
exclusive grin won't let a stranger in,
the greatest invitation: she forsakes
the pleasure; therefore, I may write her books.

IV

The children have gone home; heaven allows
the snowfall through the stars turning our eyes
adrift that follow as it folds in air,
then seems to break away from earth, from trees,
circling back upon some celibate star.
Wafers of snow to earth administer
their sacrament fading into our flesh,
burdening the sky with little honesties
from heaven. Now and then the wind will flash
out of the trees establishing a throne
of air that keeps the snowfall, coming down.

My heart is full of longing after snow;
for there is so much earth and so much sky
meeting the drift behind my eyes that turn
aside to follow the snowfall down. I go
out walking; for the storm is my concern,

is mine: the snowfall coming down is mine,
is my most secret blessing and my wound
of everyday. I wish, if I can pray,
to give back good of unsuspected kind,
a subtle ecstacy like snow. The air,
this night, becomes my guardian of prayer:

how can we know it is snowing, how can we know;
how can we know it is snowing, vastly snow
and vastly snowing, vastly knowing: can
we know: how can we know; for there is so
much sky, how can we know: how can a man
expressly hope to know: what can be known:
how can we know, how can the snow be vast,
how can the sky be vast: how can we know
it is snowing, how can we know; and how express
our knowing it is snowing if we know:
how can we know, how can we know the snow.

Words can become the thing itself: I lift
the snowfall outward from my heart, adrift,
to take up flesh enforcing solitude.
A snowflake cherishes its form, the soft,
hermetic pattern of the ghost obscured
in quietude of size: my words exclude
another's eyes: my flesh is commonplace,
or seems, like snow: my ghost remains, the gift
of prayer and puzzle of my happy days:
for words make visible the world, the rhyme,
the measure of its harmony and form.

                    V

We take the weather in our arms like song
turning digressions of our days along
a white periphery up from the drift
of snow: days pass. The children do no wrong
establishing a form drawn from the shaft,
collapsible, of faded air to lift
up lovely men of snow. I see that they
are unaware of me; they are among
some wing of angels singing pointlessly,
for they are at their game and, knowing how
to play out prayer, their flesh is turned to snow.

So, reader, in the snow, do not invade
my prayer; our blank encounters are well made
to pass without hello. Allow my way
in isolated sacrament, applied
to stars; for it must keep its secrecy.
Give me farewells. As I release a day
of little bliss into the sky, don't breathe
it down into the drift before its played
its circuit of my heart. Days pass; the earth
turns on itself. So, reader, you will do
me well; and I will do the same for you.

Hello, Miss Stein, farewell; we will do well
together keeping to ourselves. The fall,
the swell of snow recalls your hermitage
in words, clean to invasion, simple,
white and white as snow, as snowfall, page
on page of comedy and prayer, as sage,
opaque, as days. Miss Stein, your eyes and grin
exclude a friend as you extend to all
the courtesy of fun. Farewell, Miss Stein.
Days pass; the world turns on itself like snow.
This is the most exclusive prayer I know.

GERTRUDE STEIN

Mina Loy

Curie
of the laboratory
she crushed
the tonnage
of consciousness
congealed to phrases
to extract
a radium of the word

A LETTER TO GERTRUDE STEIN

Lindley Williams Hubbell

The roots have struck deep; tree-root and flower-root
   and the small absurd weed nourished by dust;
In this rich soil a whole generation that would have found death
   in the wind and the black ice,
But the roots were fast, the loam was packed tightly about them,
   the serried stalks were secure,
The earth was stronger than the deep ice, the earth gave back laughter
   to the laughter of the wind, the ice cracked.

In the cities it was the same: people leaned out of windows
   and sniffed the air and laughed,
Children flew past in a clatter of roller skates, children screamed,
   their voices louder than the clatter of their skates,
The older ones played ball in the street, chairs were brought out
   on the pavements, women rocked back and forth,
In all the cities it was like this, and in the little towns
   no one stayed in the houses when work was done.

The miracle was this: that a man could look at his friend
   and say without shame,
"It is better to be dead than to laugh at a perfectly simple thing.
   To do that is worse than death."
The miracle was that sweetness was not gone out of the sap,
   that the stem was not ashamed to bear blossoms.
That the roots were glad of the rain, that the slow wind was permitted
   gladly,—that the boughs were fed willingly.

Love, the bright flower, the homage,
   the proud spear-head of the tall flower,
And laughter, a spoke of mullein, whatever is simple and without harm,

whatever is unashamed of the dust it wears on its leaves,
And the sanity of the grass, the wide cool sanity of the grass that asks
    one inch, two inches of earth, and one inch, two inches of air,
These shall be plaited into a sign to be given from hand to hand
    as a token and a remembrance.

AS GERTRUDE SAID TO ALICE ONE CHRISTMAS

Sarah White

maybe a cake's
as important
at times
as a poem
to make
or

maybe
what's
not too important
anyway
is
important
to make

EPITAPH: IN MEMORIAM GERTRUDE STEIN 1874–1946

William Alfred

To love the world is not an evil.
I swear to you, you who pass,
Though you see both God and Devil
Locked on the broken grass.

I tell you this, here's a high place and a hilly.
Some of you have been here before,
You who have seen the ancient heights burned silly,
And the darkness not held back by any door.

I asked my question of two nations
Till I was out of heart and breath.
Who like me would not lose patience
And expatriate to death.

OR AS GERTRUDE STEIN SAYS...

Vassar Miller

The sky is as blue as itself,
and the tree is as green as its leaves.
How shall I write a poem about today?

The tree stands—
but the tree has no feet.
The tree leans its head—
but the tree is not tired,
growing without resting,
resting without pausing.

Let me try again.

The wind blows.
How, having no whistle?
The wind sings.
How, having no tune?
The wind sighs.
How, having no heart?
Yet it is lovers who borrow
from the wind their softness and storms.

Well then, the wind moves.
How, having no body
but the motion of bodies?

When the sky is as blue as itself,
and the tree is as green as its leaves—
a poem is only
taking a child's downy skull

gentle between your hands
and, with not so much breath as might startle a gnat's wing,
whispering,
"Look!"

Leo, Gertrude, and Michael Stein at 27 rue de Fleurus, c. 1907. (private collection)

Gertrude Stein's signet for sealing wax, from "Sacred Emily," 1913. (editor's collection)

Alice Toklas, c. 1906. Photograph by Arnold Genthe. (private collection)

Sarah Stein (in hat), her husband Michael, and Gertrude Stein (smoking), at 27 rue de Fleurus, c. 1909. Photograph probably by Leo Stein. (private collection)

Gertrude Stein at 27 rue de Fleurus, 1920. Photograph by Man Ray. (private collection)

"Portrait of Mabel Dodge at the Villa Curonia," 1911. Photograph by Jacques Émile Blanche. (editor's collection)

Leo Stein in Paris before 1914. (private collection)

Carl Van Vechten, 1916. Photograph by Herman Mishkin. (editor's collection)

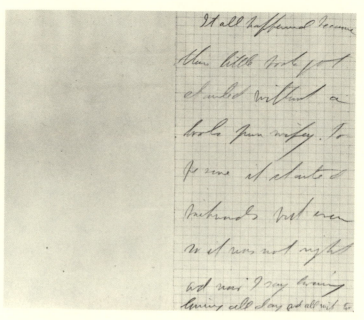

A Gertrude Stein *carnet*, c. 1925. Gertrude Stein often began her work in *carnets*, 3½ × 5½-inches memorandum books. Sometimes she inscribed them to Alice Toklas before beginning, and sometimes she dedicated them at both ends. This magical act assured her of her capacity to write. Failure to inscribe a *carnet* could be blamed if something went wrong, even if she had begun writing from the end. (Courtesy Collection of American Literature, Beinecke Rare Book and Manuscript Library, Yale University)

It all happened because this little book got started without a look from wifey. To be sure it started backwards but even so it was not right and now I say loving loving all day and all night too.

An Unlikely Guest at an Unlikely Party: Gertrude Stein flanked by politician William Jennings Bryan and poet Edwin Markham, actors Douglas Fairbanks and Minnie Maddern Fiske, and writer Ring Lardner at an adjacent table, 1923. Detail from a drawing by Ralph Barton. (Courtesy Diana Barton Franz)

A Gertrude Stein *carnet*, c. 1925. A *carnet* in which Gertrude Stein and Alice Toklas exchange notes or play verbal parlor games. (Courtesy Collection of American Literature, Beinecke Rare Book and Manuscript Library, Yale University)

[GS] Baby has
her husband
here to give
her good cheer.
[AT] And likes it
Baby has a cheerful
husband? [GS] A question
mark is not admitted
by us moderns.
[AT] Then you'll have to
learn to read
[GS] She is a wonderful
mind reader.
She is a wonderful
mine reader

Gertrude Stein and Alice Toklas, sempre fidelis, 1982. Papier mâché, gesso, and acrylic sculpture by Currell Benek. (editor's collection)

Gertrude Stein's manuscript *cahier* for "A Bouquet. Their Wills." French *cahiers*, about 6½ × 8½-inches, offer ideas for compositions through their cover illustrations, titles, and directions. In *L'art de faire un bouquet*, Gertrude Stein applies floral arranging to a bouquet of words. The 1927 manuscript became the text for "A Bouquet. Their Wills." First published in *Operas and Plays* five years later, it is more concerned with her Baltimore relatives than it is with flowers. (Courtesy Collection of American Literature, Beinecke Rare Book and Manuscript Library, Yale University)

The way to make a bouquet and/or to receive flowers the way to make drawings acceptable or a needle make points of different additional distances which result in a man and a basket at an advantage of consequence

Gertrude Stein with Basket on the terrace at Bilignin, 1934. Photograph by Carl Van Vechten. (Courtesy Carl Van Vechten Estate)

Thornton Wilder, 1929. (private collection)

Alice Toklas, Gertrude Stein, and United Airlines flight crew during American lecture tour, 1934. (Courtesy Carl Van Vechten Estate)

ROSE IS A ROSE IS A ROSE ✸ *ROSE IS A ROSE IS A ROSE*

PLAYS AND WHAT THEY ARE
A LECTURE BY
MISS GERTRUDE STEIN
AT THE RESIDENCE OF
MRS. JOHN W. ALEXANDER
170 EAST 78TH STREET
NEW YORK CITY
TUESDAY EVENING, OCTOBER THIRTIETH
AT NINE O'CLOCK

ADMIT...
SUBSCRIPTION $2.00

*THIS CARD MUST BE
PRESENTED AT THE DOOR*

ROSE IS A ROSE IS A ROSE ✸ *ROSE IS A ROSE IS A ROSE*

Invitation to Gertrude Stein's first lecture in America, 1934. (editor's collection)

Four Saints in Three Acts, original production, 1934. Photograph by White Studios. (private collection)

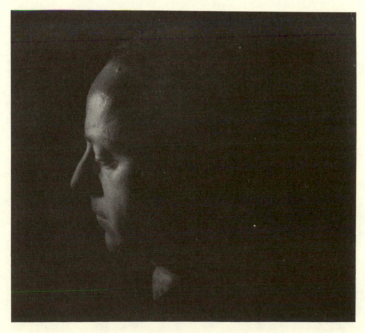

Virgil Thomson, 1932. Photograph by Carl Van Vechten. (Courtesy Carl Van Vechten Estate)

I am Rose my eyes are blue
I am Rose and who are you
I am Rose and when I sing
I am Rose like anything

The World Is Round advertisement, 1939 by Gertrude
Stein. Illustration by Clement Hurd. (editor's collection)

Gertrude Stein and Alice Toklas, 1934. Photograph by Carl Van Vechten. (Courtesy
Carl Van Vechten Estate)

The Mother of Us All, Santa Fé Opera production, 1976. Photograph by Ken Howard. (Photograph courtesy The Santa Fé Opera, 1976 production of Virgil Thomson's *The Mother of Us All*)

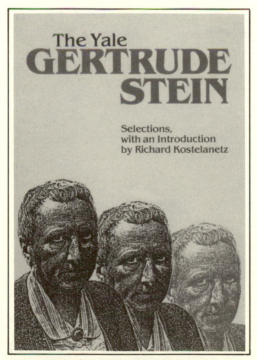

The Yale Gertrude Stein, 1980. Jacket design by Christopher Harris, cover illustration from a photograph by Carl Van Vechten. (Courtesy Yale Univesity Press)

"Gertrude's Follies," 1979. Gertrude Stein and Alice Toklas permanently entered American mythology in 1978 with the advent of Tom Hachtman's brilliant and irreverent comic strip. It ran in several newspapers on both coasts including the *Los Angeles Weekly* and the *Soho* (New York) *Weekly News* for nearly a decade. Selections were collected for *Gertrude's Follies* (1980) and *Fun City* (1985). Drawing by Tom Hachtman. (Courtesy Tom Hachtman)

Gertrude Stein and Alice Toklas at 5 rue Christine, 1945. Photograph by Cecil Beaton. (private collection)

Illustration for *A Book Concluding with As a Wife Has a Cow a Love Story*, by Gertrude Stein, 1926. Lithograph by Juan Gris. (Courtesy Gertrude Stein Estate)

PART III

Friends and Enemies:
A Biographical Dictionary

ABDY, SIR ROBERT HENRY EDWARD, 11 September 1896–16 November 1976, collector. In *Everybody's Autobiography*† Gertrude Stein wrote, "Bertie Abdy . . . is the Sweet William who had his genius and who looked for his Lillian. . . . he dislikes with a violence that is disconcerting all modern art and all Americans, and to prove that the exception proves the rule he is very fond of me and he is going to print for me the two hundred Stanzas of Meditation" (299–300). The proposed edition of *Stanzas in Meditation*† was, however, ultimately abandoned. Abdy, a wealthy English baronet, was interested in finely printed and bound books, antiques, china, furniture, and eighteenth-century French painting, and opened his own gallery after having been associated with the Wildenstein galleries in Europe. He and his second wife, Lady Diana Bridgeman, whom he married in 1930, met Stein early in 1932. They became good friends, according to Alice Toklas, who remembered dining with them at their fabulous house in Saint-Germain. Abdy was a great gourmet, she wrote, who spent an hour each evening with his cook discussing the food to be prepared for the next day. After listening to Stein discuss her early days in Paris, Abdy suggested that she write a history of that time and her friends, which Stein "put . . . together as it later was written in The Autobiography of Alice B. Toklas" (*EA* 300). On a visit to Stein and Toklas in Bilignin, the Abdys offered to arrange lectures for Stein at Cambridge and Oxford for the following winter. In 1936 Stein and Toklas stayed with the Abdys at their eighteenth-century estate in Cornwall during part of that lecture tour. Lady Diana was "charming lovely and an awfully good friend," Stein wrote to Carl Van Vechten* in 1938, recommending that he photograph her (*GSCVV* 586). The Abdys, who had one son, were divorced in 1962; Lady Diana died in 1967. Sir Robert's third marriage also ended in divorce. Stein's "Portrait of the Abdys" was published in the English literary magazine *Janus* in May 1936, and Sweet William and Lillian, their characters in that portrait, also appear in "Listen to Me," in *Last Operas and Plays*†.

REFERENCES: *EA*, 1937; *LO&P*, 1949; *WIR*, 1963; *CC*, 1974; *WWW*, 1971–1980, 1981; *GSCVV*, 1986.

Priscilla Oppenheimer

ACTON, SIR HAROLD, 5 July 1904–   , poet, historian. Harold Acton was born into a wealthy English family living in Florence, Italy, at the time. He was educated in private schools and studied with Bernard Berenson* there before attending Oxford in the 1920s. As a child he knew Gertrude Stein in Florence at Mabel Dodge's* Villa Curonia. In his *Memoirs of an Aesthete*, he tells how as a student he considered parodying Stein's experimental style in his school assignments but decided against it, fearful of his teacher's reaction. When Acton was president of his literary society at Oxford, he invited Stein to speak. After an earlier lecture at Cambridge, she arrived accompanied by Edith, Osbert, and Sacheverell Sitwell* to speak at Christ Church on 7 June 1926. In his memoir, Acton gives his version of the event. Stein drew a standing-room audience in contrast to the somewhat smaller one at Cambridge the day before. It was arranged that "her tall bodyguard of Sitwells" sat on the platform with Stein to give her confidence. The audience was expecting an "eccentric visionary" instead of "a placid reading of 'Composition as Explanation.' " Acton observed "there was no nonsense about her manner, which was in deep American earnest, as natural as could be . . . " (161–62). Following the lecture, Stein read her word portrait, "Sitwell Edith Sitwell," during which the subject tried not to seem embarrassed when she was introduced into it halfway through:

> Miss Edith Sitwell have and heard.
> Introduces have and had.
> Miss Edith Sitwell have and had.
> Introduces have and had introduces have and had and heard.
> Miss Edith Sitwell have and had and heard. (*WAM* 51)

Harold Acton divided his time in the twenties between England, France, and Italy and was often a guest at 27 rue de Fleurus. In *How to Write*† the chapter "Regular Regularly in Narrative" portrays him briefly but vividly in one of Stein's familiar patterns involving days of the week and counting, concluding "Harold Acton famous in life and death" (235–38). By the thirties, Acton was teaching at the University of Peking, China, and in later years he has lived most of the time in one of the Medici palaces in the Via Bolagna in Florence.

REFERENCES: *HTW*, 1931; *WAM*, 1940; Sir Harold Acton, *Memoirs of an Aesthete*, 1984.

Paul Padgette

ADLER, MORTIMER, 28 December 1902–   , writer, lecturer. Mortimer Adler decided at the age of fifteen to become a philosopher. Although he never took a degree, he wrote books and delivered lectures on a wide range of subjects.

He was a natural choice as editorial chairman of the *Encyclopædia Britannica*, a post he still holds. When Robert Hutchins* became president of the University of Chicago in 1929, he invited Adler to administer the Great Books program, for which the university—and Adler—became famous. Adler edited the *Great Books of the Western World* and compiled the list of 102 Great Ideas, the heart of the Great Books program. He himself wrote many of the lengthy essays defining the Great Ideas. Great books and great ideas continue to be his passion. During Gertrude Stein's American tour in 1934 she visited the University of Chicago in response to Hutchins's invitation. At a dinner at Hutchins's home Stein objected to Adler's notion that there were no Great Ideas in English. The argument between Stein and Adler became so heated that when the police arrived, everyone assumed they had come to break up a fight; in fact they had come to give Gertrude Stein and Alice Toklas a ride in a patrol car. Adler continues to be actively involved in philosophical research and to write and lecture. While he is largely ignored by professional philosophers, he may justly be called the philosopher for the common man. Such books as *How to Think about War and Peace*, *How to Read a Book*, *How to Think about God*, and *Reforming Education* have attracted vast numbers of readers. His autobiography, *Philosopher at Large*, appeared in 1977. Always an iconoclast, Adler now devotes much of his energy to Paideia, a revolutionary program in the schools of Atlanta, Chicago, and Oakland. He has over forty books to his credit and has been called "the last great Aristotelian" (*Time*, 4 May 1987, 84).

REFERENCES: *CB*, 1940; *CC*, 1975; *Time*, 6 May 1985, 4 May 1987.

Margaret Woodbridge

ALDRICH, MILDRED, 16 November 1853–19 February 1928, writer. Mildred Aldrich, born in Providence, Rhode Island, is best known for several volumes of autobiography she wrote late in life. Earlier, she had been a critic for the Boston *Transcript*; then she moved to London where she continued as a critic, an editor, and occasional agent for other writers. Shortly after the turn of the century, she settled in France where she met Gertrude Stein. Stein at that time described Aldrich at fifty-one as a female version of George Washington with her long face and abundant white hair. Aldrich introduced many people to the Stein circle through the years, among them the art patroness Mabel Dodge* and Henry McBride,* the American art critic who became one of Stein's most faithful promoters in his columns of the New York *Sun*. In June 1914, Aldrich moved to the farmhouse she called La Creste, on the top of a hill overlooking the Marne River in Huiry, south of Paris, where she spent the rest of her life. From her garden she witnessed the unfolding battle of the Marne in 1915 and wrote her impressions of it in *A Hilltop on the Marne*. It became a publishing success, reprinted twenty times, and remains her most famous book. It was followed in the next few years by several other volumes of memoirs mingled with local history. During World War I she spent most of her limited funds helping refugees and the schoolchildren of her village, aided by Gertrude Stein and Alice Toklas during the first winter of the war. In 1922, in recognition of her efforts, Aldrich was awarded the French Legion of Honor, largely through a campaign that Stein organized. When she was in her seventies and in failing health, Aldrich received help from Stein, Toklas, and the sculptor Janet Scudder,* who initiated a fund, with contributions from her many friends in the past, to see her through her last years. Aldrich discovered the source of her good fortune after an appeal was printed in the *Atlantic Monthly*, a magazine to which she had been an early contributor. In the twenties, Stein wrote two word portraits of Aldrich, "Mildred's Thoughts," first published in *American Caravan* in 1927 and later in the 1973 collection, *Reflection on the Atomic Bomb*.† The second portrait, "Mildred Aldrich Saturday," written in 1924, was printed a decade later in *Portraits and Prayers*.† When Aldrich was seventy-five years old, she died of a stroke and was buried in the cemetery at Huiry. Her personal papers were bequeathed to Stein, but she never made the trip to Huiry to collect them; evidently they were destroyed when the house was sold. Among Aldrich's correspondents was French playwright Maurice Maeterlinck, whom she had served as American agent. A part of her extensive library of important first editions, many with inscriptions to her, was left to the American Library in Paris.

REFERENCES: *ABT*, 1933; *P&P*, 1934; *EA*, 1937; *RAB*, 1973; *CC*, 1974.

Paul Padgette

ALFRED, WILLIAM, 16 August 1922–   , playwright, educator. William Alfred began writing to Gertrude Stein while he was still in high school, and they met after the second world war when he was in the army in France. He wrote his "Epitaph" for her the day he learned of her death, "uncannily," he has observed, before having heard of the now celebrated deathbed exchange between Gertrude Stein and Alice Toklas about questions and answers. Alfred's poem won the Atlantic Contests for College Students, sponsored by *The Atlantic Monthly*, in 1946–1947. Subsequently, he joined the faculty of Harvard University where he is now Professor of English. In 1965, Alfred's widely regarded play, *Hogan's Goat*, was first produced. He has written other plays as well, and a substantial body of poetry.

REFERENCES: *SOA*, 1973; Alfred letter, 24 Feb 1988.

Bruce Kellner

ALSOP, JOSEPH, JR., 11 October 1910–   , journalist. Even before meeting Gertrude Stein, Joseph Alsop, Jr., was impressed by her *Four Saints in Three Acts*.† As a reporter for the *New York Herald Tribune* he attended a rehearsal of the opera, intending to do a humorous piece on it, but liked what he heard and changed his mind. In October 1934, when Stein arrived in New York to begin her American tour, he asked her why she did not write as clearly as she talked. "Oh, but I do" was her reply. "After all, it's all learning how to read it'' (*CC* 455). This was the first of several interviews Alsop had with her, during which the two learned to like each other and temporarily became fast friends. After attending Stein's first lecture, "Pictures," Alsop noted that "with Miss Stein there is never a dull moment" (*CC* 462). Throughout her tour he continued to give her friendly coverage in the *Herald Tribune*. Alsop went on to become famous as the good friend of President Franklin D. Roosevelt. His book *Men around the President* received acclaim for its impartiality. His journalistic work continued, sometimes through collaboration with Robert Kintner and often with his brother Stewart Alsop. Several books and articles authored by Joseph Alsop reflect his lifelong interest in art and especially in China. He loathed the communist regime, but after a visit in 1983 he surprised his readers by observing that it had worked out better than he had expected.

REFERENCES: *WWA*, 1974; *CC*, 1975; B. Rose, "Art of Value," *Vogue*, 1983.

Margaret Woodbridge

ANDERSON, MARGARET, 16 August or 24 November 1886, 1891, or 1893–18 October 1973, editor. Born and educated in Indiana, Margaret Anderson moved to the more worldly atmosphere of Chicago in 1914. She coincided there with the Chicago Renaissance, a good time to get a foothold in the arts. Anderson began as a book reviewer for the *Dial* and the *Chicago Evening Post*, and through these positions she formed a circle of literary friends to organize the *Little Review*. In the first issue, in March 1914, she stated her aim for the magazine was to "produce criticism of books, music, art, drama, and life that shall be fresh and constructive" (Hoffman 53). The content of the magazine in subsequent issues moved from criticism to poetry. Harry Hanson, a leading journalist of the Chicago scene at the time, reflected on the early days of the *Little Review* and its founder: "It had few friends, and meagre resources, and nobody knew when and where it was going to be published next, but it provided inspiration and spiritual sustenance for . . . men and women whose names have emerged from obscurity into literary fame" (103). Margaret Anderson herself, Hanson continued, "was always vivid . . . and beautiful to look upon, and lovely in her mind" (105). In 1917 she engaged Jane Heap,* an art student in Chicago, to co-edit the *Little Review*; with their roster of emerging writers, they moved the magazine briefly to Muir Woods, California, and then on to New York City. In 1918 Anderson and Heap published early installments of James Joyce's *Ulysses*, resulting in a trial and conviction for printing obscene literature. Anderson paid the fine of $100 in December 1920, losing her case even though she had been defended by the well-known attorney and bibliophile John Quinn. In 1922 Anderson and Heap moved the *Little Review* to Paris and thereafter Heap assumed the burden of the editorial work, although Anderson's name remained on the masthead. Anderson was not fond of Gertrude Stein, although she encouraged publication of Stein's work in the *Little Review*. She was critical of *The Making of Americans*,† which she found boring and endlessly repetitive; consequently, Stein's involvement with the magazine was conducted through Jane Heap, who acted as an unofficial agent in other outlets as well. During the years of its tenure, the *Little Review* published T. S. Eliot,* Ezra Pound,* Hart Crane, Djuna Barnes, Amy Lowell, Sherwood Anderson,* and William Carlos Williams.* Gertrude Stein's "Vacation in Brittany" appeared in the spring 1922 issue. One of her most famous poems, "Idem the Same. A Valentine to Sherwood Anderson," appeared in the spring 1923 number. Other contributions followed, and in the last issue of the magazine, in May 1929, appeared her word portrait of her friend, "J. H. Jane Heap. Fairly Well. An Appreciation of Jane." The magazine ceased publication, Anderson wrote, because "self-expression is not enough, . . . all the arts have broken faith or lost connection with their origin and function" (Hoffman 65). She did not mention that she never paid any of her contributors when she wrote her own histories of the *Little Review*, *My Thirty Years' War* and *The Fiery Fountains*.

REFERENCES: Harry Hanson, *Midwest Portraits*, 1923; Margaret Anderson, *My Thirty Years' War*, 1930; *ABT*, 1933; Frederick J. Hoffman, *Little Magazine*, 1947; Margaret Anderson, *The Fiery Fountain*, 1951.

Paul Padgette

ANDERSON, SHERWOOD, 13 September 1876–8 March 1941, writer. Sherwood Anderson's childhood and growing up experiences were good training for his adult writing career. He was born in Camden, Ohio, the third child in a family of seven. His harness-maker father moved the family about the state until 1884 when they settled in Clyde, the Ohio town that Anderson called Winesburg in his most famous book. He attended school irregularly after the age of fourteen and worked as a newspaper boy, farmhand, and laborer. His mother's early death at forty-two of consumption decided Anderson to pursue a business career, and he left for Chicago in 1895. After a period of casual labor, he enlisted in the army during the Spanish-American War and afterward studied at Wittenberg Academy for a college education that he never completed. He married the first of his four wives in 1904, the daughter of a successful businessman in Elyria, Ohio. In 1912 he suddenly walked away from his wife, children, and Ohio, returning to Chicago with some manuscripts he had worked on while in business and took employment as a copywriter. Over a period of time Anderson came to know some of the figures associated with the Chicago literary world: Carl Sandburg, Ben Hecht, Edgar Lee Masters, Margaret Anderson,* and Harriet Monroe, editor of the new magazine *Poetry*. Anderson reworked some of his unfinished manuscripts and in 1916 published *Windy McPherson's Son* and several of the Winesburg stories. Now divorced from his first wife, he married Tennessee Mitchell, a painter, in 1916. He was beginning to be known as a writer of promise, but the financial rewards remained meager. Anderson had read the special number, dated August 1912, of Alfred Stieglitz's* *Camera Work*, containing Gertrude Stein's word portraits "Matisse" and "Picasso." He later said that the creative inspiration from these and Masters's *Spoon River Anthology* made him concentrate on the tales in *Winesburg, Ohio*. In 1919 he found a publisher for his struggles at communication, and that book was born. In 1921 he was awarded the $2,000 prize from *Dial*'s editors for his contributions to American literature in the short story form, which allowed him to travel to Europe. Shortly after arriving in Paris in May 1921, Anderson discovered Sylvia Beach's* Shakespeare and Company bookshop. He noticed *Winesburg, Ohio* on display in its window and introduced himself as the author. Beach then took him to meet Gertrude Stein. In addition to *Camera Work*, he had read *Tender Buttons*† and *Three Lives*.† The meeting proved important to both of them, since Stein was famous but largely unpublished, and Anderson was an established writer from America. In a notebook he kept of his Paris impressions, he wrote that Gertrude Stein "is the very symbol of health and strength, . . . she laughs, . . . tells stories with an American shrewdness in getting the tang and the kicking into the telling" (Fanning 51). After he returned to America, Stein wrote him requesting that he write a preface to her first important anthology, *Geography and Plays*,† which she was collecting for publication. He answered, "It's a literary job I'd rather do than any other I know of" (*SAGS* 13), and in his preface he declared "the work of Gertrude Stein consists in a rebuilding, an entire new recasting of life, in the city of words" (*G&P* 8). In the *New Republic* for 11 October 1922, he went on to say this "worker in words" was "laying word against word, relating sound to sound, feeling for the taste, the smell, the rhythm of the individual word" (*SAGS* 24–25). In a letter to Anderson in April 1923, Stein expresses her impressions of his own writing in a direct and compelling manner: "I tell you honestly Sherwood and this is straight you are the best writing America does and you are in the great tradition" (*SAGS* 27). Her first published tribute to him came in the form of "A Valentine to Sherwood Anderson," first published in the *Little Review*, spring 1923, which says, in part,

> Very fine is my valentine.
> Very fine and very mine.
> Very mine is my valentine very mine and very fine.
> Very fine is my valentine and mine, very fine very mine and mine is my valentine. (*P&P* 152).

Anderson continued to pay tribute to Stein in his work. In *A Story Teller's Story*, the first of three autobiographies he published, he said that "reading Miss Stein had given me a new sense of my own limited vocabulary, had made me feel words as more living things" (*SAGS* 41). In March 1925, Stein wrote one of her rare reviews of another writer's work in *Ex Libris* (a publication of the American Library in Paris), identifying Anderson with Mark Twain, William Dean Howells, and James Fenimore Cooper in a quartet of writers whose "essential intelligence" is best equipped to "express life" (*SAGS* 45). In December 1926, Anderson and his third wife, Elizabeth, and two of his children by his first marriage, arrived in Paris for a three-month stay. He saw Stein several times, and their correspondence resumed as before when he returned to America. Anderson settled in Virginia in 1927, purchasing a farm, where he remained for the rest of his life. During Stein's American lecture tour in the mid-thirties, she saw Anderson only twice—in Minnesota and in New Orleans—because their schedules would not allow for further meetings, but in New Orleans Anderson amused Stein by driving her about in his car, and the *Chicago Tribune* published Stein's review of Anderson's recently published *Puzzled America* to coincide with the conclusion of her tour in May 1935. After her return to France, Stein wrote *Everybody's Autobiography*† in which her meetings with Anderson are recorded. Their letters continued until February 1941 when Anderson and his fourth wife, Eleanor, sailed from New York for South America. At the Canal Zone Anderson died of peritonitis. Gertrude Stein's last published tribute to Anderson was in a special memorial issue of *Story* in 1941, "Sherwood's Sweetness," in which she summed up her emotions: "And he was everything and he did everything" (*SAGS* 114). Earlier, in *The Autobiography of Alice B. Toklas*,† she had contended that "Sherwood Anderson had a genius for using the sentence to convey a direct emotion, this was in the great american tradition and that really except Sherwood there was no one in America who could write a clear and passionate sentence" (*ABT* 268).

REFERENCES: *ABT*, 1933; *P&P*, 1934; *EA*, 1937; *SAGS*, 1972; Michael Fanning, *France and Sherwood Anderson*, 1976.

Paul Padgette

APOLLINAIRE, GUILLAUME, 26 August 1880–10 November 1918, poet, dramatist, critic, journalist. Long regarded as the advocate of cubism, a fun-loving prankster, a pornographer, a poet of erotic love, a man who would embrace any new "ism" in art or politics, Guillaume Apollinaire has come to be recognized as a very important figure of the twentieth century. Born Guillaume Apollinaire de Kostrowitsky of a Polish mother and probably an Italian father, he had a chaotic boyhood. At twenty he came to Paris, a city he soon learned to love, and established himself as one of the most colorful members of the avant-garde. His best friend was Picasso,* for whom he often sat for sketches. His art criticism, collected under the title *The Cubist Painters*, shows his often penetrating understanding of the work of his young painter friends, although they liked to claim that he knew nothing about painting. Inevitably, this ardent disciple of new art made his way to 27 rue de Fleurus. Apollinaire and his mistress—at that time the painter Marie Laurencin*—became regular members of the group. Gertrude Stein was quite fond of him for his brilliant and amusing conversation, though she seems to have held his writing in low esteem. (It has been pointed out that she was surprisingly ignorant of French poetry.) Even though they had similar goals and methods they seem never to have conferred about writing, nor did Stein ever express an opinion about his work. A long, unpunctuated poem of an early fruitless love, "La Chanson du Mal-Aimé," first drew attention. Apollinaire always regarded punctuation in poetry as unnecessary. He had to work on various kinds of writing projects in order to make money, all the while working on his poetry.

The event that had the greatest impact on his poetry occurred in 1911, when he was accused of stealing the Mona Lisa from the Louvre. Although hardly anyone believed he was guilty, he found his six days in prison a devastating experience. It is speculated that the French chauvinist public had never ceased to regard him, a foreigner and a radical, with suspicion. By contrast, one of the happy episodes of these years is the birthday party he organized for the painter Henri Rousseau.* The accounts are hilarious, full of youthful high spirits. Gertrude Stein and Alice Toklas were present on this occasion and apparently enjoyed the merriment as much as the others. Apollinaire's most famous work, *Alcools*, written in prison, is a collage-like group of fifty-five poems, chiefly autobiographical, full of allusions to history and literature. For this reason, an unfriendly critic called it "an old junk shop" (Steegmuller 250). Although the critic later recanted, the review hurt Apollinaire, who had worked long and carefully over the poems and had tried to use his erudition to suggest simultaneity of experience. The poems contain striking, often shocking, images drawn from the dark, instinctive side of his nature. Many images came from dreams, a distinctly Freudian characteristic. These poems show his complete understanding of the male sex drive, yet they have a haunting lyrical beauty. Later work includes "Calligrammes," a half-mocking, half-playful collection inviting comparison with François Villon; several novels; and a surrealist libretto for Francis Poulenc's opera, *Les Mamselles de Tirésias*, a farce on overpopulation that caused a riot in 1918 when it was first performed. Though he was not French and need not have served, he enlisted during World War I, one of the first to recognize the close relationship between male sexual desire and war. Unfortunately, he received a head wound for which trepanning was necessary. Stein and Toklas visited him in the hospital and found him looking "handsomer than ever" (*WIR* 87). The trepanning weakened him considerably, making him an easy victim of influenza. He died the day before the Armistice was signed. His last hours were tragically disturbed by crowds of people in the street outside his window shouting, "A bas Guillaume!" He assumed that they were directing their shouts to him, when in fact they were referring to the Kaiser. Gertrude Stein felt his death keenly because she thought that the warm-hearted Apollinaire had helped to keep the group together. Picasso telephoned the news, then drew a portrait of himself staring morosely into the mirror. As Stein said, "now that he [Apollinaire] was gone everybody ceased to be friends" (*ABT* 74). Critics of twentieth-century poetry consider Apollinaire's achievement considerable. He assimilated all the movements of his day, and in turn influenced everyone, perhaps even Gertrude Stein.

REFERENCES: Francis Steegmuller, *Apollinaire, Poet among the Painters*, 1963; Cecily Mackworth, *Guillaume Apollinaire and the Cubist Life*, 1963; *WIR*, 1963; *CC*, 1975.

Margaret Woodbridge

ASHTON, FREDERICK, 17 September 1906– , dancer, choreographer. Frederick Ashton grew up in Lima, Peru, where he saw Anna Pavlova's company dance. This event marks the beginning of an illustrious career in ballet. In London he saw the Diaghilev corps and in 1924 he became a pupil of Leonid Massine. He began to compose ballets noted for their elegance and charm. In 1933, when the producers were looking for someone to do the choreography for *Four Saints in Three Acts*,† Virgil Thomson* suggested Ashton. He accepted the job for a ticket to New York plus expenses, without salary. He was considered difficult at rehearsals, but he charmed the cast with his English manners and audiences with his staging. In 1935 he joined Sadler's Wells (subsequently renamed the Royal Ballet), with which he has ever since been associated. In 1937 he staged Gerald Lord Berners's* version of Gertrude Stein's "They Must. Be Wedded. To Their Wife." as *A Wedding Bouquet*.† Ashton joined the RAF in 1940 as a flight lieutenant. After the war, his work acquired greater depth. He created many ballets and often danced leading roles. A partial list of titles indicates the importance of his contribution to dance: *Façade*, *Les Patineurs*, *Dante Sonata*, *Tales of Hoffman*, and *Cinderella*. In 1950 he was made a Commander of the Order of the British Empire.

REFERENCES: *EA*, 1937; *Current Biography*, 1951; *CC*, 1975.

Margaret Woodbridge

ASWELL, EDWARD, 19 October 1900–5 November 1958, editor, publisher. Born in Nashville, Tennessee, Edward Aswell received his B.A. degree from Harvard in 1926. He is noted for his work as a publisher and editor, having served with many of the most famous houses and periodicals: *Forum*, *Atlantic Monthly*, Harper's, McGraw-Hill, and finally, Doubleday. In his capacity as editor he made the acquaintance of most of the writers of the period and became a good friend to many. He was especially encouraging to Thomas Wolfe by accepting his novels for Harper's when the writer despaired of finding a publisher. When Gertrude Stein submitted *The Autobiography of Alice B. Toklas*† to the *Atlantic Monthly* in 1933, Aswell was so fascinated by it that he forgot about time completely, he claimed. Finding that the room had darkened, he thought a storm had come up and was astonished to discover that night had fallen. The result was that the *Atlantic Monthly* serialized the book with delight.

REFERENCES: *NYT*, 6 November 1958; *CC*, 1975.

Margaret Woodbridge

ATHERTON, GERTRUDE [FRANKLIN HORN], 30 October 1857–14 June 1948, novelist. Gertrude Atherton was born in San Francisco, the daughter of a tobacco merchant who arrived in the early 1850s from Connecticut and became a member of the Vigilante Committee. After her parents separated when she was two years old, she was raised under the guidance of her grandfather, the owner of a large, private library that gave her a taste for reading. Later, at private schools, her progress with conventional education was uneven, and she ended up mostly self-taught and possessing a strongly rebellious nature. At the age of nineteen she married George Atherton, an adventurer who had earlier courted her mother. He came from monied Colonial New England stock, and she spent her married life at the San Francisco Peninsula country estate he owned, now the town of Atherton. She began writing for her own amusement as a child and had published in the prestigious San Francisco *Argonaut*; it was not until after her husband's death in 1887 that she wrote for fame and money. Her husband's family did not approve of her unconventional behavior and refused to support her, so she moved to New York and continued her writing career. In the next half-century Gertrude Atherton published fifty-six books. The most critically successful was *The Conqueror*, a novel based on the life of Alexander Hamilton. She was an exhaustive researcher and published a series of novels on early California history; *The Californians* and *The Splendid Idle Forties* were the most popular. Atherton lived at various times in England, Germany, and France researching her novels. During the twenties while living in Paris, she was introduced to Gertrude Stein by their mutual friend, playwright Avery Hopwood.* Atherton later remarked that she was pleased to sit with Stein instead of being relegated to the side with Alice Toklas and the wives as was the custom for most female visitors at 27 rue de Fleurus. In 1935 when Gertrude Stein arrived in San Francisco on her lecture tour, Gertrude Atherton, by now in permanent residence and the reigning figure of local literary circles, acted as Stein's hostess as a favor to their mutual friend, Carl Van Vechten.* By the time Stein ended her San Francisco sojourn, Atherton had been won over by her guest's celebrated charisma. Atherton arranged the season's most glittering cocktail party for her guests, guiding Stein and Toklas through San Francisco society, skillfully adhering to Stein's requests and suggestions. The two Gertrudes crossed the Bay by ferry to visit the Dominican Convent College in San Rafael and meet Gertrude Atherton's granddaughter, a teaching nun at the College. Stein toured Oakland to revive old childhood memories; searching for familiar places and not finding them, she wrote the line—usually quoted out of context—"There is no there there" (*EA* 289). Stein spoke at Mills College for Woman in Oakland and lectured at the International House at the University of California at Berkeley. The conservative university would not permit her to speak in a campus setting, but the two Gertrudes won the day by arranging the International House locale, and Stein delivered one of her most successful lectures of the tour. Although their literary styles and aspirations were vastly different, they liked each other personally and said so in print. Stein honored Atherton by including her as a character in a play written shortly after her return to France, "A Play Called Not and Now."

REFERENCES: *EA*, 1937; *TCA*, 1940; Emily Leider, "A Tale of Two Gertrudes," San Francisco *Examiner and Chronicle*, 30 November 1980; *GSCVV*, 1986.

Paul Padgette
Bruce Kellner

AUZIAS, NINA, 1883–?, model. Leo Stein's* intermittent love affair with Nina Auzias lasted a dozen years, from the time they met in 1909 until they married in 1921. Auzias was an artist's model, having failed at the singing career to which she aspired. After Alice Toklas moved to 27 rue de Fleurus, Leo Stein moved to Italy, taking Auzias with him. Gertrude Stein's portrait of her, "Elise Surville," reflects a woman who "has been helping some one to be one not succeeding in living, to be one coming to be a dead one and that one was one perhaps not coming then to be a dead one." Later she is "an interesting one to some" who is "not needing much from any one to be one being living" (*TWO* 316–18). As the portraits from this early period reflected character more often than profession or occupation, Stein's "Elise Surville" may suggest more of Nina Auzias's selfless devotion to Leo than it suggests of her highly active love life. In 1909, at the time of the portrait, she was engaged in three separate affairs. She remained married to Leo Stein until his death in 1947, apparently adding credence to Gertrude Stein's early Surville-servile pun.

REFERENCES: *JS*, 1950; *TWO*, 1951; *CC*, 1974.

Bruce Kellner

BALMAIN, PIERRE, 18 May 1914–29 June 1982, fashion designer. Pierre Alexander Balmain was born in Savoy, France, and came to Paris as a young man to attend L'École des Beaux Arts. He did so well that from 1934 to 1939 he was a designer for Molyneux, and from 1939 to 1945 for Lucien Lelong. During World War II he was a refugee in Aix-les-Bains, where he became acquainted with Gertrude Stein and Alice B. Toklas. When their clothing became threadbare he made warm suits for both of them. After the war Balmain went to Paris to establish himself as the young designer of liberated France. He set up his own fashion salon, and Gertrude Stein sponsored his first showing. She and Alice Toklas attended, dressed in the suits he had made for them. Toklas warned Stein not to tell anyone they were wearing Balmain's clothes because she thought they looked "too much like gypsies" (*WIR* 171). Stein continued to take friends to his showings and to write articles about him for *Vogue*. He enjoyed huge success in the postwar fashion world, about which he wrote in an autobiography entitled *My Years and Seasons*.

REFERENCES: John Malcolm Brinnin, *The Third Rose*, 1959; *WIR*, 1963; *WW*, 1973; *CC*, 1974.

Margaret Woodbridge

BALTHUS [BALTHASAR KLOSSOWSKI DE ROLA], 1908–   , painter. "I took some interest in a new man, he was a Pole named Balthus. I found him the day I was leaving for the summer but when I came back at the end of the summer I did not bother," Stein wrote in *Everybody's Autobiography*,† but apparently her enthusiasm for Balthus later revived (98). She wrote Sherwood Anderson* in December 1940 that "Balthus, perhaps one of the most interesting of the young painters and who is also passing winters and summers not far from us had bicycled over. . . . you have probably heard of him" (*SAGS* 112). Stein and Alice Toklas exchanged visits with Balthus frequently during the summers in Bilignin in the late thirties, according to Sir Francis Rose.* Balthus has purposely remained out of the limelight, and the facts of his autobiography are obscure. He was born in France to a family of Polish artists and was encouraged as a child by the German poet Rilke to become a painter. A member of no particular group or movement, he looked to the masters of the Italian Renaissance for inspiration. His first one-man show took place in Paris in 1942, and his reputation grew steadily. His portrait of André Derain* is considered by many to be one of the great portraits of the twentieth century. A retrospective was held in London in 1968, and in 1984 an exhibition of his work at the Pompidou Center in Paris, which later moved to New York, drew enormous crowds. Robert Hughes writes that Balthus has "painted some of the best landscapes of his time," and calls him a painter who is "fetishized and underrated to an equally striking degree" (*Time*, 16 April 1984, 75).

REFERENCES: *EA*, 1937; Sir Frances Rose, *Saying Life*, 1961; *Praeger Encyclopedia of Art*, 1971; *SAGS*, 1972; *Time*, 16 April 1984, 75.

Priscilla Oppenheimer

BARNEY, NATALIE CLIFFORD, 31 October 1876–3 February 1972, hostess, poet, memoirist. Natalie Barney, beautiful and witty heiress from Dayton, Ohio, made the improbable transition from respectable Washington society to Paris of the Left Bank, where she established the most influential literary salon in Europe and became the most notorious lesbian of her time. Her love affairs were legendary. Barney's book of lesbian love poems appeared in 1900, and the following year a novel by the famous courtesan Liane de Pougy chronicled her seduction by the young American. Barney appears as a character in six novels and is described in numerous memoirs. The French author and critic Remy de Gourmont brought her fame as a literary personage with the publication of his *Letters to an Amazon*, essays based on their conversations, in 1914. De Gourmont was one of several men of letters impressed with her intelligence and charm and with whom she developed close friendships. As George Wickes points out, she had a "genius for friendship" and many talented women, some her former lovers, became her friends for life (9). In 1909 Barney moved to a house at 20 rue Jacob on the Left Bank, where she lived until her death and where she realized her true vocation. Her Friday evenings "at home" continued for sixty years and brought together the leading scholars, political figures, publishers, artists, and writers of Paris. Among her guests at various times were Auguste Rodin, Anatole

France, André Gide, Rainier Maria Rilke, Paul Valéry, Gabriele D'Annunzio, Max Jacob,* Colette, Jean Cocteau,* and Remy de Gourmont. The salon was in its heyday after World War I, when English and American writers came there to meet their French counterparts and to be met: James Joyce,* Ezra Pound,* T. S. Eliot,* Ernest Hemingway,* F. Scott Fitzgerald,* and Sherwood Anderson.* Her salon was, however, as conventional as her life was unconventional—formal and old-fashioned, established with the deliberate goal not of pushing her own career as a writer, but of fostering the work of other artists. Barney herself wrote in French, a language she had mastered and spoke in an elegant, eighteenth-century style. Although she published her own work, she was undisciplined as a writer and refused to polish and revise, preferring to consider her life itself her major work of art. Her writing was a by-product of her life, according to Wickes: poems written to lovers, theatricals designed to entertain, memoirs of friendships and two volumes of *Pensées*, epigrammatic collections of her witty remarks made on social occasions. Shari Benstock, however, believes that a reevaluation of Barney's work from a feminist critical standpoint would uncover its deeper significance.

Gertrude Stein had kept her distance from Barney's salon, not wanting to become someone else's literary lion, but in 1927 Barney prevailed upon her to attend a program to be held in her honor, one of a series featuring the work of women writers. Barney's Académie des Femmes presented readings of the work of French women of letters and introduced the work of English and American women, often in translation. Barney translated passages from *The Making of Americans*,† which were read by Mme. Langlois. A presentation by Mina Loy* opened the program, and Virgil Thomson* played and sang music he had written to Stein's "Susie Asado" and "Preciosilla." Subsequently, Stein occasionally attended Barney's parties, where, according to one observer, "with her stout tweeds, her sensible shoes, she seemed like a game warden scrutinizing the exotic birds" (Wickes 242). Barney introduced Stein to the Duchess of Clermont-Tonnerre,* who became a good friend, and they lunched or had tea often, corresponded, introduced their friends, and, as Virgil Thomson noted, "exchanged literary people" (Wickes, 248). Barney and Romaine Brooks* usually stopped to visit at Bilignin summers on their way to the Riviera. Stein and Barney became even closer friends after Stein moved to 5 rue Christine, near the rue Jacob. They walked together often in the evenings, engaging in light conversation while Basket II* ran on ahead, and Barney found Stein a good listener and advisor. She wrote Stein while she was living in Florence with Brooks during World War II that she looked forward to resuming their walks after the war. When it was over, the irrepressible Barney, now in her seventies, continued her Friday night gatherings, now somewhat stuffy anachronisms in the life of postwar Paris, looked after ageing friends, edited books by and about other friends, established a poetry prize, and published two more volumes of memoirs. After Stein's death she took pains to include Alice Toklas in her circle. Although she had rarely attended previously, Toklas became an honored habitué of the salon.

In 1954, Barney wrote the foreword to *As Fine as Melanctha*,† the fourth volume of the Yale edition of Gertrude Stein's unpublished writings, remembering her "staunch presence, pleasant touch of hand, well-rounded voice always ready to chuckle," and she recalled that her friend "never appeared to hesitate or reflect or take aim, but invariably hit the mark" (viii). Natalie Barney died in Paris at the age of ninety-five, after one more love affair, begun when she was past seventy, which had as its unfortunate consequence a bitter break with her greatest friend, Romaine Brooks, when they were both over ninety.

REFERENCES: *AFAM*, 1954; *VT*, 1966; George Wickes, *The Amazon of Letters*, 1976; Shari Benstock, *Women of the Left Bank*, 1986.

Priscilla Oppenheimer

BARRY, JOSEPH [AMBER], 13 June 1917–   , author, journalist. Born in Scranton, Pennsylvania, Joseph Barry received his A.B. degree from the University of Michigan in 1939. Subsequently he did graduate work at the Sorbonne. He returned to Paris during the war as part of the army that liberated Paris. After this event, when Gertrude Stein and Alice Toklas were once more in Paris, he met them and asked Stein to lecture to some American troops. He became a good friend of her last years, calling himself "her adopted nephew" (*CA* 45). When it seemed that Gertrude Stein would benefit from a rest at Luceau, about 200 kilometers from Paris, Barry offered to drive her and Alice Toklas there. On the journey, Stein was taken ill and returned to Paris, where she died a few days later. Barry was referred to as "Jo the Loiterer" from an incident in his student days when he was picketing and charged with "loitering," there being no law against picketing at that time. As "Jo the Loiterer" he appears in *The Mother of Us All*.† Barry has enjoyed a long career as a journalist, writing for *Newsweek, The New York Times, The New York Post, House Beautiful*, and other magazines. He has also authored several books, mainly on France. He says that Paris, the French, and Gertrude Stein were the greatest influences on his life.

REFERENCES: *FF*, 1953; *WIR*, 1963; *CC*, 1975; *CA*, 1976.

Margaret Woodbridge

BASKET, Spring 1929–c. 15 November 1938, poodle. At a dog show in Paris, Gertrude Stein bought a white poodle with blue eyes that had jumped into her arms—a leap, as it turned out, into literary immortality. Alice Toklas had wanted a white poodle since she had read *The Princess Casamassima* years before, and the puppy became "Basket" because she thought he would look elegant enough when grown to carry a basket of flowers in his mouth. "Which he never did," but rarely has a poodle carried more literary and philosophical freight than Basket (*WIR* 124). He collaborated in his mistress's exploration of grammatical structure and in her search for identity through language. Stein wrote that "listening to the rhythm of his water drinking made her recognise the difference between sentences and paragraphs, that paragraphs are emotional and that sentences are not'' (*SW* 233). In ''Identity a Poem'' she wrote ''I am I because my little dog knows me even if the little dog is a big one'' (*WAM* 77–78). Earlier in the piece, she declared, ''The person and the dog are there and the dog is there and the person is there and where oh where is their identity, is the identity there anywhere'' (*WAM* 72). When *The Autobiography of Alice B. Toklas*† turned out to be a financial success, Basket received material rewards as well: an expensive coat and two studded collars. Companionable and good-natured, yet discriminating, Basket tolerantly shared Stein's affections variously with Byron and his successor Pépé*, chihuahuas given her by Francis Picabia,* but frankly detested Picasso's* dog Elf, an oaf of an Airdale who had no consideration for box hedges. Basket hobnobed with notables, was photographed by Cecil Beaton,* napped on Stein's ample lap, and became a cherished member of the ménage. When he died, Toklas later wrote, ''it did us all up and we are just now able to smile and tell you about it'' (Rogers 97).

REFERENCES: W. G. Rogers, *When This You See Remember Me*, 1948; *SW*, 1962; *WIR*, 1963; *CC*, 1974.

Priscilla Oppenheimer

BASKET II, c. 1938–24 November 1952, poodle. After Basket's* death, it comforted Gertrude Stein and Alice Toklas to think of the poodle puppy they bought in Bordeaux as Basket's baby. Basket II stepped gracefully into his predecessor's footsteps, becoming Stein's inseparable companion on long afternoon walks in the country around Bilignin and Culoz, wintering in Paris at 5 rue Christine. Like his mistress he was ''both affable and woolly,'' a reporter observed (*CC* 420). He shared the hardships of wartime exile from Paris, when walks sometimes had to be curtailed, and he shivered from the sound of bombs exploding in the distance. When Paris was liberated, an elegantly clipped Basket participated in the celebration in Culoz with Stein, although, still a bit nervous, he was frightened by the victory trumpets. He took up the good life again in Paris, where he attended Pierre Balmain's* first press showing after the war and accompanied Stein to restaurants where dogs weren't usually allowed. Stein had become a celebrity among the American GIs who visited her apartment and yelled and waved when they saw her on the street on her daily walks with Basket. Often they recognized her because of Basket; often they took turns holding his leash. After Stein's death the following year, Basket stayed on for six more years to comfort the bereft Toklas, who mentions him frequently in her letters. ''He has filled the corners of the room and the minutes and me so sweetly these last years,'' she wrote in 1949 (*SOA* 149). Also, she was pleased with the portrait of her by Dora Maar, in which Basket occupies the foreground. They grew old together, and because Toklas's hearing was poor, Basket served as her ears, barking when the doorbell rang. Then he too became deaf, and eventually his sight dimmed, as hers was to do before she died. On 24 November 1952, Toklas wrote to Carl Van Vechten,* "Basket is no more—he died quite suddenly at the vets today. . . . for some time I have realised how much I depended upon him and so it is the beginning of living for the rest of my days without anyone who is dependent upon me for anything" (*SOA* 268).

REFERENCES: *SW*, 1962; *SOA*, 1973; *CC*, 1974; *BABT*, 1977.

Priscilla Oppenheimer

BEACH, SYLVIA, 14 March 1887–6 October 1962, publisher, bookseller. Born Nancy Beach, she changed her name to Sylvia during her adolescent years. She was a sickly child who had grown up with little formal education as the second of three daughters born to a Presbyterian minister and his socially conscious wife. She learned to read at four years of age and from then on immersed herself in reading and developed a love of books, although there was always a conflict between her pious father's instructions and her mother's preoccupation with the arts. In 1902, the Reverend Beach moved his family to Paris where he became associate pastor of the American Church serving American students in the Latin Quarter. Then, after three exciting years for the bookish teenager, Sylvia returned with her family to New Jersey and a new pastorate at the first Presbyterian Church in Princeton. Ten years later, Sylvia Beach moved with her mother to Spain, despite the outbreak of the war, where they lived for two years, after which she moved to Paris.

In the fall of 1919, Sylvia Beach opened Shakespeare and Company at 8 rue du Dupuytren, with the assistance of friends, especially Adrienne Monnier, who operated a French bookstore nearby and with whom she lived for many years. In March 1920, Gertrude Stein was the first American subscriber to the shop's circulating library; then she wrote "Rich and Poor in English. To Subscribe in French and Other Latin Languages," which Alice Toklas typed and mailed to friends on the Left Bank, encouraging them to join the subscription list. It read in part: "Can any one remember much. / Say it to touch an edition say it to bury a collection. / When this you see remember me. . . . I have almost a country there." It concluded with a request: "Do make orders yesterday. . . . Do press cards. Do write letters. / Do make full names" (*PL* 95, 97). The library's records show that Gertrude Stein borrowed seventy titles over the years from Shakespeare and Company. Sylvia Beach believed that Stein was less interested in the books than in the atmosphere created by the people who congregated there. It gave her a sense of American life and satisfied a recurring nostalgia. Beach wrote in an unpublished section of her memoirs that "Gertrude had a way of looking at the French without seeing them, something like a tourist passing through their country, glancing with amusement at the inhabitants as she passed" (Fitch 56). Since Shakespeare and Company was a gathering place for writers in Paris, it was natural that Sylvia Beach arranged meetings between them. In the early days she introduced both Stephen Vincent Benét and Sherwood Anderson* to Gertrude Stein, and during the thirties she introduced Stein to James Joyce. In July 1921, to accommodate its growing patronage less than two years after it first opened,

Shakespeare and Company moved the short distance to 12 rue de l'Odeon, across the street from Adrienne Monnier's French bookshop; Beach had living quarters on the fourth floor. Gertrude Stein did not renew her membership on the new premises after 1922 as a display of her displeasure when Sylvia Beach published Joyce's *Ulysses* that year. In fact, she rarely came into the shop for some years. An exception occurred in 1931 when Edith Sitwell* gave a reading at Shakespeare and Company. Gertrude Stein attended, assuming wrongly that selections from her own work were going to be read. A few years later, after Sylvia Beach's estrangement from Joyce over contracts was complete, Gertrude Stein arrived at the bookshop to discover Ernest Hemingway* browsing the shelves. After their bitter break some time before, it must have been a tense moment for both of them. Good manners saved the day as they hugged and exchanged hearty greetings. Subsequently, Gertrude Stein and Alice Toklas enjoyed dropping in, and if Sylvia Beach were there they would chat. The visits were reciprocated at 5 rue Christine where Gertrude Stein lived after 1938.

Shakespeare and Company continued until December 1941, when under threat from the Nazis, Sylvia Beach closed the shop and moved its contents to safer quarters. She later suffered internment by the Germans in 1942 because of her Jewish affiliations. After the war she lived in her apartment above the bookshop, but Shakespeare and Company did not reopen. Adrienne Monnier died in 1955, leaving a permanent void, and Sylvia Beach died at seventy-five, still in Paris, following numerous honors and celebrations heaped upon her for her unique labors in the world of books.

REFERENCES: *PL*, 1955; Sylvia Beach, *Shakespeare and Company*, 1959; Noel Reiley Fitch, *Sylvia Beach and the Lost Generation*, 1983.

Paul Padgette
Bruce Kellner

BEATON, SIR CECIL [WALTER HARDY], 14 January 1904–18 January 1980, photographer, writer. Although he was born into the English working class, Cecil Beaton received an upper-class education at Harrow and Cambridge. He showed no aptitude for anything but photography and never took a degree, preferring to work on the student revue rather than prepare for his examinations. His photographs failed to attract attention until ballet impresario Serge Diaghilev endorsed them. When the Sitwells* decided to have Beaton photograph them, his career was launched. He began to build a reputation for glittering portraiture, especially of women. Believing that setting was just as important as the sitter, he often painted backgrounds, works of art in themselves. In seeking the unusual effect he went so far as to photograph some people with their heads under glass domes, or wrapped in silver cloth, or (for Edith Sitwell) laid out in damasks for burial. In 1929 he went to New York to make money but failed to get commissions until Elsie DeWolfe loaned him a gallery for an exhibit. That led to a contract from Condé Nast to take pictures exclusively for *Vogue*. Over the years Beaton worked for all three *Vogues*—American, British, French—as well as *Harper's Bazaar*. In 1936 he turned his attention to stage designing. He had always loved ballet, and he designed for both Sadler's Wells and the Ballets Russes de Monte Carlo. Inevitably, on a European trip, he met Gertrude Stein and Alice Toklas, photographing them extensively: Stein stolid in the foreground and Toklas wispy at the rear, with a large bent wire depending above them; Stein playing with the dogs at Bilignin; finally a 1945 profile in old age showing how admirably he captured the nobility of her countenance. He called her "the best sitter any photographer could hope to have," particularly because of "the magnanimity that shone in her trusting eyes" (Hobhouse 207). Just on the eve of the German occupation of France, Beaton visited the women at Bilignin. He was alarmed by Stein's optimism and her obstinate refusal to believe in war's reality, but when the local butcher told Toklas that all meat had been requisitioned for the army, Stein faced the truth. She sent Beaton and her other guests, Sir Francis Rose* and Samuel Steward,* on their way. On the last day of the visit, however, Beaton got drunk and disappeared. Stein was alarmed enough to get a troop of Senegalese soldiers called out from the Belley *caserne* to find him, only to discover he had been with them all afternoon, according to Steward (78–79). Subsequently, Beaton served the British War Ministry as a photographer, although his technique became more journalistic for its purposes. After the war his work returned to its earlier elegance when he designed the universally admired sets and costumes for the musical version of George Bernard Shaw's *Pygmalion, My Fair Lady*, and the film version of Colette's *Gigi*. By that time his photographs were regarded as old-fashioned, though the royal family remained loyal to him. In 1957 he was made a Commander, Order of the British Empire.

REFERENCES: Sir Francis Rose, *Saying Life*, 1961; Samuel M. Steward, *Dear Sammy*, 1977; Janet Hobhouse, *Everybody Who Was Anybody*, 1975; James Danziger, ed., *Beaton*, 1980; *NYT*, 19 January 1980.

Margaret Woodbridge

BÉRARD, CHRISTIAN, 1902–12 February 1949, painter, stage designer. Christian Bérard, who had studied at the Académie Ransom under Vuillard, painted and exhibited with the artists known as the Neoromantics (the Berman* brothers, Pavel Tchelitchew* and Kristians Tonny* in the mid-twenties and became one of the group of young artists surrounding Gertrude Stein and competing for her approval. Among these high-strung painters, who sometimes engaged in café brawls, Tchelitchew in particular was a rival of Bérard, pointing out to Stein that he was a mere copier. Virgil Thomson,* however, who had introduced Bérard and the others to Stein and who owned many Bérard paintings, thought that he was the creative power behind the neoromantics. Stein was doubtful. Bérard's pictures "are almost something and then they are just not," she wrote *SW* 215). She did keep the two wash impressions he had made of her all her life, however, although she gradually disposed of the rest of her neoromantic collection. Stein wrote a portrait of Bérard which is included in *Dix Portraits*.†

By the time Stein and Thomson considered asking Bérard to design sets and costumes for *Four Saints in Three Acts*,† which however never worked out, his career had taken a turn for the better. He became well-known as a designer of theater, ballet, and film sets, creating many productions with Jean Cocteau* in the thirties and early forties. His feeling for fantasy lent itself to designs for Cocteau's poetic vision, to which their memorable collaboration on the 1945 film *Beauty and the Beast* attests.

REFERENCES: *SW*, 1962; *Praeger Encyclopedia of Art*, 1971; *CC*, 1974; Samuel Hunter, ed., *Oxford Companion to Twentieth Century Art*, 1981.

Priscilla Oppenheimer

BERENSON, BERNARD, 26 June 1865–6 October 1959, art critic, writer. Bernard Berenson, born in Lithuania, educated at Harvard, was a man of many and varied interests, but he made his reputation as a critic, historian, and connoisseur of Renaissance art. Always witty and urbane, B.B., as he was called, retained his youthful enthusiasm and vigor into his old age, much like his idol, Goethe. Over his long lifetime he wrote extensively on Renaissance art in such works as his four-volume series on Italian painters, *Study and Criticism of Italian Art*, and *Venetian Paintings in America*. Of a more general nature, but just as illuminating and gracefully written, are *Seeing and Knowing* (1954) and *Essays in Appreciation* (1959). He also wrote books of his observations on many facets of life, such as *Rumor and Reflection* (1952). All his life he had a reputation as a brilliant and opinionated conversationalist. Leo Stein* made Berenson's acquaintance in Florence in 1900, when Berenson was living near there with the woman he later married. He taught Stein to share his enthusiasm for fourteenth-century Italian painting. Stein was fascinated by Berenson and at the same time annoyed by his self-centeredness. They frequently met to converse, and Stein availed himself of Berenson's huge library. Both Berenson and his wife found Leo something of a bore, but they liked Gertrude. Leo was a man, according to Berenson, who was "always inventing the umbrella" (Brinnin 54). In September 1902 Leo and Gertrude Stein went to Haslemere, England, to spend a few days with the Berensons. They liked the area so much that they took a cottage nearby. They dined frequently with the Berensons and their brilliant group of friends and especially enjoyed the lively after-dinner conversations, in which Gertrude fully participated. It was Berenson who introduced Leo to the work of the modern painters, recommending Cézanne through Ambroise Vollard's* gallery. Leo bought a Cézanne immediately and continued buying the next year. Thus Berenson developed his taste for modern art and awakened his passion for collecting. Many of Berenson's insights have become commonplaces in art criticism today. Perhaps his greatest contribution is his insistence on what he considered the highest value of art—the moments of pure transcendence we experience through it. Berenson remained actively engaged in writing and adding to his library almost to the day of his death. He spent his last years at his beloved estate, I Tatti, in the hills above the beautiful Arno Valley.

REFERENCES: John Malcolm Brinnin, *The Third Rose*, 1959; John Walker, introduction to *A Bernard Berenson Treasury*, 1962; *CC*, 1975.

Margaret Woodbridge

BERMAN, EUGÈNE, 4 November 1899–14 December 1972, painter, stage designer. Born in Saint Petersburg, Eugène Berman fled to Paris after the Russian revolution where he studied painting under Bonnard and Vuillard. Fascinated with classical ruins, Berman painted for a time in Italy and attempted to interpret older periods in modern terms. He joined the group of young artists who painted in a more traditional style in a revolt against abstraction. An exhibition of the neoromantics was held in Paris in 1926, where Gertrude Stein became mildly interested in Berman's work. She considered him the creative force behind the movement, studied his work carefully at his studio, and bought two of his landscapes. Thereafter Berman became one of the group of artists and writers for whom Stein was mother-patron-muse during the late twenties. A word portrait of Berman appears in *Dix Portraits*,† published in 1930, but by that time Stein had lost interest in his work "though he was a very good painter he was too bad a painter to have been the creator of an idea," she wrote (*SW* 217). A decided break had occurred on one of his visits to Bilignin, and whether she was dissatisfied with the sketches he had been making for portraits of her and Alice Toklas, or whether she was annoyed with his lack of appreciation of her word portrait of him, she rather rudely asked him to leave. Although he later was to refer to her as "an *impossible* woman," he wrote her a flattering and effusive note and sent her a self-portrait—"courteous revenge," he said, for her dictatorial behavior *(CC* 340). Berman came to New York in 1935 and became known as a designer of settings for ballet and opera both there and in Paris. His designs for the Metropolitan Opera House were highly acclaimed, in particular those for the 1957 production of *Don Giovanni*. That same year he designed the sets for the New York City Ballet Festival in honor of his old friend of twenty-five years, Igor Stravinsky. Also, in 1957, Berman moved to Rome where he continued to paint, design sets, and illustrate books until his death.

REFERENCES: *SW*, 1962; *NYT*, 15 December 1972; *CC*, 1974.

Priscilla Oppenheimer

BERNERS, GERALD [TYRWHITT], LORD, 18 September 1883–19 April 1950, composer, writer. One of the century's genuine eccentrics, Lord Berners returned the word "dilettante" to its original meaning, "a lover of the arts." A scion of nobility and great wealth, he was educated at Eton and then studied art and music on the Continent, notably in Dresden and Vienna. He was an honorary attaché to the British Embassy in Constantinople from 1909 until 1911 and then in Rome until 1920. Influenced by Erik Satie,* and taught composition by Ralph Vaughan Williams, his music was admired by Alfredo Casella and Igor Stravinsky. He composed a modest body of chamber music, an opera, a film score, many songs, and four ballet scores, including *The Triumph of Neptune* for Serge

Diaghilev, and one which set his own cutting of Gertrude Stein's "They Must. Be Wedded. To Their Wife." as *A Wedding Bouquet*,† performed by Sadler's Wells in 1937 and still in the repertory of more than one ballet company. He was scheduled to set her "Doctor Faustus Lights the Lights" as an opera, but World War II had so depressed him that he gave up composing and returned to painting, in which he had earlier dabbled, and fiction. He wrote five novels: *The Camel*, 1936, in which the eponyn falls in love with an English vicar's wife; *Far from the Madding War*, 1941, in which the heroine unstitches a large and priceless German tapestry as her contribution to the war effort; *Count Omega*, 1941, in which a musician falls in love with a blonde trombonist guarded by a eunuch; *The Romance of a Nose*, in which Cleopatra has hers bobbed in an attempt to look like Helen of Troy; and a privately printed, pseudonymous lesbian spoof, *The Girls of Radcliffe Hall*. All five are snaked out in a hilarious, deadpan prose style, guaranteeing the "perilous laughter" of which he spoke in his 1934 memoir, *First Childhood*, that "sometimes wells up within one with such violence that the human frame is nearly shattered in the course of its suppression" (34). It informed all his work, but he was a serious composer, painter, and writer, if only minor in these pursuits. English novelist Nancy Mitford captured him as Lord Merlin in *The Pursuit of Love*, 1934, but he was equally fantastic in real life, dyeing the pigeons and doves at Faringdon, his country estate, in various rainbow hues; blowing soap bubbles in public restaurants; jogging through his hosts' houses to aid digestion; inviting a white horse into his drawing room for coffee; draping the Van Dykes and Corots there with strings of fake pearls from Woolworth's; composing on a piano in the back seat of his Rolls Royce. His self-characterization as Lord Fitzcricket in *Far from the Madding War* is perhaps a wiser assessment than the fictional re-creations or gossipy legends: "He was astute enough to realise that, in Anglo-Saxon countries, art is more highly appreciated if accompanied by a certain measure of eccentric publicity. This fitted well with his natural inclinations" (128). Lord Berners met Gertrude Stein and Alice Toklas when they went to Oxford for lectures in 1936 and were his house guests at Faringdon; he visited them, in turn, in Paris and in Bilignin—a brief but apparently warm friendship.

REFERENCES: *EA*, 1937; Sir Francis Rose, *Saying Life*, 1961; Berners, *First Childhood* and *Far from the Madding War*, 1983.

Bruce Kellner

BLOOD, FLORENCE, ?–?, philanthropist. Florence Blood, a wealthy American woman living in Europe, seems to have been a friend of both Leo* and Gertrude Stein. On one occasion, in Florence, Gertrude and Alice Toklas were entertained by her and her friend the Princess Ghika at their beautiful villa. Leo wrote that she showed him and other friends the Berensons'* garden, all the while hugely enjoying making fun of its bad taste. Gertrude did a prose portrait of Miss Blood which both pleased and mystified her. She found the phrase "pink pepper" especially intriguing. She liked and admired the cubist painters and expressed a wish to meet Picasso.* Accordingly, Gertrude Stein invited her to 27 rue de Fleurus for an evening during which Picasso informed her that he was "le bec Auer," a gas mantle, of painting (*WIR*, 55). During the war Florence Blood's casual life radically changed. She and a friend turned the latter's house in the Basses Pyrénées into a hospital for convalescent soldiers. She considered it a privilege to serve them and apparently ran the enterprise well. On the strength of this she suggested to Gertrude Stein that she might want to add a postscript to her portrait. Written in 1913, "A Portrait of F. B." is in the manner of the image-filled portraits of Constance Fletcher and Mabel Dodge, brief paragraphs largely of complete sentences composed in seeming non sequiturs. It bears little resemblance to portraits written after the war and was therefore unrevised when it first appeared in print in *Geography and Plays*† in 1922.

REFERENCES: *G&P*, 1922; *FF*, 1953; *WIR*, 1963; *CC*, 1974.

Margaret Woodbridge

BOOKSTAVER [KNOBLAUCH], MAY [MARY, MRS. CHARLES], 1874–29 November 1950, friend, feminist. May Bookstaver was one of the group of educated, free-thinking women whom Gertrude Stein met in Baltimore. She was a courageous, unconventional, beautiful young woman with whom Stein developed an intense, unhappy relationship. Stein's novel *Q.E.D.*† recounts the progress of this affair. Written in 1903, it was unpublished in Gertrude Stein's lifetime. She claimed to have forgotten about it, but its content is a more likely explanation for its long suppression. Perhaps she found writing the novel a release from the pain of the affair. According to Leon Katz, Bookstaver served as the real life model for a character in *Q.E.D.* He became aware of the possible link when he was doing research for his doctoral dissertation on *The Making of Americans.*† In the novel, Helen Thomas (Bookstaver) is loved by Adele (Stein) whom she treats badly. Mabel Neathe (in real life, Mabel Haynes)* also loves Helen and is jealous of Adele. The story of this triangular love affair, of necessity, had to be told in veiled terms. For all that, it is a remarkable account of a lesbian relationship in the years 1900 to 1903. James Mellow observes that the title, *Q.E.D.*, was chosen because it "pointed up the scientific nature of the affair" (*CC*, 78); however, for publication in 1950 the book was retitled *Things as They Are*. Just how closely the novel parallels events in real life is difficult to determine, for the letters between Gertrude Stein and Bookstaver have not survived. In an interview with Katz, Alice Toklas admitted that she had destroyed Bookstaver's letters to Stein "in a passion" (*CC*, 80). From *Q.E.D.* it can be concluded that the affair caused Stein considerable pain. Bookstaver's behavior on her return to Baltimore was observed with disapproval by another friend, Emma Lootz, who reported that Bookstaver showed Stein's letters to anyone who cared to see them and enjoyed herself at dinner parties by making fun of Stein, surely an act of cruelty. On 16 August 1906, May Bookstaver was married in Newport to Charles Knoblauch. According to Mabel Weeks,* he was "what the American magazine story would call a 'man's man' " (*CC*, 159). In 1908 Bookstaver tried to place Stein's *Three Lives*† with a publisher, finally succeeding in getting Grafton Press to agree to publish a limited edition at Stein's expense. She also tried, unsuccessfully, to get *The Making of Americans* accepted for publication by Mitchell Kennerley. No deal was made, and the manuscript of *The Making of Americans* was returned. In her obituary, *The New York Times* reported that May Bookstaver Knoblauch had been an active supporter of the women suffrage movement and birth control.

REFERENCES: *ABT*, 1933; *NYT* Obit. 29 November 1950; *C.C.*, 1975.

Margaret Woodbridge

BOWLES, PAUL FREDERICK, 30 December 1910–   , composer, poet, novelist. Although he published his first poem at the age of nineteen in *transition*, Paul Bowles began his career as a composer and music critic before turning to the writing of poetry and fiction. Born in New York City, Bowles studied composition with Aaron Copland in New York and Berlin from 1930 to 1932, and with Virgil Thomson* and Nadia Boulanger in Paris until 1934. His compositions include film and theater scores, chamber music, suites, and two operas, *The Wind Remains* (1941) and *Yerma* (1948). From 1942 to 1946 he was music critic for the *New York Herald Tribune*. In 1931, having made Gertrude Stein's acquaintance by writing her "engaging letters from America," Bowles, with Aaron Copland, visited Stein and Alice Toklas in Bilignin. Stein said of him that "he [was] delightful and sensible in summer but neither delightful nor sensible in the winter." Stein, who sought to advise the young man, was pleased that Copland told him "if you do not work now when you are twenty when you are thirty, nobody will love you" (*SW* 236–37). Stein and Bowles, whom she always called Freddy, became lifelong correspondents. In 1934 Bowles sent her reams of clippings on the New York run of *Four Saints in Three Acts*,† until there were so many he had to stop. In 1938 Bowles married Jane Auer, a writer; Stein never met Jane Bowles, later author of the remarkable *Two Serious Ladies*. A planned visit as Stein and Toklas were leaving for Bilignin at the start of World War II couldn't be managed. Paul Bowles began to write short stories after his marriage, and in 1938 his first novel, *The Sheltering Sky*, was published. He has published poetry, travel books, novels, translations, and an autobiography, *Without Stopping*. In 1950 Bowles won the National Institute of Arts and Letters Award. Bowles has traveled widely in Africa and South and Central America, often collecting folk music. On his 1931 visit to Bilignin, Toklas had suggested he visit Tangier, which became an inspiration for his music, poetry, and fiction, and where he ultimately settled.

REFERENCES: *SW*, 1962; *CC*, 1974; Ruth E. Anderson, ed., *American Composers*, 1982; *DLB*, 1982.

Priscilla Oppenheimer

BRADLEY, WILLIAM ASPENWALL, 8 February 1879–10 January 1939, literary agent, editor. William Aspenwall Bradley was born in Hartford, Connecticut, worked as an editor in New York, and served in France in World War I. He married a Frenchwoman in 1921 and settled there as a translator of French writers into English. Subsequently, he was literary representative for many writers: Henry Miller, Ezra Pound,* Thornton Wilder,* Anaïs Nin, Natalie Clifford Barney,* and John Dos Passos among others. Bradley helped Gertrude Stein have two wishes fulfilled. He arranged for her work to be published in the *Atlantic Monthly* after years of rejections, when an abridged version of *The Autobiography of Alice B. Toklas*† appeared in four issues, May through August 1933; and he arranged for her "money" series of five brief articles to appear in the *Saturday Evening Post*, between June and October 1936. Further, he placed *The Autobiography of Alice B. Toklas* with Harcourt Brace in America and with the Bodley Head in England. When Gertrude Stein was planning her American lecture tour, Bradley was able to give her sound advice, and on the strength of the tour he persuaded Harcourt Brace to publish Bernard Faÿ's* abridgment in English of his abridged French translation of *The Making of Americans*.† Before Bradley's death, he and Stein had a series of misunderstandings, but Jennie Bradley, his widow, continued his work as a literary agent and helped Alice Toklas in placing her *Alice B. Toklas Cook Book* with Harper and Row in 1954.

REFERENCES: *EA*, 1937; *CC*, 1974.

Paul Padgette

BRAQUE, GEORGES, 13 May 1882–31 August 1963, painter, sculptor. Born in Argenteuil, France, Georges Braque came to Paris in 1900 to study at the École des Beaux Arts. His friend Otto Friesz aroused his interest in the fauvist group of artists. However, Cézanne and Picasso,* with their emphasis on structural composition, proved to be stronger influences. Braque and Picasso became inseparable friends, and together they created cubism. The Steins overlooked Braque's contribution, however. Gertrude thought he was merely competent and did not buy a single one of his paintings until the 1920s, when she purchased two small still lifes and kept them for a few years. Nevertheless, Braque continued to go often to 27 rue de Fleurus, usually with Henri Matisse.* The close collaboration with Picasso continued, even to the point of signing each other's paintings in order to confuse the public. In 1911 both began to put fragments of real objects in their pictures, calling them *papiers collé*. The fragments might be pieces of newspapers, oilcloth, or wallpaper. When World War I came Braque enlisted and received a serious head wound. In 1918, while convalescing near Avignon, he was visited by Gertrude Stein and Alice B. Toklas. The two women had adopted such an unusual type of war uniform that Braque was embarrassed by the attention they attracted on that visit. He continued to see Gertrude Stein into the 1920s when the old crowd had scattered. By this time he and Picasso were no longer friends. Braque was one of those who objected to *The Autobiography of Alice B. Toklas*† on factual grounds. He participated in the publication of "Testimony Against Gertrude Stein" in *transition* in February 1935 to correct the record. The other contributors were Matisse, Tristan Tzara,* Eugene and Maria Jolas,* and André Salmon. Gertrude Stein dismissed their complaints, however. After World War I Braque abandoned his early austere style of cubistic painting for a looser, more relaxed style. He is at his best in painting still lifes of fruit, flowers, pitchers, and guitars—his favorite subjects. He did a few figure paintings, sculptures, and lithographs, but his still lifes remain his best work. His *8 Ateliers* shows him as complete master of the genre, with no mannerisms. He is universally regarded as one of the greatest of twentieth-century painters. In 1951 he was made a commander of the Legion of Honor, and in 1956 he received an honorary doctorate from Oxford.

REFERENCES: *Praeger Picture Encyclopedia of Art,* 1958; *CC,* 1975; Harold Osborne, ed., *Oxford Companion to Twentieth Century Art,* 1981.

Margaret Woodbridge

BREON, JOHN, 1923–April 1984, writer, editor. In 1945, John Breon while still in the army wrote Gertrude Stein a fan letter: "Since college, I have had a deep interest and a profound admiration for you and for your work." (*FF* 375). When he earned leave from his post in Germany, he went to Paris and visited Stein, bringing some of his manuscripts with him. It was a warm and welcome reception he received from Stein and Alice Toklas at 5 rue Christine. When he returned to Germany after his visit, he wrote her again: "you gave me the most wonderful times and the happiest I've known since coming into the Army." He hoped to remain in France after leaving the military and added, "I'll shine shoes in Paris before I'll go back to the routine of Rockford [Illinois]. I'm afraid to go back now, for I'd never leave—trapped there forever" (*FF* 389–90). Breon's personality must have impressed Stein for she included him as a character in her war novella, *Brewsie and Willie,*† a study of the GIs as she knew them at the end of the war. In 1946, she wrote a word portrait, "John Breon a Novel or a Play." In 1955, back in Rockford, Breon published a novel, *The Sorrows of Travel*, dedicated "In memory of Miss Stein and for Alice B. Toklas." Later, Breon became an editor with McGraw-Hill.

REFERENCES: *FF,* 1953; *GSP,* 1970; *SOA,* 1973.

Paul Padgette

BREWER, FRANKLIN H., 1907–   , soldier. A Harvard-educated Philadelphia Mainliner, Franklin Brewer was a GI who became "Brewsie" in Gertrude Stein's *Brewsie and Willie.*† As an infantry sergeant somewhat older than his compatriots in Company K, Brewer proved "coolest under fire" and "a calming influence on everyone," according to Harold P. Leinbaugh and John D. Campbell who wrote a history of their rifle unit of the 333rd Infantry. In a letter of 24 September 1945, Brewer wrote to thank Stein for conferring immortality upon him in her book, and to thank Alice Toklas for "unforgettable chocolate ice cream" (*FF* 388). By that time, he had become a regular visitor at 5 rue Christine, one of the dozens of soldiers who, in Thornton Wilder's* memorable phrase had "gone up to Paris to see the Eiffel Tower and Gertrude Stein" (*FIA* xxvii).

REFERENCES: *FIA*, 1947; *FF*, 1953; Harold P. Leinbaugh and John D. Campbell, *The Men of Company K*, 1985.

Margaret Woodbridge
Bruce Kellner

BREWER, JOSEPH, 19 October 1898– , publisher, educator. Joseph Brewer was brought to 27 rue de Fleurus to meet Gertrude Stein when he was a young man with the publishing firm of Payson and Clarke. He was sympathetic to her work and discussed with her the possibility of publishing some of her pieces. He decided to begin with a collection of short pieces about America under the title *Useful Knowledge*.† The book, published in 1929, was not a financial success, and Brewer suggested no further publication. In *The Autobiography of Alice B. Toklas*† Stein expresses her disappointment since she had hoped that he might be able to gradually build audience for her work (298). Brewer's next meeting with Gertrude Stein occurred on her American trip of 1934–1935. She and Alice Toklas were in a Detroit hotel when Gertrude became frightened by a report that a gunman was on the loose. She at once called her old friend Brewer, at that time president of Olivet College in Michigan, and asked him to come and get them. Brewer and three or four others complied. They remained at Olivet for several days, much to the delight of students and faculty. As Brewer, who vividly remembers the incident, said in a speech in 1974, "We had a marvelous time with them. They sat around and talked with everybody. They got a *great* deal more out of their visit, though she made no formal appearance, than I am sure the University of Michigan did where we delivered her to make a formal lecture" (Verplank). Brewer has enjoyed a long and outstanding career as an educator. After he left Olivet in 1944 he earned a M.A.L.S. degree at Columbia University. He then joined the faculty of Queen's College and helped to build the library. He is now retired and living in New York.

REFERENCES: *ABT*, 1933; *CC*, 1975; Laura Verplank, Olivet College, A letter to M. Woodbridge, 24 February 1987.

Margaret Woodbridge

BROMFIELD, LOUIS, 27 December 1896–18 March 1956, novelist, journalist, critic. Louis Bromfield, once an important best-selling novelist, has been largely ignored in recent years. Though he has a long list of novels, some short stories, and three plays to his credit, he is no longer considered first-rate. His tetralogy, *Escape*, won high praises, but subsequent work was not as highly regarded. The decline of American individualism together with the growth of industrialism is his favorite theme. He also enjoys pointing out the role of the strong woman, as in *Mrs. Parkington*. Like many American writers, he lived in France for many years, where he made the acquaintance of Gertrude Stein. She was not particularly impressed by him or his writing, but during a visit to Bilignin she handed him her lesbian novel *Q.E.D.*† and asked him to read it. He found it "vastly interesting" but thought there might be "great difficulties" in getting it published (*FF* 249–250). Stein did admire Bromfield for his knowledge of gardens and soils. He had lived on a farm in Ohio, and again at Senlis in France. He contributed to the literature of nature and organic farming in such books as *Pleasant Valley* and *Malabar Farm*. She came to have a higher opinion of Bromfield's writing and asked him to collaborate with her in writing a mystery novel. He seems never to have developed any interest in the project—probably wisely.

REFERENCES: *ABT*, 1933; *FF*, 1953; *CC*, 1975; James Vinson, ed., *American Writers since 1900*, 1980.

Margaret Woodbridge

BROOKS, [BEATRICE] ROMAINE GODDARD, 1 May 1874–7 December 1970, painter. Gertrude Stein and Alice Toklas met Romaine Brooks at the same time as they met Natalie Barney,* and saw her often through the years in Paris and Bilignin in the company of Barney. During their American tour Brooks was their hostess at lunch. Brooks was the product of a ghastly childhood, in which she was forced to be the keeper of a mentally disturbed brother by her equally mentally disturbed mother. Although she was forbidden to draw by her mother, she developed her talent at school and finally was allowed to study painting in Rome. On her mother's death she inherited a sizable fortune and, after a brief and disastrous marriage to John Brooks, she went to London and Cornwall, painting and studying the works of James McNeill Whistler. She found his subtle colors congenial and developed a palette of gradations of gray, black, and beige in which she painted from then on. Brooks moved to Paris around 1908 and became known as an interior decorator and portrait painter. In 1915 she met Natalie Barney, with whom she began a passionate, lifelong friendship. Independent and introverted, Brooks had no interest in Barney's salon, and traveled and painted on her own much of the time, although the two women shared a summer house on the Riviera in the twenties and thirties and lived together in Florence during World War II. Solo exhibitions of her works were held in London and New York in 1925. Her self-portrait of 1923 and the 1924 portrait of Una, Lady Troubridge, are among her best-known work, her portraits of women done in greys and blacks being incisive personality studies "exposing devastating self-divisions presumably hidden by external poses" (Benstock 305). No one but

Barney, who is portrayed without the usual tight, angry mouth and piercing eyes, escaped the painter's trademarks. In the late twenties, Brooks wrote an autobiography, *No Pleasant Memories*. She illustrated these memoirs with a series of unpublished drawings, mysterious poetic fantasies which are some of her most original work, calling up the nightmare of her early life.

REFERENCES: George Wickes, *The Amazon of Letters*, 1976; *NAW*, 1980; *Art News*, October 1980, 156–58; Shari Benstock, *Women of the Left Bank*, 1986.

Priscilla Oppenheimer

BROWN, BOB [ROBERT CARLTON], 1886–7 August 1959, writer. Under the influence of Gertrude Stein's *Tender Buttons*† and Guillaume Apollinaire,* Bob Brown wrote *Eyes on the Half Shell* in 1917. By the end of the twenties he had expanded this into *1450–1950*, a full collection of optical poems, foreshadowing the work of Kenneth Patchen and the concrete poets who followed. *1450–1950* was published by the Black Sun Press in an edition of 150 copies in 1929, for which Stein supplied a blurb: "I have enjoyed myself enormously, in every way enormously." The following year, she wrote "Absolutely as Bob Brown or Bobbed Brown." In 1955, it was published from a typescript copy belonging to Addison Metcalf, a private collector, as *Absolutely Bob Brown, or, Bobbed Brown* by the Banyan Press in a hand-set and -sewn edition of fifty-four copies. It was reprinted the same year in *Painted Lace*,† and in 1959 a facsimile edition of *1450–1950* was printed, quoting Stein's original blurb. In his 1930 *Readies*, Brown wrote that Stein gave him "a great kick . . . I began to see that a story might be anything. . . . I threw my typewriter into the air and huzzahed" (McAlmon 20).

REFERENCES: *PL*, 1955; Bob Brown, *1450–1950*, 1959; Robert McAlmon and Kay Boyle, *Being Geniuses Together*, 1968.

Bruce Kellner

BROWN, TILLIE [MATILDA E.], 18 June 1871–30 March 1935, girlhood friend. When Gertrude Stein and Leon M. Solomons* published their "Normal Motor Automatism" in the *Harvard Psychological Review* in the fall of 1896, Tillie Brown wrote to praise the "wondrous fame you were earning as an all round literary-scientific critic and genius, the embodiment of wisdom etc., etc." (*FF* 12). She wrote again when installments of *The Autobiography of Alice B. Toklas*† were appearing in the *Atlantic Monthly* in 1933, reminding Stein of their early association at Oakland High School. In 1914, Stein wrote "Tillie," a brief portrait that might be of this early acquaintance: two long sentences playing with the name and rhyming and punning on several verbs, "Tillie labor" occurring regularly (*BTV* 173). In "To Do," published posthumously in *Alphabets and Birthdays*,† "Tillie Brown" is one of the four characters for the letter "T" in Stein's alphabetical collection of stories for children. "Tillie Brown" is the child of a missionary father and "Thornie Rose" (obviously Thornton Wilder)* is the child of a missionary mother in China. They sing to the children and have conversations about birthdays with "all the miles and miles of Chinamen and Chinese women and Chinese children and more and more miles of them" (55). In actuality, Matilda E. Brown was born in Yokohama, Japan, and spent her adult life at 600 29th Street in Oakland, "at home" and with "no profession," according to her death certificate. She died of cancer just over a week before Gertrude Stein returned to Oakland during her lecture tour.

REFERENCES: *FF*, 1953; *BTV*, 1953; *A&B*, 1957.

Bruce Kellner

BRUCE, PATRICK HENRY, 1880–1937, painter. One of the pioneer abstractionists was born in Virginia and exhibited his work in the Independent Salon in 1914. A few years before that debut he had visited 27 rue de Fleurus on occasion. He had been "one of the early and most ardent Matisse* pupils," but Gertrude Stein found him morose over the inevitable sorrow that he felt afflicted artists. Great artists at least had their success to mitigate against it; but a "little artist," he contended, "has all the tragic unhappiness and the sorrows of a great artist and he is not a great artist" (*ABT* 140). Stein seems to have identified him as one of several people in her portrait, "Five or Six Men" but there is no immediate key to establishing his identity there. Bruce had little success in Paris, and after 1920 he was in seclusion in New York. In 1933 he destroyed all but fifteen of his works and left those to Henri-Pierre Roché.*

REFERENCES: *ABT*, 1933; *TWO*, 1951, 1971.

Bruce Kellner

BRYHER, WINIFRED, 2 September 1894–28 January 1983, novelist, editor. Winifred Bryher, pen name of Annie Winifred Ellerman, was the beautiful, wealthy English wife of Robert McAlmon,* an American editor and one-time friend of Gertrude Stein. Stein rather liked McAlmon, but she has nothing to say about Bryher, as she was always called. Yet Bryher seems to have understood Stein's conversation better than most people. She revealed later that she regretted that the tape recorder had not been invented when she first knew Stein. Bryher did not feel that Stein's mind was muddled at all, but that she fully explored a phrase. Bryher herself was too shy to participate in discussions with the group. She preferred talking to Alice Toklas, who, she thought, "had subordinated her own gifts" yet retained her own personality "intact" (*CC* 290–91). Bryher felt that Gertrude Stein had helped all writers, whether they knew it or not, by her attack on language. In 1927, Bryher, now divorced and living in Switzerland, edited a magazine called *Close Up*. She sent Gertrude Stein five guineas for her manuscript of "Three Sitting Here" and in a note expressed her enthusiasm for the piece and her thanks for Stein's good wishes. In Paris in the 1930s, Thornton Wilder,* on learning of Bryher's long friendship with the poet Hilda Doolittle, asked Stein and Toklas to introduce him. They did so, and after leaving Bryher's house Wilder observed: "Bryher is Napoleonic, she walks like him, she talks like him, she probably feels like him'' (*WIR* 136). Bryher's historical novels have received little attention, though *Reader's Encyclopedia* states that they faithfully re-create the past: Rome in *Roman Wall* (1954), Celts in *Ruan* (1960), Carthage in *Coin of Carthage* (1963), to name a few. She maintained a huge correspondence with other intellectuals in wartime and peacetime. During World War II she managed to help many Nazi victims get to the United States.

REFERENCES: *FF*, 1953; Sylvia Beach, *Shakespeare and Company*, 1959; *WIR*, 1963; William Rose Benét, *The Reader's Encyclopedia*, 1965; *CC*, 1975.

Margaret Woodbridge

BUSS, KATE, May 1884–?, writer. Massachusetts-born Kate Buss began collecting Gertrude Stein's work very early, and when she went to Paris to study at the Sorbonne, she became a regular caller at 27 rue de Fleurus. She introduced several writers there: poet Alfred Kreymborg, novelist Djuna Barnes, and Mina Loy,* although Gertrude Stein had met the latter earlier in Italy as the wife of painter Stephen Haweiss. Kate Buss contributed to *Vanity Fair*, *The New Republic*, and *Poetry*, and she published her *Studies in the Chinese Drama* through the quasi-vanity press in Boston, Four Seasons. When subsequently Gertrude Stein was searching for a publisher for her *Geography and Plays*,† Kate Buss recommended the house to her, which issued the book in 1922. In 1930, Gertrude Stein wrote a portrait of her friend, "To Kitty or Kate Buss," published in *Portraits and Prayers*† in 1934 and filled with rhymes and puns:

> Kitty Buss had the name
> Kitty Buss had the same
> Kitty Buss is the same as Kitty which is a name.
> Kate Buss came with her name.
> This is why she asked a little name to blame. (*P&P* 103)

It does not refer to Kate Buss's having been on the *Titanic*.

REFERENCES: *ABT*, 1933; *P&P*, 1934; WWNA, 1976.

Bruce Kellner

BUTCHER, FANNY, 13 February 1888–14 May 1987, journalist. Fanny Butcher was born in Kansas and educated at the University of Chicago. She became a public school teacher briefly before turning to journalism, beginning her long career with the *Chicago Tribune* as assistant to the women's editor. Subsequently she advanced to reporter, music critic, society editor, and finally literary editor. Along the way she found time to be a bookshop proprietor, to support women's suffrage, and to work for the liberalizing of expression of all writers. In the early thirties, she and a traveling friend were invited to visit Gertrude Stein and Alice Toklas at Bilignin. From college she remembered being impressed with *Three Lives*† as a work of greatness; from Bilignin she remembered Stein reading

aloud *Before the Flowers of Friendship Faded Friendship Faded,*† which she
enjoyed hearing without understanding its contents. Later Butcher said Stein's
intentions were clear to her "only in flashes, . . . but I feel that if I could read
her work as a child reads, without any preconceived ideas of what it ought to
be, I could understand everything" (418). When Stein and Toklas arrived in
Chicago in November 1934, for a lecture at the University of Chicago and to
see *Four Saints in Three Acts,*† Fanny Butcher met the plane and acted as one
of the guides. Through her influence on the *Tribune* staff, she was able to satisfy
Stein's desire to ride in a police squad car on its nightly rounds. After Stein's
lecture for the Chicago Arts Club, "What Is English Literature," Butcher commented in the *Tribune* that "some of the time everybody understood, much of
the time fewer understood, but there were always a few who understood all of
the time" (*GSRG* 55). Beginning with *The Autobiography of Alice B. Toklas,*†
Fanny Butcher reviewed nine of Gertrude Stein's books. Admitting she did not
always feel clear about their contents, she always communicated her enthusiasm
for the writing and the mental excitement she experienced in reading and writing
about it.

REFERENCES: *ABT*, 1933; Fanny Butcher, *Many Lives*, 1972; *GSRG*, 1984.

Paul Padgette

CERF, BENNETT, 25 May 1878–27 August 1971, anthologist, editor, publisher. After receiving a B.A. degree from Columbia, Bennett Cerf worked for
the *New York Herald Tribune* and then as a broker on Wall Street. In 1925,
with Donald Klopfer, he bought Modern Library and brought out inexpensive
editions of numerous classics. The venture was a huge success. For this reason
he became known as "the reader's unknown benefactor" (*CB* 1941). In 1927,
again with Klopfer, he became the American agent for Nonesuch Press, which
he admired tremendously. Because he yearned for the excitement of bringing
out new books, in 1927 he and Klopfer founded Random House. Rockwell Kent
drew the trademark, used by the firm ever since. As president of Random House
he published many important writers, among them Eugene O'Neill, Robinson
Jeffers, William Faulkner, Sinclair Lewis, and James Joyce. In 1933, after the
success of *The Autobiography of Alice B. Toklas,*† Cerf's friend Carl Van Vechten* suggested that Modern Library publish some of Gertrude Stein's earlier
works. Modern Library immediately brought out *Three Lives,*† but Cerf and
Gertrude Stein did not meet until 21 April 1934, when he called at 27 rue de
Fleurus. On that occasion Stein tried unsuccessfully to sell him the four or five
hundred copies she had left of earlier books published by her as Plain Editions.
Cerf suggested instead that he publish a new collection—*Portraits and Prayers*†—to coincide with her projected American tour. When Stein and Toklas
arrived in New York, Cerf and Van Vechten met the two women at the pier.
They marveled at the ease with which Stein handled cheeky reporters and photographers. In his memoirs, *At Random*, Cerf called her "the publicity hound

of the world—simply great'' (103). Everyone liked her, even though they wrote amusing stories about her. For the two or three weeks in New York she made Cerf her slave. In fact, he reports, she ordered everyone about and even dared to disagree with Alexander Woollcott,* to his delight. Cerf agreed to do a book a year for Stein, while admitting, even on a dust jacket, that he did not understand her writing. She could talk as plainly ''as a banker,'' but her writing was ''mishmash'' (104). Nevertheless, their relationship was an affectionate one, and Cerf always admired her tremendously. The affection he had for her was put to a severe test in 1938, when she wrote in French a monograph on Picasso.* She had given English rights to B. T. Batsford, who sold the American rights to Scribner's. Cerf was distressed but never blamed Gertrude Stein. The last time he saw her was in 1936 at Bilignin with Jo Davidson,* who had not wanted to visit these ''crazy women'' (106). As it happened, they had a wonderful time together. Five days after the publication of *Brewsie and Willie*† Gertrude Stein died. She did not live to see the publication of *Selected Writings of Gertrude Stein*† with an introduction by Van Vechten, but before her death she wrote a brief message of thanks that touched Cerf deeply. She said that ''all [the writings] that are here are those that I wanted the most'' (*SW* vii). First through the Modern Library and later in a Vintage Paperback, Random House has kept *Selected Writings* in print ever since the first edition, in 1946, was exhausted.

REFERENCES: *CB*, 1941; *SW*, 1946; Bennett Cerf, *At Random*, 1971; *CC*, 1975.

Margaret Woodbridge

CHALFIN, PAUL, 2 November 1874–?, painter. Connecticut-born Paul Chalfin was another of the young artists studying in Paris at the time Gertrude Stein was doing a series of portraits of her subjects' characters rather than their achievements. ''Chalfin'' is one of her briefest examples, the subject always referred to as ''one'' who may be or might be ''wonderful in being living'' through dozens of variant sentences. In progress, ''one'' is expanded to ''some one'' and then to ''any one'' and, finally, to ''a great many'' who are ''being living'' (*TWO* 342). Because of its brevity, ''Chalfin'' is an excellent model to demonstrate Stein's manner in many other portraits as well, sufficiently taxing patience. Chalfin was later a member of the Architects' League in New York.

REFERENCES: *TWO*, 1951; WWAA, 1985.

Bruce Kellner

COATES, ROBERT MYRON, 6 April 1897–8 February 1973, writer. As a young avant-garde writer living in Paris, Robert Coates met Gertrude Stein through Mr. and Mrs. Willie Dunbar Jewett, an American couple who had been active in wartime France. Coates became a constant enthusiast for Stein's writing and worked untiringly with others to bring *The Making of Americans*† into print. He felt that she introduced ''an almost mathematical lucidity . . . into the treatment of the English language'' (*CC* 254). Coates had graduated from Yale in 1916;

back in America in 1926, his friend, writer James Thurber, helped him get a job at *The New Yorker*. Coates wrote "Talk of the Town" pieces and book reviews, and eventually he became art critic for the magazine. In a letter to introduce Coates to Carl Van Vechten,* 4 December 1926, Stein wrote, "I like what he is doing he does not do much because he is still in the stage where he has to earn his living by regular work but it is good" (*GSCVV* 136). She had recently read Coates's surrealist novel *Eater of Darkness*, published by Robert McAlmon* in his Contact Editions, and thought his work had "an individual rhythm, his words made a sound to the eyes" (*SW* 164). Coates reviewed Stein's *Lucy Church Amiably*† for *The New Yorker*, telling his readers "one may read it for the intricate delicate embroidery of its style. One may read it for the peculiar evasive beauty of some of its passages . . . but one should never read it . . . for its plot" (*GSRG* 34).

REFERENCES: *ABT*, 1933; *SW*, 1946; *CC*, 1974; *GSRG*, 1984; *GSCVV*, 1986.

Paul Padgette
Bruce Kellner

COBURN, ALVIN LANGDON, 11 June 1882–23 October 1966, photographer. This "queer american" called on Gertrude Stein circa 1912, at the suggestion of English art critic Roger Fry, "the first photographer to come and photograph her as a celebrity and she was nicely gratified" (*ABT* 171–72). While still in his teens, Alvin Langdon Coburn came to the attention of important photographers and critics because of his imaginative work. In 1904, Alfred Stieglitz* devoted a whole issue of his influential *Camera Work* to Coburn's photographs. That same year, Coburn began making a series of photographs of celebrated artists and writers, including George Bernard Shaw and Ezra Pound,* both of whom wrote endorsements for his work. Many of Coburn's experiments and achievements were ground-breaking and influential, from youthful abstractions based on Japanese patterns to aerial photographs of New York as early as 1913; he perfected photogravuring from his negatives to insure that later prints would duplicate his original ones; he memorialized the ancient ritual stones of the British Isles, not only as documents but as works of art. Coburn is perhaps best known for his masterful portraits, however, including those of Gertrude Stein. He gave her the portraits he had made, "and then he disappeared," according to *The Autobiography of Alice B. Toklas*,† "and though Gertrude Stein has often asked about him nobody seems ever to have heard of him since" (172).

REFERENCES: *ABT*, 1933; George Walsh, et al., eds., *Contemporary Photographers*, 1982.

Bruce Kellner

COCTEAU, JEAN, 5 July 1889–1891?–11 October 1963, writer, artist. In 1917 Picasso* brought Jean Cocteau, known at the time as a poet, to 26 rue de Fleurus. He and Gertrude Stein did not meet again until 1920, this time through the sculptor Jacques Lipchitz.* Stein and Cocteau met rarely after these two occasions but maintained a lively friendship through correspondence. It seemed that Cocteau was chronically ill; every time Stein suggested a meeting, he pleaded some fresh attack or malady. Nevertheless, they always addressed each other in affectionate terms. Oddly enough, neither seems ever to have expressed an opinion about the other's work. On receiving copies of a newly published book, each of them would reply with thanks at once, obviously before the book could have been read. Cocteau did confess to Stein that he understood only half of *The Making of Americans*.† Perhaps this explains his reluctance to comment on her other writing. In 1922, for instance, Stein asked him to review her *Geography and Plays*,† but he never responded to the request. For her part, Stein may have been hesitant to comment on Cocteau's work for the same reasons that many critics find him controversial. He was a dilettante, though in the best sense of the word, multitalented and versatile. Cocteau tried almost every genre: novel, poetry, ballet, film, drama. Within each he tried every new "ism" of the day: modernism, surrealism, neoclassicism, expressionism, and so on. His experiments were technically successful but rarely profound. Perhaps his continual search for a proper medium is a reflection of his troubled life. He was homosexual and at times turned to drugs. Cocteau's best friend was Guillaume Apollinaire,* in whose manner he often shifted from one movement to another, all of them masking some secret sorrow. *Les Enfants Terribles*, 1929, is generally considered his best novel; *Orfée*, 1949, his best film; and *The Infernal Machine*, 1934, his most memorable drama. In 1955 Cocteau was made a member of the Académie Belge and of the Académie Française. He received an honorary doctorate of literature from Oxford and was made a member of the Legion of Honor of France. Gertrude Stein's word portrait of Jean Cocteau, whom one "must address with tenderness" plays with rhythms and counting (*WAM* 58).

REFERENCES: *WAM*, 1940; *VT*, 1966; *CC*, 1975; Martin Seymour-Smith, *Who's Who in Twentieth Century Literature*, 1976.

Margaret Woodbridge

CONE, CLARIBEL, 14 November 1864–20 September 1929, physician, art collector. In the late 1890s Gertrude and Leo* Stein often attended the at-home evenings of Dr. Claribel Cone and her sister Etta.* The Cone sisters had inherited a substantial fortune from their father, a Jew who had come from Germany and established a wholesale grocery business in Baltimore. Through their friendship with the Steins, the Cone sisters developed a lifelong interest in art which led eventually to an impressive collection centering on late nineteenth- and early twentieth-century painting. An independent and assertive woman, Claribel Cone had graduated from the Women's Medical College of Baltimore but preferred research and teaching to private practice. Stein saw her often when she was a student at Johns Hopkins, where Cone was engaged in research, and was impressed by her regal bearing and autocratic manner. Cone did advanced medical study in Frankfurt in the winters of 1904 and 1905. In the fall of 1905, she and her sister visited the Autumn Salon where they were stunned by the paintings of the fauves, which they thought were grotesque and not to be taken seriously, until they saw the Steins taking them very seriously indeed. The exhibition was their introduction to Henri Matisse,* whose paintings they bought regularly thereafter, and with whom they established an enduring friendship. Subsequently they steadily acquired works of the French impressionists, postimpressionists, and the fauves, including several by Bonnard, Renoir, and Cézanne, and many paintings by Picasso,* predominantly from the Rose and Blue periods. In "Two Women," one of Stein's early portraits written some time after "Ada," the vast difference in personality between the sisters is portrayed. Claribel, called Martha, is the distinguished but domineering and self-centered "rich one." Etta, the subservient, self-effacing "suffering" sister, capable of "tender feeling," is called Ada, a recognition, in James Mellow's view, of the probable similarities between the Cone sisters' relationship and that of Stein and Alice Toklas (*CC* 132). Claribel Cone "came majestically in and out," and "loved to read Gertrude Stein's work out loud and she did read it out loud extraordinarily well. . . . Everybody delighted in Doctor Claribel" (*SW* 118).

When America entered World War I, Cone was detained in a hotel in Germany as an enemy alien, having put off leaving the country earlier because she couldn't abide the uncomfortable wartime traveling conditions. Stein saw the Cones less frequently after the war, but the sisters continued to collect art and antiques, buying some things from Stein's collection as well, including Picasso's 1906 portrait of Leo Stein. Claribel Cone died suddenly on a summer holiday in Switzerland in 1929, but Stein was still thinking of her seventeen years later when, shortly before her own death, she included a favorite phrase of Cone's in *The Mother of Us All*:† "dear life, life is strife" (*LO&P* 87). Cone willed her enormous collection, after the death of her sister, to the Baltimore Museum of Art. It includes, besides forty-two oils and eighteen bronzes by Matisse, Vallotton's* oil portrait and Lipchitz's* bronze head of Gertrude Stein, and the typewritten copy of "Two Women," which Stein gave to the collection in 1932.

REFERENCES: *LO&P*, 1949; *SW*, 1962; *CC*, 1974.

Priscilla Oppenheimer

CONE, ETTA, 30 November 1870–31 August 1949, art collector. During the Baltimore years, Gertrude Stein and Etta Cone became close friends. While Stein admired Claribel's* accomplishments and forthrightness, she enjoyed the company of the patient and domestic Etta, who advised her on dress fabrics, accompanied her to museums and galleries, and was a good audience. While Claribel pursued her career, Etta took care of her parents until they died and then devoted herself to Claribel's needs. She had become interested in art while purchasing home furnishings in New York, and she listened to Leo Stein's* opinions on art with interest at their at-home evenings. The summer of 1904 Stein and Cone sailed back from Europe together, the last trip Stein was to make to America for thirty years. In 1905, while her sister continued her studies in Germany, Cone rented a flat in the same building in which the Michael Steins* were living in Paris. She had met the Steins previously, was fond of their son Allan, and maintained a friendship with them for many years. She accompanied Gertrude and Leo to art galleries and discussed their latest purchases at their flat. Cone did not care for the portrait of Stein that Picasso* was working on when Stein took her to his studio in November of that year. She found Picasso "appalling but romantic" but bought a watercolor and an etching for one hundred francs at Stein's urging, just to ease his financial situation (*ABT* 64). The following year she and her sister bought eighteen of his drawings and etchings which became in later years, as Stein points out, the nucleus of their collection. That year Etta volunteered to type Stein's manuscript for *Three Lives*,† doggedly deciphering the miserable handwriting letter by letter, until Stein told her it was permissible to read the text as she went. She was generous as well about lending Stein money when the necessity arose. Alice Toklas was less impressed with Etta than with Claribel when they first met at a luncheon in Florence in 1908, and her continuing dislike of Etta probably had less to do with a disagreement over who was to pay the bill that day than with jealousy over Etta's close friendship with Gertrude. For Toklas, one ministering angel in Stein's circle was enough. There was apparently little contact between Cone and Stein after her sister died in 1929, and an occasion for a reunion ended in disaster over a misunderstanding when Stein and Toklas were on their American tour. Stein wrote her a conciliatory note hoping that they would meet some time, signed with lots of love, but from that time on Etta saw nothing of Stein but her likenesses in oil and bronze. Those items are now to be seen in the Cone Wing of the Baltimore Museum of Art, which opened in February 1957, along with some 3,000 other artworks from the bequest of Claribel and Etta Cone.

REFERENCES: *ABT*, 1933; *SW*, 1962; *CC*, 1974.

Priscilla Oppenheimer

COOK, WILLIAM, 31 August 1881–?, painter. Iowa-born William Cook met Gertrude Stein and Alice B. Toklas in Palma de Majorca in 1915, at that time remote to tourists. He and his Breton wife, Jeanne, became their traveling companions to bullfights and, subsequently, warm friends in Paris. To support himself, Cook drove a taxicab, an old Renault, and taught Gertrude Stein how to drive. Later, when Cook inherited money, he engaged Le Cobusier to design a house for him in the south of France, and he joined Gertrude Stein in contributing to a fund to insure a comfortable old age for their mutual friend Mildred Aldrich.* William Cook's career as a painter seems not to have succeeded, but he did inspire two of Gertrude Stein's pieces: "What Does Cook Want to Do," written in 1915 about buying tickets for a bullfight, noting that he "approved of everything" and that he "had been good natured" (*PL* 31–32); "I Must Try to Write a History of Belmonte'' was published in *Geography and Plays*,† a disguised dialogue with Alice Toklas about one of the bullfighters, in which Cook puts in brief appearances.

REFERENCES: *G&P*, 1922; *ABT*, 1933; *PL*, 1955; *WWAA*, 1984.

Bruce Kellner

CORNELL, KATHARINE, 16 February 1893–9 June 1974, actress. After appearing with the Washington Square Players and the Jesse Bonstelle Stock Company, Katharine Cornell became famous in London for her portrayal of Jo in *Little Women*. George Bernard Shaw called her ''the gorgeous dark lady'' (*CB* 172). In 1921 Cornell married the director Guthrie McClintic, and together they produced many successes, often with a Shaw play. She became known as one of Shaw's leading interpreters, although she also performed in Shakespeare and Chekhov. Her favorite role, however, was as Elizabeth Barrett in *The Barretts of Wimpole Street*, which she performed seven hundred times. When Gertrude Stein and Alice Toklas came for the American lecture tour, Cornell was playing in *Romeo and Juliet*, and having met Stein and Toklas through their mutual friend, Carl Van Vechten,* Cornell invited them to a performance and entertained them afterwards. Ten years later, touring with a USO company in *The Barretts of Wimpole Street*, Cornell and members of the company read aloud an early version of *In Savoy*,† later retitled ''Yes Is for a Very Young Man,'' at 5 rue Christine. She returned with a copy to New York where she and McClintic tried unsuccessfully to find a producer. The difficulties and triumphs in Cornell's distinguished career are recorded in her reminiscences *I Wanted to Be an Actress* (1939) and *Curtain Going Up* (1943). As an actress, her most distinctive characteristic was her low, rich voice, suggesting controlled passion, and she possessed a regal bearing. It is unlikely that anybody other than Gertrude Stein ever called her ''Kitty.''

REFERENCES: *CB*, 1941; John Malcolm Brinnin, *The Third Rose*, 1959; *CC*, 1975; *GSCVV*, 1986.

Margaret Woodbridge

CREVEL, RENÉ, 10 August 1901–1939, writer. Gertrude Stein believed that René Crevel had become ''a devout surréaliste'' because both religion and patriotism had failed him. ''Young and violent and ill and revolutionary and sweet and tender'' (*ABT* 291), Crevel was a member of the group of young men whose fortunes rose and fell at 27 rue de Fleurus during the twenties. Virgil Thomson,* Georges Hugnet,* and Pavel Tchelitchew* were notable among them, but Crevel was a particular favorite. Alice Toklas adored his ''characteristic brilliant violence'' and his ''french charm'' (*ABT* 291). Crevel wrote ten books, all influenced by his ''littérature de malade énervé'' and what Bernard Faÿ* called his ''legendé vivant'' (Talvart 1089). His six novels have been described as interior autobiographies, much preoccupied with death—Crevel had tuberculosis—and suitably titled, for example, *La mort difficil* and *Mon corps et moi*. His writings against bourgeois society and the church reflect his Marxist leanings, and his surrealistic narratives have offered him some claim as a forerunner of Samuel Beckett and Eugene Ionesco, although the cases are by no means given accord by all his readers. Crevel committed suicide at the age of thirty-four.

REFERENCES: Talvart, Hector and Joseph Place, eds., *Bibliographies Auteurs Modernes De Langue Française (1801–1927)*, 1931; *ABT*, 1933; *EA*, 1937; *VT*, 1966; Richard Brooks, ed., *A Critical Bibliography of French Literature*, 1980.

Bruce Kellner

D'AIGUY FAMILY, circa 1924–1947, landed gentry. Gertrude Stein and Alice Toklas were friendly with several families who lived near Bilignin, outside Belley, where they spent their summers. They met the d'Aiguys when they needed "a garden to sit in," as Stein later synthesized a whole sequence that Toklas spelled out in her memoirs (*PL* 316). During the first summer at the hotel owned by the Pernollet family* in Belley, the old Baronne Pierlot invited them to visit her chateau at nearby Béon. On the property, there was "a small seventeenth-century house called the Cellier," Toklas recalled, where Stein was invited to "install herself" and work undisturbed (*WIR* 123). Madame Pierlot had come to this lovely region in 1870 to escape the Franco-Prussian War; by the twenties, she had buried two husbands, the first an army officer, the second a museum director, and lost one of her three sons during World War I. Descendant of a fourteenth-century family, she lived on in her chateau, "small and blue eyed and exciting," Stein described her, "elegant and generous and compelling" (*PL* 316). Her two sons, Robert and François d'Aiguy, lived with her; Robert's wife Diane translated Stein's *Paris France*† and, as *Petits poèmes pour un livre de lecture*, *The First Reader*.† Stein and Toklas were visiting the d'Aiguys when war was declared; while the d'Aiguys escaped to Tunisia where Robert was manager of a date palm company, Stein and Toklas stayed on, first at Bilignin and then, when their house was reclaimed by its owner, at Culoz where Madame Pierlot located another house for them. The daughter in the family, Rose Lucie Renée Anne, born in 1928, is the apparent model for the heroine of Stein's book for children, *The World Is Round*,† sharing not only her name but her fanciful imagination and favorite color, blue. When the old Baronne died shortly after the war, Robert "became impossible," François turned "gaga," and the family "went completely to pieces," Toklas wrote to Samuel Steward* (158). *The World Is Round* and its genesis in "The Autobiography of Rose" account for a happier time in the family, even if Rose's adventures mask some darker concerns of Stein's own, as Richard Bridgman has suggested. Stein's earlier portraits of the family—"The d'Aiguys" in 1928, printed in *Portraits and Prayers*,† and "La Baronne Pierlot" in 1937, printed in *Painted Lace*—are similarly pleasant accounts.

REFERENCES: *P&P*, 1934; *TWR*, 1939; *PL*, 1955; *SW*, 1962; *WIR*, 1963; *GSP*, 1970; Samuel M. Steward, *Dear Sammy*, 1977; *GSCVV*, 1986.

Bruce Kellner

DARANTIÈRE, MAURICE, ?–?, printer. Fifteen years after she completed *The Making of Americans*,† Gertrude Stein persuaded Robert McAlmon* to publish the book as part of his Contact Editions. McAlmon, in turn, engaged a young printer in Dijon to prepare an edition of five hundred copies for trade and five additional copies printed on vellum for collectors. Darantière, who assessed the work as containing 506,500 words, found himself caught in a crossfire of misunderstandings over distribution to British and American publishers. A few years later, when Gertrude Stein and Alice Toklas began their Plain Editions, privately financing books into print, Darantière prepared a thousand copies of *How to Write*† in 1931. The following year, he moved his press to Paris, met his employers, and suggested an economical way to issue further titles, bound in paper and slipcased. *Operas and Plays*† appeared in 1932 and *Matisse Picasso and Gertrude Stein*† in 1933, each in an edition of five hundred copies. The success of *The Autobiography of Alice B. Toklas*† made private printing no longer necessary.

REFERENCES: *ABT*, 1933; Robert McAlmon and Kay Boyle, *Being Geniuses Together*, 1968; *CC*, 1974.

Bruce Kellner

DAVIDSON, JO, 30 March 1883–2 January 1952, sculptor. "One day, wandering through the building, I found myself in a room full of plaster casts and modeling stands—and not a soul in it. I found the clay bin, put my hand in it, and touched the beginning of my life." So said Jo Davidson in his autobiography, *Between Sittings (GSCP* 94). After that moment he was hardly ever to have his hand out of clay. He was born and grew up in New York and had his first instruction at the Art Students League. Later he went to the Yale Art School and after that to Paris. There he lived the bohemian life with other struggling young artists and writers. He loved Paris, married a French girl, and eventually acquired a reputation for modeling a bust in a single sitting, best known as a portraitist rather than an abstractionist. Compared to other artists of his day he was conservative, though lively, and he always thought of himself as belonging to the avant-garde as much as anyone. After the initial years of struggle, success came rapidly, and he was commissioned to sculpt Woodrow Wilson and other war leaders. In 1923 he sculpted Gertrude Stein, whom he had known and liked since his arrival in Paris. She made him very much a part of her life, always treating him "like a second cousin," according to Virgil Thomson* (*VT* 179). Davidson did a seated figure because Stein seemed to him "a modern Buddha" for whom a head was not enough (*GSCP* 95). While she sat for him she composed his word portrait which pleased him enormously when she read it, but he admitted when it appeared in *Vanity Fair* that it made no sense to him. He seems to have sensed an almost mythic quality about her as she held court, dispensing wisdom to young artists. On Saturdays, he continued, her studios were jammed with people, gaping at the pictures and eating the excellent food. All the while, Gertrude Stein stood with her back to the fireplace looking like "a Cambodian Caryatid" who understood what they did not (*GSCP* 95). In Davidson's own home, Stein met James Joyce for the first and last time. Since Joyce was nearly blind, Stein went into another room to meet him. The two exchanged greetings and then discovered they had nothing to say to each other, as Virgil Thomson reported that historic encounter (*VT* 77). Jo Davidson sculpted many famous British and American writers, and after World War II he hoped to sculpt its world leaders at the United Nations, but a heart attack prevented that. After he had recovered sufficiently, he and his wife returned to their estate in France, where he died. Davidson's work is valued because he caught the spirit of his subjects in addition to molding their features. One way in which he was able to do this was to listen when they talked, thus enabling him to catch the essential personality. His statue of Gertrude Stein—cast large in stone and small in bronze—admirably conveys the massiveness of her figure as well as the strength of her presence. In addition to her portrait of Jo Davidson, Stein wrote one of his wife, actually a triple portrait: "And So. To Change So. Muriel Draper Yvonne Davidson Beatrice Locher." Both were included in *Portraits and Prayers*.†

REFERENCES: *P&P*, 1934; *CB*, 1945; *VT*, 1966; Wayne Craven, *Sculpture in America*, 1968; *GSCP*, 1974.

Margaret Woodbridge

DAVIES, ARTHUR BOWEN, 26 September 1862–24 October 1928, painter, printmaker. As president of the Society of Independent Artists, Arthur Davies organized a major exhibition at the 69th Regiment Armory in New York in 1913 which was to become a watershed in the recognition of modern European and American painting by the American public. Born in Utica, New York, Davies studied painting there and in Chicago and became known for his friezes of nude figures and mythological creatures in romantic landscapes. In 1908 he organized the exhibition of contemporary artists known as the Eight or the Ashcan School. In preparation for the Armory Exhibition, Davies and the painter Walt Kuhn visited Gertrude and Leo* Stein in Paris to arrange for the loan of some paintings. They chose two Picasso* still lifes and *Blue Nude* by Matisse* in addition to two Matisses which they borrowed from the Michael Steins.* The cooperation of the Stein family helped to reassure Paris art dealers who were asked to lend works for the show. The Armory Exhibition was a sensation, providing fodder to the press for months, but the ridicule in newspapers and magazines aroused the interest of thousands of people who were exposed to "modern" art for the first time. Davies wrote an article on the new art in the March 1913 issue of *Arts and Decoration*, in which an article by Mabel Dodge* on Gertrude Stein, comparing her aim in writing to Picasso's methods as a painter, also appeared. Davies briefly adopted the cubist style in his own paintings, but later went on to work in etching and color lithography and to design Gobelin tapestries.

REFERENCES: *CC*, 1974; *Encyclopedia Americana* 8, 1983.

Priscilla Oppenheimer

DE GRAMONT, ELISABETH, LILY DUCHESSE DE CLERMONT-TONNERRE,
1875–1954, writer. The model for Marcel Proust's Duchesse de Guermantes in *A la recherche de temps perdu* met Gertrude Stein through Natalie Clifford Barney,* whose friendship with Barney endured far beyond the duration of their long love affair. Elisabeth de Gramont wrote four volumes of memoirs as well as other autobiographical works, travel books, and two studies of Proust's work, largely to make money after a divorce ending her unhappy marriage and after the war had depleted her estate. She worked for a time ministering to the French wounded in both Normandy and in Paris. In 1927, Virgil Thomson's* musical setting for four male singers and piano of Gertrude Stein's *Capital Capitals* was given its first performance at one of Elisabeth de Gramont's celebrated masked balls, and at other evenings in her musical salons in Paris Gertrude Stein's work was given readings. Following her 1933 tour of the United States, lecturing on French culture, she acted as messenger—"Duchesse Xpress"—to transport packages, notably a large Mexican pottery pig from Carl Van Vechten,* but her role in Gertrude Stein's life is perhaps less public and more personal: in the late twenties, imitating the popular fashion, the duchess had her hair bobbed; when she unveiled her new coiffure, Gertrude Stein demanded that her own hair be cut off. Alice Toklas continued snipping until the crew cut that thereafter identified Gertrude Stein had been achieved.

REFERENCES: *ABT*, 1933; *WIR*, 1963; George Wickes, *The Amazon of Letters*, 1976; Shari Benstock, *Women of the Left Bank*, 1986.

Bruce Kellner

DEMUTH, CHARLES, 8 November 1883–23 October 1935, painter. Born into
a well-to-do family in Lancaster, Pennsylvania, Charles Demuth was encouraged to pursue his interest in art. After graduating from the Pennsylvania Academy of the Fine Arts, he went on a trip to Europe in 1907 and again in 1912–1914. These years were especially important for Demuth, for it was then that he met, among others, Jo Davidson,* Ezra Pound,* and Gertrude Stein. Under their influence Demuth's own painting attained greater maturity. His watercolors of flowers, still his most sought-after type of work, remind one of Matisse,* with their bright colors and elegance. His interest in cubism is evident in his oil paintings of buildings and machinery, a complete change of subject. He next turned to subjects drawn from vaudeville and night life, again showing the Matisse influence. In the 1920s he became interested in the "poster portrait," a composition in which words, letters, and numerals are elements of an abstract

design. His famous poster portrait of Gertrude Stein, entitled *Love, Love, Love*, consists of a mask floating in space in the midst of the words and numbers. Demuth always had to struggle to overcome severe handicaps. He was crippled from the age of four on, possibly from a childhood injury, unattractive in appearance, diabetic, consumptive, and homosexual. But he was known and valued as a witty, engaging companion and friend. Demuth went often to 27 rue de Fleurus during his stay in Paris. Gertrude Stein liked the rather dandified young man. She thought at first that he was more interested in writing than in painting, but about 1930 he left at her door the small painting that he had promised he would do for her one day, a "remarkable little landscape" that reminded her of Nathaniel Hawthorne and Henry James (*SW* 110–11). Demuth's reputation as an artist seems to be growing at present, though some critics of his work find no "spiritual resonance" in it; Sam Hunter points out that no spiritual resonance was intended, however (153). Demuth is interested in rendering concrete objects with a plainness and simplicity that make his paintings "subtle" and "mysterious," as Stein found his "little landscape." Some consider his illustrations for *Nana* and *The Turn of the Screw* decadent, quite unlike the freshness and elegance of his still lifes.

REFERENCES: *SW*, 1946; Emily Farnham, *Charles Demuth*, 1971; *Phaidon Dictionary of Twentieth Century Art*, 1973; *CC*, 1975; Samuel Hunter, ed., *Oxford Companion to Twentieth Century Art*, 1981; Betsy Fahlman, *Pennsylvania Modern, Charles Demuth of Lancaster*, 1983.

Margaret Woodbridge

DERAIN, ANDRÉ, 10 June 1880–8 September 1954, painter. One of the original fauves, friend and follower of Matisse,* André Derain was becoming known at the Independent Salon when he met Stein and her brother at lunch at the Matisses. He and Stein had an argument over philosophy. He based his ideas on "having read the second part of Faust in a french translation," she sniffed, and she disliked him and his work thereafter (*SW* 39). Although "he had a sense of space that was quite his own," his pictures lacked life, depth, and solidity; he looked like a modern but smelled of museums, she thought (*SW* 36, 39, 204). Derain became a part of Picasso's* circle after being introduced by Apollinaire,* painted with him in Spain in 1910 and visited the Steins in his wake, but after he enlisted in 1914, never saw Picasso again. After the war, Derain designed productions for the Ballets Russes, illustrated books and continued to paint traditional subject matter—landscapes, nudes, and still lifes—although with a more somber palette than in his earlier works. He painted with power and vision, but his style changed little after 1920.

REFERENCES: *SW*, 1962; *Praeger Encyclopedia of Art*, 1971.

Priscilla Oppenheimer

DRAPER, MURIEL, 1891–26 August 1956, writer, hostess. The Massachusetts-born wife of tenor Paul Draper (whom she divorced in 1916) was first known for her London salon in "Edith Grove," where musicians like Pablo Casals and writers like Henry James called regularly. Before that, however, she and her husband had settled in Florence in 1909 and met Gertrude Stein at Mabel Dodge's* Villa Curonia two years later. "A hard, slender, polished ivory figure carved from an elephant's tusk" with a "blonde negroid profile," in Dodge's later recollections (*EE* 255), Muriel Draper survived a philandering alcoholic husband; raised two sons (one of whom, Paul, became a celebrated dancer); and achieved some notoriety in New York, first as an interior decorator and later as a patron of the arts. With Carl Van Vechten,* she was much involved with popularizing the Harlem Renaissance of the twenties, although she lived through that period in what Virgil Thomson* called "resplendent poverty" (140). In a renovated stable on 40th Street and then in a 53rd Street apartment, she gave impoverished teas every Tuesday, with sufficient refreshments—usually supplied by friends—for about a third of the guests. Her memoir, *Music at Midnight* (1929), gives no hint of her later social conscience that manifested itself through her various interests in psychoanalysis, Gurdjieff's teachings, and Marxism. Gertrude Stein included her in a "fantasy on three careers" (*GSCVV* 102) as one of a trio including Jo Davidson's* wife Yvonne and Robert Locher's* wife Beatrice Howard. Written in 1924† and included in *Portraits and Prayers*† in 1934, the portion of the portrait devoted to Muriel Draper might serve to summarize her whole career, beginning, "Muriel has made Muriel has made it, apparently Muriel has made it an advantage, apparently Muriel has made it more than an advantage" (145).

REFERENCES: *P&P*, 1934; *EE*, 1935; *VT*, 1966; Bruce Kellner, ed., *The Harlem Renaissance*, 1984.

Bruce Kellner

DUCHAMP, MARCEL, 28 July 1887–2 October 1968, painter. "It is possible that Marcel Duchamp . . . has been the most destructive artist in history. At the same time . . . he has been the most influential in the adventurous course of modern art except Picasso,"* John Canaday wrote in *The New York Times* (3 October 1968, 51). Stein saw the handsome and utterly charming Duchamp, "looking like a young norman crusader," at dinner at the Picabias* shortly after the Armory Exhibition of 1913, and rubbed shoulders with him in the Paris art world and at her home both before and after World War I. "I was always perfectly able to understand the enthusiasm that Marcel Duchamp aroused," she wrote in *The Autobiography of Alice B. Toklas.*† "Everybody loved him. So much so that it was a joke in Paris that when any american arrived in Paris the first thing he said was, and how is Marcel" (*SW* 125–26). Born in Normandy, Duchamp was mainly self-taught as an artist. He was influenced early in his career by the work of Cézanne, then turned to fauvism and cubism. His *Nude Descending a Staircase*, dubbed by a critic "explosion in a shingle factory" (*CC* 171), was the *succès de scandal* of the Sixty-Ninth Armory Exhibition, seized upon by the press as a symbol of the insanity of modern art. The wave of notoriety brought him to New York in 1915, where with Man Ray,* Francis Picabia, and Alfred Stieglitz* he founded the review *291*. His paintings of whimsical, useless machines and his ready-mades, assemblages of everyday objects elevated to the status of art, were actually forerunners of the dada movement of 1916. He satirized the machine age in one of his best-known works, *The Bride Laid Bare by Her Bachelors*, a huge composition of oil paint and lead wire, embedded in glass, on which he worked for eight years, until 1923, but never actually finished. Duchamp rebelled against the sacred view of art which prevailed among critics and collectors, and in the mid-twenties he abandoned his career as an artist. Moving permanently to New York, he devoted the rest of his life to writing studies of chess and experimental optical theory, and to editing reviews and surrealist publications. In 1938 he organized the International Surrealist exhibit in Paris. His "aesthetic nihilism," as it was often called, was a constant influence on younger artists, culminating in the Pop Art movement of the early sixties, when interest in his work was revived. Duchamp had visited Gertrude Stein in 1919. The next year, along with Henry McBride* and Walter Arensberg, he discussed the possibility of bringing out a new book of Stein's work, and the best ways of promoting it, but he concluded that it would have to be printed at her own expense. Duchamp became an American citizen in 1955. Most of his work, collected by Arensberg, can be seen in the Philadelphia Museum of Art.

REFERENCES: *SW*, 1962; *NYT*, 3 October 1968; Bernard Myers, ed., *McGraw-Hill Dictionary of Art*, 1968.

Priscilla Oppenheimer

DUDLEY, KATHERINE, DOROTHY, AND CAROLINE, ?–?, friends. Caroline Dudley Reagon took Josephine Baker and the *Revue Nègre* to Paris in 1925 and met Gertrude Stein at a party given for the company by the American socialites Gerald and Sara Murphy. Stein's "Among Negroes," published in *Useful Knowledge*,† resulted from the evening. Dorothy Dudley Harvey wrote a study of Theodore Dreiser, *Forgotten Frontiers* in 1932, in which she devoted a few pages to Stein's writing. Their sister Katherine, a friend of Carl Van Vechten* from the turn of the century when they were students at the University of Chicago, married the French writer Joseph Deltiel. Imprisoned by the Germans in a concentration camp during World War II, she proved herself a practical friend when she returned to Paris after its liberation. She engaged a former Stein-Toklas handyman, a Russian named Svidko, to restore some order to 5 rue Christine before the women returned from their exile in the south of France. Gestapo agents had broken into the apartment, threatening to destroy the paintings and trying on Gertrude Stein's Chinese coats, until the police ousted them after a woman who worked in the building called in a complaint.

REFERENCES: *FF*, 1953; *SOA*, 1973; *GSCVV*, 1986.

Bruce Kellner

DUFY, RAOUL, 1877–23 March 1953, painter. Although Raoul Dufy was identified sequentially with the postimpressionists, the fauvists, and the cubists, and was even Georges Braque's* roommate circa 1909, Gertrude Stein did not mention his name in her writing until 1946. Indeed, the Julian Sawyer* extension of the 1941 Yale University Library *Catalogue of the Published and Unpublished Writings of Gertrude Stein*, utilized by Richard Bridgman, places her appreciative essay about the painter and his work in the last month of her life. It even followed the ''Message'' she wrote as a preamble to *Selected Writings of Gertrude Stein*† and mailed off 24 June 1946 (*GSP* 385, *GSCVV* 826). ''One must meditate about pleasure. Raoul Dufy is pleasure,'' it begins (*RAB* 63). The painter studied in Paris at the École de Beaux Arts and first exhibited at the Independent Salon in 1903. Three years later, Dufy had his first one-man show, but his work was various and imitative until 1910 when he began designing fabrics for couturier Paul Poiret. After World War I Dufy returned to painting with a style all his own, based on the decorative lines and brilliant colors by which his work is now easily identified. During World War II he encountered Gertrude Stein and Alice Toklas in Aix-les-Bains, near Culoz where they had been sitting out the German occupation. Their meeting motivated her essay about him, although the bulk of it was given over to an account of her return to Paris. It was published post-humously, in 1949 in *Harper's Bazaar*, four years before Dufy's death. During the interim, there was some discussion of Maurice Darantière* printing Stein's ''To Do'' (eventually published in *Alphabets and Birthdays*)† with illustrations by Dufy and a book of colored plates by Dufy with Stein's essay about him, but his ill health prevented either project.

REFERENCES: *RAB*, 1973; *Praeger Encyclopedia of Art*, 1971; Samuel M. Stewart, *Dear Sammy*, 1977.

Bruce Kellner

DUNCAN, ISADORA, 27 May 1878–14 September 1927, dancer. On the flyleaf of the manuscript notebook for ''Orta or One Dancing,'' Gertrude Stein wrote ''Isadora,'' and in the piece itself she considered as alternate titles ''Orta Davray,'' ''Alma Davray,'' and ''Isadora. Dora. Ra'' (Steiner 66). Apparently she had seen Isadora Duncan onstage and perhaps knew her through her brother Raymond Duncan, a neighbor on the rue de Fleurus. Born in California, Isadora Duncan is widely considered the founder of modern dance as a reaction against traditional ballet, although in fact her remarkable inventions evolved when she was unable to afford professional lessons. By the time Stein wrote her portrait, Duncan had danced widely in the United States, England, France, Italy, Greece, Austria, Germany, and Russia. One of the great legendary personalities as well as dancers of the twentieth century, Duncan bore two children to stage designer Gordon Craig; she was mistress to the scion of the Singer Sewing Machine

Company; she married Russian poet Serge Essenin; and she gave dozens of recitals of her unique, often improvisational dances. Swathed in diaphanous veils or (at least on one occasion) in the American flag, she scandalized or converted her vast audiences. Her schools in Germany and France made no attempt to establish some professional system, nor was she "seeking to invent or devise anything," as dance critic John Martin later observed, "but only to discover the roots of that impulse toward movement as a response to every experience, which she felt in herself and which she was convinced was a universal endowment" (3). Gertrude Stein had suggested much the same attitude forty years earlier in "Orta or One Dancing," its eighteen or twenty pages of circuitous and repetitive patterns echoing dance itself, synthesized in a passage like this: "This one is the one being dancing. This one is the one thinking in believing in dancing having meaning. This one is one believing in thinking. This one is one thinking in dancing having meaning. This one is one believing in dancing having meaning. This one is one dancing" (*TWO* 289). Isadora Duncan was still dancing at the age of forty-nine when she died as melodramatically as she had lived, her neck broken when her trailing scarf caught in the wheel of a Bugatti racer in which she was about to take a drive.

REFERENCES: *ABT*, 1933; John Martin, "Isadora Duncan and the Basic Dance," *Isadora Duncan*, 1947; *TWO*, 1951; Wendy Steiner, *Exact Resemblance to Exact Resemblance*, 1978.

Bruce Kellner

EDSTROM, DAVID, 27 March 1873–13 August 1938, sculptor. In *The Autobiography of Alice B. Toklas*,† Gertrude Stein recalled David Edstrom as "the fat swedish sculptor who married the head of the Christian Science Church in Paris and destroyed her" (141). During the period of her early portraits, however, later printed in *Two*,† she commemorated him in "A Man" as "a very fat one" who "had been a thin one," playing protracted verbal exercises with her subject's fluctuating weight, with his "working, "winning," and "being one being talking" (235–38). During the same period, she included him as one of a homosexual trio in "Men," along with Hutchins Hapgood* and Maurice Sterne,* "kissing" and "fighting." The latter activity was based on a specific physical encounter involving Sterne and Edstrom. The portrait may also reflect the circumstances in which Edstrom, thinking himself on the verge of death, confessed an embarrassing autobiography to Hapgood who converted it into an ugly narrative. Stein persuaded him not to publish it. Edstrom's own eventual autobiography, *The Testament of Caliban*, is in the manner of Benvenuto Cellini's, as Rupert Hughes's foreword avers, garrulous and preposterous in its account of a man of huge appetites and colossal conceptions. Edstrom numbered among his wives the daughter of a Swedish official, who wore men's attire; and Cora Downer, the Christian Scientist. Edstrom bragged a great deal about his sexual prowess, and cried a great deal as well in the process. "Woman's only power lies in her sex appeal," he contended in his autobiography (305), the pages of which spill over with his conquests and rejections. (Alice Toklas even records his mild flirtation with her San Francisco friend, Harriet Levy,* although nothing came of it.) In addition to his career as a sculptor, Edstrom accounts for himself as, variously, a minister, a hobo, a farmer, and a voluntary prisoner at Sing-Sing. He and Gertrude Stein renewed acquaintance briefly in Pasadena during the American lecture tour. He was working on a statue of Florence Nightingale. Seeing him again reminded her that he "used to complain so that I liked everybody in character" (*EA* 6).

REFERENCES: *ABT*, 1933; *EA*, 1937; David Edstrom, *The Testament of Caliban*, 1937; *TWO*, 1951; *WIR*, 1963; *CC*, 1974.

Bruce Kellner

ELIOT, T[HOMAS] S[TEARNS], 26 September 1888–4 January 1965, poet, critic. From 1922 until 1939, T. S. Eliot—during that period perhaps the most influential voice in modern poetry—edited the magazine *Criterion*, sponsored by Lady Rothmere. Mutual friends wanted Gertrude Stein and him to meet, but she was reluctant. Then, on 15 November 1924, Lady Rothmere brought Eliot to 27 rue de Fleurus unexpectedly. The two writers solemnly discussed the split infinitive. Eliot asked Stein for her most recent work for the *Criterion*, so she wrote a portrait of Eliot entitled "The Fifteenth of November," containing not a word about him. He delayed publishing it, thereby annoying her, but finally put the piece in a January issue—two years later. After this unpromising beginning, relations between the two did not improve. Some time later, Stein was mollified to hear that Eliot had pronounced her work "very fine but not for us," although, according to John Malcolm Brinnin, Eliot actually said her work "is not improving, it is not amusing, it is not interesting, it is not good for one's mind. . . . If this is the future, then the future is, as it very likely is, of the barbarians. But this is the future in which we ought not to be interested" (244). Eliot's reservations were founded in his background and training. Born in St. Louis, Missouri, educated at Harvard and the Sorbonne, in Munich and at Oxford, he became learned in philosophy and various literatures before World War I. He settled permanently in England in 1915, having written his remarkable "Love Song of J. Alfred Prufrock" four years before at the age of twenty-three, in a stream-of-consciousness style, laced with allusiveness and ironic wit to express the despair of twentieth-century man. *The Waste Land*, probably his best-known poem, appeared in 1922, conveying the exhaustion of modern civilization in haunting images and often obscure allusions, as well as something of his difficult first marriage. Later work includes his meditations in verse, *Four Quartets*, collections of literary criticism, and several plays, notably *Murder in the Cathedral* and *The Cocktail Party*, all reflecting a deep yearning for salvation. Eliot produced a small body of work that defines the first half of the twentieth century. He became a British subject and joined the Church of England in 1927. Always a believer in tradition, he was, as he put it, "classicist in literature, royalist in politics, and Anglo-Catholic in religion" (Abrams 2163). His detractors accuse him of a narrow range and a lack of passion. Nevertheless, his craftsmanship and power won for him the Nobel Prize in 1948 and a secure place in literature.

REFERENCES: *ABT*, 1933; John Malcolm Brinnin, *The Third Rose*, 1959; *WIR*, 1963; *CC*, 1974; M. S. Abrams et al., eds., *Norton Anthology of English Literature* 2, 1974.

Margaret Woodbridge

EVANS, DONALD, 24 July 1885–26 May 1921, poet, publisher. Born and educated in Philadelphia, Donald Evans moved to New York's Greenwich Village about 1912. He became a copy editor for *The New York Times* and through its assistant music critic, Carl Van Vechten,* he joined a band of aesthetes calling themselves "The Post-Decadents," including Walter Conrad Arensberg, Wallace Stevens, and Allan and Louise Norton. After Van Vechten introduced him to Mabel Dodge,* Evans became a regular visitor at her 23 Fifth Avenue salon. After reading Gertrude Stein's "Portrait of Mabel Dodge at the Villa Curonia," he voiced enthusiasm for her writing and, on Van Vechten's advice, wrote to request permission to publish some of her plays. He had recently established a small private press—called Claire Marie after the actress Claire Burke—in order to publish his own poems and the work of his friends. Stein sent him the manuscript for *Tender Buttons*,† which he brought out in 1914, a fragile book in yellow boards in an edition of one thousand copies and retailing for one dollar apiece. Through Van Vechten and Mabel Dodge's circle, it created a stir among the avant-garde. Evans claimed to be profoundly inspired by *Tender Buttons* and was proud of his perfect typesetting of the esoteric pieces. Evans himself wrote several collections of poems, among them *Discords* (1911) and *Sonnets from the Patagonian* (1914), and a monograph on his own work, *The Art of Donald Evans* (circa 1916) under the pseudonym Cornwall Hollis, calling himself the "most interesting personality in contemporary American poetry, . . . the chameleon of modern verse" (1). He enlisted in the army "for the aristocracy of thought, to make life comfortable once more for the decadent, the iconoclast, the pessimist" (Kellner 56). Evans's position in the literary world hangs by a slender thread, although his latter-day admirers have included poet-critics Alfred Kreymborg and Yvor Winters. He was personally eccentric in the extreme, a Firbankian personality whom Mabel Dodge called a "strange genius" (74). Donald Evans committed suicide at the age of thirty-six.

REFERENCES: Cornwall Hollis, *The Art of Donald Evans*, circa 1916; Alfred Kreymborg, *Our Singing Strength*, 1929; Mabel Dodge Luhan, *Movers and Shakers*, 1936; Horace Gregory and Marya Zaturensky, *A History of American Poetry*, 1946; Bruce Kellner, "The Origin of the *Sonnets from the Patagonian*," *Hartwick Review*, Spring 1967.

Paul Padgette
Bruce Kellner

FAŸ, BERNARD, 3 April 1893–22 December 1977, historian, translator. Bernard Faÿ was born into a conservative Catholic family in Paris. He graduated from the Sorbonne after an earlier private school education, served as a captain in World War I, and was decorated for bravery in Belgium and at Verdun. After the war he was awarded the Victor Emmanuel Chapman Memorial Fellowship and studied for two years at Harvard. He became professor of history for ten years at the University of Clermont-Ferrand, located not far from Gertrude Stein's summer home at Bilignin. In 1932, the College de France created a chair of American civilization and called Faÿ to head it. At thirty-nine he was the youngest person ever appointed to that faculty. His authority as a scholar of American history and culture was demonstrated in his highly regarded biographies of Benjamin Franklin (1929) and George Washington (1931). By 1935, he had made his twenty-second visit to the United States, this time as president of the French Committee of the Academy for the Rights of Nations. In 1940, Faÿ was appointed as general director of the French National Library, the Bibliothèque Nationale. Gertrude Stein first met Faÿ in 1926 when he was lecturing at the University of Clermont-Ferrand. She was pleased by his knowledge and appreciation of her writing and they became fast friends. Faÿ was also a promoter of Sherwood Anderson's* writing and Virgil Thomson's* music, both close Stein friends. In 1929, Gertrude Stein wrote a word portrait, "Bernard Faÿ," published in *Portraits and Prayers*,† in which Faÿ's vocation as a linguist is suggested in three passages: "A is an article. / They are usable. They are found and able and edible. . . . / Articles are a an and the. / When this you see remember me. . . . / A noun is the name of anything" (41–43). Faÿ abridged *The Making of Americans*† to less than half its original 925 pages and then, with the Baroness J. Seillière, he translated it as *Américains D'Amérique* for publication by Librairie Stock in 1933; Harcourt Brace published his English abridgment the following year. Also, in 1934, Gallimard published Faÿ's translation of *The Autobiography of Alice B. Toklas*.† Faÿ's appointment to the National Library under the Vichy government made him a highly regarded advisor to Marshal Pétain,* and during monthly meetings at Vichy he would frequently visit Stein and Toklas at Culoz to keep them posted on possible dangers from the advancing German army. He defended his action by saying he had obtained from Pétain orders that the Préfet and the Sous-Préfet should help and watch over them. During the war the German military invaded the Stein-Toklas Paris apartment filled with its art treasures. Picasso* got in touch with Faÿ (still an influential person), who took the necessary steps to see that such an invasion did not recur. Faÿ was arrested in September 1944, charged as a collaborator with the enemy, tried, and sentenced to life imprisonment. Stein thought he was the victim of injustice and wrote a lengthy testimonial in his defense, but it was rejected. After Stein's death in 1946, Alice Toklas made numerous attempts to assist in Faÿ's release. In 1948 the life sentence was reduced to twenty years, and when amnesty for political prisoners was issued in 1957, he was pardoned. Gertrude Stein's affection for Faÿ never wavered, and she said that his was one of the four permanent friendships of her life. His admiration for her can be summed up in his preface to his abridgment of *The Making of Americans*: "the greatest and most beautiful of her gifts is her presence'' (xi). It was to Faÿ's country house, 200 kilometers south of Paris in mid-July 1946, that Stein and Toklas were going to rest when Stein became seriously ill, and they turned back to Paris and to the hospital where she died a few days later.

REFERENCES: *MOA*, 1934; *P&P*, 1934; *TCA*, 1942; *SOA*, 1973; *CC*, 1974.

Paul Padgette

FITZGERALD, F. SCOTT, 24 September 1896–21 December 1940, writer. Ernest Hemingway* first brought F. Scott Fitzgerald to 27 rue de Fleurus in May 1925. Gertrude Stein and Fitzgerald immediately assumed an amused, friendly relationship which continued in person (though their meetings were few) and in their letters. Stein thought that both *The Great Gatsby* and Fitzgerald's earlier *This Side of Paradise* ''really created for the public the new generation'' (*ABT* 268). In spite of his bouts of drinking, Fitzgerald always appeared at the Stein atelier in a sober condition. During a visit on his thirtieth birthday he said he felt his youth was going and wondered aloud what was to become of him. Stein assured him he should not worry and that he had been ''writing like a man of thirty for many years.'' She said he should do a big novel, and she drew a line to indicate its thickness. When *Tender is the Night* was published in 1934, Fitzgerald sent her a copy inscribed, ''Is this the book you asked for?'' (*CC* 276). In a letter to Fitzgerald in May 1925, Stein told him he was ''creating the contemporary world much as Thackery did in *Pendennis* and *Vanity Fair* and this isn't a bad compliment'' (Bruccoli 164). On her lecture tour of America, Gertrude Stein made a special effort to visit Fitzgerald on Christmas Eve 1934 in Baltimore. All accounts confirm it was a fine evening of talk and remembrance. In a letter to Stein following the visit Fitzgerald wrote her, ''You were the same fine fire to everyone who sat upon your hearth—for it was your hearth, because you carry home with you wherever you are—a home before which we have all always warmed ourselves. . . . Christmas eve was well spent in the company of your handsome face and wise mind—and sentences 'that never leak' '' (*FF* 294). Upon returning to France in the spring Stein wrote Fitzgerald thanking him for seeing her at Christmas. ''I did like being with you all in Baltimore and . . . I wonder . . . what you are doing, and I hope you are doing it very well whatever it is, you know that I am very fond of you and hope this finds you the same . . . love to you over and over again'' (Bruccoli 412–13).

REFERENCES: *ABT*, 1933; *FF*, 1953; *CC*, 1974; Matthew J. Bruccoli and Margaret M. Duggan, eds., *Correspondence of F. Scott Fitzgerald*, 1980; James R. Mellow, *Invented Lives*, 1984.

Paul Padgette

FLANNER, JANET, 13 March 1892–7 November 1978, journalist. As ''Genêt,'' Janet Flanner wrote the semimonthly ''Letter from Paris'' for *The New Yorker* for nearly fifty years. Born in Indianapolis, Flanner had studied at the University of Chicago, worked as a film critic, made speeches for women's suffrage, and had a brief marriage before settling in Paris in 1921 to pursue a writing career. With an assignment from Harold Ross to report to *The New Yorker* on the French character, she developed a remarkable knowledge of Gallic life, writing on politics, art, theater, and society in an elegant and colorful manner. She worked hard at her style, she admitted, molding each sentence like a sculpture. She knew most of the artists and writers in Paris between the wars and became a strikingly memorable figure on the Left Bank. Shortly after Flanner arrived in Paris she met Gertrude Stein and became a close friend; but owing to the pressure of her work, Flanner did not visit 27 rue de Fleurus as often as Stein might have liked. She admired the integrity of Stein's literary processes if not always the results. In her *New Yorker* letters she referred more often to Stein as an art collector than as a writer, and her interest in the paintings extended to helping Stein and Alice Toklas make an inventory when they moved to 5 rue Christine in 1938. Flanner was connected with other writers as well. After World War I, she became a close friend of Ernest Hemingway* and championed his work, and she supported efforts to legalize publication of James Joyce's *Ulysses* in America. After 1934 she shuttled between Paris and London, having added a "Letter from London" to her assignments. In 1940 she published *An American in Paris* to considerable acclaim, and from that time until the end of World War II she lived in New York. Back in Paris, Flanner proved a loyal friend to Alice Toklas after Gertrude Stein's death, assisting her financially and with the painful move to a new apartment when Toklas was eighty-six. Flanner continued to write her "Letter from Paris" until 1974, when she returned permanently to New York. Her only novel, *The Cubical City*, was published in 1926, and in the late twenties she translated some of the works of Colette. Collections of Flanner's *New Yorker* articles were issued as *Men and Monuments* in 1957, *Paris Journal 1944–1965* in 1965, which won the National Book Award that year, and *Paris Journal 1965–1971* in 1971. In 1951 she wrote the introduction to *Two*,† the first volume of the Yale edition of Gertrude Stein's unpublished writings, concluding cogently: "Her theory about writing was that if you saw a thing clearly in writing it, you had seen it so well that it became part of the explanation. She thought reading had nothing to do with writing. If the reader had a sufficiently strong reaction, that reaction was what he had left to work on afterward, in sympathy and intelligence, without prejudice. . . . She thought she had no personality aside from her writing" (xvii). Like Gertrude Stein, Janet Flanner perpetuated her personality in her own writing.

REFERENCES: *TWO*, 1951; *CC*, 1974; *NYT*, 8 November 1978; *DLB* 4, 1980.

Priscilla Oppenheimer
Bruce Kellner

FLETCHER, CONSTANCE, 1858–10 June 1938, writer. Constance Fletcher encountered Gertrude Stein only once, at Mabel Dodge's* Villa Curonia, circa

1911, but she made a sufficient impression to serve as subject matter in a crucial Stein text. "Portrait of Constance Fletcher," unpublished until 1922 in *Geography and Plays*,† sharply defines the break between the style of the early portraits, complicating simple statements through circuitous repetitions, and the manner that led to *Tender Buttons*,† highly charged with startling combinations of images, puns, rhymes, and oblique word patterns. The portrait begins with sentences like this: "She was one having, she was one who had had family living" (157); it concludes with sentences like this: "The one who is a sun is the last flower that is not open when all the petals falling feel the whole of all intention" (164). Nothing of Constance Fletcher's remarkable history is discernible in the portrait, however. A glamorous intimate of Oscar Wilde and Henry James, and a reviewer for the London *Times*, as popular for her baby blue eyes and gilded curls as she was for her novels and plays, Constance Fletcher perpetuated her past into legend suitable for one or another of her florid melodramas. When she was twelve, her mother eloped to Italy with Eugene Benson, a minor English painter. She lived with them in Venice, scandalized by the romance and subsequent divorce. Their Palazzo Capello became a celebrated salon, where Constance Fletcher's mother paraded the rose petal–strewn marble staircases to hold court. At eighteen, Constance Fletcher wrote *Kismet*, the first of six novels under the pseudonym George Fleming, and shortly became a successful playwright as well, with a dramatization of Rudyard Kipling's *The Light That Failed* for Forbes Robertson and *The Canary* for Mrs. Patrick Campbell. Wilde dedicated his *Ravenna* to her, and James based *The Aspern Papers* on her thwarted love affair with Lord Byron's grandson, Lord Lovelace. Into her old age she clung to the poet's miniature and a packet of his love letters, returning to Venice to continue the rose petal ritual in her mother's memory and to help Benson into his own old age. By 1911, she had grown extremely nearsighted, lost her teeth, and ballooned to Gertrude Stein's elephantine proportions, though still gowned in the dresses of her youth, apparently very witty, talented at free-hand embroidery, and comfortable with one of the ghosts at the Villa Curonia. Gertrude Stein and Alice Toklas "particularly liked Constance Fletcher" whom they found "attractive and impressive" (*BT* 158–59). If Constance Fletcher is difficult to perceive in her 1911 portrait, she is clear enough in Gertrude Stein's final work, *The Mother of Us All*,† her opera libretto about women's suffrage. As the object of John Adams's affection, she is "blind as a bat and beautiful as a bird, . . . white and cold as marble, beautiful as marble, yes that is marble but you you are the living marble dear Constance Fletcher, you are" *(LO&P* 85).

REFERENCES: *G&P*, 1922; *ABT*, 1933; *LO&P*, 1949; *EE*, 1935; Oscar Wilde, *Letters*, 1961.

Bruce Kellner

FORD [HUEFFER], FORD MADOX, 17 December 1873–26 June 1939, novelist, editor. Ford Madox Hueffer changed his name to Ford Madox Ford because one of his early mistresses, the writer Violet Hunt, was mistakenly identified as Mrs. Hueffer, his wife. When she sued the publication, it caused a scandal in English society. Partly for that reason, he moved to Paris to live—with a succession of mistresses. In 1908 he founded the *English Review*, in which he published Thomas Hardy, Joseph Conrad, D. H. Lawrence, H. G. Wells, and Wyndham Lewis. After its demise he turned his attention to fiction and in 1915 brought out *The Good Soldier*. In the twenties he persuaded John Quinn, the wealthy American collector and patron, to put up money for *Transatlantic Review*, another little magazine he edited. From April to December 1924 Gertrude Stein's *The Making of Americans*† ran serially in its pages. They had met before the war, "at the tea table," with Violet Hunt (*ABT* 264). Ford inaccurately claimed that he had seen Stein regally steering her Ford down the Champs-Elysées circa 1913, but she had no car then nor had she learned how to drive. Stein and Toklas were always kind to Ford's mistresses and his young daughter Julie, whose mother was the painter Stella Bowen. Stein and Toklas always went to their Christmas parties for the neighborhood children. As a writer, however, Ford seems to have enjoyed no great popularity with Stein and the rest of the literary crowd in Paris. His novels were too conventional for their tastes. Nor did they all care much for him personally. Overbearing to many people, he reminded Robert McAlmon* of Lord Plushbottom in the comic strip *Moon Mullins*, and Ernest Hemingway* called him "the golden walrus," probably because of his blond mustache, and satirized him in *The Sun Also Rises*; in contrast, Sylvia Beach* said that he was jolly and well liked, and Alice Toklas confessed that she always "had a weakness for him" (*WIR* 113). He often dipped into his own pocket to produce money for writers when his magazine's funds were exhausted. Apparently Stein was never paid for all of the installments he published of *The Making of Americans*, however. Ford was also occupied in the twenties with writing his Tietjens tetralogy, a series of novels on the decline and fall of the prewar order of society. In 1938 he brought out an ambitious work, *The March of Literature from Confucius to Modern Times*. Opinion is divided about Ford's writing. His novels have always had readers, but he never attained the stature of his contemporaries. Robert M. Adams writes that Ford was a man "of intellectual talent and resource," but "whose life needs a good deal of forgiving" (455).

REFERENCES: *ABT*, 1933; Sylvia Beach, *Shakepeare and Company*, 1956; *CC*, 1975; Robert M. Adams, *The Land and Literature of England*, 1983.

Margaret Woodbridge
Bruce Kellner

FROST, ARTHUR, ?–?, painter. Arthur Frost labored under the shadow of his father, the well-known illustrator A. B. Frost whose drawings for *Tom Sawyer* and many popular magazines in the late nineteenth century had made him famous. Arthur Frost studied with Matisse* for a time, disappointing his father, who would have preferred him to work commercially. Another Matisse pupil commiserated that "You can lead a horse to water but you cannot make him drink." "Most horses drink," Mr. Frost replied (*ABT* 140). Arthur Frost was pleased with Gertrude Stein's portrait of him largely because it was three pages longer than the portraits of Picasso or Matisse, but like most of those early portraits, "Frost" treats his character rather than his potential or his achievement. Throughout, he is "completely a young one." He asks questions and he understands and he does "listen and listen again and again"; he amuses and he does not disappoint, but he concludes as he has begun, "a young one" (*TWO* 330–32).

REFERENCES: *ABT*, 1933; *TWO*, 1951.

Bruce Kellner

GALLUP, DONALD CLIFFORD, 12 May 1913– , bibliographer, editor. Donald Gallup was for thirty-three years curator of the Collection of American Literature, now housed in the Beinecke Rare Book and Manuscript Library, at Yale University. The collection includes Gertrude Stein's manuscripts and correspondence, some of her books and pictures, and the papers of such old friends of hers as Neith Boyce and Hutchins Hapgood,* Marsden Hartley,* Mabel Dodge Luhan,* Henry McBride,* Thornton Wilder,* and Carl Van Vechten.* Most of Gallup's work on Stein has been based on the Yale Collection. In 1941, he and Norman Holmes Pearson arranged a Stein exhibition at Yale, and in connection with it Gallup published *A Catalogue of the Published and Unpublished Writings of Gertrude Stein*, compiled in his free time after library hours, into which was incorporated Robert Bartlett Haas's* revision of Stein's own bibliography that had been printed in *transition* in 1929. In 1947, Gallup saw through the press *Four in America*† and arranged a memorial exhibition featuring Stein's correspondence. This developed eventually into *The Flowers of Friendship* in 1953, a selection of some 450 letters to Stein between 1895 and 1946. With Donald Sutherland* and Thornton Wilder as members of a three-man advisory committee, Gallup helped Carl Van Vechten prepare for publication by the Yale University Press, between 1951 and 1958, the Yale Edition of the Unpublished Writings of Gertrude Stein. In the eighth and final volume, Van Vechten turned over his "stewardship" to Gallup, as his "more-than-adequate successor" (*NOTY* xiv). Gallup carried out the obligation in 1971 with his edition of *Fernhurst, Q.E.D., and Other Early Writings*,† published by Liveright. Gallup continues to serve as literary advisor to the Stein estate. He has contributed numerous articles about Gertrude Stein and her work to various publications. Three appeared in the *Yale University Library Gazette*: "The Gertrude Stein Collection," October 1947, describes the papers at Yale; "Carl Van Vechten's Gertrude Stein," October 1952, is about the long friendship between the two writers; and "Gertrude Stein and *The Atlantic*," January 1954, deals with her correspondence with editor Ellery Sedgwick.* The subjects of other articles have ranged widely: "A Book Is a Book" in *New Colophon*, January 1948, tells the story of the publication of *Three Lives*;† "The Weaving of a Pattern" in *Magazine of Art*,

November 1948, uses letters to illuminate Marsden Hartley's friendship with Stein; "Picasso, Gris, and Gertrude Stein" in the San Francisco Museum of Art's 1948 exhibition catalog, *Picasso, Gris, Miro*, discusses Stein's relationships with two of the three painters; "Always Gertrude Stein" in *Southwest Review*, summer 1949, prints Stein's ten letters to Gallup, written between 1941 and 1946, enhanced with his commentary "The Making of *The Making of Americans*,"† again in *New Colophon*, 1950, accounts for the long publication history of the novel Stein considered her major achievement; "Du Côté de Chez Stein" in the London *Book Collector*, summer 1970, demonstrates how the presence of the Stein papers helped the Yale Collection of American Literature to attract other materials; and "Introducing Gertrude Stein," in the issue of *Widening Circle* devoted to her work in the fall of 1973, reports on her talk— "L'Amérique Mon Pays, La France Mon Chez-moi"—at the Reformed Church of Choisy-le-Roi near Paris, in March 1945, detailing Gallup's personal and professional friendship with Gertrude Stein and Alice Toklas. In addition to these articles, he supplied the introduction to the penultimate volume of the Yale edition of Stein's unpublished writings, *Alphabets and Birthdays*,† in 1957.

He has written about other authors as well, and is probably best known for the standard bibliographies of T. S. Eliot* in 1969 and Ezra Pound* in 1983, both models of clarity and precision for all contemporary bibliographers. He has edited Pound's *At the Círculo de Recreo* in 1985 and *Plays Modelled on the Noh* in 1987. He edited Carl Van Vechten's *Fragments from an Unwritten Autobiography* in 1955, and he continues to serve as Van Vechten's literary trustee. As Thorton Wilder's literary executor, he has been responsible for three posthumous volumes: *The Alcestiad* (1977), *American Characteristics and Other Essays* (1979), and *The Journals* (1985). Gallup has also edited Eugene O'Neill's *Inscriptions* (1960), *More Stately Mansions* (1964), *Poems* (1979), *Work Diary* (1981), and *The Calms of Capricorn* (1981), and Kathryn Hulme's *Of Chickens and Plums* (1982). In 1988, Yale's Beinecke Library published Gallup's memoirs, *Pigeons on the Granite*, about the Collection of American literature including material about Gertrude Stein and Alice Toklas.

Donald Gallup was born on Ekonk Hill near Moosup, in Sterling, Connecticut. He completed his bachelor of arts degree in 1934 and his doctor of philosophy degree in 1939, both at Yale, working part-time in the library during that period. He taught English at Southern Methodist University in Dallas, Texas, before returning to Yale as a cataloger in the library there in 1940. His first contact with Gertrude Stein was a letter to her in December of that year, to clarify titles and dates for the projected checklist to be published in connection with the exhibition scheduled for February 1941 of her writings. Two days before it opened, on 22 February, Gallup entered the army to spend five years on active duty, mostly overseas. While he was stationed in Paris, he hand-delivered a note to 5 rue Christine, not trusting the efficiency of the postal system, to suggest that he would like to call. They met on Thursday, 5 January, the first of many Thursdays prior to his transfer in July. His army career ended with Michaelmas

Term at Magdalen College, Oxford—under an armed services quota—and made possible two further visits to Paris. In October, Stein inscribed a copy of the special number of *Camera Work* from August 1912, devoted to her portraits of Matisse* and Picasso* and to their work: "To Donald our very dear friend this almost my first printed book, in memory of such pleasant Thursdays, there was Donald all through that cold winter after the liberation there was Donald himself and packages, full of comfort himself and packages, Dear Donald, he was a Thursday child, and we were the happier welcomers of the Thursday days, Always Gertrude and Alice Paris October 1945 All happiness" (Gallup, "Du Côté,"[188]). On his penultimate visit, Gallup, Virgil Thomson,* and Joseph Barry* discussed with Stein and Toklas the writing of *The Mother of Us All*,† and all five became members of the opera's cast of characters. Gallup had only a small role, but his line is memorable and accurate enough: "Last but not least, first and not best, I am tall as a man, I am firm as a clam, and I never change, from day to day" (*LO&P* 86). Discharged as lieutenant colonel in the spring of 1946, Gallup returned again to Yale and in July 1947 became Curator of the Collection of American Literature, Assistant Professor of bibliography, editor of the *Yale University Library Gazette*, and Fellow of Jonathan Edwards College. He visited Alice Toklas several times before her death in 1967, returning with an early Picasso oil given to her by the artist and Marie Laurencin's* portrait of Basket II,* both for the Gertrude Stein Collection at Yale. In 1971, Colby College in Waterville, Maine, gave Gallup an honorary Litt.D. degree. He retired from his official duties at Yale in 1980, but he continues to write and edit from his apartment, within walking distance of the Beinecke and Sterling libraries, where for more than four decades he has worked to preserve the writings of Gertrude Stein and many others.

REFERENCES: *LO&P*, 1949; *FF*, 1953; *NOTY*, 1958; Donald Gallup, "Du Côté de Chez Stein," *Book Collector*, Summer 1970; *SOA*, 1973.

Paul Padgette
Bruce Kellner

GIBB, HARRY PHELAN, 8 April 1870–25 October 1948, artist. Harry Gibb was born in the north of England and became a successful animal painter in his youth. He later studied in Germany and then migrated to Paris to investigate the new school of painting evolving at the time. He was interested in the techniques of Picasso* and Matisse,* and his later work shows the influence of both masters. He did not find a French market for his work and returned to England. In 1912 he went to Dublin where he enjoyed the attention of a few patrons, and in 1913 his friend Oliver St. John Gogarty arranged an exhibition of his work that turned out to be the high point of his career. From that time he found himself at odds with the critics and public alike and died in obscurity in 1948. Gertrude Stein met Gibb during her early days in London and developed a fondness for him that she frequently expressed in conversation and letters. He was a loyal publicist for her work, and it was he who suggested to Alice Toklas that she publish the Plain Editions, those works by Stein that did not interest commercial publishers. Stein wrote "A Portrait of One: Harry Phelan Gibb," published in the *Oxford Review*, 7 May 1920. It was later included in the 1922 collection, *Geography and Plays*.†

REFERENCES: *G&P*, 1922; *ABT*, 1933; *FF*, 1953.

Paul Padgette

GOODSPEED [MRS. CHARLES B.], ELIZABETH FULLER ["BOBSIE"], 1893–8 September 1980, art patron. Gertrude Stein's Chicago hostess came to Bilignin with Fanny Butcher* in early 1934 to encourage an American lecture tour, convinced that engagements in and around Chicago alone would pay for more than half the trip. Wife of one of the regents of the University of Chicago, Bobsie Goodspeed served for ten years as president of the Arts Club of Chicago, sponsoring exhibitions by a number of young painters, including two in whom Stein had taken an interest, Elie Lascaux* and Sir Francis Rose.* Also, she was responsible for organizing the art exhibition during the Chicago World's Fair of 1933. Of Mrs. Goodspeed's generosity, Stein recalled that she had two sets of seats at the Chicago performance of *Four Saints in Three Acts*,† both in a box for the first half and down quite close in the orchestra for the second, and Toklas recalled the "perfect cuisine," especially a clear turtle soup to begin and a nougat with roses and cream and tiny candles to conclude (*ABTC* 125). To commemorate the visit—from about 15 November until 5 December 1934—Mrs. Goodspeed arranged to have printed as her Christmas card *Chicago Inscriptions*, a pamphlet of Gertrude Stein's inscriptions in copies of books belonging to several of her friends as well as to herself: "To Bobsy," Stein had written in a copy of *The Making of Americans*,† "who helped me way away in France and Switzerland to know the American way and it is a nice way the nicest way the very nicest way that American way" ([15]). Subsequently, Elizabeth Fuller Goodspeed married Gilbert Chapman, president of the New York Public Library.

REFERENCES: *EPH*, 1934; *EA*, 1937; *ABTC*, 1954; *GSCVV*, 1986.

Bruce Kellner

GRIS [GONZALEZ], JUAN [JOSE VICTORIANO], 23 March 1887–11 May 1927, painter. "Gertrude Stein always says that cubism is a purely spanish conception and only spaniards can be cubists and that the only real cubism is that of Picasso* and Juan Gris. Picasso created it and Juan Gris permeated it with his clarity and his exaltation. To understand this one has only to read the life and death of Juan Gris by Gertrude Stein, written upon the death of one of her two dearest friends . . . both spaniards" (*SW* 85). Gris began studying art in Madrid at the age of fifteen. In 1906 he moved to Paris and settled near Picasso. A gifted draftsman, he supported himself with drawings for the satirical press. He began painting in the cubist style of Picasso and Braque,* although he differed with them on points of theory, and exhibited at the Section d'Or and the Independent Salon in 1912. He produced highly inventive collages and stressed rhythm and composition in his paintings, but he admitted they lacked a sensitive and sensuous aspect. In 1914 the art dealer Daniel-Henry Kahnweiler* committed himself to buy Gris's entire production and continued to represent him the rest of his life. Stein bought three Gris still lifes from Kahnweiler in 1914 and bought several more after World War I, by which time she and Gris had developed a close friendship. Gris respected her judgment on his work; she saw a similarity in their approach, a "passion for exactitude" (*SW* 198). Stein supported his career as well as she could afford to do, and promoted the special Juan Gris issue of the *Little Review* in 1924, to which she contributed an essay. Gris provided lithographs illustrating Kahnweiler's luxury edition of Stein's *A Book Concluding with As a Wife Has a Cow: A Love Story*.† Widely respected by artists and critics, he lectured at the Sorbonne in 1924. When many other artists had abandoned the style, Gris remained a cubist. He was also a prolific illustrator of books and worked with Serge Diaghilev, designing sets for ballets and operas. Gris had suffered from ill health for several years but was nevertheless a "very gay, delightful companion," Toklas wrote of a seaside holiday they spent with Gris and his wife (*WIR* 135). When Gris died from uremia at the age of forty, Stein was deeply affected. She felt he had not had the success he deserved and wrote her tribute to him, "The Life and Death of Juan Gris," published in *transition* in July 1927, which she considered the most moving thing she had ever written. Gris's death was the occasion for a quarrel between Stein and Picasso. Earlier, Picasso had resented her intimacy with Gris and had accused her of not honestly liking Gris's work. Stein vented her grief on Picasso and told him he had no right to mourn Gris's death, that he had never really understood him. Earlier, she had identified them together as "Two Spaniards," and disguised with Anglicized names with Daniel-Henry Kahnweiler, in "Relieve," both printed in *Painted Lace*† posthumously.

REFERENCES: *PL*, 1955; *SW*, 1962; *WIR*, 1963; *Praeger Encyclopedia of Art*, 1971; *CC*, 1974.

Priscilla Oppenheimer

GROSSER, MAURICE, 1903–22 December 1986, painter, scenarist. "I always remember . . . he had a way of knowing how it was possible to play the plays that I have written," Gertrude Stein recalled (*EA* 75). Alice Toklas remembered Grosser as a "poor painter but a charming person—intelligent, witty and sensitive" (*WIR* 129) who was an excellent cook as well. Born in Huntsville, Alabama, Grosser entered Harvard in 1920 and became interested in painting after attending art classes in Boston. As a member of the Harvard Liberal Club he met Virgil Thomson,* who became a lifelong friend. After graduation Grosser went to Europe to study painting on a Harvard Fellowship and shared a flat in Paris with Thomson, in whose company he was a regular visitor of Stein's both in Paris and in Bilignin. In 1929 at Thomson's invitation, Grosser, who "among us all really understood the text," devised the scenario for *Four Saints in Three Acts*,† a clear plan of action that allowed it to be staged which was "bedrock to our production" (*VT* 229). His scenario has been used in many subsequent productions of the opera. Grosser also wrote a scenario for a projected film to be made from two of Stein's plays with music by Paul Bowles,* but the film was never made. In 1946 he developed a scenario for *The Mother of Us All*.† During the thirties Grosser lived and painted in France, and after his first art show in Paris in 1930 he gradually began to sell his paintings. He painted "over-life-size fruit and bread and vegetables in high bright colors; he also painted very striking portraits" (*VT* 291). Grosser returned to the United States at the outbreak of World War II and exhibited in New York. He was the author of four books, including *Painting in Public*, 1948, and *The Painter's Eye*, 1951, and for a time he was art critic for *The Nation*.

REFERENCES: *EA*, 1937; Maurice Grosser, *Painting in Public*, 1948; *WIR*, 1963; *VT*, 1966; *NYT*, 24 December 1986.

Priscilla Oppenheimer

HAAS, ROBERT BARTLETT, 20 January 1916–   , teacher, editor. As a student at the University of California at Berkeley in 1935, Robert Bartlett Haas met Gertrude Stein after one of her lectures in the Bay Area. Their ensuing correspondence lasted until her death a decade later, during which time, and subsequently, Haas did much to further her career. In a letter to Carl Van Vechten* in February 1937, Stein asked, "Will you send a photo to a very charming fellow who is writing [a] doctorate about me . . . and could it be the profile that you made . . . that I like so much, I hate to ask so much, but he would like it so" (*GSCVV* 534). At the time, Haas was researching a Stein checklist that eventually became part of the Yale catalog he compiled with Donald Gallup* in 1941. At various times in her letters and in print, Stein called Haas "Barkeley Bobbie," "Bobolink," and "Bobchen." When he married in 1939, Stein wrote a "Prothalamium—for Bobolink and His Louisa." Also titled "Love Like Anything" and "Very Well I Thank You," variously in its five small printings—as few as 25 and as many as 100 copies—none was ever for sale (*GSBIB* 43–44). In turn, Haas expressed his enthusiasm for Stein's writing by seeing through publication one of her important manuscripts, "What Are Masterpieces and Why Are There So Few of Them." Written in 1935 and delivered as a lecture at Oxford and Cambridge in 1937, it was printed with the contents of the 1926 *Composition as Explanation*,† a second lecture, "An American and France," and a play entitled "Identity a Poem." Haas supplied the introduction for *What Are Masterpieces*,† published in 1940, assessing Stein as "a truly philosophical poet" (17). The following year, Stein wrote a word portrait, "To Bobchen Haas," which reached print thirty years later in *A Primer for the Gradual Understanding of Gertrude Stein*,† a chronology in miniature with selections from her work and his helpful explanatory notes. Also, it included the full text of "Gertrude Stein Talking—A Transatlantic Interview," made a few months before her death in 1946 when Haas had posed a series of questions to her about her work, through an intermediary in Paris. Subsequently, Haas edited two volumes of Stein's uncollected pieces, *Reflection on the Atomic Bomb*† in 1973 and *How Writing Is Written*† in 1974. In his introduction to the latter, he observed, "Her genius as a writer lies in her sense of the immediate" ([8]).

REFERENCES: *WAM*, 1940; *HWW*, 1974; *GSBIB*, 1975; *GSCVV*, 1986.

Paul Padgette
Bruce Kellner

HAPGOOD, HUTCHINS, 21 May 1869–18 November 1944, writer. Mabel Dodge Luhan* described Hutchins Hapgood as "an intellectual anarchist," gently pursuing God and social reform among the lowly, "an old bloodhound on a leash" held by his novelist wife Neith Boyce (45–46). Author of several quasi-autobiographical works, notably *The Spirit of Labor* (1907), *The Story of a Lover* (1919), and *A Victorian in the Modern World* (1939), he was born in Chicago and educated at Harvard. En route to Japan, he met Leo Stein* in 1895, and he met Gertrude Stein in Heidelberg the following summer; for several years he was a regular caller at 27 rue de Fleurus and a strong ally. In 1906 Gertrude Stein sent him the manuscript for *Three Lives*,† which he found "full of reality, truth, unconventionality," although he balked at the repetitions as "an affectation of style" (*FF* 31). Nevertheless, he sent it to an American publisher he knew, and in later years he called attention to her and her work in his columns in the *New York Globe*. Hapgood was much a part of Mabel Dodge's 23 Fifth Avenue salon, where artists and anarchists rubbed shoulders with various left-wing groups in Chicago, and with young playwrights in Provincetown and Greenwich Village. Reflecting back on the Steins from his old age, Hapgood contended that Leo could have been a significant critic had he been able to control his neuroses, and that Gertrude's self-absorption had undermined her career. Hapgood was one of three subjects for Gertrude Stein's portrait of a homosexual trio, "Men" (*TWO* 310–15), the others identified in manuscript as Maurice Sterne* and Swedish sculptor David Edstrom.*

REFERENCES: *MS*, 1936; Hutchins Hapgood, *A Victorian in the Modern World*, 1939; *FF*, 1953.

Bruce Kellner

HARCOURT, ALFRED, 31 January 1881–20 June 1954, publisher. Alfred Harcourt began his career in the book world with Henry Holt & Company in 1904. In 1919 he founded Harcourt, Brace & Howe, and he was the originator of the Blue Ribbon Books that reprinted editions of popular titles. In 1933 he published *The Autobiography of Alice B. Toklas*† following its serialization in four issues of *Atlantic Monthly*. This first commercial success for Gertrude Stein earned her

$4,495.31 in royalties. A few months later, Harcourt saw *Four Saints in Three Acts*† in its New York production and reported to Stein on "a thrilling evening and a really splendid performance." Arturo Toscanini was sitting behind him "completely absorbed" (*FF* 227). When Gertrude Stein arrived in the fall of 1934 for her lecture tour, she and Alice Toklas accompanied Harcourt to the Yale-Dartmouth football game as his guests. It reminded her of a bullfight (*EA* 195). Harcourt wanted to publish Stein's memoir of the lecture tour, *Everybody's Autobiography*,† but she had already promised it to Bennett Cerf* of Random House, who remained her primary publisher for the rest of her life.

REFERENCES: *EA*, 1937; *FF*, 1953; *CC*, 1974.

Paul Padgette
Bruce Kellner

HARTLEY, MARSDEN, 4 January 1877–2 September 1943, painter. In *Adventures in the Arts*, first published in 1921, Marsden Hartley lauded the French custom of discussing art and ideas in the sunlight in outdoor cafes, "where you feel the passing of the world and the poetry is of one piece with life itself. . . . The studio of Gertrude Stein, that quiet yet always lively place in the rue de Fleurus, is the only room I have ever seen where this spirit was organized to a similar degree, for here you had the sense of the real importance of painting, . . . you had a fund of good humor thrust at you, and the conversation took on . . . a kind of William James intimacy, . . . bringing the universe of ideas to your door in terms of your own sensations" (194). Hartley was introduced to Stein on his first visit to Europe in April of 1912. Born in Maine, Hartley had studied art in Cleveland and New York and had his first one-man exhibition at Alfred Stieglitz's* 291 gallery in 1909. He became a regular member of the Stieglitz circle and held a second show at 291 in 1912. Stein took an immediate interest in Hartley, in part because there was "nothing mystic or strange about his production," she wrote to Stieglitz in 1913; it was "genuinely transcendant": "He deals with color as actually as Picasso* deals with form" (*CC* 187–88). Hartley and Stein kept up a regular correspondence, and she bought four paintings from him in 1913. Later that year when he was in Berlin she sent him money for his support. Hartley had become interested in German painting through his acquaintance in Paris with Arnold Rönnebeck,* a German sculptor. He painted in Berlin in 1913–1914 and exhibited with the Blaue Reiter group. In late 1914, moved by repulsion and fascination with the trappings of war, and by the death in action of a dear friend, Hartley began his series of German military paintings, dramatically colored examples of Synthetic Cubism, which are considered to be among his best work. Stein's words of German were one of the inspirations for the portraits of German officers in this series. A portrait of Hartley, "M——N H——," from Stein's play *IIIIIIIIII*, was included in the brochure of Hartley's January 1914 exhibition at the 291 gallery, a rare instance of Stein's willingness to publish her work in sections. Hartley had a major show in Berlin before belatedly leaving Germany for the United States in 1915. On his return he lived and painted in Santa Fe, New Mexico, but for the next twenty years he moved frequently and experimented with various painting styles. He lost touch with the Stieglitz group and seemed to lose all direction as well. The last ten years of his life marked a return to his roots. He moved back to Maine where he produced a series of expressive landscapes which surpassed the achievement of his German military series. In 1921 Hartley had given a reading of works by Stein, along with Henry McBride,* Katherine Dreier, and Mina Loy,* at the Society Anonyme in New York, but in later years he had little contact with Stein.

REFERENCES: Marsden Hartley, *Adventures in the Arts*, 1972; *CC*, 1974; Barbara Haskell, *Marsden Hartley*, 1980.

Priscilla Oppenheimer

HAULLEVILLE, ERIC DE, 1900–20 March 1941, poet. Eric de Haulleville is one of the subjects for a series of brief portraits Gertrude Stein wrote circa 1929–1930. De Haulleville's portrait—four sentences that begin promisingly about keeping a goat in a boat—appeared in *Portraits and Prayers*,† but the subject himself is nowhere mentioned in her memoirs. Born in Belgium to a family long involved with arts and letters—his grandfather was a well-known historian and his father founded a museum for African art—de Haulleville published his first poems in 1921. In Paris during the twenties he was one of Virgil Thomson's* early companions, a group of poets, painters, and musicians collectively identified as neoromantics. His *Le Genre Épique* was published in 1928, a collection of poems, fables, and playlets. After his marriage to Aldous Huxley's sister-in-law, Rose Nys, de Haulleville returned to Brussels; then, during World War II, he hitchhiked with his wife and child, through cities and landscapes destroyed or in flames, to seek a cure in France for a long-term problem with his circulation. De Haulleville died in Vence while seeing his last poems, *L'Anneau des Années*, into print. Admirers of his work have compared its lyricism with Shelley's.

REFERENCES: *P&P*, 1934; *Columbia Dictionary of Modern European Literature*, 1947.

Bruce Kellner

HAYNES, MABEL, ?–?, medical doctor. As "Mabel Neathe," Mabel Haynes appears in the unhappy lesbian triangle in Gertrude Stein's *Q.E.D.*† in 1903. Born in Boston and a Bryn Mawr graduate in 1898, she was a first-year student at Johns Hopkins when she met Stein, then in her second year of medical studies. Her later history is related in "Regular Regularly in Narrative" in *How to Write*.† She married twice, first Heissing and then Leick, and she was twice widowed. Long after the events involving Mabel Haynes and May Bookstaver* in *Q.E.D.*, Gertrude Stein maintained communication with many college friends.

REFERENCES: *HTW*, 1931; *ABT*, 1933; *CC*, 1974.

Bruce Kellner

HEAP, JANE,   1887–18 June 1964, editor. Margaret Anderson met Jane Heap, then an art student in Chicago, in 1916 and later described her "handsome features" as "strongly cut, rather like those of Oscar Wilde in his only beautiful photograph" (5). Anderson realized that Heap's persuasive personality would be a decided asset for her *Little Review* and made her co-editor. When the magazine moved from New York to Paris in 1923, it was Jane Heap who interested Gertrude Stein in contributing to it. Heap never faltered in her enthusiasm and devotion to Stein and her work. In *The Autobiography of Alice B. Toklas*,† Stein said that Heap "had never appreciated the quality of Gertrude Stein's work until she proof-read it" (139). In the final years of the *Little Review*, Heap shuttled between Paris and New York on magazine business, and in its last issue, May 1929, faced her own Stein word portrait, "J. H. Jane Heap. Fairly Well. An Appreciation of Jane." In the middle twenties, Heap acted as one of Stein's unofficial agents and tried repeatedly to get *The Making of Americans*† under contract and in print in America and England, by arranging for a publisher to take unbound sheets already printed in France for Robert McAlmon's* Contact Editions. She negotiated with Dial, Huebsch, Boni, and, in England, Nott; financing was always a stumbling block. Heap even tried to sell *The Making of Americans* to the book collector, A.S.W. Rosenbach, "but he [was] busy buying pages of the Gutenberg Bible, for millions of dollars the page," Heap commiserated in a letter from New York, 26 March 1926 (*FF* 189). In later years, Heap became a disciple of Gurdjieff, the Russian mystic popular in the twenties. Alice Toklas described her as "one of the heroines of the Blitz in London" (*SOA* 158). She died there at the age of seventy-seven.

REFERENCES: *ABT*, 1933; Margaret Anderson, *The Fiery Fountains*, 1951; *FF*, 1953; *SOA*, 1973; *CC*, 1974.

Paul Padgette
Bruce Kellner

HÉLÈNE, CLOTHILDE, ET AL.,   circa 1905–circa 1967, domestics. "Unfortunately there have been too many of them in my service," Alice Toklas wrote in her *Cook Book* (169) of the long succession of servants she and Gertrude Stein had experienced singly or shared together. Notable among those at 27 rue de Fleurus, Hélène, a superb cook and housekeeper, ran the household from 1905 until 1914. Practical, efficient, thrifty, and something of an autocrat, she expected punctuality of all guests. On her account, Stein was reluctant to hold up dinner when Picasso* was late. Hélène knew the subtleties of choosing the appropriate menu to honor a guest and to snub one she didn't like, such as Matisse,* for whom she would fry eggs but not make an omelet. She had a talent for meat dishes—a special meal might include a filet of beef with Madeira sauce followed by a saddle of mutton and an exquisite chicken dish—but she declined to do elaborate desserts, preferring instead the simplicity of a soufflé. One of her peculiar culinary failures occurred on Carl Van Vechten's* first dinner at 27 rue de Fleurus: "For some reason best known to herself she gave us course after course of hors d'oeuvres finishing up with a sweet omelet" (*SW* 129). Hélène did not encourage Toklas's interest in learning from her; a lady, she believed, should leave the cooking to the servants. What she thought about being quoted for posterity in the celebrated cookbook is not known. Although she was herself humorless, her freely expressed opinions provided amusement for Stein and Toklas. She assumed America must be devoid of artists, for example, because they were all studying in Paris. Most Americans, she thought, must be dentists. In his "Pastiches et Pistaches" in 1923, Van Vechten saluted Hélène as "the super cook. Like all artists, she takes her work easily. Show me an artist who labors and you show me a mediocrity. Hélène builds complicated dishes with the ease that you and I make letters. . . . Supreme test of a cook, she can boil potatoes. On those days when Hélène prepares a plain lunch of cottage cheese and boiled potatoes you will fare as well as you would elsewhere on a five-course déjeuner with all the delicacies of the season" (243). When in 1914 her husband insisted she give notice and devote herself to taking care of him, Stein was sorry to lose her. But, as Hélène had always said, "all men are fragile" (*SW* 205). Fifteen years later, after her son had died and her husband had fallen on hard times, she came back to work for Stein and Toklas for a year and discovered to her amazement that all the nobodies she had cooked for were now famous artists.

Following the formidable Hélène, a long series of cooks and servants began, most of them accounted for in *The Alice B. Toklas Cook Book*, though not always in chronology and not always by name. Hélène was succeeded by Muggie Moll, as Gertrude Stein nicknamed her, a good-looking woman with a cast in one eye and a gendarme for a husband, but she left when Gertrude Stein and Alice Toklas returned to France from England after the battle of the Marne. Jeanne Poule came next, a good cook, excellent at cleaning, and reliable when unexpected guests turned up. Before the war was over, however, she married and left. Léonie came next, energetic to the point of recklessness. She had been engaged only to clean, but her cooking was so successful that she and Alice Toklas more or less switched jobs. Léonie cooked by inspiration, neither weighing nor measuring, relying instead on instinct and prayer. Only teasing, Alice Toklas "told her she did not always pray to the right saint" (*ABTC* 174). Léonie lasted less than three years. Then a second Jeanne arrived, gentle, naive, illiterate, strange but agreeable, and capable of miraculous concoctions, mysterious sauces, delicate chicken croquettes, and a claim that she could prepare eggs or potatoes one hundred ways. When Jeanne simply drifted away in 1921, a parade of domestics came and went. The first left almost immediately, terrorized by the collection of paintings on the walls. The second, Louise, was a gourmet who liked Alice Toklas's cooking better than her own; she left in tears when she was not allowed "a small amputation" for herself from a Thanksgiving turkey in advance of its being served to guests. The third was an Austrian from Ohio who departed because the household "lived French." Then a trio of Bretonne sisters came in succession: another Jeanne, who "cooked the classical French kitchen" (*ABTC* 192) until she got pregnant; Caroline, whom they called "Heart of Gold" (*ABTC* 193), adding peach-pit liqueur and an unforgettable strawberry jam to the Stein-Toklas pantry; the third sister, Margot, came when Caroline departed to care for her infant niece, tossing crêpes, flaming desserts, and constructing pretty salads until she married. After a series of unsuccessful French and Italian couples, Gertrude Stein and Alice Toklas commenced their "insecure, unstable, unreliable but thoroughly enjoyable experiences with the Indo-Chinese" (*ABTC* 198). Trac came first, talented in the kitchen, terrified of phantoms and ghosts from his homeland, and perpetually chattering. Apparently he took other work during the American lecture tour. In the winter of 1935–1936, Stein and Toklas employed Otto Baumgartner, "a gay and enchanting Austrian" Toklas chose to call "Frederich" in her cookbook. He was a "perfect cook," having trained at the celebrated Sacher Hotel in Vienna, and made complicated cakes like a book for Gertrude Stein and a little dog for Alice Toklas, spun sugar nests for ice cream, and of course the Sacher Torte (*ABTC* 43). "[W]e try not to grow fat," Stein wrote to Carl Van Vechten (*GSCVV* 457). Otto—or Frederich—was torn between an "angel" as sweet and frothy as his concoctions and a "devil" who tried to poison him with tokay. He eloped with the devil, and Stein and Toklas sent the angel back to Austria with his wages where she made a prosperous marriage (*ABTC* 46). Then they waited for Trac to return to them, his first of several departures.

When Trac grew restless and left to cook briefly for Elisabeth de Gramont,* the Duchess of Clermont-Tonnerre, they employed a Russian named Yvan briefly, followed by a series of other Indo-Chinese, a gambler, a tippler, a womanizer, a drug addict. Nguyen proved more successful, helped with the housework in Bilignin by the Widow Roux. Nguyen found the temptations of Paris too strong, however. Agnel, a Polish-American woman, replaced him, and Trac returned to replace her when she went on vacation. Then he married a Bretonne named Lucienne and opened a restaurant. Next, a Finn named Margit came to 27 rue de Fleurus, whom Alice Toklas described as "for several years the joy of our household, though not a radiant presence"; one of their friends called her "Mademoiselle Hamlet" (*ABTC* 206), but she was a superb cook until, under the threat of the war, she returned to Finland. Gertrude Stein and Alice Toklas waited out the war in Bilignin, attended by two sisters, the younger Olympe, who cleaned the house, and Clothilde, "old, tired and pessimistic, . . . indifferent, inert and too discouraged" by the German occupation of her country (*ABTC* 223). Gertrude Stein included these two final servants in her play *In Savoy*† (in which they speak in unison), later retitled *Yes Is for a Very Young Man* (in which their lines are divided but more or less interchangeable). Clothilde, a cook who was famous in the area but woefully underpaid, came with the house that Stein and Toklas rented near Culoz in February 1943 after they had lost their lease for the manor house at Bilignin. Clothilde "couldn't cook the plainest meal without a pint of dry white wine a pint of cream and the yolks of at least six eggs," and the food shortages of the long war had stifled her enthusiasm (*SOA* 157). She sat by in a depressed state while Toklas learned to make do in the kitchen, turning out a meat loaf with one cup of veal and three cups of breadcrumbs and plenty of herbs and white wine. Clothilde paid no attention (*ABTC* 210). She was outraged when German officers were billeted briefly in the house, as much by their menu as by their presence. When they offered her some of their canned bread and potato substitute, she was gratified that even her hens refused to eat it. When the Americans arrived in August 1944, Clothilde came to life again and produced wonders: "She had fresh trout . . . and enormous apple pies fresh from the oven from early morning to late at night," Toklas wrote to her old friend Annette Rosenshine* afterward. "I learned more from her . . . than she cared to learn from me—she despised economy and saving in detail," she continued. "She was a great person" (*SOA* 157). None who followed was so colorful as either Hélène or Clothilde, in the long series of anonymous domestics serving Alice Toklas after Gertrude Stein's death, although one did claim to be the offspring of Brigitte Bardot and Jesus Christ. A Spanish maid, Jacinta, attended her finally.

REFERENCES: Carl Van Vechten, "An Artist Cook," 1923; *ABT*, 1933; *ABTC*, 1954; *SW*, 1962; *SOA*, 1973; *CC*, 1974; *BABT*, 1977; *GSCVV*, 1986.

Priscilla Oppenheimer
Bruce Kellner

HEMINGWAY, ERNEST, 21 July 1899–2 July 1961, writer. Ernest Hemingway was twenty-three years old when he arrived in Paris from Chicago, carrying a letter of introduction from Sherwood Anderson* to Gertrude Stein. He had worked for the *Kansas City Star* before serving as an ambulance driver in World War I, and at the time he met Stein in 1922 he was a correspondent for the Toronto *Star*. From the beginning, there was a strong emotional response between them, and their relationship seemed secure. Stein was able to help Hemingway place his early work, *Ten Stories and Three Poems*, with Robert McAlmon's* Contact Editions in 1923. She reviewed the book in the Paris edition of the *Chicago Tribune*, 27 November 1923, as "very pleasantly said. So far so good" (*GSCVV* 89). In an early letter to Stein concerning his work, Hemingway wrote, "It used to be easy before I met you. I certainly was bad, gosh, I'm awfully bad now but it's a different kind of bad" (*FF* 165). Hemingway always credited Stein in helping him to concentrate on his writing, and at the beginning he was a willing student. As his circle enlarged, he brought other writers to meet his mentor, including F. Scott Fitzgerald* and his wife Zelda in 1925. Stein's word portrait "He and They, Hemingway" first appeared in *Ex Libris* in December 1923 and later in *Portraits and Prayers*† in 1934, hardly a description but suggestive. Hemingway expressed his appreciation by arranging with Ford Madox Ford* to serialize part of *The Making of Americans*† in *Transatlantic Review*, running from April through December 1924.

Long afterward, Hemingway re-created his early impressions in *A Moveable Feast*: "Miss Stein was very big but not tall and was heavily built like a peasant woman. She had beautiful eyes and a strong German-Jewish face that . . . reminded me of a Northern Italian peasant woman with her clothes, her mobile face and her lovely, thick, alive immigrant hair" (14). Of her work, he wrote about her discovery of "many truths about rhythms and the uses of words in repetition that were valid and valuable and she talked well about them" (17). In *The Autobiography of Alice B. Toklas*,† Stein remembered Hemingway as "an extraordinarily good-looking young man, twenty-three years old . . . , rather foreign looking, with passionately interested, rather than interesting eyes" (261). But the relationship turned bitter. The student began to believe he was the teacher. Stein's version of the falling-out admitted that she and Sherwood Anderson "were both a little proud and a little ashamed of the work of their minds," concluding they had "a weakness for Hemingway because he [was] such a good pupil." Alice Toklas insisted he was "a rotten pupil" because "he looks like a modern and he smells of the museums." Even in the days when Stein said he was "so wonderful" she told him he was "ninety percent Rotarian. Can't you, he said, make it eighty percent. No, said she regretfully, I can't" (*ABT* 265–66, 270). Hemingway attributed Stein's celebrated observation about those young men who served in the war being "a lost generation" to her garage keeper (29); she contended that the eponymous owner of the Hôtel Pernollet* in Belley deserved the credit (*EA* 52); but he had the last word, in *A Moveable Feast*, with an ugly account he overheard between Stein and Toklas, concluding that she grew to resemble "a Roman emperor and that was fine if you liked your women to look like Roman emperors" (118–19). Time partially healed their wounds and in the thirties they accidentally met in Sylvia Beach's* bookshop. Good taste prevailed, as it did again at the end of World War II when, upon another accidental meeting, they embraced on discovering they had survived. In *Charmed Circle*, James R. Mellow suggested that "with unerring instinct, Gertrude had wounded him where he was most vulnerable—in that image of untarnished courage and masculinity that he wished to project. He countered it, very effectively, by exposing her lack of 'manliness' " (282).

REFERENCES: *ABT*, 1933; *P&P*, 1934; *EA*, 1937; *FF*, 1953; Ernest Hemingway, *A Moveable Feast*, 1964; *CC*, 1974; *GSCVV*, 1986.

Paul Padgette
Bruce Kellner

HOCKADAY, ELA, 1875–26 March 1956, educator. In 1913 Ela Hockaday founded a junior college for girls in Dallas, Texas, and made it an outstanding institution. The original school had 10 girls and $1,200 in equipment. In 1946, when Ela Hockaday retired, there were 425 girls and millions of dollars' worth of equipment. Gertrude Stein and Alice Toklas visited the school during their American tour of 1934–1935. Stein lectured and met informally with the girls, finding them extremely knowledgeable. What Toklas liked best was the modern kitchen, the finest she had ever seen. Both pronounced the food the best they had enjoyed on the trip. A special new favorite were the southern corn sticks. They liked them so much that before they left, Ela Hockaday presented them with a corn stick pan. This was one of the items stolen by the German soldiers who looted their flat at 5 rue Christine.

REFERENCES: *NYT*, 28 March 1956, 31; *CC*, 1974.

Margaret Woodbridge

HOPWOOD, AVERY, 28 May 1882–1 July 1928, playwright. After graduating from the University of Michigan in 1905, Avery Hopwood became a reporter on the Cleveland *Leader* and moved to New York as its special correspondent there. He changed professions almost immediately, co-authoring his first play, *Clothes*, with Channing Pollock in 1906. Subsequently, he became one of the most prolific and successful playwrights in America. During the 1919–1920 season, Hopwood had four plays running simultaneously on Broadway. His most famous play, *The Bat*, written with mystery writer Mary Roberts Rinehart, was produced in 1920 and ran for 867 performances. His work was admired by Carl Van Vechten,* who claimed Hopwood "contrives to do in English very much what [Georges] Feydeau does in French" (*The Merry-Go-Round* 237). Hopwood met Gertrude Stein by a curious route. He had met Van Vechten in New York shortly after they both arrived there in 1906. A few years later, after Van Vechten introduced him to Mabel Dodge,* Hopwood carried a note from her when he first visited 27 rue de Fleurus circa 1915. His friendship with Stein did not mature until 1923 when their meetings were more frequent. Once they attempted a literary collaboration. Stein had read Hopwood's play *Our Little Wife*, a farce about wife-swapping and reversing identities, and charmed by the amusing aspects she wrote "A List" in 1923. Van Vechten submitted it to Edmund Wilson,* then an editor for *Vanity Fair*, but he thought it was too long for the magazine and asked permission to cut it. Gertrude Stein replied, "I am awfully sorry not to be able to consent to your cutting . . . , but the quality of it is in the way it fills itself out and so I must say no" (*GSCVV* 81). "A List" reached publication a decade later in *Operas and Plays†* in the Plain Edition. On a visit in May 1925, Hopwood brought his friend Gertrude Atherton* because, "he said so sweetly, I want the two Gertrudes whom I love so much to know each other," and as Atherton had been Alice Toklas's "youthful idol" everyone was "pleased and charmed" (*ABT* 170–71). Other encounters were less successful, even embarrassing, when a drunk Hopwood clumsily broke glasses and splashed wine on other guests, but Gertrude Stein always forgave him. They had a last pleasant evening in Paris before Hopwood moved to Juan-les-Pins in the south of France in June 1928. On the first day of July he went wading, suffered a heart attack, and died in the water, but not from drowning as was first reported. In a letter to Van Vechten, Stein wrote, "I was awfully fond of him and we did have a charming time together this spring. . . . He was a very wonderful creature and I was always awfully pleased that you had made us friends" (*GSCVV* 165). Hopwood bequeathed the bulk of his substantial estate to the University of Michigan to create awards for aspiring writers. The fund is still in operation.

REFERENCES: Carl Van Vechten, *The Merry-Go-Round*, 1918; *ABT*, 1933; Bruce Kellner, *Carl Van Vechten and the Irreverent Decades*, 1968; Jack Frederick Sharrar, "Avery Hopwood: American Playwright," 1984; *GSCVV*, 1986.

Paul Padgette
Bruce Kellner

HOUSEMAN, JOHN, 22 September 1902– , director, actor, writer. Born Jacques Haussmann in Romania, John Houseman was educated in France and England but has spent much of his life as an actor and director in the United States. In 1933 Virgil Thomson* asked him to direct *Four Saints in Three Acts*,† the opera by him and Gertrude Stein, even though Houseman had not directed previously, and without the promise of a fee. Houseman agreed, thus beginning an association between the two that lasted for over thirty years. The success of the opera brought Houseman favorable attention, and he has participated in a long list of productions ever since in the theater, cinema, radio, and television. In 1937 he joined Orson Welles at the Mercury Theatre, where their most effective venture was *Julius Caesar* in modern dress. He also helped Welles with the famous "War of the Worlds" broadcast and the film classic, *Citizen Kane*. During World War II he worked with the Voice of America broadcasts. Houseman has gone on to enjoy great success in all theatrical media. His films have picked up seven Oscars. In 1973 he himself won an Oscar for best supporting actor for his portrayal of Kingsfield in *The Paper Chase*. His autobiography appeared in 1983.

REFERENCES: *VT*, 1966; Gerald Martin Bordman, ed., *Oxford Companion to American Theatre*, 1984.

Margaret Woodbridge

HUBBELL, LINDLEY WILLIAMS, 3 June 1901– , writer, librarian. Among the young writers on whom Gertrude Stein made a strong impact, Lindley Hubbell was "a nice young man," according to Alice Toklas (*SOA* 55), who had been reading Gertrude Stein's work, and writing to her about it, since the twenties. He published his first collection of poems, *Winter Burning*, in 1938, and sent it as well as his subsequent books to Gertrude Stein. Never an intimate friend or visitor though a sometime correspondent, he was nevertheless the most distinctively literary member of the coterie of young American writers with whom Gertrude Stein was connected during her later years, among the others Samuel Steward,* Max White,* and Wendell Wilcox.* Hubbell wrote a distinguished volume of lectures about Shakespeare as well as other volumes of verse. He was employed at the New York Public Library from 1925, his collected poems were published in 1965, and his autobiography was published in 1971. "A Letter to Gertrude Stein," his moving tribute in verse to her, was published in *Pagany*, April-June 1930, acknowledging her influence. It is printed on pages 115–16 of this book. In 1960 he became a Japanese citizen, and in 1970 he retired from the faculty of Doshisha University in Japan.

REFERENCES: *FF*, 1953; *AAUB*, 1972; *SOA*, 1973.

Bruce Kellner

HUGNET, GEORGES, 1906–26 June 1974, poet, publisher. Georges Hugnet was part of the group of young poets and painters who met in Paris in the 1920s. Virgil Thomson* introduced him to Gertrude Stein in 1927, who took to him "with all her heart" (181). According to Thomson, Hugnet was "small, truculent, and sentimental"; his conversation was "outrageous" and his wit "guttersnipe" (94). Nevertheless, he and Stein developed a special relationship, she apparently taking a maternal interest in the young poet. Hugnet wrote sweet, tender lyrics, but Thomson says that his greatest contribution to literature was his history of Dada (94). He also worked as a publisher, bringing out editions of his own poetry, as well as the writings of others, under the imprint of Editions de la Montagne. Hugnet translated and published Gertrude Stein's portraits and selections from *The Making of Americans*,† and together they translated her "Composition as Explanation."† She then began to work on a translation into English of his suite of poems called *Enfances*. The need to try to catch Hugnet's tone opened up a new vein of poetry to her, and she became very excited about it. For this reason Thomson feels that Hugnet was a strong influence on Stein's own writing. Unfortunately, Stein's free translation of *Enfances* caused a rift between her and Hugnet, and for a time between her and Thomson. The two versions were printed on facing pages in the little magazine *Pagany* in winter 1931. Then Hugnet decided to publish the two versions in book form, again side by side, but without giving equal credit on the title page to the translator. As a result, Stein withheld her version from the publisher, Jeanne Bucher, and at their next meeting she refused to shake hands with Hugnet. He regretted the break and begged Virgil Thomson to do what he could to heal it. Thomson's solution was to use print of equal size for both names. Stein agreed, but Alice Toklas did not, and the break with Hugnet became permanent. However, in 1931 Toklas brought out a limited edition of the translation of *Enfances* under her own strangely appropriate title, *Before the Flowers of Friendship Faded Friendship Faded*.† In the years that followed, Hugnet continued his association with other members of the artistic circle, but his friendship with Gertrude Stein had truly faded.

REFERENCES: *VT*, 1966; *CC*, 1975.

Margaret Woodbridge

HURLBUT, BYRON SATTERLEE, 1865–1929, educator. It is probable but unverifiable that the subject of Gertrude Stein's portrait "Hurlbut" was an English instructor at Harvard during her Radcliffe years. He graduated from Harvard in 1887. From 1895 until 1902 he was the university's recording secretary, and in 1901 he was promoted to assistant professor. "Hurlbut," written in 1927 and published posthumously in *Painted Lace†* gives no hint of its subject's profession; the odd name may be only coincidental.

REFERENCES: *PL*, 1955; *WWA*, 1978.

Bruce Kellner

HUTCHINS, ROBERT MAYNARD, 17 January 1899–14 May 1977, educator. Robert Maynard Hutchins was born in Brooklyn, New York. He attended Oberlin College for two years, but left to spend two years in the U.S. Army with the ambulance corps and two years with the Italian Army. After the war he received his B.A. and LL.B. degrees from Yale, where he later served as dean of the law school. In 1929 he became president of the University of Chicago. In this capacity he was widely known either as the "Boy President" or as "The most dangerous man in American education." He felt that American higher education had lost its true direction, which was to teach students to think. Like Matthew Arnold, he believed that education consisted in putting students in touch with great minds of the past. To achieve this, he brought Mortimer Adler to Chicago, and together they launched the Great Books program. He felt that vocationalism and specialization were the downfall of higher education. Most "dangerous" of all, he cared nothing for athletics and developing social contacts in college. Not for him was the Dewey concept of the well-rounded man. Needless to say, his ideas and concepts still have an impact on American higher education. During Gertrude Stein's American tour Hutchins invited her to speak at the University of Chicago. She gave her "Poetry and Grammar" lecture, with great success. Afterwards, at a dinner at Hutchins's house she, Adler, and Hutchins engaged in an argument about the Great Books program. Stein noted that their list included no books in English. That was because, said Hutchins, there were no ideas in English. To that Gertrude responded angrily; thereupon, Hutchins invited her to teach a seminar at Chicago. Although she had never taught before and was apprehensive, she managed to draw out the students very adroitly on the topic of the epic, much to Hutchins's delight. In 1945 Hutchins was made chancellor of the University of Chicago. He was offered many jobs outside the field of education, but always turned them down. He continued to write and lecture on the need to reform American education. In 1952 he became editor in chief of *Great Books of the Western World* and chairman of the board of the *Encyclopaedia Britannica*.

REFERENCES: *CB*, 1940; *WIR*, 1963; *CC*, 1974.

Margaret Woodbridge

IMBS, BRAVIG, 8 October 1904–early June 1946, writer. Bravig Imbs played the violin and wrote poetry as a child in Milwaukee, Wisconsin. He studied at Dartmouth for two years and then in Paris with composer George Antheil. He worked as a proofreader on the Paris edition of the *Chicago Tribune* and later as music critic for the Paris *Times*. Pavel Tchelitchew's* sister Choura took Imbs to 27 rue de Fleurus for the first time in 1926. He later spent short vacations with Gertrude Stein and Alice Toklas in Belley, near their eventual summer home at Bilignin. He was in their favor until he married a Latvian woman in 1928 with whom neither Stein nor Toklas was taken. They had been generally attentive to the couple's first child, attending the christening and offering gifts; but when his wife became pregnant again, and Imbs planned to situate her on her own near Bilignin—presumably so Stein and Toklas could look after her— the impertinence led to a permanent break. In 1936, Imbs published his auto- biography, *Confessions of Another Young Man*, with an interesting account of the relationship and some of the Stein-Toklas eccentricities. Once he and Stein were out sight-seeing alone, pleasantly enough apparently, until she felt the need to return to her friend who had remained behind: "We must be getting back to Alice. If I'm away from her long I get low in my mind" (240). During World War II, Imbs was with the Office of War Information as a civilian, and in 1944 he established the first open radio station in Cherbourg, following the German occupation in France. Imbs was killed in an automobile accident there in 1946, never reconciled with Gertrude Stein who had declared early on, in *The Auto- biography of Alice B. Toklas*,† that "his aim was to please" (293). He may have been aiming for that when he changed his name from Wilbur Eugene Kenneth Bravig Ingebrechtson.

REFERENCES: *ABT*, 1933; Bravig Imbs, *Confessions of Another Young Man*, 1936; *VT*, 1966; *CC*, 1974.

Paul Padgette
Bruce Kellner

JACOB, MAX, 11 July 1876–5 March 1944, poet, painter. The puzzling Max Jacob was born in Brittany of Jewish parents. After an unhappy childhood he was drafted into the army where he was a miserable failure. Afterward, as a poor young man, he went to Paris and became an inseparable companion of Picasso* and Apollinaire.* Jacob was the clown of the group, already showing the wit and sense of fun that endeared him to many people for the rest of his life. His first book, a children's tale, was published in 1903, by which time he was dabbling in painting, doing gouaches from the dregs of coffee cups, cigarette ashes, and so on. No one took him seriously in 1915 when he tried to convert to Catholicism following his vision of Jesus Christ at a cinema. Finally a priest sanctioned Jacob's mystical Christianity and baptized him; Picasso was godfather. In 1921 Jacob deserted Paris for the cloister of Saint Benoît-sur-Loire, where he lived a life of strict piety like a monk. In 1928 he returned to Paris, but again in 1936 he retreated to the abbey, expecting to end his days there. In 1944 he was arrested by the Gestapo and sent to a concentration camp at Drancy. As his health had never been good and Drancy conditions were hard, he contracted pleurisy and died within a few weeks, after writing a farewell to Jean Cocteau.* Cocteau had been trying to obtain his release but succeeded too late. Max Jacob seems always to have lacked confidence in himself; his puny appearance disappointed him, and his homosexuality filled him with disgust. Picasso's occasional rebuffs further hurt him deeply. Alice Toklas says that Gertrude Stein stopped seeing Jacob because he was dirty and "did not amuse" (*WIR* 132), and Virgil Thomson* agrees, adding that he could be "hard to take" (201). Nevertheless, for a time at least, Jacob was a regular at 27 rue de Fleurus and seems to have known everyone. Like Stein herself at one period, Jacob was attempting to apply the principles of cubism to writing. Much of his poetry—filled as well with anguish over his Jewish heritage and homosexuality—is unintelligibly puzzling, if oddly amusing. Stein always spoke of his work with respect. Much of it remains unpublished, but there is a selection in English, *Drawings and Poems* (1951), and a French selection in *Poésie* (1951).

REFERENCES: *WIR*, 1963; *VT*, 1966; Gerald Kamber, *Max Jacob and the Poetics of Cubism*, 1971; *CC*, 1975; Martin Seymour-Smith, *Who's Who in Twentieth Century Literature*, 1976.

Margaret Woodbridge

JAMES, WILLIAM, 11 January 1842–26 August 1910, psychologist, philosopher. William James, brother of novelist Henry James, is certainly America's most influential philosopher. He came to philosophy by way of painting, medicine, and psychology. His *Principles of Psychology*, 1890, long a classic text, broke new ground in the infant science of psychological investigation and inspired further research. When his interest shifted to philosophy he became the most popular philosopher in America. His collections of essays, *The Will to Believe* and *Varieties of Religious Experience*, investigate religion from the point of view of common sense. James's emphasis on practical value and human happiness led to his pragmatism, a term he adopted from C. S. Peirce. His pragmatism was never of the simplistic kind, which asserts that if something works, it's good, but it was definitely of a kind to appeal to the deepest instincts of Americans, an optimistic belief based on faith in human progress. According to Gertrude Stein herself, James was the most significant influence upon her of anyone at Harvard, and one of the most important influences of her whole life. James was at this time at the height of his powers, with an almost legendary ability to inspire students. He awakened Stein's interest in human personality, which remained her dominant interest throughout her life. She participated eagerly in discussions and experiments on the subconscious, a topic of great interest to James, although, to be sure, she never accepted belief in the subconscious.

James more than once showed his understanding of this highly independent student. On the lovely spring day of the final examination for his seminar, Stein read the questions, then turned in her paper with a note at the top: "Dear Professor James, I am so sorry but really I do not feel a bit like an examination paper in philosophy to-day." James replied: "Dear Miss Stein, I understand perfectly how you feel I often feel like that myself" (*ABT* 97–98). She claimed he gave her the highest grade in the class, but in fact he gave her a C (*GSP* 21). From James she learned stream-of-consciousness, a concept of obvious importance in her writing. After the publication of *The Autobiography of Alice B. Toklas*† the psychologist B. F. Skinner accused her of using automatic writing, a subject she had investigated at Radcliffe. She denied the charge and insisted that her writing was not at all automatic. It was James who advised Gertrude Stein to enter Johns Hopkins University to study medicine and then to go into psychology. She took his advice but did not finish her degree. The two remained in touch and saw each other occasionally through the years. In Paris, when Stein took James to see her pictures, he gasped, then recovered himself and said, "I always told you that you should keep your mind open" (*CC* 182). Clearly, she had taken his advice. Just before his death he wrote to apologize to her for not yet having read *Three Lives*.†

REFERENCES: *ABT*, 1933; Elizabeth Sprigge, *Gertrude Stein: Her Life and Work*, 1957; *Encyclopaedia Britannica* 12, 1962; *GSP*, 1971; *CC*, 1975.

Margaret Woodbridge

JOHNSON, LAMONT, 30 September 1922–   , actor, director. Born in Stockton, California, Lamont Johnson graduated from Pasadena Junior College and UCLA. After touring in Europe as an actor with the USO in 1945 in *The Barretts of Wimpole Street*, with Katharine Cornell,* he studied acting with Sanford Meisner at the Neighborhood School of Theatre and with Lee Strasberg. He married actress Toni Merrill, who had been in the USO company, in 1945. Cornell, visiting Gertrude Stein in Paris with members of the company, read an early version of "Yes Is for a Very Young Man" and took a copy of it back to New York with her. No producer could be found, but Lamont Johnson, who had read a part at 5 rue Christine, began his own negotiations for its production. He impressed Stein as having a sympathetic understanding of the play, and after an extended correspondence between France and California, Johnson arranged to have a production at the Pasadena Playhouse. Stein accepted his suggestions and additions for the text prior to the play's premiere on 13 March 1946. Johnson played the role of Ferdinand, his wife played Constance, and other actors from the USO company were in the cast as well. Thomas Brown Henry directed the production. The first New York production opened at the Cherry Lane Theatre, 6 June 1949, directed by Johnson and Robert Claborne, with Kim Stanley and Beatrice Arthur in the cast. In 1960, Johnson's letters and scripts concerning "Yes Is for a Very Young Man" were given to the Stein Collection at Yale.

Lamont Johnson continues as a director in motion pictures and for television; among his credits is the television dramatization of William Bradford Huie's *The Execution of Private Slovik* in 1974.

REFERENCES: *LO&P*, 1949; *WWA*, 1967; *GSCVV*, 1986.

Paul Padgette
Bruce Kellner

JOLAS, EUGENE, 1894–26 May 1952, editor. Eugene Jolas was born in Union City, New Jersey, but when he was two years old his family moved to Lorraine, culturally divided by French and German occupations. He grew up there, trilingual, always curious about his origins. At sixteen he migrated back to America and worked at menial jobs until he was employed by the New York *Daily News*. After serving in the army during World War I, he returned to his family in Lorraine in 1923. A year later he became a reporter in the *Chicago Tribune* Paris office and then its literary editor, writing a widely read column, "Rambles through Literary Paris." In 1925 Jolas married Maria McDonald from Louisville, Kentucky, and in 1927 they joined forces with Elliot Paul* to create *transition*. It became the leading "little magazine" in the English-speaking world in the late twenties. The first issue, in April 1927, included Gertrude Stein's "An Elucidation," her first effort to explain her creative tactics, but there was trouble between Stein and *transition* from the beginning. The printer jumbled the text of "An Elucidation," and she insisted that a separate, corrected pamphlet be printed; Paul—who had been a friend before the magazine began publication— supplied an apology for the corrected copy. Realizing the significance of Stein's work, the Jolases encouraged further contributions. Nine pieces of various length appeared during the ensuing months, and in the fall of 1928 *transition* carried the full text of *Tender Buttons*.† Stein's own bibliography of her work appeared in February 1929 and the full text of *Four Saints in Three Acts*† in June of that year. Those early issues also included contributions by Hart Crane, Kay Boyle, Archibald MacLeish, Allen Tate, Harry Crosby, and Katherine Anne Porter. An ongoing series of excerpts called "Work in Progress" by James Joyce, later part of his *Finnegans Wake*, irritated Stein, for her own work began to appear less often than his. 1932 saw the last of her *transition* appearances, the same year that she wrote "A Play without Roses" about the Jolases, its first line portending what followed: "It is out of the question that we will meet" (*P&P* 200). When *The Autobiography of Alice B. Toklas*† appeared in 1933, the Jolases joined Henri Matisse,* Georges Braque,* André Salmon, and Tristan Tzara* in publishing a pamphlet, as a supplement to *transition* (February 1935), *Testimony against Gertrude Stein*, to take issue with her references to them. Maria Jolas contended that Stein could "tolerate no relationship that did not bring with it adulation. This was undoubtedly lacking in our otherwise entirely and correct and cordial attitude toward her," and Eugene Jolas said "her attitude was remote from anything I felt or thought. . . . I found her artistic approach both gratuitous and lacking in substance'' (McMillan 73–76). The criticism only served as publicity for Stein's autobiography. Questioned by reporters in Chicago during her lecture tour, she said the charges were ''babyish'' and ''infantish,'' and as for her unflattering comparison of Madame Matisse to a horse, at which her husband had taken offense, Stein claimed she had meant it as a compliment: ''I'm crazy about horses'' (*CC* 402). The Jolases continued *transition* until 1938.

REFERENCES: *ABT*, 1933; *P&P*, 1934; Frederick J. Hoffman, *The Little Magazine*, 1947; *CC*, 1974; Dougald McMillan, *Transition*, 1976.

Paul Padgette
Bruce Kellner

KAHNWEILER, DANIEL-HENRY, 25 June 1884–11 January 1979, art dealer, publisher. Born in Mannheim, Germany, Daniel-Henry Kahnweiler moved to Paris, and in 1907 opened an art gallery. He became what Gertrude Stein later called a dealer who ''like[d] adventure'' (*ABT*, 297), meaning that he was willing to take risks on unknown artists. He began by supporting the fauves, then became a friend and supporter of all the cubists. Among those he especially championed are Pablo Picasso,* Georges Braque,* and Juan Gris.* He mounted a Braque show after the artist had been refused by the Autumn Salon, and he gave Gris financial help until World War I, when, as a German, Kahnweiler had to take refuge in Switzerland and could send no money. As a result, Gris's situation became desperate. Through their mutual interest in painting Kahnweiler had met Gertrude and Leo* Stein shortly after their arrival in Paris. He always preferred Gertrude to Leo, and later on grew to admire Alice B. Toklas. The Kahnweilers became frequent guests at 27 rue de Fleurus. Because of the close relationship Kahnweiler saw between Gertrude Stein's prose and cubist painting, Stein's writing interested him and he decided to publish some of it. In 1924 he planned to bring out ''The Gertrude Stein Birthday Book'' for Picasso's son, Paul, with etchings by Picasso. This project never reached fulfillment, but his second project, *A Book Concluding with As a Wife Has a Cow a Love Story*,† illustrated with lithographs by Gris, was successfully executed by the three in 1926 and published in a limited edition. In 1928 Kahnweiler published Stein's *A Village*,† after which he had to abandon the publishing business altogether. While he admired Stein's knowledge of English poets, he found her lack of interest in French poets, especially Apollinaire* and Max Jacob,* shocking. Although Kahnweiler had become a French citizen before World War II, as a Jew he had to go into hiding in the country. He and his wife lived under false names in the department of Lot-et-Garonne. After the war he joyfully reunited with his Paris acquaintances. Kahnweiler was always a good friend to Gertrude Stein and to the young artists and poets whose work he admired. Through his support he made it possible for them to continue. After Gertrude Stein's death he wrote a warm tribute to her in his introduction to *Painted Lace*,† the fifth volume in the Yale edition of her unpublished work.

REFERENCES: *ABT*, 1933; *PL*, 1955; *CC*, 1975; *Samuel Hunter, ed., Oxford Companion to Twentieth Century Art*, 1981.

Margaret Woodbridge

LANE, JOHN 14 March 1854–2 February 1925, publisher. John Lane was the British publisher of the Bodley Head, founded in 1887, and of *The Yellow Book*, edited by Aubrey Beardsley and Henry Harland, published between 1894 and 1897. Born in Devon, Lane came up to London to work as a clerk in the railway clearing office when he was fourteen. He had a feeling for old books and spent his off-hours browsing in bookshops, and by 1887 he had collected enough of them to open one of his own, the Bodley Head, in Vigo Street. The name was inspired by the Rembrandt Head Galleries, located on the same street, and by Bodley, the most notable name from his village in Devon. Lane and his partner, Elkin Mathews, also from Devon, soon began publishing in a limited way, first with a slim volume of poems by the then unknown Richard Le Gallienne, *My Ladies' Sonnets*. This led to books by Oscar Wilde, Max Beerbohm, Saki (H. H. Munro), H. G. Wells, and Arnold Bennett. By the time Gertrude Stein first met him, Lane was one of the most respected and important British publishers. Their meeting has a complicated history. Myra Edgerly, a San Francisco miniaturist painter famous in London for portraits of the royal family, had come to Paris for further study. Mildred Aldrich* brought her to 27 rue de Fleurus, delighting Alice Toklas, who remembered having seen Edgerly in their youth in San Francisco at a Mardi Gras ball, "very tall and very beautiful and very brilliant" (*ABT* 154–55). Edgerly knew John Lane, wrote to him of her enthusiasm for Stein's writing, and urged Stein to go to London to meet Lane. Lane considered bringing out an English edition of *Three Lives*,† encouraged by his wife's positive reaction to the book, but no contract was signed. In the spring of 1914, Lane visited Stein in Paris, still interested in *Three Lives*. On the last day of July that year she signed a contract at the Bodley Head office in London and, later in the day, departed with Toklas for a weekend with their new friends, Evelyn and Alfred North Whitehead,* at Lockridge near the Salisbury Plain. They stayed on at the Whiteheads' urging, only to find themselves stranded for several weeks when the war broke out. John Lane issued *Three Lives* the following year, 1915, made up of imported, unbound copies of the 1909 American edition of the book, with his own imprint on the title page. In 1920 Lane reprinted the volume, and in 1927, two years after his death, the Bodley Head firm asked to republish it, probably because of the favorable publicity created in England following Stein's lectures at Cambridge and Oxford. Instead, *Three Lives* was published by John Rodker in London in 1927, but the Bodley Head published *Useful Knowledge*† in 1929, prepared from imported American sheets. In 1933 the house John Lane had founded published its own edition of *The Autobiography of Alice B. Toklas*† and again in 1935 as part of its Weekend Library.

REFERENCES: *ABT*, 1933; Sheila Birkenhead, *Peace in Piccadilly*, 1958; *GSBIB*, 1975.

Paul Padgette

LASCAUX, ELIE, 5 April 1888–? 1968, painter. "His painting has a white light that is a light and anything a village, green trees any part of Paris, Bourges, all and any french thing can be in that white light which is the light that Elie Lascaux has inside him," Gertrude Stein wrote for the catalogue of an exhibition of Lascaux's works held at the Arts Club of Chicago in 1936 ([2]). Born in Limoges, Lascaux worked as an actor and singer as well as draftsman for an architect and as a porcelain painter. He taught himself to paint as a German prisoner of war during World War I, and exhibited with the Autumn Salon in Paris beginning in 1921. He painted landscapes, street and city scenes, and still lifes in a manner influenced by Japanese painting. Lascaux was married to the sister-in-law of art dealer Daniel-Henry Kahnweiler,* and in 1928 illustrated Stein's *A Village. Are You Ready Not Yet*,† published by Kahnweiler. He also illustrated *Tric Trac du Ciel* by Antonin Artaud. On her return from her American tour, Stein discussed with Lascaux the excellence of American design in everyday objects, for which the best materials are used for the cheapest things, "the square books and the old Ford car" (*EA* 232). She wrote that Lascaux "having always lived in an isolated country and coming to Paris thought the automobiles going around the Arc de Triomphe were a carousel and it only slowly dawned on him that they were always different cars not the same ones" (*EA* 232). Alice Toklas visited an exhibition of his works in Paris in 1951 and wrote to Donald Gallup* about a change in his painting: "the color is warmer more closely related to the composition and without losing any of the light which was so characteristically his special gift. . . . The integrity of Lascaux's character is beyond mere praise" (*SOA* 245).

REFERENCES: *EPH*, 1936; *EA*, 1937; Hans Vollmer, ed., *Allegemeines Lexicon der Bildenden Künstler des XX Jahrhunderts*, 1956; *CC*, 1974.

Priscilla Oppenheimer

LAURENCIN, MARIE, 1885–9 June 1956, painter, illustrator. As a young art student, Marie Laurencin had been introduced to the poet and art critic Guillaume Apollinaire* by Picasso,* who brought them both to 27 rue de Fleurus in the early years of the Stein salon. Laurencin inspired some of Apollinaire's best love lyrics and blossomed in the world of artists and poets into which he took her. She painted industriously, exhibited at the Independent Salon after 1907, and sold her first picture to Gertrude Stein, a group portrait of herself, Apollinaire, Picasso and Fernande Olivier,* and their dog. Laurencin was nearsighted and plain, with a high, beautifully modulated voice, and "temperamentally reminded us of some strange mythological animal," Alice Toklas wrote (*WIR* 35). Since Apollinaire's mother refused to allow them to marry, Laurencin lived with her mother, who hated men, in a strange convent-like atmosphere. According to

Stein's report of the famous Rousseau* banquet of 1908, Laurencin had drunk too many aperitifs beforehand and had to be dragged up the hill to Picasso's studio, where Olivier at first refused to let her in. Later, Olivier said, Laurencin fell into a tray of jam tarts and went around in her sticky state hugging the guests until Apollinaire sent her home. Stein reported that she returned later, bruised but sober, and sang some old Norman songs. After her mother's death Laurencin went through a period of emotional instability and broke with Apollinaire around 1912. She married a German painter with whom she lived unhappily in Spain during the war, at which time she provided illustrations for Francis Picabia's* *Dada Review*. She returned happily to Paris, divorced, after the war and designed sets and costumes for the Ballet Russes de Monte Carlo and the Comédie Française and painted portraits of Parisian society women. Besides her work in oil and watercolor, Laurencin did etchings, lithographs, and book illustrations, and she wrote poetry. Her work was exhibited in France and in New York until her death, and she was made an officer of the Legion of Honor by the French government in 1949. Stein and Laurencin met from time to time by accident during the twenties and thirties. Laurencin had begun to teach to supplement her income, Stein wrote in *Everybody's Autobiography*,† and her pupils found her very amusing: "She had grown stout by then. . . . but it made her just that more pleasing" (*EA* 33). Laurencin had not been pleased with what Stein had written in *The Autobiography of Alice B. Toklas*,† but Stein listened to her explain at length how she felt, and they embraced as they had always done. Laurencin remained a valued friend of Alice Toklas after Stein's death. Toklas was distressed by Laurencin's sudden death, probably from exhaustion, in 1956, and remembered her then as having been an enchanting and legendary character in the good old days.

REFERENCES: *EA*, 1937; *NYT*, 9 June 1956; Roger Shattuck, *The Banquet Years*, 1968; *SOA*, 1973; *CC*, 1974; Chris Petteys, *An International Dictionary of American Women Artists*, 1982.

Priscilla Oppenheimer

LEVY, HARRIET LANE, 1867–1950, writer. Harriet Levy was born in San Francisco to an upper-middle-class Jewish family and graduated from the University of California at Berkeley in 1886. She accompanied her friends, Michael* and Sarah Stein to Paris in 1904–1905 and stayed with them at 58 rue Madame. In San Francisco she had lived next door to Alice Toklas*—a friendship she described in her memoir, *920 O'Farrell Street*—and when she returned to Paris in December 1906, Toklas accompanied her. They took an apartment not far from the Michael Steins. As travelers in Italy the following year, they shared quarters again, by which time they knew all the Steins. Levy's account of the legendary and amusing 1908 banquet in honor of Henri Rousseau,* unpublished until long after her death, claims that she was called upon to sing—she shouted it, she wrote—the yell of the University of California, garnering a hearty response from everybody: "Gertrude beamed her approval. To this day I have never relinquished the memory of myself on my feet . . . and the enthusiastic reception'' (2–3). Levy returned to San Francisco in the summer of 1910, by which time the Stein-Toklas alliance was firmly rooted. They had not wanted to hasten Levy's decision to leave, but she was aware that they were contemplating a shared life. Toklas moved to 27 rue de Fleurus in September 1910. These events and arrangements resulted in a wry word-portrait, ''Harriet,'' beginning, ''She said she did not have any plans for the summer,'' and ending, ''she was not then answering anything when any one asked her what were her plans for the winter'' (*P&P* 105–7). The playful parallel smooths over what must have been difficult in actuality. In addition to her 1947 memoir, Harriet Levy published a volume of poems, *I Love to Talk about Myself*, in a limited edition. She died in Carmel at age eighty-three. Her impressive collection of paintings, including Henri Matisse's* sketch of her, is in the San Francisco museum of Modern Art.

REFERENCES: *P&P* 1934; Harriet Lane Levy, *920 O'Farrell Street*, 1947; *CC* 1974; *Babt*, 1977; ''A Supper in Montmartre,'' *Bancroftiana*, April 1986.

Paul Padgette
Priscilla Oppenheimer

LEWIS, LLOYD DOWNS, 2 May 1891–21 April 1949, journalist, historian. Born in Indiana of Quaker parents, Lloyd Lewis wrote for newspapers and worked as a publicist before publishing *Myths after Lincoln* and *Chicago: The History of Its Reputation* in 1929. In 1932 his standing as a scholarly historian was secured with *Sherman: Fighting Prophet*. During her 1934–1935 lecture tour, Gertrude Stein let him read the manuscript of her biographical meditation on Ulysses S. Grant from her then unpublished *Four in America*.† After he had written favorably of it in one of his newspaper columns, she urged him to write a book with her about Grant. ''I like the word collaboration,'' she wrote, ''and I have the kind of imagination of how it could take place'' (*EA* 270), although nothing came of the proposal. Subsequently, she wrote one of her rare reviews when Lewis co-authored *Oscar Wilde Discovers America* with Henry Justin Smith, declaring of Lewis, ''Anything that is American is in him and he is in it'' (*RAB* 56). Lewis's final work, *Captain Sam Grant*, was published posthumously in 1951.

REFERENCES: *EA*, 1937; *FF*, 1953; *RAB*, 1973.

Bruce Kellner

LIPCHITZ, JACQUES, 22 August 1891–26 May 1973, sculptor. Born in Lithuania, student of engineering at the insistence of his father who opposed an artistic career for him, Chaim Jacob Lipchitz had become by his death one of the foremost sculptors of the twentieth century. In 1909 his mother sent him to Paris to study at the École des Beaux-Arts, and after a brief stint in the Russian army and a medical discharge he returned to Paris in 1913. Introduced to cubist painting by Diego Rivera, he was one of the first to apply the principles of cubism to sculpture, and according to Hilton Kramer became ''an artist of intense power and originality who helped create the basic grammar of modern art and then aspired to go beyond his own creation'' (*NYT* 18). Stein had known Lipchitz only slightly before World War I, but shortly after the war they ran into each other on the street and Lipchitz asked her to pose for him. Although she did not like sculpture, she agreed to do so. Stein enjoyed the posing and Lipchitz's gossip, but she grew annoyed as the sessions went on all the warm spring of 1920 in his excessively hot studio. Lipchitz's elegant bronze head of Stein, now in the Baltimore Museum of Art, shows her as a ''massive inscrutable Buddha,'' the hollowed eyes giving an impression of ''shadowed introspection'' (Lipchitz 60). Although it pleased her, she did not buy it, and for many years thereafter they did not see each other. Then, through Jane Heap,* they had a tender reunion in 1939, when she claimed Lipchitz said he was fonder of Stein than almost anybody (*SW* 192). Stein looked to him at that time like ''a shrivelled old rabbi,'' and he began to do another portrait of her which, however, progressed only as far as two preliminary models in bronze (Lipchitz 60). During the twenties Lipchitz had turned from cubism to more fluid forms, and during the following decade began sculpting monumental allegorical subjects such as his *Myth of Prometheus*. He spent most of World War II in the United States, and in 1958 became an American citizen. Stein wrote ''one of her most lovely protraits of him,'' in 1926, she said in *The Autobiography of Alice B. Toklas*† (*SW* 192), using the German spelling of his name *Lipschitz* as she had in the portrait: ''Like and like likely and likely likely and likely like and like,'' it begins; ''When I know him I look at him for him and I look at him for him and I look at him for him when I know him,'' it concludes. ''I like you very much'' (*P&P* 63–64).

REFERENCES: *P&P*, 1934; *SW*, 1962; *NYT*, 28 May 1973; Jacques Lipchitz, *My Life in Sculpture*, 1972; *CC*, 1974.

Priscilla Oppenheimer

LOCHER, ROBERT, 1888–18 June 1956, illustrator, decorator. Robert Locher was the closest friend of Charles Demuth.* They were playmates as children and later shared artistic interests. Locher became a designer, interior decorator, illustrator for *Vanity Fair* and several avant-garde magazines, and was an associate editor of *House and Garden*. His interiors appeared in many public buildings and, in addition, he taught at the Parsons School of Design and the Franklin School of Professional Art in New York. In the 1920s he made numerous trips to Paris, where he became acquainted with Gertrude Stein, who later did a word portrait of his wife, Beatrice Howard. Stein and Alice Toklas saw the Lochers socially as well as frequently by accident at the bank they shared. ''[I]n fact we met them at two banks,'' Stein wrote to Carl Van Vechten* through whom she had met them, ''the less money we all have the more we seem to meet in banks but that again is on strictly classic lines'' (*GSCVV* 98).

REFERENCES: *NYT*, 21 June 1956; Betsy Fahlman, *Pennsylvania Modern: Charles Demuth of Lancaster*, 1983; *GSCVV*, 1986

Margaret Woodbridge

LOEB, HAROLD, 18 October 1891–20 January 1974, writer. As editor of the avant-garde literary quarterly, *Broom*, Harold Loeb requested that Gertrude Stein write something for it "as fine as Melanctha," her story in *Three Lives*† (*ABT* 253). Promptly, then, she wrote "As Fine as Melanctha," although the lengthy verbal doodle didn't get into print until 1954. Loeb did publish some other pieces in *Broom*, however: "If You Had Three Husbands" in three installments in 1922, and "Wear" in 1923. Loeb began his career far removed from the Paris literati, first in Canada and then in California in various commercial business enterprises. He was associated with poet Alfred Kreymborg in *Broom*, which during its brief life published work by many later celebrated figures from the twenties. Loeb wrote three novels, notably *The Professors Like Vodka*, about the Paris literary scene, in 1927, and his memoirs, *The Way It Was*, in 1959. Stein's portrait of Loeb is about three people, "La Fontaine and the pair" (*P&P* 208), but a more familiar portrait lies in the character of Robert Cohn in Ernest Hemingway's* *The Sun Also Rises*.

REFERENCES: *ABT*, 1933; *P&P*, 1934; *AFAM*, 1954; Harold Loeb, *The Way It Was*, 1959; *DLB* 4, 1980.

Bruce Kellner
Priscilla Oppenheimer

LOY [LOWY HAWEISS CRAVAN], MINA [GERTRUDE], 27 December 1882–25 September 1966, poet, artist. Mina Loy—"beautiful, intelligent, sympathetic and gay" according to Alice Toklas (*WIR* 76)—first came to 27 rue de Fleurus in 1905 as the wife of painter Stephen Haweiss. They were among the first to become interested in Gertrude Stein's work. Haweiss "did however plead for commas" in *The Making of Americans*;† Stein allowed him two, then took them back, noting that Mina Loy "had always been able to understand," even without commas (*ABT* 162). Mina—or perhaps Jemima—Lowy was born in England and studied art in Munich with Angelo Jank and in London with Augustus Johns before settling in Paris, where she changed her name to Loy. Her remarkable life has been outlined and the best of her work preserved in *The Last Lunar Baedeker*, sensitively edited by Roger Conover, on her centenary anniversary, following intermittent decades of obscurity, many of them self-imposed. In 1906 she was elected to the Autumn Salon; in 1913 her paintings and drawings were exhibited in London; and in 1914 her poems began to appear in little magazines in America, *Camera Work, Trend*, and *Rogue* among others. Mabel Dodge* had become a friend in Italy, and Carl Van Vechten* had begun to act as her unpaid press agent in America. At about the same time, she was abandoned by Haweiss, by whom she had three children, one of whom had died in infancy. Also, in 1913, she was identified both personally and professionally with the futurists, and in 1914 she became a nurse in an Italian hospital. In New York after 1916, she acted with the Provincetown Playhouse; she edited little magazines; she gave poetry readings; she made her living by creating lampshades and designing dresses; and she met Arthur Cravan, poet, boxer, art historian, and mock suicide, with a penchant for removing his clothes in public. They were married in Mexico City in 1918 and opened a boxing school that failed. When Loy became pregnant she left for Europe by way of Buenos Aires; Cravan was to follow, but she never saw him again, and there is no record of what happened to him. After longer and shorter periods in New York and Florence, Loy settled in Paris in 1923 with her daughters—in 1921 Haweiss had kidnapped their son who died shortly thereafter—and supported herself making more lampshades and copyrighting attendant lighting devices. By that time she seems to have encountered everyone from Sigmund Freud to Kiki of Montparnasse and virtually the full membership of Gertrude Stein's Lost Generation. On 4 February 1927 she gave a lecture on Stein's work at Natalie Clifford Barney's* salon, and two years later she published a two-part sympathetic dissection of Stein's work in Ford Madox Ford's* *Transatlantic Review*. This protracted series of one- and two-sentence paragraphs, reprinted in *The Last Lunar Baedeker*, anticipates some of the critical attitudes of Thornton Wilder* and Donald Sutherland,* free of biographical readings and predicated entirely on "a most dexterous discretion in the placement and replacement of her phrases, of inversion of the same phrase sequences" in Stein's early work and telescoping "time and space and the subjective and objective in a way that obviates interval and interposition" in what followed (289–91). Loy leaves "the ultimate elucidation of Gertrude Stein to infinity" (299). After serving as her art-dealer son-in-law's Paris agent for a few years, Loy settled into two decades of virtual obscurity on and around New York's Bowery, still writing and painting; then she moved to Aspen, Colorado, to live near her daughters. When in 1957 someone wanted to issue a book of her poems, she claimed she had never been a poet, and in 1959 when an exhibition of her work was given in New York, she did not attend. Mina Loy's early poem about Gertrude Stein is reprinted on page 114.

REFERENCES: *ABT*, 1933; *WIR*, 1963; Mina Loy, *The Last Lunar Baedeker*, 1982.
Margaret Woodbridge
Bruce Kellner

LUHAN, MABEL [GANSON EVANS] DODGE [STERNE], 26 February 1879– 18 August 1962, writer, arts patron. Mabel Ganson was born into a wealthy Buffalo family and educated at private schools in New York City. In 1900 she married Karl Evans as a step in abandoning Buffalo. She bore him her only child, John, two years later, and the following year Evans died in a hunting accident. En route to Paris with her son, Mabel Evans met wealthy Edwin Dodge of Boston. He pursued her for some weeks until she agreed to marry him, and they settled in Florence in the fall of 1905 where their combined wealth allowed them to purchase the Villa Curonia, a Renaissance palazzo built by the Medicis in the fifteenth century. It became famous during the next few years as a gathering place for celebrities from both sides of the Atlantic. In the spring of 1911 Mildred Aldrich* took Mabel Dodge to 27 rue de Fleurus to meet Gertrude Stein. They became immediate admirers of one another's vastly different talents. Carl Van Vechten* later described Mabel Dodge's peculiar attraction: "She spends her energy in living, in watching other people live, in watching them make their silly mistakes, in helping them make their silly mistakes. She is a dynamo. She will give you a good deal" (119). She returned to Florence from that first meeting with Stein bearing several chapters from *The Making of Americans*,† later judging it "one of the most remarkable things I have ever read. . . . It is almost frightening to come up against reality in language in this way" (*FF* 52). A few months later, Gertrude Stein wrote "Portrait of Mabel Dodge at the Villa Curonia" while she and Alice Toklas were guests there. After its accessible, familiar opening line, "The days are wonderful and the nights are wonderful and the life is pleasant" (*SW* 465), its abstractions suggest some of those in *Tender Buttons*.† Mabel Dodge had three hundred copies printed and bound in Florentine wallpaper and took them back to America in the fall of 1912 when she returned to enroll her son in school. The portrait was then available to a wide variety of callers at the justly celebrated salon she had soon established at 23 Fifth Avenue, just on the fringe of Greenwich Village. At the suggestion of muckraker Lincoln Steffens, and encouraged by an old friend Hutchins Hapgood,* and a new one, Carl Van Vechten, she held a weekly open house, supplying not only space but food for a remarkable confluence of the artistic and political worlds then operating in New York. Emma Goldman, Walter Lippmann, Bill Haywood, and Margaret Sanger represented various social issues, and the young engagé poet John Reed bridged the gap between their concerns and those of the artists in attendance. (By that time Mabel Dodge had separated from her second husband and was soon to become Reed's lover.) Max Eastman was another socialist poet in regular attendance. So were establishment poets like Edwin Arlington Robinson and effete pretenders like Donald Evans.* Marsden Hartley,* Andrew Dasburg, Charles Demuth,* Arthur B. Davies,* and Max Weber represented serious painting at the 23 Fifth Avenue evenings; stage designers Robert Edmond Jones and Lee Simonson attended too; so did novelists Neith Boyce and Edna Kenton; actresses Fania Marinoff* and Helen Westley; and Alfred Stieglitz.* Once the salon was firmly established, Mabel Dodge became involved in the then notorious 69th Armory Exhibition in February and March 1913, the first avant-garde art exhibition in America, and wrote "Speculations, or Post-Impressionists in Prose" for *Arts and Decoration*, which contained the first critical analysis of Gertrude Stein's writing to appear in America. Stein was "as proud as punch," she wrote after the article had eventually reached her (*MS* 35), although the publicity Dodge received from her efforts began to have a cooling effect on their friendship. It had been in the making. In Florence the year before, according to Dodge, Gertrude Stein "sent me such a strong look over the table that it seemed to cut across the air to me in a band of electrified steel—a smile traveling across on it—powerful—Heavens!'' Toklas interpreted it as a flirtation and fled from the room. Subsequently, Dodge believed, Toklas had labored to separate them (*EE* 332–33). Mabel Dodge spent the summers of 1913 and 1914 in Italy, but she did not see Stein again. In 1917 she married painter Maurice Sterne* and moved to New Mexico, settling in Taos where she created an art colony. By 1923 she had divorced Sterne to marry Antonio Lujan—Americanized to Lu-han—a Pueblo Indian. Until her death at the age of eighty-one, she acted as hostess and patron to many visitors, including D. H. Lawrence, Georgia O'Keeffe, Willa Cather, Andrew Dasburg, Marsden Hartley, Christopher Isherwood, and many others. Her friendship with Gertrude Stein was professionally as well as personally over by 1913, but they were kept abreast of each other's activities by their mutual friend Carl Van Vechten. In 1934, when Stein made her lecture tour across the United States, Mabel Dodge Luhan made two overtures to see her, but Toklas successfully prevented any encounter. Mabel Dodge Luhan's six volumes of memoirs are a valuable record of a significant contribution to American arts and letters: *Lorenzo in Taos*, 1932; *Background*, 1933; *European Experiences* and *Winter in Taos*, 1935; *Movers and Shakers*, 1936; *Edge of Taos Desert*, 1937; *Taos and Its Artists*, 1947.

REFERENCES: Carl Van Vechten, *Peter Whiffle*, 1922; *EE*, 1935; *MS*, 1936; *FF*, 1953; Lois Palken Rudnick, *Mabel Dodge Luhan*, 1984; Patricia Everett, *Mabel Dodge: The Salon Years*, 1985.

                                                                              Paul Padgette
                                                                              Bruce Kellner

LUTZ, [JOHN] MARK, 31 March 1901–24 November 1968, journalist, publicist. Born in the midwest but raised in Richmond, Virginia, Mark Lutz was a book reviewer and reporter for the city's two newspapers, the *Times-Dispatch* and *News Leader*. Reclusive by nature, he seemed to his contemporaries well-bred but aloof, and everything in his behavior seemed ''correct, guarded, and carefully planned,'' according to his biographer Larry Hall (6). Lutz knew Hunter Stagg* but apparently he had no close friend until Stagg introduced him to Carl Van Vechten* in 1931. Despite the twenty-year difference in their ages they were intimate companions for ten years and warm friends afterward until Van Vechten's death. In June 1934 they visited Gertrude Stein and Alice Toklas in Bilignin; when Stein and Toklas in turn came to Richmond, Virginia, Lutz arranged for Stein's lecture at the Women's Club there—her only lecture in a nonacademic setting—and at the University of Richmond; also, he seems to have been involved in arranging her other appearances in Virginia as well, a lecture at William and Mary College and an impromptu chat at Sweet Briar College. Subsequently, Lutz and Stein corresponded casually, usually about her work, candidly and admiringly on both sides. Lutz moved from Richmond to Philadelphia in 1937 to become a publicist for Philco; he died there of a heart attack at the age of sixty-seven, leaving his collection of 13,000 photographs by Carl

Van Vechten to the Philadelphia Museum of Art; an eclectic collection of paintings that included works by Georges Braque,* Georgia O'Keeffe, Florine Stettheimer,* Alexandre Cabanel, Kristians Tonny,* Giorgio de Chirico, Mrs. Thomas Eakins, Mina Loy,* Andrew Dasburg, Abraham Walkowitz, Mary Bell, Don Bachardy, Alfred Sisley, Maurice Grosser,* and a number of late Florentine and Venetian canvases, eventually dispersed through bequests and at auction; and a valuable collection of modern first editions, which he willed to to the University of Richmond, including full runs of Ernest Hemingway,* William Faulkner, F. Scott Fitzgerald,* Ronald Firbank, James Joyce, and of course Carl Van Vechten and Gertrude Stein.

REFERENCES: *EA*, 1937; Bruce Kellner, *Friends and Mentors*, 1979; Larry Hall, "A Van Vechten Pose," *Glasgow Newsletter*, October 1982, March 1983.

Bruce Kellner

LYNES, GEORGE PLATT, 15 April 1907–6 December 1955, photographer. When he was eighteen years old, George Platt Lynes published Gertrude Stein's *Descriptions of Literature* as the second of his As Stable pamphlets, a name Stein had given to his fledgling enterprise. Other booklets were of work by Ernest Hemingway* and René Crevel.* At the time, Lynes was working in bookshops— eventually his own—the Park Place Bookshop in Englewood, New Jersey—but he turned to photography as a permanent career in 1928. In addition to a masterful portrait of Gertrude Stein in 1931, he "fixed the face of nearly every artist and writer and musician of importance in his epoch, in a unique attitude," as Lincoln Kirstein later wrote of his work (Walsh 463). Lynes's fashion photographs in *Harper's Bazaar* and *Vogue*, his male nude studies, and his ballet photographs give further evidence of his talent. He is one of "The Five Georges" in Stein's 1932 *Operas and Plays*; and in *To Do*, her 1940 alphabetical children's book, under *G*, he is the "George" along with "Jelly Gus and Gertrude," a gray-haired boy born on April Fool's Day who tries to take photographs of cookies (*A&B* 13–14). A more accessible portrait of George Platt Lynes than either of these may be found in Donald Windham's novel *Tanaquil*.

REFERENCES: *EPH*, 1926; *O&P*, 1932; *A&B*, 1957; Donald Windham, *Tanaquil*, 1977; George Walsh, et al., eds., *Contemporary Photographers*, 1982.

Bruce Kellner

McALMON, ROBERT, 9 March 1896–2 February 1956, writer, publisher. Some years after their break, Gertrude Stein allowed that Robert McAlmon's "abundance" appealed to her: "he could go on writing, but she complained that it was dull" (*ABT* 269). He was born in Clifton, Kansas, the tenth child of a Presbyterian minister, and spent his childhood moving with his nomadic family through South Dakota. He attended the University of Minnesota briefly and enrolled at the University of Southern California at Los Angeles when his family moved west in 1917. Whatever the school, however, McAlmon was discontented with his teachers, so he joined the newly formed air corps briefly during the war. In 1919 he spent another year at the University of Southern California, writing short fiction and poetry, some of which was published in Harriet Monroe's *Poetry*. A year later he left California for Greenwich Village, where he and William Carlos Williams* founded and edited *Contact*, publishing material by Wallace Stevens, Marianne Moore, Hilda Doolittle, and of course by themselves in its four issues, 1921–1922. McAlmon's future took a new turn when Williams introduced him to Winifred Bryher,* daughter of the English shipping magnate Sir John Ellerman. After they married, McAlmon was surprised that the family not only accepted him but supported him. Much of his publishing capital came from his father-in-law all through his subsequent publishing career, although his marriage was one of convenience. McAlmon settled in Paris; his novelist wife shuttled between England and France. In 1922, touring the Dôme-Rotonde-Coupolé circuit, he met William Bird, owner of the avant-garde Three Mountains Press, to found Contact Editions at 29 Quai d'Anjou. They published Ernest Hemingway's* *Three Stories and Ten Poems* as well as work by James Joyce, Ezra Pound,* and William Carlos Williams. One of their first titles was Mc-Almon's own *A Hasty Bunch*, issued in 1922. Although he did not meet Gertrude Stein until 1924, when Mina Loy* introduced them, he had asked her to contribute to a proposed volume, *The Contact Collection of Contemporary Writers*. She sent him "Two Women," word portraits of the Cone* sisters, Baltimore art collectors who were her longtime friends. After their first meeting, McAlmon left 27 rue de Fleurus "thinking that one could become fond of Gertrude Stein if she would quit being an oracle, descend from the throne-chair, and not grow panicky every time someone doubted her statements, or even bluntly disagreed" (Knoll 202). In his autobiography, *Being Geniuses Together*, written in 1934 and published in 1938, McAlmon recounts his version of publishing Stein's *The Making of Americans*,† the largest single venture of Contact Editions. In January 1925, when he agreed to do it, there was mutual disagreement and frustration over the contract. An edition of five hundred copies was agreed upon when Stein assured him of the sale of fifty copies to her friends. Gentlemen's agreements are often open to misinterpretation. Independent of McAlmon, Stein negotiated through her self-appointed agent, Jane Heap,* to interest New York and London publishers in distributing part of the edition. When the cost of printing the 925-page volume came into dispute, McAlmon offered to let Stein purchase the books or bid for them, since not even those fifty copies had all sold; otherwise, he wrote, he would simply pulp them all a year after publication (*FF* 190). Stein did not buy the run, nor did McAlmon carry out his threat; the books simply disappeared and, with them, any further dealings between Stein and McAlmon. In 1927, he and Bryher divorced; he traveled to Spain, Germany, France, and Mexico, finally settling in Desert Hot Springs, California, after he developed tuberculosis. In editing selections from McAlmon's writings, Robert E. Knoll assessed him as "the prototype of the lost generation of whatever century. Impatient with inherited values, he was yet unable to arrive at new values he could accept. . . . At the end his integrity was all that remained of his high aspirations'' (355).

REFERENCES: *ABT*, 1933; *FF*, 1953; Robert E. Knoll, ed., *McAlmon and the Lost Generation*, 1962; Robert McAlmon and Kay Boyle, *Being Geniuses Together*, 1968.

Paul Padgette

McBRIDE, HENRY, 1867–31 March 1962, art critic. *The Autobiography of Alice B. Toklas*† pays tribute to ''Henry McBride who used to keep Gertrude Stein's name before the public all those tormented years. Laugh if you like, he used to say to her detractors, but laugh with and not at her, in that way you will enjoy it all much better'' (149). Stein and McBride met through Mildred Aldrich* in the spring of 1913. After that, he kept her name before the public in his regular essays in art criticism in the New York *Sun*, aligning her writing with her collection of paintings as ''a strange jargon quite as queer as the pictures'' (51), and identifying her as ''Patron Saint of the new artists'' (53) in his columns, preserved posthumously in *The Flow of Art*. Moreover, he attempted to have her early plays produced in America, and in his columns printed ''M. Vollard and Cezanne'' and passages from one of her plays and one of her letters. McBride's ''congenital contempt for successful people,'' as Mildred Aldrich described it to Gertrude Stein, may have had some influence on his attraction to her writing (*CC* 193). He was distrustful of success, aware of how an audience's demands could influence an artist's work. ''It ruins you, it ruins you,'' he told her: ''the best that I can wish you, he always said, is to have no success. It is the only good thing. He was firm about that'' (*ABT* 149). Stein's own preoccupations with ''identity'' and ''entity,'' writing for herself or for the audience she suddenly had in the mid-thirties after so many years of obscurity, must have reminded her of McBride's early attitude. This ''most astute and entertaining art critic of his generation,'' as James Mellow described him (*CC* 193), was born into a Pennsylvania Quaker family and from an early age sought a career as an artist. He began by illustrating seed catalogs, but by the turn of the century he was affiliated with the Educational Alliance, and shortly he had numbered among his pupils the sculptors Jacob Epstein and Jo Davidson* and Isadora Duncan's* immortalizer in the graphic arts, Abraham Walkowitz. For three decades the New York *Sun* carried his byline as art critic, and he served in that capacity after 1920 for the magazine *Dial*, and as editor of *Creative Art* in 1930–1932. During that long and productive career, he counted among his discoveries the work of the American painter Thomas Eakins and the English poet-artist William Blake. He covered the notorious 69th Regimental Armory Exhibition and the first Cézannes at the Metropolitan in 1913, the debuts of Charles Demuth* and Georgia O'Keeffe, the openings of the Museum of Modern Art and the Whitney Museum, retrospectives of Mary Cassatt and introductions of Jackson Pollock, even the work of Walt Disney. In the remarkable span and scope of Henry McBride's work, the art of the first half of the twentieth century has an engrossing critical chronology. It is firmly grounded in his early academic training in the Artists and Artisans Institute, his efforts at painting and sketching, his teaching, an all-embracing self-education influenced by art critics Bernard Berenson* and Roger Fry, and by his own visionary eye. As many subsequent critics have pointed out, McBride's work was always marked by the fullness of its information and the soundness of its judgments, laced with wit. Inevitably, Gertrude Stein wrote a portrait of her friend, although Lincoln Kirstein called it "a genre picture, a portmanteau composition of picture dealing, art manipulation, the salon world of Miss Stein's domesticated power-politics during the first World War" (McBride 7). "Have They Attacked Mary. He Giggled" was subtitled "A Political Caricature"; it appeared in part—abbreviated for reasons of space—in *Vanity Fair* in June 1917 and then was issued as a pamphlet with its missing thirty-five lines restored. Divided into forty-six "pages," many of which are only one line long, the piece mentions the ostensible subject only once: "Who is Mr. McBride" (*SW* 474). His long career, extending well into his eighties, answers that question better than her portrait does.

REFERENCES: *ABT*, 1933; *SW*, 1946; *CC*, 1974; Henry McBride, *The Flow of Art*, 1975.
Bruce Kellner

McCOWN, EUGENE, ?–?, writer, pianist. Eugene McCown majored in journalism at the University of Missouri and then studied art with Andrew Dasburg. In 1921 he began his fourteen-year sojourn in Paris, playing the piano at the celebrated nightclub, Le boeuf sur le toit, and was identified with the neoromantic artists and musicians of the decade. Gertrude Stein included him in a joint portrait with his friend Virgil Thomson* because they came from the same state. "To Virgil and Eugene" begins "Show me I am from Missouri" and then plays variations on the familiar counting song, "one two three four five six seven all good children go to heaven" (*PL* 311). McCown returned permanently to the United States in 1935, but during the second world war he served with army intelligence as a French translator in London. Odd-eyed and elegant, he published his roman à clef about artists in Paris, *The Siege of Innocence*, in 1950.

REFERENCES: Eugene McCown, *The Siege of Innocence*, 1950; *PL*, 1955; *VT*, 1966.
Bruce Kellner

MAN RAY [EMANUEL RADNITZKY], 27 August 1890–18 November 1976, photographer, painter. Man Ray looked like "an Indian potentate in miniature, very pretentious," although he was actually a simple person, Alice Toklas recollected (*WIR* 110). Born in Philadelphia, the son of Russian-Jewish immigrants, Man Ray moved to Brooklyn after his high-school graduation, gave himself a new name, and supported himself with odd jobs while trying to begin a career as an artist. He exhibited for the first time in 1912, after Alfred Stieglitz* had introduced him to the work of modern artists, in 1913 at the 69th Armory Exhibition and in a one-man show in 1915. Under the influence of Marcel

Duchamp* he eventually developed his own iconoclastic style. In 1921 Man Ray moved to Paris and became a personality in the cultural life of the city. His work encompassed cubism, Dada, and surrealism and was exhibited in the surrealist show of 1925. He had been introduced to photography as well by Stieglitz, developing his own Rayograph prints, and became the fashionable photographer of Parisian aristocrats, artists, and writers. After he was introduced to Gertrude Stein by an American couple, Man Ray asked her to pose for him. Stein was fascinated by his use of lights and was pleased with his photographs of her, and he photographed her and Alice Toklas and the studio frequently thereafter. During long photo sessions he asked Stein to keep moving so that the results would have a spontaneous quality; she seems to have been pleased with the results, although some people have noted they make her look like a football linebacker. Man Ray depicted her even more unflatteringly in his autobiography, and in interviews he referred to her as a dictator of art. Man Ray was also a maker of classic avant-garde films. In 1944 his work received a large retrospective show in New York, and he is represented in museums in America and Europe.

REFERENCES: *WIR*, 1963; *CC*, 1974; *NYT*, 19 November 1976.

Priscilla Oppenheimer

MANGUIN, HENRI CHARLES, 1874–1949, painter. One of the minor painters whose works were among those that hung early on at 27 rue de Fleurus, Henri Manguin was an early admirer of Henri Matisse.* He was briefly identified with the fauvists, but after 1905 he moved to Saint Tropez and spent his career painting from the luminous natural landscape there. He had studied with Gustav Moreau, but Cézanne and Gauguin seem to have been stronger influences on his work than either Moreau or Matisse. In 1909, Gertrude Stein wrote "Manguin a Painter," suggesting that he had some trouble in completing altogether satisfying work: "To finish a thing so that any one can know that that thing is a finished thing is something"; "To make a pretty thing . . . is something" (*P&P* 54). The two adjectives never appear in the same sentence.

REFERENCES: *ABT*, 1933; *P&P*, 1934; *Praeger Encyclopedia of Art*, 1971.

Bruce Kellner

MARATIER, GEORGES, ?–?, art dealer, publisher. Gertrude Stein called Georges Maratier "everybody's friend" (*ABT* 283), and his loyalty over the years bore out the compliment. One of the group of young artists and writers who came into Stein's circle in the mid-twenties, Maratier was unique in being only creative in ancillary ways. His Editions de la Montagne issued the French translation of selections from *The Making of Americans*† in 1929, after which he turned the operation over to Georges Hugnet, who issued *Dix Portraits*.† Maratier then became an art dealer, responsible for securing Stein's early purchases of works by Sir Francis Rose,* and in 1937 he opened his Galerie de Beaune. Virgil Thomson* observes that Stein eventually quarreled with everyone in the group; Pavel Tchelitchew,* Allen Tanner, Georges Hugnet,* Kristians Tonny,* Bravig Imbs,* René Crevel,* Eugène and Leonid Berman,* Christian Bérard,* and only afterward made up with himself and with Maratier. One proved as loyal as the other. In the early thirties, Maratier helped Alice Toklas interview prospective servants; he took care of the chihuahua Pépé* during the American lecture tour; after Stein's death he assessed the art collection. In the latter instance, the lawyer for the Stein estate, Edgar Allan Poe (whom Toklas referred to as "the grumpy grandpapa"), required a detailed inventory indicating "their present value . . . for his reassurance," Toklas wrote to Carl Van Vechten.* "He will be breathless with surprise when he sees the value Georges Maratier put upon them—which he kindly did—saving the fee of an expert—which he is" (*SOA* 358). Stein's 1929 portrait of this "stout middle-sized Frenchman" (*EA* 166) was included in her 1934 anthology, *Portraits and Prayers*.† "G. Maratier" is brief and elliptical, but its conclusion may speak well of its subject: "Think well with or without thinking with or with or without. Think well with or with or with or without, thinking" (184). Maratier is one of "The Five Georges" in *Operas and Plays*,† written in 1931, along with George Platt Lynes, the American photographer. "George M." and "George L." and "George of England" are easy enough to identify; "George G." is not, and "George S." was "George H." for Hugnet in manuscript and then altered when Stein fell out with him. At one point in the play, "George M." is "made to marry" (311), perhaps a reference to his brief marriage in 1930 to Florence Tanner, sister of Allen Tanner, the pianist.

REFERENCES: *O&P*, 1932; *ABT*, 1933; *P&P*, 1934; *EA*, 1937; *VT*, 1966; *SOA*, 1973.

Bruce Kellner

MARCOUSSIS [MARKOUS], LOUIS, 1878–1941, painter. Gertrude Stein met the Polish-born Marcoussis when Pablo Picasso* and his then-mistress Fernande Olivier* brought him and his own mistress, Eve, to 27 rue de Fleurus one evening. Strongly influenced by impressionism until 1907, his subsequent identification with the cubist painters continued until after World War I. Stein did not see him again, following their initial encounter, until after *The Autobiography of Alice B. Toklas*,† had been published in 1933. Then he told her that Picasso, Guillaume Apollinaire,* Max Jacob,* and he himself had been involved in "series production." The poets wrote one poem every day and the painters completed one painting every day, believing "there would be such an accumulation that it would completely force a market for the poems and the pictures and this is what would happen" (*EA* 42). Marcoussis turned to engraving in the thirties, but his interest in pure form carried over into it.

REFERENCES: *ABT*, 1933; *EA*, 1937; *Praeger Encyclopedia of Art*, 1971.

Bruce Kellner

MARINOFF [VAN VECHTEN], FANIA, 20 March 1887–7 November 1971, actress. Carl Van Vechten's* second wife was born in Odessa, Russia, but her family immigrated to Boston when she was five years old. When her stepmother died, the thirteen children were scattered; she went to Denver, Colorado, to live with one of her brothers. Before she was ten she was reciting and singing at political rallies in which her brother was involved, but at twelve, schooling abandoned, she joined successive touring theatrical troupes that brought her to New York in 1903. By the time she met Van Vechten in August 1912, she had appeared in several Broadway productions, including George Bernard Shaw's *You Never Can Tell*. They were introduced by the mutual friend who had appeared as a witness against Van Vechten when Anna Snyder* divorced him two months earlier. Their love affair was nearly two years old when they sailed together for Europe in the spring of 1914. Van Vechten sent a note to Gertrude Stein when they arrived: "I'm in Paris for a few days. . . . and I should like to bring over a little Russian called Fania" (*GSCVV* 22–23). She returned to New York later in the summer to begin rehearsals for a new play; Van Vechten was caught in Italy when war broke out and could not return until October. They were married a few days later. Prior to her semiretirement in the early twenties, Marinoff's greatest successes came as Ariel in Shakespeare's *The Tempest* and as Wendla in Frank Wedekind's controversial *Spring's Awakening*. She appeared in a number of films as well, including a 1915 version of Frank Norris's *MacTeague*. In the postwar decade, Marinoff was often in France without Van Vechten and saw Gertrude Stein and Alice Toklas on several occasions. In May 1927, for example, after a visit, Stein wrote to Van Vechten, "Fania has been here and gone [to London] and we liked her being here immensely" (*GSCVV* 146). Two months later, back in Paris, Marinoff had a note at her hotel after another visit: "[W]e did enjoy having you for it kind of brings us closer not that we were not awfully close but it kind of bridged the physical years and you know how much I love Carl and you" (*GSCVV* 149–50). In August 1930 Marinoff and Van Vechten were in Bilignin for a few days' visit, and during the lecture tour Stein and Toklas attended a performance of Elmer Rice's *Judgment Day*, in which Marinoff had a featured role. She had returned to the stage in 1931. Her last appearances were as Charmain in Tallulah Bankhead's catastrophic production of Shakespeare's *Antony and Cleopatra* in 1937 and as the Fortune Teller in Thornton Wilder's* *The Skin of Our Teeth* in 1943. Gertrude Stein never mentioned Fania Marinoff in her published writings, but the relationship seems to have been uncomplicated during its thirty years, and for another ten with Alice Toklas after Stein's death—ever since Van Vechten had asked if he could bring over "a little Russian called Fania."

REFERENCES: Bruce Kellner, *Carl Van Vechten and the Irreverent Decades*, 1968; *GSCVV*, 1986.

Paul Padgette
Bruce Kellner

MARLOWE, JULIA, 17 August 1866–12 November 1950, actress. Gertrude Stein included a portait of this celebrated Scots-American actress among those written at the time she was attempting to treat the character of her subjects rather than their achievements. "Julia Marlowe" is a rare instance of Stein's having used someone widely recognized long before she was herself well-known. Marlowe's theatrical career began in childhood and developed into one of the most distinguished in performing history, notably through a wide number of performances in Shakespeare. Stein may well have seen Marlowe onstage, but the actress is not mentioned in any of her autobiographical writings. The early portrait suggests something of "being a successful one in being one being living" (*TWO* 328) but little else.

REFERENCES: *Who's Who in the Theatre*, 1939; *TWO*, 1951.

Bruce Kellner

MARS, ETHEL, AND MAUD HUNT SQUIRE,   ?–?, salon visitors. Gertrude Stein immortalized two women friends—early habitués at 27 rue de Fleurus— as "Miss Furr and Miss Skeene" in her 1908 short story about them. Helen Furr and Georgine Skeene both have pleasant voices; they live together, travel together, cultivate their voices together, spend some time sitting with some dark and heavy men, but most of their time is spent in "being gay," being "regularly gay" (*G&P* 17–18). Stein may be the first to have employed the word as double-entendre. When Alice Toklas first met them at 27 rue de Fleurus, she and Miss Mars spent the evening talking about how to put on makeup (*ABT* 16); a quarter of a century later, Miss Squire wrote from Vence, where they lived then, to say that Miss Furr still liked "being gay & wanting everybody & everything else to be gay" (*FF* 269).

REFERENCES: *G&P*, 1922; *ABT*, 1933; *FF*, 1953.

Bruce Kellner

MASSON, ANDRÉ,   4 January 1896–November 1987, painter. Another of the young painters of the twenties in whom Gertrude Stein took an interest that was "permanent and vital" (*ABT* 258), André Masson had a grim early life. He was seriously wounded during World War I, then decorated ceramics, worked as a deliveryman in a glass factory, and free-lanced as a proofreader, all to sustain him while he developed as an artist. Strongly influenced by Gertrude Stein's protégé Juan Gris,* and subsequently by the surrealists, Masson is best known for ballet designs during the thirties and theater designs during the forties.

REFERENCES: *ABT*, 1933; Muriel Emanuel et al., eds., *Contemporary Artists*, 1983.

Bruce Kellner

MASSOT, PIERRE DE,   ?–circa 1930, writer. Gertrude Stein met Pierre de Massot through Virgil Thomson* when he was a member of the circle of younger artists and writers in Paris later identified as neoromantics. In his modest output, de Massot included a preface for Georges Hugnet's* French translation of selections from *The Making of Americans*,† published by Hugnet's Editions de la Montagne as *Morceaux Choisis de "La Fabrication des Américains."* Gertrude Stein's brief portrait of de Massot begins, "I remember very well when you came. / I was pleased. English and French. / I was very pleased. I never forgot the pleasure. / I never forgot you. I know that very well." (*PL* 311). She wrote it just about the time of his early death brought on by ill-health and opium addiction.

REFERENCES: *PL*, 1955; *VT*, 1966.

Bruce Kellner

MATISSE, HENRI, 31 December 1869–3 November 1954, artist. Born in Le Coteau, France, in 1869, Henri Matisse did not begin to paint until he was twenty. After becoming acquainted with the work of early impressionists, he turned to experimenting with color as the most important ingredient of his painting. In 1905 he became identified with André Derain, Maurice de Vlaminck, and others as the fauves when their exhibition at the Autumn Salon caused a riot. Parisians thought Matisse's *Woman with the Hat* a hoax, but Gertrude and Leo* Stein bought it for $100. Michael Stein's* wife Sarah had wanted to buy it too. In compensation, she and her husband became Matisse's most ardent collectors. Matisse and his wife became welcome guests on both the rue Madame and the rue de Fleurus. Gertrude Stein called him "cher maître" for a time, and even after she had lost interest in his work, she maintained a lively interest in the Matisses as friends. Her admiration waned when she began to feel there was no longer a sign of struggle in his painting, and she bluntly told him so. However, her 1909 word portrait of Matisse builds its case on his becoming "a great one," "clearly expressing something being struggling" (*SW* 290–92). At that point he was producing some of his finest works, full of great bursts of color together with a clarity of line. Gertrude Stein had always admired his hard work, but as his security and fame grew she seemed to admire him less; nor did she seem to understand his preoccupation with design, one of the attributes that give his work its distinction. Also, her relationship with Matisse cooled because she had grown increasingly interested in Picasso.* Matisse's vast creativity continued into old age, in sculptures, lithographs, and ballet settings, as well as paintings. At the age of seventy-two, an invalid confined to beds and wheelchairs, he discovered paper cutting for spectacular and simplified collages and made it an art all his own. His last great work, in 1944, was the design for the Chapel of the Rosary of the Dominican nuns at Vence, its stained glass windows, vestments, pyx, and other ecclesiastical accoutrements, all showing his skill with color and flat surfaces to full advantage. Matisse's final contact with Gertrude Stein seems to have come through *Testimony against Gertrude Stein*, the pamphlet, printed as a supplement to *transition* 23 and issued by Eugene Jolas* and others to protest various declarations in *The Autobiography of Alice B. Toklas*.† Matisse resented Stein's having said his wife looked like a horse.

REFERENCES: *ABT*, 1933; *SW*, 1946; John Russell, ed., *The World of Matisse*, 1969; *CC*, 1975.

Margaret Woodbridge

MAURER, ALFRED, 1868–1932, painter. One of the earliest habitués of the Stein salon, "Alfy" Maurer was a "little dark dapper man . . . with hair, eyes, face, hands and feet all very much alive," of whose witty company Gertrude Stein was quite fond, although she felt his artistic talent was more derivative than innovative (*SW* 10). It was Stein who had introduced him to the fauves, bringing about an abrupt change in his painting style. Maurer, born in New York, the son of a well-known lithographer for Currier and Ives, came to Paris in 1897 and gained some recognition for his paintings in the Whistlerian style. After 1906 he adopted the style of Matisse,* but it is not known whether Stein bought any of his fauve landscapes. Maurer's works were exhibited by Alfred Stieglitz* in New York in 1909 and 1910 and at the Armory Exhibition of 1913, for which Maurer had helped collect paintings in France. Maurer appears as "Alf," a character in Stein's play *IIIIIIIIII*, written in 1913 and printed in *Geography and Plays*† in 1922. On his way back to America in 1914, having narrowly escaped the advance of the German army on the Marne, Maurer stopped for a last visit with Stein. Maurer's father, who had been supporting him, had forced him to return to New York by cutting off his funds, and their relationship, always a stressful one, was exacerbated by the necessity of making their home together thereafter. Maurer, now painting in a semi-abstract style, which later became more expressionistic, exhibited a few times during the early twenties, but interest in his work waned as interest rose in the type of work his father had always done. After severe bouts with depression, Maurer committed suicide shortly after his father had died at the age of one hundred.

REFERENCES: *SW*, 1962; *Praeger Encyclopedia of Art*, 1971; *CC*, 1974; Harold Osborne, ed., *Oxford Companion to Twentieth Century Art*, 1981.

Priscilla Oppenheimer

MOODY, WILLIAM VAUGHN, 8 July 1869–17 October 1910, poet, dramatist. William Vaughn Moody entered Harvard College in 1889 after teaching for several years in public and private schools. He took his degree in three years, and then traveled to Europe before returning to Harvard as a graduate student and instructor. During this time Gertrude Stein, then a sophomore at Radcliffe, came under his tutelage in English 22, a composition course. Her college themes were rambling and careless, conventional undergraduate efforts, riddled with mechanical errors. They often had to be revised, a task she disliked. In the end Professor Moody gave her a grade of C, but he noted: "Your work has shown at times considerable emotional intensity and a somewhat unusual power of abstract thought. It has frequently been lacking in organization, in fertility of resource, and in artfulness of literary method" (*RAD* 155). Subsequently, Moody taught with the English department of the University of Chicago until 1902, then quit teaching to devote himself to writing plays and poetry. His lyrics are often "exquisite and magnificent in phrasing," according to Arthur Hobson Quinn (773). His poems on political subjects show his desire that his country remain true to its ideals. His best plays are *The Great Divide* and *The Faith Healer*, both reflecting a new realism and higher intellectual quality than had heretofore been evident in American theater.

REFERENCES: Arthur Hobson Quinn, ed., *Representative American Plays*, 1925; *RAD*, 1949; *CC*, 1975.

Margaret Woodbridge

MÜNSTERBERG, HUGO, 1 June 1863–16 December 1916, psychologist. Hugo Münsterberg was born in Danzig, received a Ph.D. at Leipzig and a medical degree at Heidelberg. Initially, his academic interest was in philosophy, but his work received little attention. In 1892 William James* brought him to Harvard to lecture and to direct the psychology laboratory. He became one of the group at Harvard who "lived very closely and very interestingly together" (*ABT* 95). His lasting contributions are in the field of applied psychology. He supervised and conducted research by his students, among them Gertrude Stein whom he called "the ideal student" (*FF* 4). As a result, James asked her to attend his seminar in her junior year and to conduct more experiments. Together with Münsterberg, Gertrude Stein worked on a series of experiments in automatic writing, the results of which were published in the *Harvard Psychological Review*. (Later on, B. F. Skinner cited this article as proof that Stein's works were examples of automatic writing.) Psychology was then in its infancy, and Münsterberg was the first to investigate many problems now considered commonplace matters. For instance, he established a relationship between fatigue and job monotony and the efficiency of workers. He contributed to law by pointing out how changes in blood pressure affect memory, a principle used in the polygraph for lie detection. William James called Münsterberg "the Rudyard Kipling of psychology," no doubt intended as high praise at a time when Kipling was poet laureate. Münsterberg died suddenly while lecturing at Radcliffe at the age of forty-eight.

REFERENCES: Edward R. A. Seligman and Alvin Johnson, eds., *Encyclopedia of the Social Sciences* 10, 1930–1935; *ABT*, 1933; *FF*, 1953; *CC*, 1974.

Margaret Woodbridge

NADELMAN, ELIE, 1882–28 December 1946, sculptor, draftsman. One of the many minor artists whose portraits Gertrude Stein wrote, "in all manners and in all styles" (*ABT* 140), Elie Nadelman was a Polish-born sculptor working in Paris shortly after the turn of the century in the manner of Rodin. He was much preoccupied with curves and curving lines in his pieces, and in relationships in volume. In 1914, the doyenne of beauty aids for women, Helena Rubenstein, brought him to America, where he made a considerable career in decorative arts. Stein's use of Nadelman as a portrait subject, however, lay in his character rather than in his work. Dating to 1911, "Nadelman" is built of Stein's incremental repetition as "one certainly doing thinking," "one expressing thinking," "one completely expressing completely working," "one not expressing completely loving women," "one expressing light being existing" (*P&P* 51–53). These locutions, as Janet Flanner* observed in her introduction to *Two*,† were designed for "reading long enough and sufficiently to become interested in the character of the portraits" (x). "Nadelman" is one of over two dozen portraits written between 1908 and 1912.

REFERENCES: *ABT*, 1933; *P&P*, 1934; Lincoln Kirstein, *The Sculpture of Elie Nadelman*, 1948; *TWO*, 1951.

Bruce Kellner

OLIVIER, FERNANDE BELLEVALÉE, 1885–4 February 1966, model. Fernande Olivier, a prospective teacher separated from her husband, who was "very large, very beautiful and very gracious," took shelter from a summer rainstorm in Picasso's* doorway in 1904 (*SW* 43). Picasso invited her in; she stayed for seven years. An "odalisque" beauty with "sensational natural coloring," dark hair and almond-shaped eyes, Olivier was the model for Picasso's Rose period paintings (*WIR* 27). She accompanied Picasso on his frequent visits to the Steins, read aloud from La Fontaine when Gertrude Stein began to pose for her portrait, and on trips to Spain with Picasso wrote Stein long letters describing the land, the people, and the earthquakes. Alice Toklas, who took French lessons from Olivier three times a week, often "took her off Picasso's hands" by going on shopping trips, attending dog and cat shows and art exhibits. Olivier was very interested in clothes and perfume, Toklas remembered (*WIR* 34). In 1911 Olivier went off with a young Italian painter, but by the time she had a change of heart and returned, Picasso had fallen in love with Marcelle Humbert, whom he called Eva. Olivier wrote a dignified letter to Stein breaking off their friendship. She had appreciated Stein's sympathy and affection, but she realized that Stein's relationship with Picasso had been the reason for their connection. *Picasso and His Friends*, a memoir describing Olivier's life with the artist from 1904 to 1913 (which includes her version of the famous Rousseau* banquet), was published in 1933. Picasso tried unsuccessfully to prevent its publication to placate his wife Olga. Many years later he paid for Olivier's care when she became ill. Toklas remarked that when she saw Olivier again in 1954 she had grown "enormous," but still had "vestiges of her old beauty" (*SOA* 295).

REFERENCES: *SW*, 1962; *WIR*, 1963; *NYT*, 4 February 1966, 31; *SOA*, 1973; *CC*, 1974.

Priscilla Oppenheimer

PACH, WALTER, 1883–27 November 1958, painter, art historian. Walter Pach, a noted art historian and professor of art at City College of New York and New York University, studied with Henri Matisse* in Paris as a young man and was a frequent guest at 27 rue de Fleurus, where Leo Stein's* discussions had awakened his interest in modern art. He brought other young artists to visit the Steins, among them Joseph Stella, exhibited his own work at the Independent Salon, and helped acquire loans from Paris art dealers for the Armory Show of 1913. Alice Toklas shared Pach's interest in music and typed some articles for him. Although his articles on artists were often considered too avant-garde for publication, he persevered in trying to gain recognition for modern art, an effort which impressed Gertrude Stein. He was the subject of one of her word portraits, but his youth apparently made her somewhat undecided as to his future: "If he is a young one now he will perhaps be succeeding very well in living" (*TWO* 338). Pach exhibited in New York after 1917, and his etchings and paintings are in the permanent collections of the Metropolitan Museum of Art and other museums. He wrote introductions to art books, translations, and reviews, and is the author of *The Classic Tradition in Modern Art,* published in 1959, and of several biographies of artists.

REFERENCES: *TWO*, 1951; *NYT*, 28 November 1958; *CC*, 1974; *BABT*, 1977.

Priscilla Oppenheimer

PÉPÉ, 1932–1943(?), chihuahua. Pépé, born in France of Mexican descent, was a present from Francis Picabia* to Gertrude Stein to replace his predecessor, Byron. Byron, so named because "he was to have as a wife his sister or his mother," died suddenly one night either of typhus, as Stein thought, or from the horror of living up to his name (*EA* 49). Although they looked so much alike they could not be told apart in photographs, Byron and Pépé were temperamentally quite different. Byron had a "strange and feverish nature, he was very fierce and tender and he danced strange little war dances" (*EA* 49). Pépé, on the other hand, was constitutionally and emotionally delicate; his health was often a concern to his mistresses. "Pépé had une petite intervention chirurgicale on his hinder end," Alice Toklas reported to Carl Van Vechten* in 1935, "but he's frisking about now" (*GSCVV* 459). A year later Stein informed Van Vechten about Pépé's attack of kidney trouble: "he used to be the roi de pipi and then there was none" (*GSCVV* 529). When Pépé was told he was to be represented in a ballet, he threw up from excitement at first, but then was quite pleased. Joyce Farron danced the part of Pépé in *A Wedding Bouquet,*† based on Stein's 1931 play *They Must. Be Wedded. To Their Wife.* In April 1937, Stein and Toklas flew to London for the first performance of the ballet, set to music by Lord Gerald Berners,* with choreography by Frederick Ashton,* and Robert Helpman and Margot Fonteyn as principal dancers. Later Lord Berners drew Pépé's head on a carpet for Toklas to tapestry. Everybody was "so pleased and occupied with Pépé first on the stage and now on a carpet," Stein wrote (*GSCVV* 552). Everybody but Basket,* that is, whose nose was severely out of joint; the much-photographed, painted and written-about canine companion was not accustomed to taking a back seat to Pépé. A darker period in Pépé's life occurred not long afterwards, however, when Basket died and he tried unsuccessfully to console Stein and Toklas. When Basket II* was brought home he felt so neglected he had to get an attack of rheumatism. During World War II, Pépé went into exile in Savoy with his mistresses, but did not live to see the liberation. Although he wore his coat, he suffered so from the cold he eventually refused to go outside. When the vet reported there was no saving him, Toklas wrote, she "kissed little Pépé and put him in the basket I had brought him in, a very pretty Spanish one. . . . I could not see where I was walking for the tears" (*WIR* 164).

REFERENCES: *EA*, 1937; *WIR*, 1963; *GSCVV*, 1986.

Priscilla Oppenheimer

PERNOLLET FAMILY, 1924–1933, hotel keepers, Touring in 1924 through the south of France in Lady Godiva—their Ford so named because of its lack of ornamentation—Gertrude Stein and Alice Toklas stopped at the Hôtel Pernollet in Belley, a family establishment stretching back five generations. The husband cooked and the wife managed. In her *Cook Book*, Alice Toklas pronounced the food "undistinguished" and even "mediocre" (92), but she and Gertrude Stein were so pleased with the landscape that they returned for several summers until they were able to rent the manor house in the nearby hamlet of Bilignin. Monsieur Pernollet is responsible for the observation attributed by Ernest Hemingway* to Gertrude Stein, "You are all a lost generation." According to Gertrude Stein, Pernollet contended that men became civilized between eighteen and twenty-five; those who missed out on that civilizing period because of the war were "a lost generation" (*EA* 52). Madame Pernollet contributed to the Stein canon as well when, in 1933, in despair over her unfaithful husband, she died after being discovered on the cement courtyard of the hotel following an apparent fall. This unsolved mystery, coupled with other odd occurrences that summer, led to Gertrude Stein's *Blood on the Dining-Room Floor*.†

REFERENCES: *ABT*, 1933; *EA*, 1937; *BDRF*, 1948; *ABTC*, 1954.

Bruce Kellner

PÉTAIN, HENRI PHILIPPE [BENONI OMER JOSEPH], 24 April 1856–23 July 1951, French marshal, premier. General Henri Pétain came into prominence in World War I as the hero of Verdun. After the war, promoted to marshal, Pétain was instrumental in shaping France's disastrous defensive military policy. Closely allied to his conservative military policy was his equally conservative political philosophy. He was contemptuous of democracy and made no secret of his fondness for dictatorships which made their countries strong. With the defeat of France in 1940, Pétain was made premier, at the age of eighty-four, of the Vichy government, the puppet regime set up under Hitler to govern the southern part of France. In this capacity he was both scorned and admired. He cooperated with the Germans, which meant that Vichy France was anti-Semitic. Gertrude Stein tried to sympathize with and understand his motives, though as a Jew her own life was in danger. In 1942 she began to translate Pétain's speeches into English but never completed the project. She may have given up because the work seemed a pointless task or because of her increasing dislike for the Vichy government. During this time Bernard Faÿ,* a good and influential friend, received assurances from Pétain that Gertrude Stein and Alice Toklas would be protected. Even so, they were warned in 1943 that they were about to be placed in a concentration camp. Under the postwar government headed by Charles De Gaulle, Pétain was tried and sentenced to death, later to life imprisonment.

REFERENCES: *CB*, 1940, 1950; John Malcolm Brinnin, *The Third Rose*, 1959; *CC*, 1974.

Margaret Woodbridge

PICABIA, FRANCIS, 22 January 1879–30 November 1953, painter, poet, designer. It was not until 1910 that Gertrude Stein heard anything about Picabia, although he later told her she must have seen his work at the exhibition where they had first seen Picasso's* work, and it was not until the thirties that they developed a deep affection for one another. Picabia had discussed Stein with Mabel Dodge* at the 69th Armory Exhibition in 1913, and when she met him at dinner shortly thereafter, Stein was annoyed with his incessantness and vulgarity. He was fresh from his triumph in New York, handsome, flashy, erratic, with enough money to indulge his fondness for nightlife, women, and cars. His two large cubist paintings in the Armory Exhibition had attracted press attention and ridicule; seizing the opportunity for publicity, Picabia had issued a manifesto announcing a new school of "amorphist" art. Born in France, the son of a wealthy Cuban father and a French mother, he had begun painting in an impressionist style after studying at the École des Beaux Arts and the École des Arts Décoratifs. He took up cubism and was a founding member of the Section d'Or in 1911, but shortly injected emotional and symbolic themes into the typically austere cubist style. He stayed in New York with several other European artists, Marcel Duchamp* and Max Ernst among them, for the duration of World War I and in 1915 exhibited at Alfred Stieglitz's* 291 gallery and contributed to the reviews *291* and *Camera Work* that year. His object portraits of that period may have been inspired by Stein's word portraits, as were others of the Stieglitz circle. In 1917 Picabia and Duchamp published another short-lived review, *391*. In 1918 Picabia moved to Switzerland where he published *Poèmes et dessins de la fille sans mère*, joined the Dada demonstrations, and collaborated with Tristan Tzara* on issues 4 and 5 of *Dada*. He published two issues of another review, *Canibale*, in 1920. By 1921 he had joined the surrealist André Breton in repudiating Dada, and 1926 saw his return to figurative art. He began another facet of his career in 1924 when he wrote the scenario and designed sets and costumes for the ballet *Relâche* by Erik Satie* and René Clair. Stein, who had acquired some of his landscapes and drawings, enjoyed many visits from Picabia and his wife during the thirties, both in Paris and Bilignin, where they discussed theories of art. "Nothing is real to him that is not painting and so knowing

anything cannot frighten him," she had written in *Everybody's Autobiography*†
(*EA* 21) in 1937. "The surréalists are the vulgarisation of Picabia," she wrote,
who "is struggling with the problem that a line should have the vibration of a
musical sound" (*SW* 198). Picabia presented Stein with her chihuahuas, Byron
and his successor Pépé, of whom she was very fond. In 1936 Stein and Picabia
worked on a plan to stage her "Listen to Me," which, however, never came to
fruition. Stein wrote introductions for the brochures of Picabia's shows in New
York in 1934 and in Paris in 1937: "In his later painting and certainly in his
drawing he has achieved a transparence which is peculiarly a thing that has
nothing to do with the surface seen," she wrote ([3]).

REFERENCES: *EPH*, 1934; *EA*, 1937; *SW*, 1962; Bernard Myers, ed., *McGraw-Hill
Dictionary of Art* 4, 1969; *CC*, 1974; *GSCVV*, 1986.

Priscilla Oppenheimer

PICASSO, OLGA KHOKHLOVA, ?–11 February 1955, dancer. Olga Khokhlova,
the daughter of a Russian colonel, was a member of the troupe of the Ballets
Russes when she met Pablo Picasso,* who had gone to Italy in 1917 to design the
sets for *Parade*. On the occasion of their marriage in July 1918, Picasso sent a
small painting to Gertrude Stein. Olga's attitude that her husband's wealth and
reputation could open the right doors for her socially led to an abrupt change in
Picasso's lifestyle—a move to a fancy apartment, the wearing of business suits
and ties, the frequenting of fashionable resorts. The marriage caused a break in
the Picasso-Stein friendship, but shortly after the Picassos' son Paolo was born in
1921, a reconciliation initiated by Picasso occurred. Another two-year break took
place in 1933 when Olga Picasso was upset by the references to Fernande Olivier*
in *The Autobiography of Alice B. Toklas*.† It was painful for Olga to have memoirs and photographs of Picasso's early life and mistresses published, Toklas said,
as it "reduces her to an episode of respectability which he has repudiated" (*SOA*
117). The Picassos separated in 1935—their Russian and Spanish temperaments
were too opposed, Alice Toklas theorized—but were never divorced. After
Stein's death, Olga Picasso and Toklas remained friends, visiting and gossiping,
going to the ballet. Olga had mellowed, Toklas observed, and had been an "angel" to her when Stein died. In her later years Olga lived in Cannes, where Toklas
and Basket II* visited her several times, "a nice frail thing with her lovely eyes,"
wearing the "heavy jewelled bracelets which Picasso of course had given her"
(*SOA* 317). She died in a clinic there after a long illness. Picasso had treated Olga
well, according to Toklas, supporting her generously and insisting on specialists
and trained nurses, and visiting her in the clinic. Although he exhibited the portraits he had painted of her, he never sold them.

REFERENCES: *NYT*, 9 April 1973; *SOA*, 1973; *CC*, 1974.

Priscilla Oppenheimer

PICASSO, PABLO, 25 October 1881–8 April 1973, painter, sculptor. In the winter of 1906, Gertrude Stein posed about eighty times while Picasso tried to finish his portrait of her. Dissatisfied with the head, he finally painted over it and gave up for a time. Then "Upon his return from Spain he painted in the head without having seen me again and he gave me the picture and I was and I still am satisfied with my portrait, for me, it is I, and it is the only reproduction of me which is always I, for me" (*PIC* 8). So began a lifelong, intense friendship between the writer and the artist. The colors in the portrait mark a turn away from Picasso's Rose period toward the use of earth tones—terracotta and gray—and the stylized, masklike face which Picasso finished in a fit of inspiration shows the influence of recently discovered ancient Iberian sculptures which had interested him; the sharp outlines and angles of the massive body prefigure the development of cubism. Three years later Picasso returned again from Spain with the first cubist landscapes. "I was alone at this time in understanding him, perhaps because I was expressing the same thing in literature," Stein wrote (*PIC* 16). Picasso's influence on the course of art in this century is incalculable. His phenomenal energy, power, and inventiveness were the catalyst for a profound change in the way people looked at art, and he inspired myriads of his contemporaries through his monumental achievement, the founding of cubism, and his innovations in sculpture and the graphic arts. Picasso had arrived in Paris from Barcelona in 1900 and was little known to the public when Leo Stein,* introduced to his work by the dealer Clovis Sagot, bought his first Picasso in 1905. That same year he and Gertrude bought *The Woman with a Fan* and *Young Woman with a Flower Basket*, and Picasso painted Leo's portrait and that of his nephew, Allan Stein. Shortly thereafter he embarked on his portrait of Gertrude. The Steins continued to buy several Picassos each year, supporting him in a difficult period, and Gertrude kept his small painting *Homage to Gertrude* over her bed in a room already crowded with paintings. By this time Stein and Picasso had forged a friendship that survived several quarrels of some duration during the course of their lives. They conversed familiarly and often about painting, writing, theory and gossip of the art world, as well as about what "makes you a genius" (*EA* 84). Earlier, in *The Autobiography of Alice B. Toklas*,† Stein's narrator had voiced the conviction that Stein and Picasso were two of the only three "first class" geniuses she knew (*SW* 5). Picasso met Matisse* for the first time at the Steins' salon, and Matisse soon became dismayed at Gertrude's enthusiasm for his rival. In fact, the rivalry with Matisse as well as his visits to the Steins may have been in part the inspiration for Picasso's groundbreaking *Les Demoiselles d'Avignon*, which parodied a large Matisse painting that hung in the Steins' flat. *Les Demoiselles* also marked the beginning of Leo's withdrawal of admiration for Picasso, whose later work he abhorred.

Gertrude Stein wrote her first word portrait of Picasso in 1909, in which she describes the work "coming out of him" as both perplexing, disconcerting, and repellent, and simple, clear, charming, and lovely (*SW* 333–35). About this time Picasso began collaborating with Georges Braque* at the birth of cubism and developed the collage painting, an innovation with far-reaching influence. A calling card Stein left on Picasso's door even found its way into one of his collages, a painting she acquired in 1912. Picasso was represented by eight works in the New York 69th Armory Exhibition of 1913, including two still lifes loaned by Leo Stein. Mabel Dodge's* article in the March 1913 issue of *Arts and Decoration*, comparing the experiments of Picasso and Stein, linked them in the attention of press and art public and contributed to the spread of her reputation begun the previous year with Stein's portraits of Picasso and Matisse published in *Camera Work*. That summer Stein sold Picasso's *Three Women* to buy his *Man with a Guitar*.

In 1916, Picasso wrote to Stein disconsolate over the death of his mistress, Eva Humbert. In 1918 he sent Stein a little painting to commemorate his marriage to the Russian ballet dancer Olga Khokhlova,* but shortly thereafter a rift between Stein and Picasso occurred, caused by Stein's disapproval of the marriage. The rift lasted for about two years, until the birth of Picasso's son Paolo, one day before Stein's birthday in 1921. Stein wrote "A Birthday Book" for Paolo, which was to have been published by Daniel-Henry Kahnweiler* with illustrations by Picasso, but Picasso never got around to doing the illustrations. Another break in the relationship occurred on the death of Juan Gris* in 1927. Stein accused Picasso of not properly appreciating Gris, but it was possible that she was angry with him for his treatment of Olga, whom she had come to like, when he became involved with a young model, Maria-Thérèse Walter. By 1930, however, they had made up, the Picasso family visited Stein and Toklas in Bilignin, and Picasso designed chair covers which Toklas worked in needlepoint. Stein's new word portrait of Picasso was included in Tom Masson's 1925 *Annual;* and *Dix Portraits*† appeared in 1930, reprinting the portrait and including three of Picasso's sketches. In 1931 Stein was forced to sell one of her early Picasso purchases, *The Woman with a Fan*, in order to finance the Plain Edition of some of her unpublished work. Picasso had become an international star; her Picassos had become an investment to be drawn on. Picasso's wife precipitated the next two-year hiatus in their friendship. When *The Autobiography of Alice B. Toklas*† was being read to them, Olga walked out of Stein's flat in consternation over the description of Picasso's early mistress, Fernande Olivier.* The next quarrel ended more quickly. Picasso, shaken after his final separation from Olga, stopped painting and began to write poetry. After an evening in which he read his work to friends, Picasso was eager to learn Stein's opinion of his work. Not only was it not poetry in her estimation, but Picasso had recently disparaged the work of two of her current favorites, Francis Picabia* and Sir Francis Rose.* After several days of evasion and minor insults, the dispute reached a heated climax. Stein grabbed Picasso by the lapels and shook him hard, reminding him of his limits, which to be sure were extraordinary, but she was not ever going to tell him she liked his poetry. A kiss restored them to amicable relations (*EA* 36–37).

In her monograph *Picasso*, published in 1938 in France and England, Stein summed up his achievement: "As everything destroys itself in the twentieth century and nothing continues, so then the twentieth century has a splendor which is its own" (50). Early on in her monograph she had observed: "Picasso was the only one in painting who saw the twentieth century with his eyes and saw its reality and consequently his struggle was terrifying" (22). And, in conclusion: "He has that strange quality of an earth that one has never seen and of things destroyed as they have never been destroyed. So then Picasso has his splendor" (50).

REFERENCES: *EA*, 1937; *PIC*, 1938; *SW*, 1962; Bernard Myers, ed., *McGraw-Hill Dictionary of Art*, 1969; *CC*, 1974; William Rubin, ed., *Picasso, a Retrospective*, 1980.

Priscilla Oppenheimer

POUND, EZRA, 30 October 1885–1 November 1972, poet. Ezra Pound has probably had greater influence than any other poet on the development of twentieth-century poetry. His influence did not, however, extend to Gertrude Stein. When he came to dinner and talked about T. S. Eliot* and Japanese prints, among other things, she "liked him but did not find him amusing. . . . he was a village explainer, excellent if you were a village, but if you were not, not" (*SW* 189). The next time he came, with the editor of the *Dial*, a violent argument ensued, so vehement that Pound fell out of his chair—Stein's "favourite little armchair." She was "furious," probably not as much about the chair as that he opposed her opinions. Pound, accustomed to heated and frank disputes, did not understand why she didn't want him to visit again. Her answer, that "Miss Toklas has a bad tooth and beside we are busy picking wild flowers," upset him, according to Stein, and they never saw him again (*SW* 190). Erudite and opinionated, Pound was devoted to the advancement of all the arts. Born in Idaho, he studied at Hamilton College and the University of Pennsylvania and taught briefly in America, but he spent most of the rest of his life in Europe. When he met Stein, shortly after World War I, he was serving as literary agent for *Poetry*, the *Dial*, and the *Little Review* in Paris. He lived in London from 1908 to 1919, where his poetry, criticism, and lectures quickly made him a member of the literary establishment. He devoted prodigious energy and time to the promotion of other writers. He advised, published, and reviewed the works of T. S. Eliot, William Carlos Williams,* James Joyce, W. B. Yeats, Marianne Moore, Hilda Doolittle and Ernest Hemingway,* among others. Pound moved to Italy in 1923. During World War II his opposition to the economic corruption of the Western democracies led him to support Mussolini and to broadcast propaganda to American troops. He was arrested for treason in 1945 but was adjudged insane and committed to St. Elizabeth's Hospital in Washington, D.C., until 1958. He continued to study and write poetry during his confinement, and in 1949 received the Bollingen Prize for *The Pisan Cantos*. In 1963 he was made a fellow of the Academy of American Poets.

REFERENCES: *SW*, 1962; *CC*, 1974; *DLE* 45, 1986.

Priscilla Oppenheimer

PURRMANN, HANS, 1890–1966, painter. One of the subjects of Gertrude Stein's "long series of portraits" (*ABT* 140), Hans Purrmann was a minor German painter in Paris. With the later celebrated German painter Max Weber and Alice Toklas's friend Annette Rosenshine,* he was a charter member of Henri Matisse's* first painting class. Purrmann continued his studies with Matisse until World War I, then returned to Germany and subsequently created a number of murals in Berlin. They attempted to marry Matisse's decorative manner with German expressionism. Stein's interest in Purrmann lay in his character rather than in his work, however, as was true of most of the portraits of the 1908–1912 period of their composition. She calls him "Carman" throughout, whose size and strength are debatable subjects. The portrait, titled "Purrmann," is built of repetitions and locutions similar to those in Stein's first portrait of Picasso: he is "one who was working and he was one needing this thing needing to be working so as to be one having some way of being one having some way of working" (*P&P* 19); Purrmann is "one steadily working, not any one knowing him, knowing of him could ever have any doubt in them of this thing" (*TWO* 334).

REFERENCES: *ABT*, 141; *P&P*, 1934; *TWO*, 1951; Bernard Myers, ed., *McGraw-Hill Dictionary of Art*, 1969.

Bruce Kellner

RIBA-ROVIRA, FRANCESCO, 1913–   , painter. Gertrude Stein discovered a young Spanish artist painting along the banks of the Seine when she was out walking Basket II* after the war. Nicknamed "Paco," Riba-Rovira designed sets for an aborted production of "Yes Is for a Very Young Man" at Biarritz, and he painted Stein's portrait. In May 1945, his exhibition carried an enthusiastic Stein endorsement, later reprinted in the French magazine *Fontaine*, and ten years later a brief passage from it was translated into English and printed for the Riba-Rovira exhibition in New York at the Passedoit Gallery.

REFERENCES: *EPH*, 1955; *GSCVV*, 1986.

Bruce Kellner

ROBESON, PAUL, 9 April 1898–23 January 1976, singer, actor. Although he briefly joined a law firm, Paul Robeson, all-American football player, Phi Beta Kappa graduate of Rutgers, and holder of a law degree from Columbia University, was more interested in a theatrical career. He appeared in New York and London in *Taboo* in 1922 and during the twenties played in Eugene O'Neill's *All God's Chillun Got Wings* and *The Emperor Jones*, in *Porgy* and *Showboat*, and began a film career. During the late twenties Robeson and his wife, at the behest of Carl Van Vechten,* visited Gertrude Stein in Paris. Although she was very interested in him—"he knew american values and american life as only one in it but not of it could know them"—the experience cannot have been for him an entirely positive one. After 1925, Robeson's magnificent voice had brought him acclaim as a singer of spirituals in America and Europe, but Stein did not like to hear him sing spirituals. "They do not belong to you any more than anything else, so why claim them," she said. Robeson said nothing; nevertheless, he did sing, and the party according to Alice Toklas went off very nicely. Another time one of Stein's guests, a southern woman, told Robeson it was a pity he wasn't from the South. "Not for me," he answered. Stein's ideas about blacks must have been puzzling to Robeson. She believed they were suffering from "nothingness" rather than "persecution": "the african is not primitive, he has a very ancient but a very narrow culture and there it remains. Consequently nothing does or can happen" (*SW* 224). Robeson appeared with great success on the stage, in films, and on radio, and he made numerous recordings during the thirties. In 1943 he played in a long-running production of *Othello*. During the forties he became increasingly interested in the rights of labor and minorities. He was a supporter of Henry Wallace and admired what he saw as the advances the Soviet Union was making in these areas. In 1950 he was denied an American passport, and lived for a time in the Soviet Union, where he was awarded the Stalin Peace Prize in 1952. He sang again in New York in 1958 and toured Europe thereafter, but ill health prevented his performing for the last decade and a half of his life. Gertrude Stein memorialized the Robesons in "Among Negroes" in 1925 and published in *Useful Knowledge*† three years later. She wrote this multiple portrait after attending a party given for the all-black cast of the Hotsy-Totsy Company in Caroline Dudley Reagon's *Revue Nègre*. Three of the performers are the portrait's focus: Maude DeForest, Ida Lewelyn, and Josephine Baker, the latter who became an internationally celebrated entertainer. "Mr. and Mrs. Paul Robeson" put in a brief appearance at the beginning, "whom they had never met," and at the conclusion a brief paragraph marks their having called on Stein and Toklas (60–61) when they were invited for tea with Donald Angus, the young white regisseur of the Hotsy-Totsy Company. "Robeson is a dear," Stein wrote to Carl Van Vechten, "and he sang for us and I had a long talk with him and everybody liked him and Angus is a nice boy and they all together made a nice party and everybody I think was pleased" (*GSCVV* 123).

REFERENCES: *SW*, 1946; *WIR*, 1963; *CC*, 1974; Bruce Kellner, ed., *The Harlem Renaissance*, 1984; *GSCVV*, 1986.

Priscilla Oppenheimer
Bruce Kellner

ROCHÉ, HENRI-PIERRE, 1880–9 April 1959, writer. When Gertrude Stein took her nephew Allan Stein to model for the sculptor Kathleen Bruce, she met "a very earnest, very noble, devoted, very faithful and very enthusiastic man who was a general introducer" (*ABT* 54). Henri-Pierre Roché was a would-be writer who introduced Gertrude and Leo Stein* to Pablo Picasso* shortly after they had purchased their first of his paintings. Roché greatly admired *Three Lives*,† but Gertrude Stein's subsequent portraits frustrated him mightly. He allowed that repetition could be intoxicating, but when it was so uncontrolled he suspected the author of being merely lazy, and said so, as kindly as he could. Gertrude Stein wrote two portraits of him, both written circa 1909. The first, titled "Roche," was included in *Geography and Plays*† in 1922, about "one completely listening" who was "really completely listening" (141–43). The second portrait is buried in "A Long Gay Book," unpublished until 1933 in *Matisse Picasso and Gertrude Stein*.† It was Roché's habit to respond to very nearly everything by saying, "Good, good, excellent," including *Three Lives*, and as that was the truth from Gertrude Stein's point of view, the portrait is entirely comprehensible: "Vrais says good good, excellent. Vrais listens and when he listens he says good good, excellent. Vrais listens and he being Vrais when he has listened he says good good, excellent" (*MPG* 53). Roché is perhaps best known for *Jules et Jim*, on which François Truffaut based his film.

REFERENCES: *G&P*, 1922; *MPG*, 1933; *ABT*, 1933; *FF*, 1953.

Bruce Kellner

ROGERS, W[ILLIAM] G[ARLAND], 29 February 1896–1 March 1978, writer. W. G. Rogers grew up in Springfield, Massachusetts, graduated from Amherst College, and shortly afterwards became a doughboy attached to the Amherst Ambulance Unit in France in 1917. On a ten-day furlough in Nîmes, where he had gone to see the Roman ruins, he met Gertrude Stein and Alice Toklas. After they had observed him several times in the hotel dining room, they introduced themselves, saying he was the first American soldier they had seen there, and invited him for tea in the lobby. Rogers, whom they called "the Kiddie" behind his back, remembered that in short order Stein and Toklas had "pumped me . . . for all they were worth. . . . One spelled the other, like police grilling a prisoner for hours on end, until they dragged my whole history out of me." Stretched out through his stay, however, he found the questions to have "an oddly comforting effect" (8–9). At the time, Stein and Toklas were engaged in Red Cross work, supplying food, cigarettes, and other comforts to troops in the field. Stein had bought an old Ford that she named "Aunt Pauline" or "Auntie" to carry them from place to place. Now it also carried Rogers along during the next several days on a tour of historic landscapes and landmarks. Afterward, they wrote to each other briefly; then Rogers returned to Massachusetts to teach in the Springfield public schools and later at Deerfield Academy. In 1931 he joined the staff of the Springfield *Union* newspaper. When *The Autobiography of Alice B. Toklas*† was published in 1933, he wrote again: "For perhaps 10 years I have been trying to write a letter to you, and I should probably not be doing it now if you had not, in The Autobiography, wondered how many of the soldiers you met in Southern France knew today who you are" (*FF* 273); then he reminded them of their holiday together, and a warm friendship commenced. In 1934 Rogers renewed acquaintance first in Paris and then for a few days at Bilignin. "They looked just as they had before; to me, they have always looked the same, as if my fond eyes growing older adjusted themselves to my friends growing older," he remembered in his memoir after Stein's death (42). At the time of that visit, Stein was still considering the possibilities of a lecture tour in America, and Rogers was one of the people who most influenced her decision to go. He was at the dock to greet them when they arrived in New York in October 1934, and later they visited Rogers and his wife, the poet Mildred Weston, in Springfield. In the summer of 1937, Rogers and his wife made a "Sentimental Journey," as he titled its account in his memoir, with Stein and Toklas, retracing that holiday twenty years before. That was his last meeting with Gertrude Stein although their correspondence continued until her death, by which time she had written him two hundred letters. Alice Toklas wired Rogers immediately: "Gertrude died this afternoon. I am writing. Dearest love. Alice" (*SOA* 3). From 1943 until 1961, Rogers was with the Associated Press as a reporter and arts editor. Later he was an associate editor of the Saturday Review syndicate. He visited Toklas in 1947; he published his memoir, *When This You See Remember Me, Gertrude Stein in Person*, in 1948; in later years he wrote a biography of the Gotham Book Mart Founder, Frances Steloff, *Wise Men Fish Here*; a children's biography, *Gertrude Stein is Gertrude Stein is Gertrude Stein*; and a study of several women in the arts, *Ladies Bountiful*. Rogers died at his home in Gallitzin, Pennsylvania, at the age of eighty-two.

REFERENCES: *EA*, 1937; W. G. Rogers, *When This You See Remember Me, Gertrude Stein in Person*, 1948; *FF*, 1953; *SOA*, 1973.

Paul Padgette
Bruce Kellner

ROHAN, HERMINIE, DUCHESS OF, 28 July 1853–13 April 1926, writer, humanitarian. Virgil Thomson* identifies the Duchess of Rohan as "a naïve writer often unconsciously comical whom certain French compared to the naïve painter, Henri (le Douanier) Rousseau" (115). In a 1928 concert of Thomson's music he substituted his settings for three of her poems, rather than risk his singer's French accent on Gertrude Stein's texts he had similarly turned into songs. Stein's portrait, written the year before, declares that "The Duchess of Rohan was a woman who wrote poetry with a rhyming dictionary but that is very well. Poetry consists in a rhyming dictionary and things seen"—an occasionally appropriate definition for her own poems. She concludes that the Duchess's poetry is "determinate and interesting" (*PL* 310). Born the descendant of the Marquis de Vertelliac, she married in 1872 into one of the great feudal families of France. During La Belle Époque she was a popular Parisian hostess, particularly attracted to American men who, she claimed, had the chivalry of knights, the manners of kings, and in their business dealings the imagination of poets. When the war broke out in 1914 she converted her house on the Boulevard des Invalides into a hospital, and for five years she supervised its nursing staff. She was awarded the Legion of Honor in 1920.

REFERENCES: *NYT*, 14 April 1926; *PL*, 1955; *VT*, 1966.

Bruce Kellner

RÖNNEBECK, ARNOLD, 8 May 1885–14 November 1947, sculptor. The American-born "rich son of a not so rich father," as he told Gertrude Stein (*ABT* 122), German artist Arnold Rönnebeck studied sculpture with Aristide Maillol in Paris, at which time his friend Marsden Hartley* brought him to the Saturday evenings at 27 rue de Fleurus. He was an avid amateur photographer, and he translated some of Gertrude Stein's portraits—notably "Portrait of Mabel Dodge at the Villa Curonia"—first into German and then into French, accomplishments that interested her more than his sculpture. Subsequently, Rönnebeck married Louise Harrington Emerson, also an artist, and taught at the University of Denver. He died in Germany.

REFERENCES: *ABT*, 1933; *WAA*, 1984.

Bruce Kellner

ROSE, SIR FRANCIS, 18 September 1909–circa 11 January 1980, painter. The last of Gertrude Stein's protégés seems to have had no other collectors during his lifetime nor after it. When the Museum of Modern Art, in collaboration with the Baltimore and San Francisco Museums of Art, mounted "Four Americans in Paris" in 1971, an exhibition drawing together the bulk of the paintings at one time in the collections of Michael* and Sarah, Leo,* and Gertrude Stein, only one of his several portraits of Gertrude Stein was included, and none of the more than one hundred paintings she had purchased in his support. He has been ignored in virtually every study of twentieth-century art, and few museums, collectors, or dealers have bothered to endorse him. Born in England of a Scots father and French mother, he came to Gertrude Stein's attention through a painting of a poet and a waterfall that she bought for 300 francs. She kept right on buying. Rose went "quite pink with emotion" when he saw them all hanging at 27 rue de Fleurus, according to *The Autobiography of Alice B. Toklas*† (308), and became ardent in his subsequent devotion. Gertrude Stein, in turn, found him "elegant, unbalanced and intelligent and certain to be right not about everything" but about himself (*EA* 57). Rose exhibited a hundred pictures in Paris when he was twenty-two years old, and Gertrude Stein later reported that "he painted eleven pictures in eight days and do not think they were not painted, they were, each one was, each one was all painted" (*RAB* 56). Rose was independently wealthy and seems to have taken his career as an international lounge lizard with equally resolute superficiality, spawning illegitimate children, hanging around the ballet, Natalie Clifford Barney's* salon, Riviera café society, or entertaining on his yacht, witnessing the Reichstag fire, and hobnobbing among the Nazis with his best friend, Ernst Roehm, founder of Hitler's Storm Troopers. He detailed all this in *Saying Life*, an autobiography remarkable for its specious observations, name-dropping, factual inaccuracies, and colossal misspellings. Kristians Tonny,* for example, is Christian Toni. Rose claims to have extracted a promise from Hermann Göring that "should anything happen to France, he would see that Gertrude Stein and Alice Toklas would be safe and never in financial need" (401). Sir Francis Rose supplied illustrations for the English edition of *The World Is Round*;† he supplied the line drawings for *The Alice B. Toklas Cook Book* and *The Gertrude Stein First Reader*;† and he designed Gertrude Stein's headstone.

REFERENCES: *ABT*, 1933; *EA*, 1937; *EPH*, 1947; Sir Francis Rose, *Saying Life*, 1961; *RAB*, 1973.

Bruce Kellner

ROSENSHINE, ANNETTE, 14 April 1880–22 July 1971, sculptor. Annette Rosenshine was born in San Francisco, the oldest of four children, in a comfortable, middle-class Jewish merchant family. Her birth defect—a harelip and cleft palate—were largely corrected by a series of operations, but she was psychologically crippled by it all her life. In searching for the beauty she felt nature had denied her, she turned her considerable creative energies at an early age to art, first in painting, and later in creating miniature sculptures, or grotesques, inspired by probing into her own psyche, she claimed. Rosenshine was a neighbor of Alice Toklas, and as children they shared mutual interests in art and music. When Michael* and Sarah Stein returned to San Francisco after the 1906 earthquake and fire to inspect the damage to their property, Toklas introduced Rosenshine to them. When the Steins returned to Paris in December that same year, Rosenshine sailed with them to study the art scene they had described to her. She enrolled in Henri Matisse's* first class which included as students Max Weber, Hans Purrmann,* and Oscar Moll, as well as Leo* and Sarah Stein. Inevitably, she met Gertrude Stein too, and was responsible for introducing her to Alice Toklas the following year. With their mutual friend, Harriet Levy,* Toklas had come to Paris for a visit. In Rosenshine's unpublished autobiography, "Life's Not a Paragraph," she describes Gertrude Stein at that time: "I was aware of a dynamic magnetism, an inner distinction which, while quite sensible, remained indefinable. There was power in the beauty of her splendid head with its heavy coil of brown hair which dominated her squat, rotund body. No one feature was outstanding, but an intellectual luminous quality shown in her face. Her hands were the only adult hands I had ever seen that resembled those of a small child—dimpled, with the bony structure well concealed. Her infectious chuckle and low guffaw seemed delightful" (72–73). At that time Stein was writing *The Making of Americans*,† including in it a word portrait that vividly described the psychological trauma that plagued Annette Rosenshine: "This one then was puzzling for many years to me and then slowly this one came to be a whole one to me. . . . Often, as I was saying, it is very irritating . . . just to be hearing repeating" (308). Then, after a forty-page digression, she returned to her subject: "slowly then some felt in this one the muggy resisting bottom that kept her from ever giving herself to any one" (352). Family pressures caused Rosenshine to give up her art studies and return to San Francisco after two years. In the decade that followed she abandoned art for social service work in settlement houses, although in correspondence Stein encouraged her to continue in her artistic pursuits. (Late in life, Rosenshine admitted with dismay that at a particularly dismal time she had destroyed all of Stein's letters to her.) During the twenties, after extensive sojourns as a patient at the Jungian Institute in Zurich, Switzerland, and other institutions, Rosenshine began a series of miniature sculpture portraits of people she met who inspired her by their unusual and individual personalities and accomplishments. In a few years she had created dozens of portraits, including journalist H. L. Mencken; novelist Rebecca West; singers Paul Robeson,* Florence Mills, and Fannie Brice; and Alice Toklas. Her technique in creating one was somewhat parallel to Stein's building up a portrait in words. In a social situation or during an interview, Rosenshine's prospective subject's unique qualities were impressed upon her in such a manner that on returning to her studio she could transfer, as if from her mind to her fingers, to soft clay the portrait that gradually appeared. Rosenshine returned to France three times, always contacted Stein and Toklas, but changes in all of their lives had eroded the relationship. She lived in New York City for a few years and enjoyed a modest career as an artist, returning permanently to the Bay Area where she continued with her experiments, exhibiting in local galleries and museums. Following Stein's death, she resumed a lively correspondence with Toklas, continued to sculpt, wrote her autobiography, and deposited nearly one hundred pieces of her work at the University of California at Los Angeles. She died peacefully at the age of ninety-one in Berkeley, where the Bancroft Library now houses the Annette Rosenshine Collection of papers, scrapbooks, and photographs.

REFERENCES: *MOA*, 1966; *SOA*, 1973; Paul Padgette, "Sculpture Became Her Language," *Lost Generation Journal*, Fall 1975; *BABT*, 1977; Annette Rosenshine, "Life's Not a Paragraph."

Paul Padgette

ROUSSEAU, HENRI, 21 May 1844–4 September 1919, painter. Born in northwestern France, Henri Rousseau was employed for fifteen years by the municipal toll service in Paris. He devoted most of his free time to painting, however, and eventually gave up his secure job to paint full-time. After his paintings were slashed and removed from the show at his first exhibition in the Salon des Champs-Elysées in 1885, he exhibited with the Salon des Artistes Indépendants. A major breakthrough was the acceptance of two of his works by the Salon d'Automne in 1905, but he achieved limited recognition thereafter and that mainly on the part of his fellow artists. He lived most of his later years in poverty and died penniless. Rousseau's childlike and innocent personality encouraged people to think of him as a simpleton, occasionally to play tricks on him. These characteristics, along with his painting style, have led him to be classified as a naive painter, although as Roger Shattuck points out, he was "primitive in performance but not in intention" (80). In fact, "in his 'portrait-landscapes' and lush, mysterious jungle scenes, Rousseau created a visionary world of such powerful originality that his place is secure among the great artists of history," in the view of Grace Gluek (48).

Gertrude Stein had not met Rousseau before the notorious banquet of 1908, which she recounts in detail in *The Autobiography of Alice B. Toklas*.† Picasso* planned the party in Rousseau's honor to celebrate his purchase of a Rousseau work, the *Portrait of a Woman*. Gertrude and Leo* Stein and Alice Toklas were among the thirty or so invited guests, several of whom later published their own varying versions of the affair. Picasso's studio was filled with trestle tables and borrowed chairs and decorated with Japanese lanterns for the occasion. The painting was draped with banners, and the honored guest sat next to it on a chair atop a crate, where hot wax from the lanterns dripped on his head all evening. After much consumption of food and wine, poets Maurice Cremnitz and Guillaume Apollinaire* read poems in Rousseau's honor, and the "blissful and gentle" Rousseau played on his violin a song he had written, followed by waltzes for dancing. The dizzy Marie Laurencin* fell into a tray of pastries; other guests sang, danced, and performed, and Apollinaire solemnly asked Stein and Toklas to "sing some of the native songs of the red indians," which "we did not either of us feel up to," Stein said (*SW* 101). Later the whole neighborhood, it seemed, crashed the party, eating the remains of the food and drinking what they could find—among them a troupe of Italian street singers and Frédé, owner of the Lapin Agile, leading his donkey, Lolo—until Fernande Olivier* threw them all out. The guests went on drinking and declaiming most of the night, but Rousseau, who had fallen asleep at intervals, was taken home in a cab by the Steins about three o'clock. In one major difference of opinion about the evening, Stein describes André Salmon as having drunk so much he "went off his head" and began to fight (*SW* 100). Picasso's statues tottered and little Rousseau and his violin had to be protected from harm until Picasso and others dragged Salmon into the front atelier and locked him in. As they were leaving they found Salmon asleep next to a half-chewed box of matches and Toklas's new hat with the yellow feather chewed off. As they left, Salmon went rushing down the hill with a wild yell. Salmon later claimed that he and another poet had staged an attack of delirium tremens, chewing soap to make them foam at the mouth, in order to bait the stuffy Americans in their formal dress. In any case, it is more likely that the feather on Toklas's hat had been eaten by Lolo the donkey, who was known to have a weakness for clothes. A month or so later, Toklas felt herself being followed on the street on a dark late afternoon, and hurried nervously along until someone called "mademoiselle." It turned out to be the guileless Rousseau, who was offering to see her home. He had been deeply gratified by the banquet in his honor and was a regular visitor to Picasso's studio until his death two years later. Picasso kept his Rousseau painting for the rest of his life.

REFERENCES: *SW*, 1962; Roger Shattuck, *The Banquet Years*, 1968; *CC*, 1974; Grace Glueck, "Putting Rousseau in Perspective," *The New York Times Magazine*, 17 February 1985, 48.

Priscilla Oppenheimer

RUSSELL, MORGAN, 1886–1953, painter. Morgan Russell "was a young one and he was already loving some one." Gertrude Stein wrote this minor painter's portrait at the time she was interested in her subjects' characters rather than in their achievements. Russell spends his brief portrait needing to succeed and trying to learn; eventually, however, everybody is "almost certain that he would not be succeeding in living" (*TWO* 336–37). Russell studied painting with Robert Henri before moving from America to Paris in 1905. Leo Stein* became his patron for a time, and through him Russell came to know Matisse* and Apollinaire.* Synchronism—"ensemble[s] of colors equilibrating around a generative color," a movement he founded with Stanton MacDonald-Wright—occupied Russell until 1916. It was a method, he wrote, that "used light as a series of related chromatic undulations" and considered "more profoundly the harmonic rapports between colors" (*Praeger*, 1801). Subsequently, he began to work more figuratively. He returned to America in 1946 to spend his last years painting large canvases of biblical subjects. His synchronist period he dismissed as apprentice work.

REFERENCES: *TWO*, 1951; *Praeger Encyclopedia of Art*, 1971.

Bruce Kellner

SANBORN, ALVIN F. 1866–22 October 1966, minor author, journalist. Alvin F. Sanborn was on the staff of several newspapers and magazines in Paris in the early years of the twentieth century, among them *The New York Times* and the *Saturday Review*. In 1909 he had a brief and unfortunate encounter with Gertrude Stein when the Grafton Press had agreed to publish *Three Lives*.† However, F. H. Hitchcock, the director, reported that his proofreaders had detected "some pretty bad slips in grammar" (*FF* 42). He suggested that a Paris editor whom they trusted, Alvin Sanborn, make the necessary corrections for a minimal fee. Gertrude Stein ignored the suggestion, but one day Sanborn appeared uninvited at 27 rue de Fleurus. He told her that Grafton had assumed that she was a foreigner, unfamiliar with the English language. Stein informed him that she was quite familiar with English and that the stories were to be printed exactly as she had submitted them. In 1914 Sanborn enlisted in the French army. After the war he worked for the improvement of conditions for

French war veterans. He authored numerous articles on French subjects—the Rouen Cathedral, French education, labor, and agriculture.

REFERENCES: *ABT*, 1933; *FF*, 1953; *CC*, 1974; *WWNA, 1921–1939*, 1976.

Margaret Woodbridge

SANTAYANA, GEORGE, 16 December 1863–26 September 1952, philosopher, teacher, writer. Born in Madrid, Spain, George Santayana was brought to the United States as a boy. He received his Ph.D. from Harvard in 1889 and was appointed instructor in philosophy that same year. So began an illustrious career as teacher and writer that ended in 1912, when he left Harvard and never returned. He was one of the most popular lecturers and one of the greatest—and most neglected—of American philosophers. During the Harvard years he made the acquaintance of Hugo Münsterberg,* a lasting friend and colleague, and Gertrude Stein, at that time a Harvard student. Though she does not appear to have been influenced by Santayana to the same degree as by William James,* she was interested enough to invite him to speak to the Philosophy Club, of which she was secretary. Santayana's writings are of two kinds: the purely academic and the literary. Among the former are *The Life of Reason*, a major work setting forth his materialistic philosophy, *Skepticism and Animal Faith*, and *The Realms of Being*. Like his purely literary works, they are noted for their breadth of vision and stylistic grace. Unlike his contemporary, William James, he found America's optimism a "thin disguise for despair" (*CHAL* 259). James disliked this "cynical sadness" (Vinson 516), and Santayana returned the dislike. He could never accept James's—and the American—reliance upon the will. Santayana's poems and his novel, *The Last Puritan* (1936), are also characterized by his elegant style. His novel attempts to analyze the lingering effects of a dying Puritanism on the American psyche. It was based on the lives of the young people Santayana knew at Harvard, but it never became popular. In 1912 he left for Rome, where he spent the rest of his life, devoting himself to study, writing, and travel. Today his writings of both kinds are valued for their humanistic sympathy and their richness of style.

REFERENCES: Oscar Cargill, *Intellectual America*, 1941; *CHAL*, 1945; *CC*, 1975; James Vinson, ed., *American Writers since 1900*, 1983.

Margaret Woodbridge

SATIE, ERIK, 17 May 1866–5 August 1925, composer. Gertrude Stein's references to Erik Satie are sparse, but she was much taken with his "playful wit which was sometimes biting" (*ABT* 209). Marie Laurencin* had first brought the shy composer to 27 rue de Fleurus shortly after World War I; he proved a charming as well as a welcome dinner guest, enthusiastic about food and wine and Normandy. He spoke little about music, nor did Stein become interested in his own compositions until Virgil Thomson* introduced her to his symphonic drama *Socrate*. Much of Satie's music was only deceptively simple. On the printed page it appeared to present little challenge to a second-year piano student, and even the fanciful, absurd titles encouraged the deception. At the keyboard, however, they have proven to require a penetrating sophistication and technique capable of allowing their minimalist sonorities to communicate. Satie was a strong influence on the generation of young composers identified during the twenties as Les Six: Georges Auric, Louis Durey, Arthur Honegger, Darius Milhaud, Francis Poulenc, and Germaine Tailleferre, in all of whose work Satie's acerbic manner is often apparent, melodic but spare, serious but witty, and usually on a modest scale. Gertrude Stein's 1922 word portrait of Satie is similarly minimal, its five brief lines punning on sounds. The first of them might have served for the composer: "Erik Satie benignly" (*P&P* 27).

REFERENCES: Carl Van Vechten, *Excavations*, 1926; *ABT*, 1933; *P&P, 1934*.

Bruce Kellner

SAWYER, JULIAN, 1915–?, bibliographer. Julian Sawyer first came to Gertrude Stein's attention when he reviewed the 1934 production of *Four Saints in Three Acts*.† He then wrote to advise her of the "monologue version" of the opera he had arranged for himself that "captured the philosophical and spiritual aspects of the text both in the production and performance," with floating fish for the "purgatorial" acts and "thirty symbols . . . to illustrate St. Therese's spiritual progress" (*FF* 286). In his youth he had studied for the priesthood, which may explain this interpretation. He hoped she would be able to attend a performance during her stay in New York, but whether or not she witnessed his effort has not been ascertained. Six years later, when he was twenty-five, Sawyer published an elaborate descriptive bibliography of her work, with a hectoring introduction that contended her "relativistic usage of language in making English an absolute in itself, even to the point of translation into any other language, justified her interchange of the parts of speech and reversals of syntax to parallel that which is being described, this being particularly appropiate in connection with landscape portraiture" (29–30). As for her detractors, "the perspicuity of their own perception, or rather lack of perception, in being a relative matter, has nothing to do with the absolute perspicacity of the most important writer writing to-day" (30). He then published a checklist of writings about Stein's life and work in *Bulletin of Bibliography* in 1943. After Stein's death, he participated in her memorial service at the Gotham Book Mart, reciting lengthy passages of her work from memory. She may have never had a more devoted young disciple, but he felt Alice Toklas's wrath when he gave a series of lectures at the Galerie Neuf in New York, "Gertrude Stein: Her Words and Her Ideas." Learning of them after the fact, Toklas voiced her strong objections to his "repeated references to the subject of sexuality as an approach to the understanding of Gertrude's work" (*SOA* 69). When Donald Sutherland* wrote to her to ask about seeking Sawyer's cooperation in preparation for writing his own study of Stein's work, Toklas hastened to reply: "No dont take on Julian

Sawyer—he is ignorant—unintelligent insensitive and pretentious'' because of ''interpretations that angered one'' (*SOA* 84). Sawyer repeated his lectures at the New School for Social Research in 1949.

REFERENCES: Julian Sawyer, *Gertrude Stein: A Bibliography*, 1940; *FF*, 1953; *SOA*, 1973; *GSCVV*, 1986.

Bruce Kellner

SCUDDER, JANET, 1874–9 June 1940, sculptor. Janet Scudder and Gertrude Stein had been friends from the early days in Paris, when Alice Toklas was impressed with her ''lovely drawling voice'' (*ABT* 251), but they saw each other even more frequently during the twenties. Although she didn't care for Matisse's* work at first, Stein noted, she saw a great deal of him; and although she didn't understand Stein's work, she read it aloud with great feeling. Born in Terre Haute, Indiana, Scudder had studied in Chicago and exhibited at the World Columbian Exposition there in 1893. At the age of twenty she went to Paris, where she studied sculpture and made her home for the next forty-five years. Her ''afternoons'' at her studio became favorite meeting grounds for French and American artists. Scudder was known for her exquisitely wrought fountains and garden statues, for which she won many medals at fairs and expositions. Business took her often to New York, where the sale of her work to architect Stanford White and other wealthy patrons made her a good living. Stein called Scudder ''the doughboy'' because of her solemnity and subtlety, her nice ways and her loneliness. In *The Autobiography of Alice B. Toklas*,† Stein describes in detail an automobile trip from Paris to Provence which she and Toklas in one car and Scudder and a friend in another made in 1922. Scudder had ''the real pioneer's passion for buying useless real estate,'' Stein wrote, and although her intention had been to buy a house in Grasse, she was tempted by every piece of property she saw along the way (*SW* 196). She finally bought a house in Aix-en-Provence which, true to Stein's prediction, she sold after a year. Stein and Toklas spent the rest of the summer and the winter of that year in Saint-Remy with many visits from Scudder, who also visited them often in later years in Bilignin. During World War I Scudder had turned over her house in Paris to the French while she devoted herself to working for the Red Cross and for French refugee children. Her autobiography, *Modeling My Life*, was published in 1925. She returned to New York in 1939 where she lived until her death the following year. Scudder's work can be seen in many American museums, including the Metropolitan Museum of Art in New York.

REFERENCES: *ABT*, 1933; *NYT*, 11 June 1940; *SW*, 1962; *CC*, 1974.

Priscilla Oppenheimer

SEABROOK, WILLIAM BUCHLER, 22 February 1886–20 September 1945, writer. After an early career as a journalist with the *Augusta* (Georgia) *Chronicle* and the *Alabama Journal*, William Seabrook escaped for a nomadic career, first as an ambulance driver in France during World War I, and then as a travel writer in the Near East. He wrote several books about esoteric social customs, *Magic Island* in 1929 about voodoo, *Adventures in Arabia* in 1930, and *Jungle Ways* in 1931. Two years later, fresh from an enthusiastic reading of *The Autobiography of Alice B. Toklas*,† he and his novelist wife, Marjorie Worthington, traveled to Belley to call on Gertrude Stein in Bilignin. He wanted to find out, he said, whether or not she was as interesting as her book. "I said I was," Gertrude Stein replied (*EA* 66), and during the next two days she poured out her entire family history to him, including in detail her relationship with her brother Leo.* They never met again after this brief but intense exchange, discussing at length the contradictions and similarities between religion and black magic, the latter of which Seabrook had experienced during his travels, and his intention to serve as a stretcher bearer at Lourdes to try white magic. Instead, suffering from acute alcoholism, he committed himself for treatment and two years later published *Asylum*, his harrowing account of his partial recovery. In 1942 he wrote his candid autobiography, *No Hiding Place*, and three years later he killed himself with an overdose of sleeping pills.

REFERENCES: *EA*, 1937; *DLB* 4, 1970.

Bruce Kellner

SEDGWICK, ELLERY, 27 February 1972–21 April 1960, editor. Gertrude Stein began submitting her work to the *Atlantic Monthly* in 1919, at the urging of her friend Mildred Aldrich,* whose *Hilltop on the Marne* had run there serially. As a result, a long correspondence commenced between her and the magazine's editor, New England–born Ellery Sedgwick, later edited by Donald Gallup* and published in full in the *Yale University Library Gazette*. It serves as a good example of Stein's persistence in trying to get into print; Sedgwick was more patient and more candid than many other publishers and editors. In 1919, he found her work "baffling" (110), and in 1924 he feared his readers would be "color-blind and music-deaf" to it (118). In 1926, *The Atlantic Monthly* turned down her comparatively accessible Cambridge-Oxford lecture, *Composition as Explanation*,† and when he eventually read it he was "lost in the mazes" of her prose and urged her to write "an entirely intelligible comment" on her work (124). Five years later, in 1932, Sedgwick decided they lived "in different worlds, (125) but a year afterward he accepted four installments of *The Autobiography of Alice B. Toklas*.† Subsequently, *The Atlantic Monthly* published two long autobiographical rambles—"Your United States," a section of *Everybody's Autobiography*† about her lecture tour, and "The Winner Loses," her account of the German occupation in France—and it even allowed one of her abstract pieces, "Butter Will Melt" in its staid pages. Harvard-educated Ellery Sedgwick had come to his sympathetic editorship through training with other magazines, *Youth's Companion, Leslie's Weekly, American Magazine*, and *McCall's*. Apparently, he never met Gertrude Stein, too shy to call on her in

Paris prior to *The Atlantic*'s having accepted her work, and unable to arrange an encounter during her American lecture tour. Early in his career, Sedgwick wrote a biography of Thomas Paine, and after retirement he wrote his memoirs, *The Happy Profession*, in 1946, rounding out a distinguished life in letters.

REFERENCES: Ellery Sedgwick, *The Happy Profession*, 1946; Donald Gallup, "Gertrude Stein and *The Atlantic*," *Yale University Library Gazette*, January 1954; *CC*, 1974.

Paul Padgette
Bruce Kellner

SITWELL, EDITH, 7 September 1887–9 December 1964, writer. The Sitwell family descends from Norman chiefs who came into the north of England in the eleventh century, their Plantagenet countenance in the mediaeval appearance and demeanor of Edith Sitwell and, to a lesser degree, her brothers Osbert* and Sacheverell.* All three were artistically gifted in distinctive ways and were among the most intriguing literary personalities of the twentieth century; Edith Sitwell was, as well, one of the most eccentric. Like her brothers she was largely self-educated, and all three of them had been taken regularly to live for extended periods in Italy and Spain during their childhood. Her first collection of verse was *The Mother and Other Poems*, published when she was twenty-eight. She edited six volumes of *Wheels*, anthologies designed to publish young poets and to showcase all three of the Sitwells. Her most famous single work is *Façade*, a series of extravagant verbal exercises written to be spoken against music composed for them in 1922 by William Walton. Edith Sitwell's output was large, usually in limited editions of her poems, although her idiosyncratic scholarship was more widely available in biographies of Alexander Pope, Jonathan Swift, Elizabeth I, and *The English Eccentrics*. She met Gertrude Stein after reviewing *Geography and Plays*† for *Athenaeum* in July 1923, followed by two critical articles on Stein's work for the London *Vogue*. Dorothy Todd, the magazine's editor, brought Sitwell to 27 rue de Fleurus in 1924, where, three years later, Stein introduced her to Pavel Tchelitchew,* perhaps the strongest contemporary influence on Edith Sitwell's life and work. Between those two encounters, in 1926, Edith Sitwell and her brothers arranged for Gertrude Stein to lecture at Cambridge and Oxford. All three of them attended both her lectures and sat on the platform as attendants. Following the lecture, Stein read "Sitwell Edith Sitwell," a portrait to illustrate her work. Edith Sitwell had previously paid her own homage in modeling her "Jodelling Song" from *Façade* on Stein's "Accents in Alsace" from *Geography and Plays*. Following her lecture, Stein wrote a collective portrait of her hosts, "Edith Sitwell and Her Brothers the Sitwells and also to Osbert Sitwell and to S. Sitwell," although it went unpublished until after her death. In her autobiography, *Taken Care Of*, Edith Sitwell said that Stein looked rather like an Easter Island idol, whose work "for the most part is very valuable because of its revivifying qualities, and it contains to my mind, considerable beauty" (159). Long before that, Stein had described Edith Sitwell equally memorably: "Very tall, bending slightly, withdrawing and hesitatingly advancing, and beautiful with the most distinguished nose I have ever seen on any human being"(*ABT* 285).

REFERENCES: *ABT*, 1933; *PL*, 1955; Edith Sitwell, *Taken Care Of*, 1965; Victoria Glendinning, *Edith Sitwell, A Unicorn among Lions*, 1981.

Paul Padgette

SITWELL, [FRANCIS] OSBERT, 6 December 1892–4 May 1969, writer. Osbert Sitwell was the perfect model of a high-bred Englishman: brilliant in conversation and eccentric in manner. He is best known for his five-volume autobiography, collectively titled after the first, *Left Hand, Right Hand* (1945), a superb re-creation of Edwardian family life, its genuine peculiarities at the family estate, Renishaw Park, and the intellectual and emotional evolution of the remarkable literary trio he made with his siblings Edith* and Sacheverell.* In addition to many volumes of poems, Osbert Sitwell wrote over a dozen works of fiction, some plays, and several collections of essays. After he had served as one of Gertrude Stein's hosts during her 1926 lectures at Cambridge and Oxford, she remembered him as having "that pleasant kindly irresponsible agitated calm that an uncle of an english king always must have" (*ABT* 287). Osbert Sitwell was educated at Eton College; he was a captain in the Grenadier Guards and wounded in France during World War I; he was knighted in 1942.

REFERENCES: *ABT*, 1933; Osbert Sitwell, *Left Hand, Right Hand*, 1945; John Lehman, *A Nest of Tigers*, 1968.

Paul Padgette

SITWELL, SACHEVERELL, 15 November 1897–   , writer. Youngest and most conventional of the most celebrated trio of English eccentrics in modern literary circles, Sacheverell Sitwell is best known for his books on art and travel. He has written a dozen volumes of verse, biographies of composers, and memoirs, even a book on truffle-hunting, in a bibliography numbering over sixty titles. The only member of the trio to marry, he is the father of two sons. Less exotic than his sister Edith,* and less authoritative than his brother Osbert,* Sacheverell Sitwell was nevertheless memorialized in Gertrude Stein's triple-portrait, following his attentions to her during her lectures at Cambridge and Oxford in 1926. Perhaps his name, however, proved too much for her, for she titled it "Edith Sitwell and Her Brothers the Sitwells and also to Osbert Sitwell and to S. Sitwell." Sacheverell Sitwell was educated at Eton College and Balliol College, Oxford; he served in the Grenadier Guards in World War I; he was knighted in 1969.

REFERENCES: *PL*, 1955; John Lehman, *A Nest of Tigers*, 1968.

Paul Padgette

SOLOMONS, LEON M., 29 September 1873–2 February 1900, student, teacher. Leon Solomons was a student from northern California studying at Harvard at the time Gertrude Stein enrolled in its Annex for women—later Radcliffe—in 1893. In 1896 Solomons and Stein worked as a team on a series of experiments conducted under the supervision of psychologist William James.* In the first of these, Stein was the subject in an experiment in automatic writing. The results, "Normal Motor Automatism," were published in the *Harvard Psychological Review*, September 1896, listing Solomons and Stein as co-authors. In a continuation of that work, Stein wrote "Cultivated Motor Automatism," published in the May 1898 issue of the same periodical but after she had left Harvard. Stein considered Solomons an intimate friend as well as a collaborator, leaving "a definite mark on her life," as she wrote in *The Autobiography of Alice B. Toklas*† (95). Philip Redfern, a character in both "Fernhurst" and *The Making of Americans*,† seems to have been jointly based on Solomons and another Harvard student, Alfred Hodder. Solomons returned to California for a year at the University of California at Berkeley, returned to Harvard in 1897 to complete his doctorate in psychology, and then took a teaching position at the University of Wisconsin. His early death may have been from infections contracted in the laboratory, but Stein believed he died of cancer following an operation from which he was unlikely to recover. In October 1900, following Solomons's death, William James wrote to Gertrude Stein about his former student: "Exactly what he would have done had he lived, it is impossible to say, but it would have been absolutely original and remarkable, absolutely clear, and it might have been very important" (*FF* 20).

REFERENCES: *ABT*, 1933; *FF*, 1953; *QED*, 1971; *CC*, 1974.

Paul Padgette
Bruce Kellner

STAGG, HUNTER, 1895–23 December 1960, journalist. Hunter Stagg was "a young southerner as attractive as his name," according to *The Autobiography of Alice B. Toklas*† (257). As one of the editors of Richmond, Virginia's fortnightly literary quarterly, *Reviewer*, Stagg contacted Gertrude Stein in Paris at the suggestion of their mutual friend Carl Van Vechten.* She and Alice Toklas were strongly attracted to the good-looking, articulate young man and gave him two pieces for his magazine, "An Indian Boy" and "Van or Twenty Years After, A Second Portrait of Carl Van Vechten." A fitful correspondence began ten years later when Stagg learned of his one-line appearance in *The Autobiography of Alice B. Toklas*, and during the lecture tour, at novelist Ellen Glasgow's Richmond party for the visitors, they renewed acquaintance. According to Stagg, Stein recognized him immediately and "stayed firmly by my side until she left. Alice Toklas, also recognizing me, flew over the floor like a bird with waving arms crying 'The Myth—the Myth!' " (MacDonald 6). By that time, Van Vechten had broken completely with Stagg. (It was his wont to cut people off without explanation throughout his life.) Stagg and Stein continued to correspond intermittently until her death, and afterwards, he corresponded with Toklas until his own. A head injury at the age of seven afflicted Stagg with powerful seizures for the rest of his life, and he suffered from such paralyzing alcoholism that he was eventually committed to Saint Elizabeth's Hospital in Washington, D.C., where he had lived with his sister after the war. Stagg's book reviews for the *Richmond Times Dispatch* and *Reviewer* clearly indicate his wit and intelligence and perceptive assessment of the contemporary literary scene; he never completed any extensive writing for publication, but his letters to his friends—particularly those to Van Vechten—delineate the literary and cultural climate of the twenties as sufficiently as any biography might have done. "Hunter Stagg turned up . . . , a charming fellow is Stagg, with an intensive Va. enthusiasm and an appreciation of you. We like him as well," Stein wrote to Van Vechten in 1923 after their first meeting; "He is a charming fellow and has talent," Van Vechten replied (*GSCVV* 87–88). Ten years later, Stagg assessed his own failure to a friend: "I conduct myself . . . without guidance of will or prudence. . . . [I]t is not a fall, but a steady progression by a logical development which my character and nature long ago made so inevitable that I can quite understand how people came to invent Fate" (MacDonald 6).

REFERENCES: *ABT*, 1933; Edgar MacDonald, "Hunter Stagg," *Glasgow Newsletter*, October 1981, 2–15; *GSCVV*, 1986.

Bruce Kellner

STEIN, AMELIA KEYSER, 16 April 1842–29 July 1888, homemaker. Gertrude Stein's mother was born in Baltimore, Maryland, into a family of German Jews, and married Daniel Stein* when she was twenty-three years old, "a gentle pleasant little woman with a quick temper," as her daughter described her in *The Autobiography of Alice B. Toklas*† (87). Disguised as a character in *The Making of Americans*,† Amelia Stein "was never important to her children excepting to begin them" (254). There were seven: Michael,* Simon,* Bertha,* then two who died in infancy, then Leo* and Gertrude, who were conceived only as replacements. They were all born in Allegheny, Pennsylvania (now a part of Pittsburgh), between 1865 and 1874, reared between 1874 and 1879 in Vienna and Paris by Amelia's sister Rachel, a governess, and a tutor, and then returned to Baltimore for a year. In 1880, the family moved to East Oakland, California. Never robust, and never influential on her children, Amelia Stein died slowly of cancer, in 1881, but by that time they "had all already had the habit of doing without her" (*EA* 138).

REFERENCES: MOA, 1925; *ABT*, 1933; *EA*, 1937; *CC*, 1974.

Bruce Kellner

STEIN [RAFFEL], BERTHA, 10 October 1870–3 December 1924, homemaker. The two middle Stein children—Bertha and Simon*—were "a little simple minded"; Gertrude Stein thought her brother "was very funny," but she thought that her sister "was not a pleasant person," apparently with reason: "It is natural not to care about a sister certainly not when she is four years older and grinds her teeth at night'' (*EA* 135,37). When their mother died, Bertha became cook and housekeeper for the whole brood. In 1892, she and Gertrude moved to Baltimore to live with relatives. Subsequently, she married Jacob Raffel, the successful manufacturer of corrugated paper boxes. She cut herself free of her siblings at that point, raising a family of her own—Arthur, Daniel, and Gertrude—content with a punctual life devoted to homemaking, music, and flowers. According to her daughter, she never communicated with Gertrude Stein nor spoke of the other Steins, although her son Daniel served as subject for a 1928 portrait, ''Dan Raffel a Nephew,'' after he had met his famous aunt in Paris. Her second son figures as ''Arthur A Grammar'' in *How to Write*.† There are too many family names to ignore the connection—including Bertha's.

REFERENCES: *HTW*, 1931; *EA*, 1937; *PGU*, 1971

Bruce Kellner

STEIN, DANIEL, 27 September 1832–28 January 1891, clothier, investor. Gertrude Stein's erratic father was one of five sons of Michael and Hanne Stein, German Jews who immigrated to America in 1841. Until 1862, Meyer, Samuel, Levi, and Solomon were in partnership with Daniel in a clothing store in Baltimore, Maryland, at which time a family rift sent Solomon and Daniel to Pittsburgh, Pennsylvania, where their branch of the Stein Brothers Clothing Store succeeded for twelve years. While his wife and five children—two others had died in infancy—lived in Vienna and Paris from 1874 to 1879, Daniel Stein was engaged in various business ventures both in Europe and America, moving the family to East Oakland, California, in 1880. In Shasta County, he purchased 480 acres in fruit orchards and grazing land for livestock, and in San Francisco, as vice president of the Omnibus Cable Car Company, he invested in mines, railroads, and the stock exchange. A ''stocky, dominant, aggressive person with no book learning whatever,'' according to his son Leo,* Daniel Stein was ''as insistent as he was positive, and at home he was often making rules which were never observed after the first few days'' (*JS* 187–88). His influence on his children seems to have been minimal, and when he grew increasingly eccentric after his wife's death in 1888, they paid even less attention to him. He became ''more a bother than he had been, that is natural enough,'' Gertrude Stein later wrote (*EA* 138), and she did not mourn him when he died at the age of forty-nine.

REFERENCES: *ABT*, 1933; *EA*, 1937; *JS*, 1950; *CC*, 1974.

Bruce Kellner

STEIN, LEO, 11 May 1872–29 July 1947, writer. Among her four siblings, Gertrude Stein's relationship with Leo was the most profound. He was largely responsible for developing her tastes and interests during her formative years, notably her attitudes toward painting. Their intense devotion began to dissipate itself only when Gertrude began to experiment with narrative in *The Making of*

Americans† and when their discovery, Pablo Picasso,* turned to cubism, assaults on traditional paths Leo was intellectually unable to follow. For the rest of his life he suffered in the shadows cast by his sister's legend, but his own career as a critic and philosopher is interesting if eccentric in its own way. Following a miserable childhood fed by exaggerated fears of anti-Semitism, contracting communicable diseases, sex in either fantasy or actuality, and digestive disorders—the latter plagued him all his life—he grew up neurotic, sexually repressed, melancholy, and secretly shy behind his fierce red beard. Mental truculence and a hypercritical attitude toward very nearly everything led him to quit high school, then to finish two years of it in a few months so he could attend the University of California. These cruel assessments are not those of his critics but of his own, spelled out in autobiographical fragments and posthumously published in *Journey into the Self* (198–200). When his sisters went east to relatives in 1892, Leo went to Harvard, where Gertrude enrolled in the Harvard Annex (later Radcliffe) the next year. They were first separated when Leo withdrew to make a world tour with his cousin Fred Stein. They went first to Japan, where he discovered the woodblock prints of the kind that had earlier influenced the French post-impressionists. Subsequently they traveled to China, which impressed him; India, which reminded him of Rudyard Kipling's work; and Egypt, which bored him. Italy motivated his planning a tour for himself and Gertrude the next year, and they spent several summers there. Casting about for a career, Leo Stein took up history but discarded it as dishonest, like fiction; philosophy was too speculative; biology, which he attempted briefly at Johns Hopkins while Gertrude was studying medicine there, was immediately uncongenial; aesthetics and art criticism of the quattrocento bogged down; finally he tried painting itself, intermittently at least. He settled in Paris at 27 rue de Fleurus and began to collect paintings to join his Japanese prints, notably Renoir. Through Bernard Berenson,* whom he had met in Italy, he began to purchase Cézannes from Ambroise Vollard.* Gertrude joined him in 1903, and when the Stein estate suddenly offered them an eight thousand franc fringe benefit, they invested it in two Gauguins, two more Cézannes, two more Renoirs, and a Maurice Denis, the latter a present from Vollard. Later that year they purchased a Toulouse-Lautrec, although Leo yearned to add Degas and Manet who, with Renoir and Cézanne, he believed the great painters of the period. In 1905, they began to add works by Matisse* and Picasso. In 1907, Alice Toklas came into Gertrude Stein's life, and in 1909, Nina Auzias* came into Leo's, advents that must have contributed to the final break between brother and sister after a nearly forty-year alliance. His growing disenchantment with her work—and with some of its inspiration—must have had equally strong influences. "I can't abide her stuff and think it is abominable," he wrote to a friend about the kind of writing later published as *Tender Buttons*;† Picasso's recent work was "utter abomination"; together they were "turning out the most Godalmighty rubbish that is to be found" (*JS* 49, 53). Leo Stein moved to Italy with Nina Auzias, taking the Renoirs, most of the Matisses and Cézannes, and leaving the Picassos. He returned to the United

States during World War I and attempted a teaching career, but as he was hard of hearing and talked incessantly, he was unsuccessful in the classroom. He returned to Europe in 1920, married Nina Auzias, and turned to writing: *The ABC of Aesthetics* in 1927, *Appreciation* in 1947, and several articles for *The New Republic* in between. *Journey into the Self*, a selection of letters and journal entries, was published posthumously in 1950. References to Gertrude Stein peppered his work, even in some notes written a few days before his death, in which he tried to assess their relationship. Gertrude Stein never mentioned him by name again, except under the duress of identification for the family lineup in *Everybody's Autobiography*.† In *The Autobiography of Alice B. Toklas*† and in *Two: Gertrude Stein and Her Brother*,† her virtuoso analysis of their relationship and its permutations, he is only referred to as "her brother," always in third person. He tried to patch up the rift in 1916 and again in 1919; she never replied. Some time later, Gertrude Stein was stalled in the Paris traffic; Leo passed by and raised his hat; she bowed in return. Then she wrote, in part: "This was a chance. That might have happened. Minutely. . . . As she rode along. Easily. By driving. As she rode. Along. She. Bowed. To her brother. . . . Nor was there. Intention. That she. Bowed to her brother. She bowed to her brother" (*P&P* 238–40). Thirteen years earlier she had written, in "Accents in Alsace," "Brother brother go away and stay" (*G&P* 409).

REFERENCES: *G&P*, 1922; *ABT*, 1933; *P&P*, 1934; *EA*, 1937; *JS*, 1950; *PGU*, 1971; *CC*, 1974.

Bruce Kellner

STEIN, MICHAEL, 26 March 1865–13 October 1938, railroad manager, art collector. When Daniel Stein* moved his family to the West Coast, his eldest son Michael was fifteen years old. Michael later attended Johns Hopkins University and then became first assistant superintendent of the Omnibus Cable Company, of which his father was vice president. When Daniel Stein died, Michael sold the family's holdings in San Francisco street railroads to Central Pacific magnate Collis P. Huntington and went to work for him as a branch manager of the Market Street Railway Company. Sound investments and family property in Shasta County and in Baltimore made possible modest independent incomes for himself and his siblings. He was a perfect legal guardian from Gertrude Stein's point of view, as she said to him later, "Mike you always understood so well that every one wants what they want and you always let Leo* and myself have it" (*EA* 139). Before he was forty years old Michael Stein had retired with a comfortable income and spent the rest of his life collecting modern art. He moved to Paris with his wife, Sarah Samuels (1870–1953), a San Francisco attorney's daughter who practiced Christian Science, and on the rue Madame they established a Saturday evening salon. It was popularly bandied that artists and writers went to Mike and Sally Stein's for good food and elegant discourse surrounded by dozens of paintings by Henri Matisse,* and then moved on to the more raffish delights offered by Leo and Gertrude Stein at 27 rue de Fleurus, where the conversation was more bohemian and the paintings even more startling. Actually, the two Stein salons were rather closer in atmosphere if not in appearance. Shortly before World War I, Michael Stein commissioned the Swiss architect Le Corbusier to build a house at Montigny-sur-Loing, but when World War II threatened, he and Sarah returned with their art collection to California. Their only child, Allan (1897–1951), remained in France and subsequently became heir to Gertrude Stein's art collection, while Allan's son Daniel (1927–   ) inherited Michael Stein's estate and eventually, of course, Gertrude Stein's as well, after Alice Toklas died in 1967.

REFERENCES: *ABT*, 1933; *EA*, 1937; *PGU*, 1971; *CC*, 1974.

Bruce Kellner

STEIN, SIMON, 7 May 1868–circa 19 August 1913, cable car brakeman. The two middle Stein children—Simon and Bertha*—were "a little simple minded," although Gertrude Stein thought her brother "was always very funny" (*EA* 135). Genial enough to be the family clown, and obese because of his over-fondness for eating, Simon was apparently uneducable, incapable even of remembering Columbus's discovery of America in 1492, but that "was not surprising . . . to anyone" (*EA* 136). He tried to learn a trade at the Fulton Iron Works and he tried to be a house painter. Eventually he became a brakeman or gripman on one of the family's cable cars—called "street railroads"—in San Francisco, genially distributing candy to children and cigars to male passengers. He was always short of money, believing he had given out the wrong change. Gertrude Stein claimed he confused five dollar gold pieces with nickels (*EA* 136), but their brother Leo* claimed he confused twenty dollar gold pieces with nickels because they were the same size (*JS* 279). By the age of thirty-eight, Simon had grown so fat that he could no longer stand up during the transits, and he was obliged to retire, just at the time of the San Francisco earthquake and fire. His death has been reported to have coincided with that catastrophe, in 1906, but he lived for seven more years, running a stationery and cigar concession in an Italian grocery store, cared for by a Mrs. Moffat, in whose home he had a room and to whom he left his estate through a will drawn up by Michael Stein's* father-in-law.

REFERENCES: *ABT*, 1933; *EA*, 1937; *JS*, 1950; *CC*, 1974.

Bruce Kellner

STELOFF, FRANCES, 31 December 1887–   , bookseller. Frances Steloff was born into so large and so poor a family that she had to leave school at the age of ten to help support it. At twenty, she left Saratoga Springs, New York, and over the next twelve years worked in several Manhattan bookshops. At thirty-three she borrowed enough money to open her own shop, the Gotham Book Mart, now a literary landmark in New York on West 47th Street, its third successive but longest standing address. It is still one of the leading avant-garde bookshops in America. Now largely retired, Steloff has no personal taste for the work of many of the writers she championed over the decades, but their dedicated lives have appealed to her. The James Joyce Society was born at the Gotham Book Mart under the shingle proclaiming that "Wise Men Fish Here," and Marianne Moore, Anaïs Nin, and Henry Miller were among her special literary children, although she was unlikely to make distinctions among writers—other than to avoid cultivating them for their commercial possibilities. Publication day for Joyce's *Finnegan's Wake* was celebrated at the Gotham Book Mart; autograph parties for Dylan Thomas, Margaret Anderson,* Jean Cocteau,* and dozens of others were held there; Gotham Book Mart hosted Edith and Osbert Sitwell* during their lecture tour; and inevitably Gertrude Stein's work was always available through Frances Steloff's efforts to keep it in stock. She possessed a consistent astuteness in buying and selling books overlooked by regular outlets, and it has paid off in the longevity of the Gotham Book Mart. The story of meeting Gertrude Stein in 1934, during the American lecture tour, has differed slightly from time to time. In his Steloff biography, W. G. Rogers* dismissed it in a single line: "With Alice B. Toklas, stiff as a ramrod, in the lead, Gertrude Stein came in during the expatriates' triumphal invasion of the United States" (168). In her memoir, "In Touch with Genius," Steloff remembered Toklas coming toward her, smiling, while Stein lingered over the big display of her books in the shop's showcase, then came in to shake hands and chat, saying she would return. At about the same time, she related the incident again in "The Making of an American Visit: Gertrude Stein." Steloff was reading the mail when "the homeliest little woman I had ever seen walked in with a broad smile which grew even broader as she came toward me with hand outstretched." Then Stein came in, having paused over the window display, "with a lovely smile and a gleam in her eye," and promised to return (11). Both versions agree that the following day Stein was autographing books at Brentano's down the block and couldn't return to the Gotham Book Mart because she was leaving on her lecture tour the next day. Carl Van Vechten* told a different story, but privately: Toklas, having been in correspondence with Steloff over the Plain Edition she had been publishing in Paris, went in the shop to express her gratitude for its distributing copies in America, but Gertrude Stein only peered in at the doorway and cruelly, inexplicably, refused to meet the one bookseller in America who had been steadily stocking her work for nearly fifteen years. Later, Stein did autograph copies of her books when they were sent over to her hotel from the Gotham Book Mart, nor did the lecture tour take her beyond commuting distance from New York for a couple of weeks. Steloff's loyalty did not waver. In 1940 she published a special catalog, *We Moderns, 1920–1940*, listing books for sale by many of the era's leading literary figures, each writer prefaced with an introduction by another one. The Stein selection was substantial and impressive, and Gertrude Stein supplied a preface about Paris rather than about some other writer. Steloff used it as an introduction for the catalog itself. She issued a catalog for Gertrude

Stein's work alone in 1964; like *We Moderns*, it carried a warm endorsement from Carl Van Vechten. Frances Steloff sold the Gotham Book Mart in 1967 to Andreas Brown, but in her 101st year she continues to live on the third floor of the building and still comes in to take a look at the legend she created.

REFERENCES: W. G. Rogers, *Wise Men Fish Here*, 1965; Frances Steloff, "The Making of an American Visit; Gertrude Stein," Confrontations, Spring 1974, and "In Touch with Genius," *Journal of Modern Literature*, April 1975.

Paul Padgette
Bruce Kellner

STERNE, MAURICE, 13 July 1878–23 July 1957, painter. Driven from Latvia with his family when he was twelve, Maurice Sterne immigrated to America in 1889. He studied painting with Thomas Eakins—which may account in part for his essential conservatism—and later in Paris and Florence where he first knew Leo* and Gertrude Stein. Later describing them as "the happiest couple on the Left Bank" in his memoir, *Shadow and Light*, he contended that Gertrude Stein had "no taste or judgment" and considered her only "a reflection of her brother" (47–49). Picasso* he judged a fraud and Matisse* a crude colorist. In return, Gertrude Stein neglected to mention him at all in her account of the Saturday evenings at 27 rue de Fleurus in *The Autobiography of Alice B. Toklas*,† but she did include him in her portrait of a homosexual trio, "Men," the others identified in manuscript as Hutchins Hapgood* and Swedish sculptor David Edstrom.* Sterne left Paris to live in Greece, Russia, Germany, finally for two years in Bali. In 1915 he became Mabel Dodge's* lover on the rebound, following her affair with John Reed. They were married briefly and lived at her mountain compound for artists in Taos, New Mexico. In 1933, Sterne was given a one-man show at the Museum of Modern Art, and he executed a series of murals in the Justice Department in Washington, D.C. Settling in California, he seems to have kept in touch with Leo Stein.

REFERENCES: Maurice Sterne, *Shadow and Light*, 1965; *CC*, 1974; Lois Palken Rudnick, *Mabel Dodge Luhan*, 1984.

Bruce Kellner

STETTHEIMER, FLORINE, 19 August 1871–11 May 1944, painter, stage designer. Artist, poet, and hostess, Florine Stettheimer painted in a unique individual style, delicate and mock-naive. She studied at the Art Students League in New York and in Stuttgart, Munich, and Berlin. On their return from Europe at the outset of World War I, Stettheimer and her sisters Ettie and Carrie had determined to live their lives centered on art. Rarely exhibited during her life, Stettheimer's works were "unveiled" at the legendary salons she and her mother and sisters held at their home in New York City. In attendance were writers and artists of the avant-garde, Marcel Duchamp,* Georgia O'Keeffe, Pavel Tchel-itchew,* Carl Van Vechten,* Virgil Thomson,* Gaston Lachaise, and Avery

Hopwood,* among others, many of whose portraits Stettheimer painted. The eccentricity of the decor and clothing worn by the sisters at their salon created an atmosphere of wit and humor which balanced the seriousness of the conversation. Stettheimer designed the critically praised sets and costumes for the Gertrude Stein–Virgil Thomson opera *Four Saints in Three Acts*.† The 1934 production had an all-black cast, whom Stettheimer dressed in bright red, green, and purple robes and white gloves. The set featured bright, white lighting and unusual materials—ostrich plumes, lace, seashells, a looped blue cellophane sky, and palm fronds fashioned of pink muslin bows. After her mother's death in 1937 Stettheimer decorated her own bachelor apartment creatively in cellophane, chandeliers, white furniture and lace, where she "received" and held dinner parties. She embarked on a series of large paintings called "Cathedrals." Posthumous exhibitions of her work were held in New York at the Museum of Modern Art in 1946, in Detroit, and in Boston in 1980.

REFERENCES: Edward T. James, et al., eds., *Notable American Women*, 1971; *CC*, 1974; Chris Petteys, *An International Dictionary of Women Artists*, 1982.

Priscilla Oppenheimer

STEWARD, SAMUEL MORRIS, 23 July 1909– , writer, teacher. Samuel Steward's early life is typical of midwest upbringing early in the century. He was born in Woodsfield, Ohio, to a conventional, middle-class family. His father was an auditor and his mother was a teacher. Early on he developed a love for exotic literature. He completed his education at Ohio State University with a Ph.D. in 1934. During his undergraduate days there, he wrote his first book of short stories, *Pan and the Firebird*, published in a limited edition in 1930. The stories show a strong sense of fantasy inspired by his reading of James Branch Cabell. Steward's first teaching job was at Carroll College in Helena, Montana, in 1934–1935. The following year, he taught at the State College of Washington (now Washington State University) and at that time published his novel, *Angels on the Bough*, through Caxton Press. The authoritarian college president, without having read the book, decided on hearsay that it was indecorous and summarily dismissed Steward. After an investigation by the American Association of University Professors, he was absolved, and the college was censored for restricting the creative output of its faculty. While still an undergraduate, Steward had come to know Gertrude Stein's writing through one of his teachers, Clarence Andrews, one of the first American academics to include her work in classes. When Andrews died suddenly of pneumonia in 1932, Steward wrote to Stein. Her reply was the first of more than one hundred letters, eventually addressed to "Dear Sammy," as he titled his memoir of Stein and Toklas, published with their letters to him, in 1977. Although they made every effort to meet during the American lecture tour in 1934 and 1935, it was not until Steward's first trip to France, in the summer of 1937, that they did so. When *Angels on the Bough* was published, Steward had a copy sent to Stein, to which she responded, "I like it I like it a lot, you have really created a piece of something, . . . you have succeeded in reaching a unity without connecting'' (129). During his second visit to Bilignin, in 1939, Stein surprised him with a poem, "To Sammy on His Birthday." At that time she was taking notes for "To Do," a children's birthday book, completed during World War II, but not published until 1957 in *Alphabets and Birthdays*. In it, Steward said she "found the amusing use . . . of my allergies under the letter 'S' '' (64), as the finished version attests: "he could eat the candles but not the cake, poor dear Sammy" (50). In his memoir, Steward recounts his two visits with Stein and Toklas in Bilignin, claiming almost total recall through the journals in which he had written each day's experiences in detail. After Stein's death in 1946, Steward visited Toklas fifteen times, usually at Christmas. After leaving the State College of Washington, Steward taught at Loyola University and De Paul University in Chicago. Between these two appointments, he was an editor with the *World Book Encyclopedia* for two years. He left university teaching permanently in 1954, calling himself an early dropout from the student revolts of the period and suffering depression from the progressively poor aptitude of each year's new crop of students. He deliberately turned to something far removed from the academic world and became a tattoo artist for a decade. Also, he began to write erotic fiction under a series of pseudonyms, the most familiar being Phil Andros. In 1984 Steward published *Parisian Lives*, a novel containing autobiographical details, and in the same year he published *Murder Is Murder Is Murder*, a mystery in which Stein and Toklas appear as his detectives. Steward lives in Berkeley, California, in a cottage stocked with books, thirty-one clocks, two dogs, and rich memories.

REFERENCES: *EA*, 1937; *A&B*, 1957; Samuel M. Steward, *Dear Sammy*, 1977; Steward interview, 1987.

Paul Padgette

STIEGLITZ, ALFRED, 1 January 1864–13 July 1946, photographer, editor, gallery director. "He was the first one that ever printed anything that I had done. And you can imagine what that meant to me or to any one," Gertrude Stein wrote long afterward (Frank 280). Alfred Stieglitz was interested in her, although on his first visit to 27 rue de Fleurus she was uncharacteristically silent while her brother did all the talking. Stieglitz asked Leo,* who declined, to write for his magazine, *Camera Work*; he didn't catch Gertrude's name. Later, however, Stieglitz helped to make her name familiar in America. It was in the special issue of *Camera Work* of August 1912, devoted to Picasso* and Matisse,* that Stein's word portraits of the two artists appeared. In a later issue her portrait of Mabel Dodge* was published. Stieglitz devoted his life to winning recognition of photography as a creative art, and pioneered in introducing avant-garde art in the United States. In 1902 Stieglitz, along with Edward Steichen and C. H. White, founded the Photo Secession, an organization working to promote photography as an art form, and edited its quarterly publication, *Camera Work*. He opened a gallery called 291, at 291 Fifth Avenue in New York, in 1905 to show the group's work, but in a few years expanded to include modern painters and sculptors such as Picasso, Matisse, and Constantin Brancusi at a time when these artists were considered a menace to public morals. Some years earlier Stieglitz himself had been expelled from the Camera Club, which he had founded, because of his espousal of Matisse. The 291 featured the work of the Americans John Marin, Marsden Hartley,* Arthur Dove, Charles Demuth,* and Georgia O'Keeffe, whom he married in 1924. The gallery closed in 1917, but in 1929 Stieglitz opened An American Place, where he continued to exhibit new art and to urge the public to see in a new way. For Stieglitz, art was not a means to wealth; he never took money for his own photographs, and he promoted the careers of other photographers at the expense of his own. His twofold goal met with astounding success in his lifetime, however, and his own works hang today in nearly every major museum in America.

REFERENCES: Waldo Frank et al., eds., *America and Alfred Stieglitz*, 1934; *NYT*, 14 July 1946; *CC*, 1974; Sue Davidson Lowe, *Stieglitz; A Memoir/Biography*, 1983.

Priscilla Oppenheimer

SUTHERLAND, DONALD, 27 September 1915–November 1978, teacher, writer. As an undergraduate at Princeton, Donald Sutherland met Gertrude Stein after her lecture there in the fall of 1934. A decade later the strong impression she and her work had made on him had only intensified. As a member of the armed forces in France, he wrote to her in July 1945, after she had sent him a copy of a French translation of *The First Reader*,† how much satisfaction her "contradiction to normal English" gave him: "I do get a nice reminiscent feeling of the first delighted shock I had when I was 13 or 14 and came across Tender Buttons† in the Library of Congress. At any rate by this time, because I do read a good many languages without referring them to English, I read Stein as Stein just as I read Herodotus as Herodotus" (*FF* 384). During the intervening decade, Stein had continued to read his work with interest—actually he had sent her some early examples before they met—including his 1937 novel, *Child with a Knife*, and he had visited her and Alice Toklas at 5 rue Christine. Stein's death, just a year after his letter about the French *First Reader*, cut short their friendship, but his devotion to Toklas continued, and he provided the first extended critical attention to Gertrude Stein's work—it is a model of the Ezra Pound–T. S. Eliot New Criticism in its decadence—*Gertrude Stein: A Biography of Her Work*, published by Yale University Press in 1951. Quirky, cerebral, and bereft of biographical reference or implication, Sutherland's work assesses Stein's published writings more or less chronologically without tying them at all to her personal life. Sutherland was "somewhat naive about Gertrude and Alice as people," Carl Van Vechten* wrote to Donald Gallup,* 5 September 1951, although he thought the book was "brilliant, if difficult. No one can review it. No one is good enough" (246–47). With Thornton Wilder* and Gallup, Sutherland was a member of Van Vechten's advisory committee for the Yale Edition of the Unpublished Writings of Gertrude Stein, issued in eight volumes between 1951 and 1958, and he supplied the introduction for the sixth of these, *Stanzas in Meditation*.† Robert Bartlett Haas's* *Primer for the Gradual Understanding of Gertrude Stein*† includes Sutherland's "Gertrude Stein and the Twentieth Century," and his nostalgic memoir, "Alice and Gertrude and Others," was published in *Prairie Schooner*. Sutherland was a professor of classics at the University of Colorado and author of a remarkable study of classic, romantic, and modern critical approaches to literature, just as quirky and cerebral as his book about Stein, and just as singularly valuable, *Oh, Romanticism!*

REFERENCES: Donald Sutherland, *Gertrude Stein: A Biography of Her Work*, 1951; *FF*, 1953; *SIM*, 1956; *PGU*, 1971; Bruce Kellner, *Letters of Carl Van Vechten*, 1987.

Paul Padgette
Bruce Kellner

TAL COAT [JACCOT], PIERRE, 1905–?, painter. The son of a fisherman, Pierre Tal Coat grew up in a fishing village in Finistère. Artists from France and foreign countries who came to the village to paint awakened his interest in art. He worked as a designer and painter in a porcelain factory and in 1924 moved to Paris. Mainly self-taught, he held his first one-man exhibition in 1927 and in 1931 exhibited with a group called Forces Nouvelles. In 1936 his portrait of Gertrude Stein with Basket,* painted in 1934, won the Paul-Guillaume Prize. In the late thirties he worked on a cycle called "Massacres," inspired by the Spanish civil war in a style that has been called expressionistic realism. He moved to Aix-en-Provence in the forties and painted studies of the mysteries of nature, inspired by the art of the Chinese Sung dynasty. Later his work became more abstract as it dealt with the ways primitive man might have perceived the world. Tal Coat does not seem to be mentioned by name in any of Stein's writing. A paragraph in *Everybody's Autobiography*,† which in all likelihood refers to him, may explain why: "once again now I am sitting again to a painter, I sit and he sits and we do not talk together, I look out over the roofs and sit not very comfortably and he draws to get acquainted with my portrait" (*EA* 157). A second Stein portrait by Tal Coat is reproduced on the covers of *Reflection on the Atomic Bomb*† and *How Writing Is Written*.†

REFERENCES: *Praeger Encyclopedia of Art*, 1971; *EA*, 1973; Günther Metken, *Realismus, Zwischen Revolution und Reaktion 1919–1939*, 1981.

Priscilla Oppenheimer

TCHELITCHEW, PAVEL, 21 September 1898–31 July 1957, painter, stage designer. After the 1918 revolution, Pavel Tchelitchew, the son of a wealthy Russian family who had studied in Kiev, worked in Istanbul, Sofia, and Berlin as a designer of sets and costumes for theater and ballet. He also painted in an abstract style, but on settling in Paris in 1923 he became one of the neoromantic group of young painters, along with Eugène Berman* and his brother Leonid, Christian Bérard,* and Kristians Tonny,* whose works represented a reaction against abstraction. Gertrude Stein was impressed with some of his work—"the young russian. . . . was painting colour that was no colour, he was painting blue pictures and he was painting three heads in one"—but although he had some good ideas, she thought, he did not have the dominating creative power to make a new movement in art (*SW* 212–13). The neoromantics vied for her attention and patronage, but she later disposed of most of their works that she had bought. When their pictures began to disappear into the walls, she told them, "they go out of the door naturally" (*SW* 214). Stein introduced Tchelitchew to Edith Sitwell,* whose portrait he painted and who helped secure him more commissions. Stein included a word portrait of Tchelitchew in *Dix Portraits*,† but by then their friendship had chilled. Whether Stein was jealous of his very close relationship with Sitwell, or whether Alice Toklas had engineered the break because a portrait Tchelitchew had painted of her made her look—according to Bravig Imbs*—like a "sleepy vulture" is not clear (*CC* 339). Toklas wrote in 1949 that she had learned a lot about Russians from her intimacy with Tchelitchew: "You have to be of hard metal to resist them," even though Tchelitchew "was absolutely cannibal—he devoured everything—men women children— flats—furniture—everything except the original Russian ballet which he caressed" (*SOA* 154). He designed ballet sets in Paris, most notably Diaghilev's *Ode* in 1928, and moved to New York in 1934 where he achieved success as a set designer. In painting he experimented with multiple perspective and anatomical landscapes, and an exhibit at the Museum of Modern Art in 1942 included both paintings and set designs. Tchelitchew moved to Italy in 1951 where he remained the rest of his life. A comprehensive exhibition of his work was held in Paris in 1956 and a retrospective took place in New York in 1964. Gertrude Stein reprinted her portrait of Tchelitchew in *Portraits and Prayers*,† titled "Pavlik Tchelitchef or Adrian Arthur." (The alternate name is unidentifiable.) He was the partial subject of "Love a Delight," along with the pianist Allen Tanner, his lover at that period. This 1927 narrative was published posthumously in *Painted Lace*† where it was classified as a "Landscape and Geography."

REFERENCES: *ABT*, 1933; *P&P*, 1934; *PL*, 1955; *SW*, 1962; *Praeger Encyclopedia of Art*, 1971; *SOA*, 1973; *CC*, 1974.

Priscilla Oppenheimer

THOMSON, VIRGIL, 25 November 1896–   , composer, critic. Virgil Thomson showed his talent for composing and performing music during his early years in Kansas City, Missouri. As a Harvard student he became acquainted with Erik Satie's music and Gertrude Stein's *Tender Buttons*,† experiences that changed his life, he has averred and then proven in his idiosyncratic autobiography, *Virgil Thomson* (46). In France with the Harvard Glee Club, after his graduation in 1921, he soon made friends with a group of young painters, poets, and musicians living in Paris, and in 1925 the composer George Antheil took him to 27 rue de Fleurus. Stein seems to have been unimpressed by Antheil, but she and Thomson got on "like Harvard men," Thomson claimed (89). Alice Toklas did not care for him, however, until he had proven himself by setting to music Stein's "Susie Asado" as a Christmas gift. They did not meet again until the following summer, when Thomson sent Stein a postcard from Savoy, to which she replied immediately, beginning a close and intense friendship. Thomson puts it almost as Stein might have done: "we were forever loving being together" (97), although for one four-year period they did not speak. Even then, however, they wrote to each other, using business as their pretext. Early in the friendship, Thomson began to compose musical portraits in the manner Stein used for her literary portraits, reinforcing his belief that her words followed the patterns and cadences of music more than of speech and were therefore ideally adapted for music. "Miss Gertrude Stein as a young girl," for example, is a violin solo, ostensibly in waltz-time but varying its incremental repetitions by shifting the innocent theme unexpectedly into 4/4 and 5/4 time. He created musical settings for several shorter Stein texts, notably "Capital Capitals" from *Operas and Plays*† for four male voices and piano accompaniment; they sing sequentially, never in unison.

In 1927 he asked her to write a libretto for an opera; rejecting various historical subjects, they chose the lives of Spanish saints, in iconographical rather than biographical rendering, seeing parallels between the religious life of the sixteenth century and the artistic life of the twentieth, both saints and artists dividing the day equally between the lonely pursuit of worthy goals and conversations. Stein had little musical knowledge and indeed seems to have considered music an inferior art fit only for adolescents. Thomson stimulated her interest in opera for the first time since her adolescence, and she learned to respect his musical judgment. Thomson was given the responsibility for getting the opera into production, yet Stein insisted that they split any royalties fifty-fifty. He protested that such a division was unfair, but she was adamant. He might have carried the burden of most of the work, she admitted, but her name alone had "commercial value" (*CC* 438). At the time, of course, she was as little read as he was performed. Their four-year estrangement ended only with the successful production of *Four Saints in Three Acts*† in 1934. In addition to their talents, it brought together those of John Houseman* as director; Frederick Ashton* as choreographer; Florine Stettheimer* as designer; and Maurice Grosser,* who provided a workable scenario for the plotless material. Long before the actual production, and doubtless influenced by the Harlem Renaissance of the late twenties, Thomson conceived of the idea of an all-black cast because blacks sang beautifully, had perfect diction, and moved with such dignity onstage. Thomson's music makes no attempt to explain Stein's obscure libretto by somehow imitating the words. Most of the score, he says, came from his Protestant upbringing, with echoes of familiar old hymns.

Thomson went on to enjoy a prolific career as a composer, including music for another Stein opera, *The Mother of Us All.*† Based on the life of Susan B. Anthony, it is more frequently performed, perhaps because it has a traceable if fanciful plot. Grosser again supplied a scenario for the work, first produced the year after Stein's death. Thomson has composed symphonies, ballets, choral works, a cello concerto, much piano, vocal, and chamber music, and film scores for the classic American documentaries of the the thirties, *The River* and *The Plough That Broke the Plains*. From 1940 until 1954 he was chief music critic for the New York *Herald Tribune*, a post he filled with a distinction simultaneously erudite, baleful, and sassy. The best of his writings have been collected for publication as *The Virgil Thomson Reader*. In 1966 he published his autobiography, twenty years after Gertrude Stein's death, containing a lengthy account of their long association, reflecting a rare understanding of and sympathy with her as a writer and as a person. The daily routine, Stein's writing habits, her eccentricities, and above all her aesthetic theories are set forth in vivid detail, extending in part Thomson's helpful introduction and notes to *Bee Time Vine*† in the Yale edition of Stein's unpublished writings. Thomson assesses this third volume's content with rare compassion, anticipating his conclusions in his autobiography that Gertrude Stein's contributions to art were made possible by the dedication of Alice Toklas who constructed and protected the serenity Stein needed. Her work, in Thomson's view, was a great breakthrough, all the more remarkable because no literary predecessor seems to have influenced her in the least. She influenced other writers, even—he thinks—James Joyce, but her own work seems to have come from direct inspiration. Thomson had continued as a valued friend for the remainder of Stein's life, and after her death he retained the same status with Alice Toklas, giving her not only emotional support but financial aid when in her last years she was reduced to penury. When she died in 1967 she bequeathed her piecrust table to "dearest Virgil Thomson" (*CC* 570). The subsequent twenty years have seen major revivals of both of the Stein-Thomson operas, and now in his nineties Thomson continues to compose, review, and comment on the contemporary musical and literary scenes within his province.

Gertrude Stein's writings contain at least three memorials to her friend and collaborator, in addition to his appearances in her autobiographies. Her 1930 portrait of him appeared in *Dix Portraits*† and was reprinted in *Portraits and Prayers*† in 1934, a narrative in paragraphs rather than in the verse-like shapes most of her other portraits of that period were cast. She wrote "To Virgil and Eugene" that same year, a block paragraph playing with the familiar children's counting song, "one two three four five six seven all good children go to heaven some are good and some are bad one two three four five six seven all good children go to heaven" (*PL* 311). Eugene McCown,* like Thomson, came from Missouri. Finally, Stein's *The Mother of Us All* numbers "Virgil T." in its cast of characters. He sings the prologue, as one of two interlocutors in that operatic collaboration; the other one is "Gertrude S."

REFERENCES: *ABT*, 1933; *P&P*, 1934; *LO&P*, 1949; *PL*, 1955; *VT*, 1966; *CC*, 1975; John Rockwell, "Virgil Thomson's 'Saints' Goes Marching On," *NYT*, 9 November 1986.

Margaret Woodbridge
Bruce Kellner

TOKLAS, ALICE B[ABETTE], 30 April 1877–7 March 1967, homemaker. Alice Babette Toklas was born in San Francisco to a mercantile family of Polish-Jewish and German-Jewish background. She grew up in comfortable circumstances, was educated at private schools, and indulged her love of reading. When her family moved temporarily to Seattle she attended the music conservatory of the University of Washington for two years, and on their return to San Francisco, studied piano privately with the intention of becoming a concert pianist, a goal she shortly abandoned, although she did perform in public briefly. Her mother died when Toklas was twenty, and she took over the running of the household for her father and grandfather and the responsibility of raising her younger brother. When he left for college Toklas was drawn to Europe by her attraction to the world of artists and writers and by the atmosphere described in the novels of Henry James, her favorite author. One year after the great earthquake of 1906 had disrupted life in San Francisco, Toklas finally had enough money and her father's permission to go. She traveled with her journalist friend Harriet Levy,* an acquaintance of Sarah Stein, at whose home they visited their first day in Paris. There, at the age of thirty, Alice Toklas's real life began. "I met Gertrude Stein," according to *The Autobiography of Alice B. Toklas*,† and "a bell within me rang" (*SW* 5). Gertrude Stein seemed to her on that day to give off a golden radiance. She "held my complete attention," Toklas wrote, "as she did for all the many years I knew her until her death" (*WIR* 23). Stein and Toklas began spending much time together, strolling the streets of Paris, discussing Stein's writing, deepening their alliance. On a holiday to Italy the following summer, Stein proposed to Toklas, to her joy, that they spend the rest of their lives together. It was not until two years later, however, in the fall of 1910, after Harriet Levy, with whom she had been sharing an apartment, returned to San Francisco, that Toklas moved into 27 rue de Fleurus with Gertrude and Leo* Stein. In the meantime, she had spent much of her time there typing the long manuscript of *The Making of Americans*† and cooking dinner on Hélène's* night off. She studied French with Fernande Olivier,* became immersed in the world of modern art, and sat with the "wives" at Stein's salon while Stein talked to the "geniuses." The strong bond between Gertrude and Leo Stein had been deteriorating steadily for some time, in part due to Leo's dogmatic belittling of Gertrude's writing ability. When in 1912 he moved out, Alice Toklas took up in earnest her life as Gertrude Stein's spouse—and stenographer, social secretary, housekeeper, cook, gardener, and later, veterinarian for the dogs (and one cat of short-lived tenure). While she performed these domestic activities with pleasure, her contributions to the union were not limited to them. She also served as

Stein's publisher, press agent, translator, and in more than one way her perpetual inspiration. Her love, patience, humor, and willingness to run interference gave Stein the security she needed to concentrate on her writing. Further, Stein drew on Toklas's opinions and insights and on Toklas herself as a subject for her work. Stein's writing became "double-voiced," Shari Benstock has cogently observed; "it admitted the heretofore forbidden voice of irreverent, humorous erotic love . . . , a voice which punctuated the narrative, exposed pretense, corrected the storytelling, offered advice . . . and the voice belonged to Alice" (164).

Toklas first appeared in Stein's writing between late 1908 and 1910 in *Ada*, the story of a young woman that follows Toklas's life closely and imitates her narrative manner, a manner, as Virgil Thomson* points out, characterized by compactness and brevity. *The Autobiography of Alice B. Toklas*, which Stein wrote in 1932, reflects this voice and narrative style for Toklas's definitive version of events: "Every story that came into the house eventually got told in Alice's way. . . . Her memory and interests were visual; she could recall forever the exact costumes people had worn . . . , the decor of a room, the choreography of an occasion," Thomson declared (177). The outbreak of World War I found Stein and Toklas stranded in England. They spent 1915 and 1916 in Mallorca and the rest of the war delivering hospital supplies in France for the American Fund for the French Wounded. The twenties brought a revived attempt to publish Stein's work, first *Geography and Plays*† in 1922, a vanity press arrangement with the Four Seas Company in Boston. Toklas contacted publishers with more frustration than success, and finally decided to become a publisher herself. She cried when Stein had to sell one of her Picasso* paintings, *The Girl with a Fan*, to raise money for the venture, but went on to arrange for the publication of *Lucy Church Amiably*† under her imprimatur, Plain Edition. She continued with *How to Write*† and a limited edition of *Before the Flowers of Friendship Faded Friendship Faded*,† and plunged into problems of distribution, publicity, and getting the books reviewed. Plain Edition also published *Operas and Plays*† and *Matisse, Picasso and Gertrude Stein*,† but the success of *The Autobiography of Alice B. Toklas*, published in 1933, made further Plain Editions unnecessary. In running the household Toklas was constantly aware of the need to improve their financial situation. None of Stein's books brought in money, and she urged her to write something that would sell. Reluctant to write her own memoirs, Stein distanced herself by writing of events through Toklas's eyes, and when she finally struck the right tone for the narrative—Toklas's distinctive voice—she finished *The Autobiography of Alice B. Toklas* in six weeks. The resulting best-seller did not please everyone. Some people who did not come off well in the book blamed Toklas personally for their treatment, since one of the roles she had assumed in Stein's life had not endeared her to some of their acquaintances. Toklas sized up newcomers to 27 rue de Fleurus, and only if they were deemed worthy of Stein would they be invited back. It also fell to her to administer the coup de grâce to old friends and acquaintances Stein no longer wished to see, and she was often accused as well of manipulating Stein to get rid of her own rivals.

Mabel Dodge* and Ernest Hemingway,* among others, had fallen to her axe. The success of *The Autobiography of Alice B. Toklas* also brought about a trip to America, from October 1934 to May 1935, a triumphal lecture tour for Stein, through which she and Toklas could finally enjoy the taste of fame.

Toklas's happiest times, however, were the fourteen summers in Bilignin. She and Stein had spent summers after the war in Belley in Savoy, and in 1929 were finally able to rent the manoir they had admired in Bilignin, nearby. Toklas turned the grounds into abundant vegetable and flower gardens complete with berries and fruit trees. She learned the planting and weather lore of the local farmers and produced enormous harvests which they ate, canned, and transported back to Paris for the winter: "The first gathering of the garden in May of salads, radishes and herbs made me feel like a mother about her baby—how could anything so beautiful be mine. And this emotion of wonder filled me for each vegetable as it was gathered every year" (*ABTC* 266). They spent the long years of World War II in Bilignin, and Toklas with her usual adaptability and energy learned to make do with inadequate supplies. When their landlord reclaimed his house, she left her beloved gardens and managed a move of the household to Culoz, just as she had managed the move from 27 rue de Fleurus to 5 rue Christine in Paris in 1938.

At the war's end they returned to Paris and enjoyed a brief period of freedom and fame. On 27 July 1946 the golden glow went out of Alice Toklas's life when Gertrude Stein died unexpectedly of cancer. "You realize surely," she wrote to Donald Gallup,* "that Gertrude's memory is all my life—just as she herself was before" (*SOA* 54), and to W. G. Rogers,* "I wish to God we had gone together as I always so fatuously thought we would—a bomb—a shipwreck—just anything but this" (*SOA* 88). In desperate shock and grief she forced herself to go on, comforted by the presence of Basket II* and old friends who rallied around. She devoted herself to carrying out Stein's wishes, to maintaining her reputation, and to burnishing her legend. She arranged for the rest of Stein's manuscripts to be sent to Yale and agitated for their publication. She made many new friends; she carried on a voluminous correspondence; she entertained a stream of Stein admirers; she discouraged the wrong people from writing about Stein and grew bitter when they did anyway, Julian Sawyer,* for example, and Elizabeth Sprigge; she encouraged young writers; she embarked on a writing career herself. Several articles on food in *Vogue* and *House Beautiful*, as well as reviews in *The New York Times Book Review, Atlantic Monthly*, and *The New Republic*, brought in some much-needed funds. She had long considered writing a cookbook using the recipes she had collected on her travels, from friends, and those she had developed herself. *The Alice B. Toklas Cook Book* appeared in 1954, its recipes interspersed with lively anecdotes and memoirs in Toklas's own distinctive style. A second cookbook, *Aromas and Flavours*, published in 1958, was less interesting—Toklas supplied the recipes and food writer Poppy Cannon put the book together with her own commentary. In 1958 Toklas began work on *What Is Remembered*, a memoir published in 1963, in which she retells the old anecdotes and adds very little about herself; it is yet another monument to Stein's memory.

Her last years were marred by frail health and money worries. She had suffered from arthritis and deafness for some time, and her eyesight grew steadily worse. Stein had of course provided for Toklas in her will; she had a life interest in the painting collection and Stein's sanction "to reduce to cash any paintings" for her "proper maintenance and support" (*CC* 467–68). The collection was to go to Allan Stein, her brother Michael's* son, on Toklas's death. In 1961 the widow of Allan Stein, charging mismanagement, got a court order to remove the uninsured paintings from 5 rue Christine to a bank vault. Toklas returned home from a winter in Rome to find the walls bare. She took some solace in her failing sight, still able to see the pictures in her memory, but was reduced to pleading with the Stein estate to send her funds: "Gertrude Stein—in her generosity to me—did not foresee that such an occasion could arise" (*SOA* 409). Then she was evicted from her apartment, and friends had to move her when she was eighty-eight. After nearly twenty-one years of "staying on alone," almost ninety, Alice Toklas died and was buried next to Gertrude Stein in Père-Lachaise. Ten years before, she had converted to Roman Catholicism, consoled by the assurance of being reunited with her friend. Shortly after Gertrude Stein's death she had written to Carl Van Vechten,* "Oh Carlo could such perfection such happiness and such beauty have been and here and now be gone away" (*SOA* 15).

REFERENCES: *G&P*, 1922; *ABTC*, 1954; *SW*, 1962; *WIR*, 1963; *VT*, 1966; *SOA*, 1973; *CC*, 1974; *BABT*, 1977; Shari Benstock, *Women of the Left Bank*, 1986.

Priscilla Oppenheimer

TONNY, KRISTIANS, 13 September 1907–?, painter, graphic artist. The Dutch painter Kristians Tonny was one of the "young men [who] were twenty-six" (*SW* 200), the circle of poets and neoromantic artists whom Virgil Thomson* had introduced to Gertrude Stein, although Tonny was actually much younger than the others. He was, in fact, only nineteen when he exhibited with the neoromantics in 1926. A child prodigy whose father had given up his own painting career to enable his son to become an artist, Tonny came to Paris at the age of ten and exhibited for the first time when he was twelve. He studied for a time with the German caricaturist, Jules Pascin. Thomson, who owned many of Tonny's works, described him as "blond, muscular, and Dutch, with the sea at the back of his eyes" (109), "a virtuoso draftsman of Flemish fantasy" (92). Tonny painted hallucinatory images of ghosts and death-dances, grotesque landscapes in the tradition of Bosch and Brueghel. Stein persuaded Carl Van Vechten* to take some of Tonny's work to New York in 1928, where he sold eight drawings and took more to sell the next year. Stein bought several of Tonny's paintings, including an oil, *Le Bateau Ivre*, a surrealist landscape inspired by a poem of Rimbaud. A word portrait of Tonny appears in *Dix Portraits*,† for which he provided some illustrations. Tonny did a pen and ink portrait of Stein with

Basket,* which Alice Toklas said she later gave to an American soldier. By the winter of 1930 Stein had quarreled with Tonny as she had with many of the other young men of twenty-six. Tonny married a Frenchwoman and traveled widely during the thirties and early forties in Africa and North and South America. In 1937 he lived in New York, and at the invitation of the director of the Wadsworth Athenaeum, painted murals on the side walls of the theater. He returned to Holland to live after World War II.

REFERENCES: *SW*, 1962; *WIR*, 1963; *VT*, 1966; *CC*, 1974; *GSCVV*, 1986.

Priscilla Oppenheimer

TZARA, TRISTAN, 16 April 1896–24 December 1963, poet, critic, playwright. Born Sami Rosenstock, in Romania, Tristan Tzara moved to Switzerland, thence to Paris, where he at once joined forces with other young poets and painters who were protesting their disgust with bourgeois society. Part of their expression was to revolt against all previous tradition, especially in art. To this end, Tzara embraced the new Dadaism. Indeed, it can be said that Dadaism as a movement began with Tzara's first play, *La Première Aventure Céleste de M. Antipyrine*. Tzara and the other Dadaists attempted to do with words what some of the painters were doing with pictures. By juxtaposing unrelated words and images they created a fresh awareness of the world. Tzara's words often created images of gross bestiality and cruelty indicative of the disgust he felt with mankind and society. Dadaism as a movement was over by 1922, but its influence lingered on in the work of such writers as Samuel Beckett and Eugene Ionesco. Tzara's good friends were Apollinaire,* Picabia,* Picasso,* and others of the Stein circle. Gertrude Stein was friendly with him only for a short time, for she disapproved of Tzara on both philosophical and personal grounds. Along with Matisse,* Braque* and others, he was one of the signers of "Testimony against Gertrude Stein," written to correct some of the perceived inaccuracies of *The Autobiography of Alice B. Toklas*.† Although his poetry may be incomprehensible, Tzara's criticism of poetry is lucid and coherent. In it he abandons his attack on language as a rational means of communication. During World War II Tzara fought with the Resistance. He had embraced a form of Marxism in 1934 and remained a Marxist until his death in 1963.

REFERENCES: Elmer Peterson, *Tristan Tzara*, 1971; Sir Paul Harvey and J. E. Heseltine, eds., *Oxford Companion to French Literature*, 1959.

Margaret Woodbridge

VALLOTTON, FELIX, 1865–1925, painter. At the 1905 Independent Salon, Leo Stein* bought a large nude by Felix Vallotton, a Swiss-born painter who had come to Paris at the age of seventeen and was to spend his entire career there. Vallotton studied at the Académie Julian, became a friend of Pierre Bonnard and was connected with the "nabis," a group of painters centered around *La Revue Blanche*. He briefly tried his hand at pointillism but settled for a neoclassical/neo-impressionistic style which became more economical after 1900. He achieved some success as a portraitist, but it was through his revival of older woodcut techniques that he had a certain influence, particularly among the German Brücke painters. Vallotton's wife was the sister of a wealthy art dealer, and the family became friendly with the Steins. "For a time his pictures were very interesting," Gertrude Stein wrote, and she consented when he asked her to pose for him, although she later considered him a "Manet for the impecunious" (*SW* 47). She was intrigued with his portrait technique, in which he began painting straight across at the top of the canvas over his crayon sketch and worked down "like pulling down a curtain as slowly moving as one of his swiss glaciers. Slowly he pulled the curtain down and by the time he was at the bottom of the canvas, there you were" (*SW* 47). The operation took about two weeks, and in the finished product Stein appears massive but inert—an inappropriate dullness more reflective of the painter, probably, than the sitter. Everyone was pleased with it when it was exhibited at the Autumn Salon, Stein noted, but it is not seen in photographs of her studio at that time, and she later sold it to the Cone* sisters.

REFERENCES: *SW*, 1962; *Praeger Encyclopedia of Art*, 1971; *CC*, 1974.

Priscilla Oppenheimer

VAN VECHTEN, ANNA ELIZABETH SNYDER, 1880–9 May 1933, homemaker. Anna Snyder was born into the same Iowa culture and family background as her future husband, Carl Van Vechten.* They were each other's best friend during childhood and they married in London in June 1907. They spent their honeymoon in France and Germany, where Van Vechten reviewed operas and ballets, and interviewed performers, as assistant music critic for *The New York Times*. In New York his professional duties were among early problems in the marriage; Snyder, who had an independent and strong personality, did not accept her secondary position easily; they separated in January and were divorced in July 1912. She called herself "Ann Van Vechten" until her death at the age of fifty-three. A mutual friend brought her to meet Gertrude Stein in the spring of 1913: "[D]epressed and unhappy. . . . Mrs. Van Vechten told the story of the tragedy of her married life but Gertrude Stein was not particularly interested" (*ABT* 166). This encounter occurred only a week before Carl Van Vechten called at 27 rue de Fleurus for the first time. He came not knowing his former wife had preceded him. Stein was in a teasing mood and began to drop hints suggesting she knew a good deal about his marital problems. Although she did not say so, in recording the story in *The Autobiography of Alice B. Toklas*,† they were apparently sexual as well as professional. Van Vechten was bewildered; but that was the uncomfortable beginning of a comfortable friendship lasting even beyond Stein's lifetime. Anna Snyder Van Vechten taught briefly in Iowa after her divorce, and then she wandered around Europe for a decade, dying a suicide in a cancer hospital at Frankfurt am Main, Germany.

REFERENCES: *ABT*, 1933; Bruce Kellner, *Carl Van Vechten and the Irreverent Decades*, 1968.

Paul Padgette
Bruce Kellner

VAN VECHTEN, CARL, 17 June 1880–21 December 1964, writer, photographer. Born into a comfortable, middle-class Cedar Rapids, Iowa, family, Carl Van Vechten escaped in 1899 to the University of Chicago. One of his teachers was William Vaughn Moody,* who had taught creative writing to Gertrude Stein at Harvard a few years before, students destined eventually to share one of the most enduring literary friendships in modern letters. Van Vechten completed his Ph.D. in English in 1903, and after an apprenticeship with the *Chicago American* as a cub reporter, he became assistant to Richard Aldrich, the respected if conservative music critic of *The New York Times*, in 1906. After a year as Paris correspondent, 1908–1909, Van Vechten returned to become America's first dance critic writing for a daily newspaper. Before he left *The Times* to become theater critic for the *New York Press* for a season, the 69th Armory Exhibition of Post-Impressionist and Cubist art was held in February 1913, coinciding with Van Vechten's first knowledge of Gertrude Stein. Mabel Dodge*—recently returned from Europe and about to begin her 23 Fifth Avenue salon where politics and the arts joined forces—gave Van Vechten a copy of "Portrait of Mabel Dodge at the Villa Curonia." It fired his enthusiasm sufficiently to write an article about Stein's work, bolstered by an interview with Mabel Dodge and copious quotations from those then more bewildering sentences in her portrait. The article appeared in only one edition of *The New York Times*, buried on the financial page, but it carried a deathless observation: "Miss Stein has now evidently forgotten how to write" (24 February 1913). A few months later he arrived in Paris, armed with a letter of introduction from Mabel Dodge. Later, Van Vechten claimed that he and Stein first encountered each other at the first performance of Nijinsky's ballet set to Stravinsky's *The Rite of Spring*, and Stein put them at the second performance, after which she wrote "One," a portrait of an unknown young man in a fancy shirt who had shared their box. Both were perpetuating a hoax. Van Vechten didn't get to the first performance, despite his frequently reprinted description of it; Stein recognized him at the second performance since he had already called at 27 rue de Fleurus. They had only coincided two days later at the ballet, cinching the bond they must have felt immediately. They met rarely after that, but their devotion was unswerving.

Van Vechten arranged for his friend Donald Evans* to publish *Tender Buttons*;† he wrote "How to Read Gertrude Stein" for the August 1914 issue of *Trend* (a magazine he subsequently edited briefly); and he placed other Stein manuscripts with other periodicals when he could. He was unsuccessful, however, in persuading his own publisher, Alfred A. Knopf, to publish *The Making of Americans*,† but in the decades that followed, he was Stein's most ardent, congenial, and surely persistent press agent. His own career as a music, dance, and literary critic ended when he was forty, with six collections of essays behind him between 1915 and 1919: *Music after the Great War*, *Music and Bad Manners*, *Interpreters and Interpretations*, *The Merry-Go-Round*, *The Music of Spain*, and *In the Garret*. He quit, he said, because "the cells hardened and prejudices were formed which precluded the possibility of the welcoming of novelty" (*Red* ix). During the twenties, he published seven novels, managing to mention Gertrude Stein in six of them, even quoting *Three Lives†* at length in *Nigger Heaven* in 1926, his controversial story of the Harlem Renaissance, a movement for which he was partly responsible, both its aesthetic and unsavory aspects. Other novels include *Peter Whiffle*, 1922, about prewar Paris and New York; *The Blind-Bow Boy*, 1923, *Firecrackers*, 1925, and *Parties*, 1930, about contemporary New York life; *The Tattooed Countess*, 1924, about turn-of-the-century Iowa; and *Spider Boy*, 1928, a Hollywood satire. Van Vechten's reputation as a successful novelist was secure, but in 1932 with a volume of autobiographical essays, *Sacred and Profane Memories*, he closed his second career to devote full time to a new one. Photography dominated the rest of his life, and he was proud of his amateur standing: never for hire, always choosing his own subjects. He gave the pictures away to friends or fed them to archives he had established, notably the James Weldon Johnson Memorial Collection of Negro Arts and Letters at Yale. He was still at it when he died at eighty-four.

During the thirty-three years Van Vechten knew Stein, their correspondence continued on a regular basis. At the time of her death, she had written to him over four hundred times, and he had nearly matched that number. As they met rarely, they learned about each other's "daily island living," as Stein frequently called it, long distance. In its published version—masterfully edited by Edward Burns—their letters offer ample evidence in both quantity and quality of their strong bond. Although Van Vechten's second wife, the Russian actress Fania Marinoff,* visited 27 rue de Fleurus during her frequent holidays in Europe, he did not go abroad between 1914 and 1928. Stein was "a little worried," after so long a separation, she reported in *The Autobiography of Alice B. Toklas.†* "When he came they were better friends than ever. Gertrude Stein told him that she had been worried. I wasn't, said Carl" (*SW* 224). In June 1934, Van Vechten photographed Gertrude Stein, Alice Toklas, the dogs, the Bilignin gardens, even the Indonesian cook, and the church at Lucey that had inspired *Lucy Church Amiably†* all the while encouraging the lecture tour in America with which Stein had been toying. Back in New York, after the plans were set, he began to arrange for friends of his—notably novelists Ellen Glasgow and Gertrude Atherton*—to host Stein and Toklas along the tour route. Already he had written an introduction for a Modern Library reissue of *Three Lives†* and, to coincide with her arrival, an introduction to the published libretto Virgil Thomson* had arranged from *Four Saints in Three Acts†* which had recently made a success. In New York he photographed Stein and Toklas again, both in the studio in his apartment and in Chicago and, later, Richmond, Virginia. Stein and Toklas had agreed to make their first airplane flight, from New York to Chicago, provided Van Vechten traveled with them. Stein then lectured at Van Vechten's alma mater and attended a performance of *Four Saints in Three Acts* given in Chicago by the original cast.

When war began to threaten Europe, Stein's anxiety for the safety of her manuscripts—still largely unpublished—caused her to send trunks of them to Van Vechten for safekeeping; simultaneously, Thornton Wilder* had arranged for Yale University to accept some of her papers. Van Vechten later gave Yale all of his Stein materials, including his own collection of her books as well as their correspondence. Her will empowered him to bring into print all of her unpublished work, subsidized through her estate. With an advisory committee of Donald Gallup,* Donald Sutherland,* and Thornton Wilder, he edited eight volumes published by Yale University Press between 1951 and 1958. In 1949 he had edited *Last Operas and Plays*† and four months after her death, Random House issued Van Vechten's 622-page *Selected Writings of Gertrude Stein*† prefaced with her final composition, a "Message" acknowledging that Van Vechten "always knew, and it was always a comfort and now he has put down all his knowledge of what I did and it is a great comfort" (*SW* [vii]).

The Van Vechten–Stein friendship was unique for its durability and serenity for over three decades. Stein was only one of Van Vechten's advocacies in the arts, in a long list that included Igor Stravinsky, Erik Satie,* George Gershwin, Ronald Firbank, Langston Hughes, James Purdy, Wallace Stevens, Ethel Waters, Paul Robeson,* even Herman Melville long after his death, and all of them before their general recognition; but surely his dedication and affection were strongest for her. At seventy-eight, he relinquished his responsibilities as Gertrude Stein's literary executor to Donald Gallup, though at eighty-three, just a year before his death, he wrote once again of his friendship with "a great writer, a great thinker, a great conversationist, and a great woman," in "More Laurels for Our Gertrude" for Frances Steloff's* Gotham Book Mart catalog of Stein's books (11). Stein left four portraits of Van Vechten. Ten years after "One," her 1913 portrait of him in his ruffled shirt at *The Rite of Spring*, with its "touching white shining sash and a touching white green undercoat and a touching white colored orange and a touching piece of elastic" (*G&P* 200), she wrote a second one that remained undiscovered until nearly forty years after her death. "And too./Van Vechten/a sequel to One—" turned up in manuscript in her *cahier* containing "He and They, Hemingway," but Alice Toklas never typed it, nor was it ever inventoried in Stein checklists and bibliographies. It is printed as an appendix to Edward Burns's edition of the Stein–Van Vechten letters. Like "Van or Twenty Years After," written shortly afterward, it was motivated by his news that his second novel had made an apparent success. Finally, Stein included Van Vechten among the V's in "To Do," her book of stories for children arranged in alphabetical order by their characters' names. "Van" is also called "Papa Woojums," and "Mama Woojums," who is Alice Toklas and "Baby Woojums," who is Gertrude Stein, figure in as well (*A&B* 61–65). He had given the three of them these nicknames during the American lecture tour. Plenty of readers gag over the cloying appellations, but two of Gertrude Stein's most sensitive interpreters do not. Edward Burns sees them establishing "a family model that reflected the emotional importance each had come to assume for the other" (*GSCVV* 4). In that view, William H. Gass has suggested, "they are not far from the political or religious use of 'brother,' 'sister,' 'comrade,' 'father,' 'mother-superior,' and so on—uses which express a wished-for fact, however, as they project friendly or family ties into far wider, higher, remoter realms" (1236). Between themselves, Stein was "Lovey" and Toklas was "Pussy," but as they used the "Woojums" designations in their letters to Van Vechten, Gass's further observation is perhaps significant: "The names which lovers often confer on one another single out and commemorate one rather narrow area of affection. They are frequently regressive, returning the lovers to a pre-sexual condition, and signalling the presence of altered emotions, as genital urges become maternal surrounds, for instance. It is also an admission or acknowledgement of power. 'Who loves ya, baby?' is a political question" (1236). Carl Van Vechten always had the answer.

REFERENCES: Carl Van Vechten, "Cubist of Letters Writes a New Book," *NYT*, 24 February 1913, *Red*, 1925, and "More Laurels for Our Gertrude," *Gertrude Stein Catalogue 1964*, 1964; *G&P*, 1922; *ABT*, 1933; *SW*, 1946; Bruce Kellner, *Carl Van Vechten and the Irreverent Decades*, 1968; *GSCVV*, 1986; William H. Gass, "Thoroughly Modernist Intimacies," *Times Literary Supplement*, 7 November 1986, 1236–37.

Paul Padgette
Bruce Kellner

VOLLARD, AMBROISE, 1867–28 July 1939, art dealer, publisher. Ambroise Vollard was the oldest of ten children born to a middle-class family living on the island of La Réunion in the Indian Ocean. Growing up in that tropical setting, he developed a keen appreciation of color and natural harmony from the exotic vegetation and landscape. Vollard studied first medicine and then law, but in 1890 he settled in Montmartre, soon became acquainted with its artists, and apprenticed himself to Alfonse Dumas in the Union Artistique. Two years later Vollard purchased five Cézanne paintings at auction for under a hundred francs, and he began to handle Gauguin's work at an impressive personal profit. The following year, in 1893, he opened his first gallery on the "Street of Pictures," the rue Lafitte, and in 1895 he moved up from 39–41 to larger quarters, where in 1904, at 6 rue Lafitte, he sold Gertrude and Leo Stein* some of Cézanne's work. There were Picassos there too, and Matisses, and two years later, in 1906, Vollard gave an exhibition of Les Fauves. By that time his shop had already exhibited them all: Cézanne as early as 1893, when the paintings caused a small scandal; Picasso* in 1901; Matisse* in 1904. Vollard's reputation, based on his uncanny eye for talent among young and unknown artists, turned his shop into headquarters for adventurous collectors; his shrewdness made him a rich man. The art historian Bernard Berenson* introduced the Steins to Vollard. If others sometimes found him difficult to deal with, they did not. From his point of view they were ideal customers: they paid on time; they didn't pretend to great wealth; they were open to the revolution going on in painting; and, moreover, Vollard liked them. When the Stein estate suddenly offered Leo and Gertrude Stein an eight thousand franc fringe benefit, they invested it in two Gauguins, two more Cézannes, and two Renoirs. Vollard liked them so much he threw in a Maurice Denis as a present. He became a frequent visitor at 27 rue de Fleurus, recalling in his autobiography, *Recollections of a Picture Dealer*, that "People who came there out of snobbery soon felt a sort of discomfort at being allowed so much liberty in another man's house, and they did not come again. Only those who really cared for painting continued to frequent this hospitable house" (136). Vollard was the subject of a Stein word portrait in 1912, "Monsieur Vollard et Cezanne," first published in the New York *Sun* through Henry McBride's* efforts, 10 October 1915, and reprinted in *Portraits and Prayers*.† For the first time Stein arranged her words and phrases vertically rather than horizontally, as Richard Bridgman rightly observes, to emphasize her wordplay "as had never been possible when it was crowded into a paragraph" (*GSP* 139). The portrait even says so, in concluding, "Yes I have gotten a new form" (*P&P* 39). In turn but long afterward, in his autobiography, Vollard wrote, "The artist predominates in Gertrude Stein's personality. . . . If fame has come to her, it is certainly not because she has sought it" (138). Vollard died in an automobile accident in his early seventies, by which time he had published over twenty volumes and portfolios of prints and illustrations by many celebrated artists, including his first discovery Cézanne, as well as Pierre Bonnard, Rouault, Renoir, Picasso, and Degas. Two dozen unissued or incomplete works at the time of his death and Picasso's celebrated *Suite Vollard* were published posthumously.

REFERENCES: *ABT*, 1933; *P&P*, 1934; *GSP*, 1970; Una E. Johnson, *Ambroise Vollard, Editeur*, 1977; Ambroise Vollard, *Recollections of a Picture Dealer*, 1978.

Margaret Woodbridge
Paul Padgette

WEEKS, MABEL FOOTE, 14 December 1872–21 August 1964, educator. Like Mabel Haynes,* Emma Lootz, May Bookstaver,* and Marian Walker, Mabel Weeks was one of several college friends with whom Gertrude Stein continued to communicate over the years. Like Bookstaver, Weeks attempted to place Gertrude Stein's *Three Lives*† for publication in America. She maintained a full correspondence with Leo Stein* as well, serving as both sounding board and confessor for him long after he had broken with his sister. Weeks was assistant dean of social affairs at Barnard College and then an associate professor of English there until 1939.

REFERENCES: *ABT*, 1933; *JS*, 1950; *FF*, 1953; *CC*, 1974.

Bruce Kellner

WESCOTT, GLENWAY, 11 April 1901–22 February 1987, writer. Like several other midwestern American writers, Glenway Wescott developed a sophisticated patina early on. After studying poetry at the University of Chicago, he went to Paris as a reviewer and somewhat stagey poet, then turned to the simple rhythms of his past, notably in autobiographical fiction, *The Apple of the Eye* in 1924 and *The Grandmothers* in 1927. *Goodbye, Wisconsin*, published in 1930, collects stories about the midwest, and he has written other fiction and two books of essays. Perhaps his most winning work, however, is *A Calendar of Saints for Unbelievers*, first published in Paris in 1932, retellings of saints' legends with illustrations by Pavel Tchelitchew.* Gertrude Stein and Alice Toklas were impressed with his English accent and his silk cigarette case when Mina Loy* first brought him to call, "but Glenway Wescott at no time interested Gertrude Stein. He has a certain syrup but it does not pour" (*ABT* 269).

REFERENCES: *ABT*, 1933; OxCAL, 1965.

Bruce Kellner

WHITE, MAX, 1906–   , writer. Three young writers made a strong impact on Gertrude Stein during her 1934–1935 American lecture tour: Samuel Steward,* Lindley Williams Hubbell,* and Max White. Educated in New England and France, White published his first novel, *Anna Becker*, in 1937, although he had sent Gertrude Stein some of his stories some months before they met. Others followed, as well as a cookbook entitled *How I Feed My Friends*, published in 1946. When Alice Toklas began her memoires in 1958, White was engaged by the publisher to act as collaborator, and for several weeks they met on a daily basis. Then it became clear that Alice Toklas was being sometimes deliberately evasive, sometimes forgetful, even dishonest to efface herself from a finished product that would canonize Gertrude Stein into literary hagiography. White gave up the task, destroyed all his notes, and broke off his loyal friendship of over twenty years.

REFERENCES: *EA*, 1937; Harry R. Warfeel, *American Novelists of Today*, 1951; *BABT*, 1977.

Bruce Kellner

WHITEHEAD, ALFRED NORTH, 15 February 1861–30 December 1947, mathematician, philosopher, educator. Alfred North Whitehead was one of the three people Alice B. Toklas recognized as geniuses (*ABT* 5–6). When she and Gertrude Stein met Whitehead at Cambridge, England, in 1914, she says "within me something rang" as it had when she met the other two, Gertude Stein and Picasso.* Professor and Mrs. Whitehead liked Toklas and Stein at once and invited them to dinner. Thus began a warm friendship. British-born Whitehead had been educated at Cambridge and became a fellow of Trinity College. In 1913, with Bertrand Russell, he published *Principia Mathematica*, a study which brought fame to both men. After getting to know Whitehead, Gertrude Stein decided, on the strength of her own judgment, that he had contributed the major ideas to the book. At the second meeting in Cambridge the Whiteheads invited

Toklas and Stein for a weekend at their country estate, Lockridge, a visit that was expanded to eleven weeks. World War I had begun, and there was no possibility of their return to France. They did manage to get to London for their trunks and a little money. During the anxious days at Lockridge Toklas helped Mrs. Whitehead with Belgian relief work, while Stein and Whitehead took long walks and enjoyed long philosophical discussions together. As Stein says in *The Autobiography of Alice B. Toklas*,† he showed himself to be "the gentlest and most simply generous of human beings" (182). The news came at last that Paris had been saved and travel restrictions eased. In October, Toklas and Stein prepared to return to France, accompanied by Mrs. Whitehead, who wanted to take a warm coat to the Whiteheads' son North, an officer at the front. Thanks to Mrs. Whitehead's papers, which included a letter from Lord Kitchener, there were no delays. In 1924 Whitehead went to Harvard to teach philosophy. Throughout the rest of his long and productive career he wrote additional books, elucidating further his comprehensive philosophical system. He died in Cambridge, Massachusetts, at eighty-six. The impact of his ideas is still debated.

REFERENCES: *ABT*, 1933; *CC*, 1974; J. H. Johnson, "Alfred North Whitehead," *Encyclopaedia Britannica*, 1974.

Margaret Woodbridge

WILCOX, WENDELL, 5 September 1906–17 March 1981, writer. In high school in Chicago, Wendell Wilcox began to feel the urge to write, and by the time he graduated from the University of Chicago in 1929 he was writing steadily. In 1931 he married a librarian who had such faith in his becoming successful that she financially supported them. In April 1941, *Harper's Bazaar* published Wilcox's "England Is in Flames," and he won the O. Henry Prize in 1944 for "The Pleasures of Travel," which had appeared in *The New Yorker*. In the thirties he had known Thornton Wilder,* then on the faculty at the University of Chicago, and through him Wilcox attended Gertrude Stein's lectures there in November 1934 and met her briefly on her return to the university in March 1935. They began to correspond when she returned to France, and when he sent her some of his work she was favorably impressed. In *Everybody's Autobiography*,† Stein wrote that Wilcox "has a feeling for meaning that is not beyond what the words are saying and of course that does make more brilliant writing and that is what he is doing" (269). Wilcox wrote a penetrating analysis for *Poetry* magazine in February 1940, "A Note on Stein and Abstraction," to accompany her first six "Stanzas in Meditation" in the same issue. In 1945 Wilcox published *Everything Is Quite All Right*, a novel about a love affair between a servant girl and her employer, about which Stein wrote to him that, "even to its tiniest details, I am very enthusiastic, and it is a pleasure" (Galanes 378). Wilcox and his wife, Esther, managed through the assistance of friends to make an extended visit to Paris in 1950, visiting frequently with Alice Toklas who was also charmed by him, according to references in her letters. The Wilcoxes moved to Chapel Hill,

North Carolina, about 1965, where Esther died in 1975. Wilcox lived on alone there, sometimes as an archivist at the Wilson Library at the University of North Carolina, until his death.

REFERENCES: *EA*, 1937; Samuel M. Steward, *Dear Sammy*, 1977; Philip Galanes, "Gertrude Stein: Letters to a Friend," *Paris Review*, Summer-Fall 1986; Samuel Steward: interview.

Paul Padgette

WILDER, THORNTON, 17 April 1897–7 December 1975, teacher, novelist, dramatist. Shyness and modesty were the two qualities of Thornton Wilder most evident to Sylvia Beach* the first time he entered her famous bookstore in Paris. Always self-deprecating, he listed his profession as teaching even after he became known as a distinguished novelist and dramatist who received numerous awards and honors. Wilder grew up in China, where his father was in the consular service, and in California. He attended Oberlin College for a year and then transferred to Yale. During 1918 and 1919 he served in the coast artillery. All these years he had been writing short stories for college magazines and plays for college groups. In 1921, while in Rome, he wrote a novel, *The Cabala*, published in 1926 and virtually ignored. In 1925 his father got a position for him at Lawrenceville Academy in New Jersey, which he held until 1928. He continued to write, this time the very successful *The Bridge of San Luis Rey*, which won one of the three Pulitzer Prizes he received. In 1930, invited by his friend Robert Hutchins,* he agreed to lecture at the University of Chicago, where, in 1934, he met Gertrude Stein through her hostess, Mrs. Charles B. Goodspeed* (later, Mrs. Gilbert Chapman). This meeting was momentous for both, for it marked the beginning of a mutually inspiring friendship that endured until Stein's death. As Stein expressed it, "Thornton Wilder began" (*EA* 201). The two writers became fast friends and defenders of each other's work, partly because they were in philosophical agreement. When Gertrude Stein agreed to return to Chicago for a series of seminars in March 1935, Wilder gave up his apartment so that she and Alice B. Toklas could be near the university. He handpicked the thirty students who participated in her special classes at the university. She enjoyed the experience of teaching and associating with young people immensely, even when some of the students became a bit rowdy. Afterward, Wilder was a welcome guest at Bilignin until the war. He and Stein roamed the countryside together, freely confiding in one another. As John Malcolm Brinnin astutely notes, "Faith in his faith in her" (353) was the basis of their relationship. For this reason he always occupied a special place in her heart.

For her part, Stein gave Wilder the support this shy, diffident man needed. His work had been attacked, as it has since then, for shallowness and facile optimism. Thanks to her teaching he was able to remain serene even when criticism was harsh. She gave him the confidence to pursue his own path and not to lose faith in his humanism. Despite her long sojourn in Europe she remained fascinated with America and turned Wilder's attention to the American scene as

the best place to study the universal in all men. His two most popular plays—
Our Town (1938) and *The Skin of Our Teeth* (1942)—were the result. By the
time he wrote these he had decided that the stage was a better medium than the
novel through which to examine timeless human truths. *Our Town* affirms the
beauty and goodness of the lives of ordinary people in a typical American small
town; *The Skin of Our Teeth* asserts the power of the great ideas to continue to
nourish and inspire mankind. Both plays were enthusiastically received by audiences because they gave validity to deeply cherished ideas of Americans. Critics
were not so happy with them, regarding them as merely entertaining and lacking
in substance. Wilder was even accused by Henry Morton Robinson and Joseph
Campbell of plagiarizing *The Skin of Our Teeth* from James Joyce's *Finnegan's
Wake*, but most critics recognized that he had merely been influenced by it.
Unfortunately, this was not the last time he encountered the hostility of critics.
As late as 1955 he reminded himself of Stein's teaching: "Oh, it's to Gertrude
that I owe this invulnerability to the evaluations of others! Nay, I have it so
deeply implanted that I can hold in my head at one time both my confidence in
what is meritorious in my work and my real self-reproach at what is bad"
(*Journals* 239).

In 1936, back in France, Stein showed that she thought highly of Wilder as
a professional writer. She asked him to write a running commentary on her
philosophical ideas for *The Geographical History of America*,† soon to be published by Ramdom House. He agreed to do so, but chose instead to write an
introduction to the book which showed how firmly he grasped her ideas. It was
her conviction, he said, that great truths can be observed not only in great
literature but also in America because throughout its history America has been
identified with human destiny. America may produce a civilization in which
"the Human Mind . . . may in many of its aspects be distributed throughout the
people" (*GHA* 50). So complete was Stein's rapport with Wilder that she designated him as her literary executor, a decision that worried her later. She asked
herself, "will he get weak and let anyone he admires and believes in some . . .
lead him where he is led" (*EA* 301), a remark that seems directed at his gentle-
ness. As a matter of fact, before her death she did indeed change her mind and
designated Carl Van Vechten* to edit her unpublished work. For some time after
Stein's death Wilder failed to get in touch with Alice Toklas, causing her to
wonder if he felt slighted. As she says, "he seems to have so little protective
covering" (*SOA* 22), but eventually he did produce the excellent introduction
for Stein's *Four in America*,† published in 1947. Nevertheless, Toklas was
"fairly sure that T. W. finds C.V.V. unworthy [to be executor] and perhaps
common" (*SOA* 36). In this introduction Wilder states that Stein perceived that
words were "no longer precise"; they were full of "remembering"; that it was
impossible for the writer to describe anything with accuracy, and "writing must
accomplish a revolution whereby it could report things as they were in themselves
before our minds had appropriated them and robbed them of their objectivity 'in
pure existing' " (*FIA* viii). Thus, Wilder shows that he remembered his talks

with Gertrude Stein. In fact, his *Journals* contain frequent allusions to her even after her death, showing her continuing strong influence on him.

By the time they met, Gertrude Stein had ceased writing portraits of friends and acquaintances, but Wilder does turn up as "Thornie" in "To Do," her children's book of alphabetically arranged stories. "Thornie Rose" and "Tillie Brown"*—the latter one of Stein's high school acquaintances—are the children of missionaries in China. They sing "Tender and True," with "miles and miles of Chinamen and Chinese women and Chinese children and more and more miles of them" (*A&B* 55).

Wilder remained a good and loyal friend to Alice Toklas, and she returned his affection, always addressing him in letters as "Dearest Thornton." He continued to be honored for his achievements. *The Merchant of Yonkers* (1938), which later became *The Matchmaker*, and still later, *Hello, Dolly!* was chosen for performance at the Edinburgh Festival in 1954. *The Skin of Our Teeth* was sent to Paris by the State Department for the Salut à la France celebration. In 1962 he was invited by President Kennedy to read from his works to the Cabinet. His novel *The Eighth Day* received the National Book Award in 1968.

REFERENCES: *GHA*, 1936; *EA*, 1937; *FIA*, 1947; John Malcolm Brinnin, *The Third Rose*, 1959; *A&B*, 1957; Thornton Wilder, *Journals*, 1986.

Margaret Woodbridge
Bruce Kellner

WILLIAMS, WILLIAM CARLOS, 17 September 1883–4 March 1963, writer, physician. In 1910, after receiving an M.D. from the University of Pennsylvania and doing graduate study in Leipzig, William Carlos Williams settled in Rutherford, New Jersey, to a lifetime devoted to the practice of medicine and poetry. In his long and prolific writing career, Williams worked toward the expression of natural American speech which incorporated European avant-garde developments in his poetic line. He became one of the foremost American modernists and had a profound influence on later writers. His output includes novels, short stories, plays, essays, and criticism as well as poetry. His autobiography was published in 1951. Among his numerous awards are the National Book Award in 1950 for *Paterson*, poems in five volumes, and the Pulitzer Prize for poetry in 1963. Williams's meeting with Gertrude Stein, at tea in her flat during his six-month trip to Europe in 1924, was less than pleasant. Stein disparaged the manners and writing of Ezra Pound,* whom Williams admired, during the conversation. She later asked Williams what she should do with the huge pile of her unpublished work and was shocked when he replied that he would select only the best and burn the rest. Stein replied stiffly, "No doubt. But then writing is not, of course, your métier" (*CC* 291). She forgave him later when he had written an essay on her work which appeared in *Pagany* in 1930. Stein had almost single-handedly enacted the revolution of the word, Williams wrote. She had returned to words as words, not simply as carriers of scientific, religious, or philosophical lumber, which gave them "a curious immediate quality quite apart from their meaning, much as in music different notes are dropped . . . into repeated chords one at a time . . . the way one hears music when listening to Bach" (Mariani 301). Stein was delighted with his assessment, wrote to thank him, and sent him copies of her books as they were published.

REFERENCES: *CC*, 1974; *DLB* 4; Paul L. Mariani, *William Carlos Williams; A New World Naked*, 1981.

Priscilla Oppenheimer

WILSON, EDMUND, 8 May 1895–12 June 1972, writer. Born in New Jersey and educated at Princeton, Edmund Wilson saw service in France during World War I, at which time he decided to devote himself to literature. He became one of America's most distinguished men of letters. Although he wrote novels, plays, and essays, Wilson's chief literary contribution is his criticism in such works as *Axel's Castle* (1931), *The Wound and the Bow* (1941), and his remarkable notebooks and diaries, published posthumously to cover a decade at a time. *The Shock of Recognition*, his anthology of great American writers' responses to their contemporaries, is crucial to any study of the national literature. Wilson was especially perceptive in dealing with twentieth-century writers, as *Axel's Castle* demonstrates in its thoughtful assessments of the work of the French symbolists, James Joyce, and Gertrude Stein, among others. Earlier, in a review, he confessed he found the prolixity and repetitions of *The Making of Americans*† wearisome, but he gave serious attention to Stein's experiments in *Tender Buttons*† and other verbal exercises. He was kinder still to *The Autobiography of Alice B. Toklas*,† paying tribute to Stein's unacknowledged influence on the writing of others, and placing her in the great American tradition of Henry James, Edgar Allan Poe, Nathaniel Hawthorne, and Herman Melville, working "from experience toward the abstract" (579). Reviewing *Q.E.D.*, when it was published as *Things as They Are* in 1950, Wilson suggested that Stein's increasing hermeticism deliberately obscured lesbian attitudes expressed in that early novel, a suggestion he wrongly abandoned (*The Shores of Light* 581–83).

REFERENCES: *CB*, 1941; Edmund Wilson, *The Shores of Light*, 1952, *Axel's Castle*, 1959; *CC*, 1974.

Bruce Kellner

WOOLLCOTT, ALEXANDER, 19 January 1887–23 January 1943, writer, actor. Millions have applauded the satiric portrait of Alexander Woollcott in the George S. Kauffman–Moss Hart play, *The Man Who Came to Dinner*. The portrait— or caricature—contains the qualities for which he was best known: his wit, shocking language, interest in crime, furious pace of meetings with his friends, love of work. His contemporaries described him as alternately (and sometimes simultaneously) clever, rude, sentimental, insolent, and generous. His nickname behind his back was "Fidget-Bottom," and he resembled a fat owl. After graduation from Hamilton College in 1909 he landed a job with *The New York Times*, first as a reporter, later as drama critic, his real love, 1914–1922. In World War I he wrote for *Stars and Stripes*. Subsequently, writing again for *The Times*, then for the New York *Herald*, 1922–1925, and the New York *World*, 1925–1928, he contributed some of the liveliest theater criticism in any paper, always speaking his mind with clarity and wit. When Gertrude Stein met him through Bennett Cerf* during her American lecture tour, he said she had not been in New York long enough to realize that "he was never contradicted," so she contradicted him—to his delight—and they got on well. He was an occasional visitor at 5 rue Christine after that, always prefacing his arrival with a request that Stein's white poodle, Basket,* be made "pure as the drivelling snow" (Sprigge 221). Woollcott wrote several books of essays and stories, but his work is perhaps best approached through *The Portable Woollcott* in 1946. His most lasting claim to a footnote in American literature lies in his membership at the Algonquin Hotel Round Table, that group of witty New York writers who enjoyed a reputation for brilliant repartée, usually by insult. He himself realized that his special talent was as a raconteur. Woollcott died of a heart attack in Germany.

REFERENCES: *CB*, 1943; Alexander Woollcott, *The Portable Woollcott*, 1946; *FF*, 1953; Elizabeth Sprigge, *Gertrude Stein; Her Life and Work*, 1957.

Margaret Woodbridge

WRIGHT, RICHARD, 2 September 1908–28 November 1960, writer. Richard Wright recounts the terrible story of his hard, cruel Mississippi childhood in *Black Boy* (1943) and in the short story "The Man Who Lived Underground." He taught himself to write through reading good writers, he claimed—when he could get the books. His account of his self-education and its attendant struggles is one of the most interesting aspects of *Black Boy*. In 1932 Wright joined the Communist party but became disillusioned and was expelled in 1944. His savage novel *Native Son* shows his Zola-like naturalism as well as his existential beliefs. Living in Paris after World War II, he met Gertrude Stein, who encouraged him to remain there because of race prejudice in the United States, and because his intermarriage could only complicate his life further back home. She admired *Native Son*, believing that she understood how difficult life in America could be for some time for blacks of talent. Because Wright had done something superlatively well, she contended, he would arouse only further resentment among whites (*CC* 553). Clearly, her attitudes had changed since her conclusion in the twenties that blacks were not suffering from "persecution" but from "nothingness" (*SW* 224). Richard Wright died in Paris of a heart attack when he was fifty-two.

REFERENCES: *CB*, 1940; Richard Wright, *Black Boy*, 1943; *CC*, 1975; Martin Seymour-Smith, *Who's Who in Twentieth Century Literature*, 1976.

Margaret Woodbridge

PART IV

Gertrude Stein's ABC

ACCURACY

Accuracy is by and by to be slightly poisoned by inaccuracy. (*PL* 272)

ADJECTIVES

. . . adjectives effect nouns and as nouns are not really interesting the thing that effects a not too interesting thing is of necessity not interesting. (*LIA* 211)

ADVENTURE (*See* Romance)

Adventure is making the distant approach nearer but romance is having what is where it is which is not where you are stay where it is. (*WAM* 62)

ADVICE

I cannot give advice. How can I when I do not authorise success. I authorise it alright. Smile. (*PL* 6)

AGE

One thing is certain the only thing that makes you younger or older is that nothing can happen that is different from what you expected and when that happens and it mostly does happen everything is different from what you expected then there is no difference between being younger or older. (*EA* 39)

. . . I tell you old and young are better than tired middle-aged, nothing is so dead dead-tired, dead every way as middle-aged, have we the guts to make a noise while we are still young before we get middle-aged, tired middle aged. . . . (*B&W* 90)

ANSWERS

Supposing no one asked the Question, what would be the answer. (*UK* 51)

ARGUMENT

Argument is to me the air I breathe. Given any proposition I cannot help believing the other side and defending it. (*RAD* 130)

ART

As always art is the pulse of a nation. (*PF* 63)

The characteristic art product of a country is the pulse of the country. . . . (*PF* 36)

ARTICLES

Partly a the
An article is a and an and the.
Thank you for all three. (*P&P* 45)

AVANT-GARDE (*See* Communication)

A creator is not in advance of his generation but he is the first of his contemporaries to be conscious of what is happening to his generation. (*PIC* 30)

My work would have been no use to anyone if the public had understood me early and first. (*TWO* xvii)

For a very long time everybody refuses and then almost without a pause almost everybody accepts. In the history of the refused in the arts and literature the rapidity of the change is always startling. (*WAM* 28)

No one is ahead of his time, it is only that the particular variety of creating his time is the one that his contemporaries who also are creating their own time refuse to accept. (*WAM* 27)

. . . the creator of the new composition in the arts is an outlaw until he is a classic. . . . (*WAM* 27)

AVARICE

Avarice is a good thing, it would be a wonderful thing to be really avaricious and so occupying. It is true though the Americanization of everything has driven avarice out of every one and I do not like it. I am hoping a good many millions are to be avaricious again and I want to be the first one. (*EA* 128)

BEAUTY

A beauty is not suddenly in a circle. It comes with rapture. A great deal of beauty is rapture. A circle is a necessity. Otherwise you would see no none. We each have our circle. (*LO&P* 141)

BELIEF

. . . I rarely believe anything, because at the time of believing I am not really there to believe. (*EA* 98)

BOASTING

The deepest thing in any one is the conviction of the bad luck that follows boasting. (*MR* 17)

BRUTALITY

When you are weak and brutal you are very much more hated than when you are strong and brutal, that is natural enough. . . . (*WIHS* 170)

CHANGE

. . . nothing changes from one generation to another except the things seen and the things seen make that. . . . (*PIC* 10)

. . . people do not change from one generation to another generation but the composition that surrounds them changes. (*PIC* 11)

CIRCLES

A circle stretches. From San Francisco to the sun. From Tangier to the moon. From London to the water. (*LO&P* 144)

CIVILIZATION

Everybody thinks that this civilization has lasted a very long time but it really does take very few grandfathers' granddaughters to take us back to the dark ages. (*EA* 92)

CLARITY

Clarity is of no importance because nobody listens and nobody knows what you mean no matter what you mean, nor how clearly you mean what you mean. But if you have vitality enough of knowing enough of what you mean, somebody and sometime and sometimes a great many will have to realise that you know what you mean and so they will agree that you mean what you know, what you know you mean, which is as near as anybody can come to understanding any one. (*FIA* 127–28)

CLAUSES

Complications make eventually for simplicity and therefore I have always liked dependent adverbial clauses. (*LIA* 220)

COLLEGE PROFESSORS

College professors have two bad traits. They are logical and they are easily flattered. (*PL* 269)

COMMAS

A comma by helping you along holding your coat for you and putting on your shoes keeps you from living your life as actively as you should lead it and to me for many years and I still do feel that way about it only now I do not pay as much attention to them, the use of them was positively degrading. (*LIA* 220)

. . . at the most a comma is a poor period that it lets you take a breath but if you want to take a breath you ought to know yourself that you want to take a breath. (*LIA* 221)

COMMUNICATION

It was exasperating, we were patient, we said it again and meant everything. . . . (*AFAM* xv)

I am trying to say something but I have not said it. (*SIM* 126)

It is always a mistake to be plain-spoken. (*BTV* 228)

CONTRADICTIONS (*See* The French, Jews)

Revolutions come and revolutions go, fashions come and fashions go, logic and civilisation remain and with it the family and the soil of France. (*PF* 101)

Action and reaction are equal and opposite. (*NOTY* 32)

There is singularly nothing that makes a difference a difference in beginning and in the middle and in ending except that each generation has something different at which they are all looking. (*SW* 513)

COUNTING

How pleasant it is to count one two three four five six seven, and then stop and then go on counting eight nine and then ten or eleven. (*IDA* 58)

CRITICISM

Do you know because I tell you so, or do you know, do you know. (*LO&P* 88)

DANCING (*See* War)

That is what war is and dancing it is forward and back, when one is out walking one wants not to go back the way they came but in dancing and in war it is forward and back. (*EA* 107)

DEATH

. . . it is so friendly so simply friendly and though inevitable not a sadness and though occurring not a shock. (*PF* 13)

. . . you have to learn to do everything even to die. . . . (*WIHS* 126)

DISILLUSIONMENT

Disillusionment in living is finding that no one can really ever be agreeing with you completely in anything. (*MOA* 264)

THE EARTH

The earth is the earth as a peasant sees it, the world is the world as a duchess sees it, and anyway a duchess would be nothing if the earth was not there as the peasant tills it. (*EA* 63)

THE EARTH, INHABITANTS OF

After all it is very simple, we are on the earth and we have to live on it and there is beyond all there is and there is no extending it because after all there it is and here we are, and we are always here and we are always there and any little while is a pleasure, and a pleasure is a pleasure oh yes it is a pleasure is a treasure. (*EA* 154)

EDUCATION

I could undertake to be an efficient pupil if it were possible to find an efficient teacher. . . . (*QED* 60)

For some years now college students good college students tell me they want not to go on going to college and this has surprised me because we we liked going to college and I asked them why. I said perhaps they had had freedom too soon, that is before they went to college and college was for us freedom physical and mental freedom. Now they they have been free too long and so perhaps college is not where they belong perhaps not. (*HWW* 96)

Very likely education does not make very much difference. (*HWW* 94)

EXPECTATION

It is easy to feel that you cherish the impression that you feel the charm that expectation is easy. (*PL* 236)

EXPLANATIONS

Anybody knows the difference between explain and make it plain. (*FIA* 125)

FAILURE

A real failure does not need an excuse. It is an end in itself. (*FIA* 175)

FAMILIARITY

Familiarity does not breed contempt. On the contrary the more familiar it is the more rare and beautiful it is. (*PF* 14)

FAMILIES

It is extraordinary that when you are acquainted with a whole family you can forget about them. (*GHA* 106)

Every adolescent has that dream every century has that dream every revolutionary has that dream, to destroy the family. (*PF* 93)

FATHERS

There is too much fathering going on just now and there is no doubt about it fathers are depressing. (*EA* 133)

FATIGUE

Fatigue is rendered attentive by disagreeable insight. (*A&B* 89)

FEAR

Since the war nothing is so really frightening not the dark nor alone in a room or anything on a road or a dog or a moon but two things yes, indigestion and high places they are frightening. (*EA* 189–90)

THE FRENCH

. . . they are never sentimental, they are never careless, they are never intimate, in short they are peaceful and exciting, that is to say they are French. (*PF* 55)
So here are the two sides to a Frenchman, logic and fashion and that is the reason why French people are exciting and peaceful. (*PF* 43)

FRIENDSHIP

In friendship, power always has its downward curve. (*TL* 54)
Before the flowers of friendship faded friendship faded. (*NOTY* 43)

GARLIC

Do be careful in eating garlic particularly on an island. (*PL* 44)

GENIUS

The earth is covered all over with people but geniuses are very few. Interesting if true and it is true. (*EA* 164)
. . . the essence of being a genius is to be able to talk and listen to listen while talking and talk while listening but and this is very important very important indeed talking has nothing to do with creation. (*WAM* 84)
It takes a lot of time to be a genius, you have to sit around so much doing nothing, really doing nothing. (*EA* 70)

GRAMMAR

Grammar means that it has to be prepared and cooked. . . . (*HTW* 101)
Grammar is useless because there is nothing to say. (*HTW* 62)

HAMLET

A young man whose father was just murdered, would not act like Hamlet, Hamlet was not interested in his father, he was interested in himself, and he acted not like a young man who had lost a loved father but like a man who wants to talk about himself, that is psychology if you like but anybody in any village can do that. (*GHA* 216–17)

HENS

Rabbits have no habits that is the reason that we prefer hens. Besides hens lay eggs, which is a pleasant habit. (*WIHS* 154)

HISTORY

The history is always the same the product is always different and the history interests more than the product. More, that is, more. Yes. But if the product was not different the history which is the same would not be more interesting. (*HTW* 213)

History takes time. (*LO&P* 279)

HOMESICKNESS

There is no passion more dominant and instinctive in the human spirit than the need of the country to which one belongs. One often speaks of homesickness as if in its intense form it were the peculiar property of Swiss mountaineers, Scandinavians, Frenchmen and those other nations that too have a poetic background, but poetry is no element in the case. It is simply a vital need for the particular air that is native. . . . The time comes when nothing in the world is so important as a breath of one's own particular climate. If it were one's last penny it would be used for that return passage. (*QED* 99)

HONESTY

Honesty is a selfish virtue. Yes I am honest enough. (*QED* 65)

HOPE

It is natural to indulge in the illusions of hope. We are apt to shut our eyes to that siren until she allures us to our death. Is it that we are among the number of those who see not and who hear not the best that leads us to salvation shall we be among the number of those who having ears hear not and having eyes see not the things that lead us to salvation. (*AFAM* 138)

IDENTITY

If nobody knows you that does not argue that you be unknown. (*IDA* 84)

The minute you or anybody else knows what you are you are not it, you are what you or anybody else knows you are and as everything in living is made up of finding out what you are it is extraordinarily difficult really not to know what you are and yet to be that thing. (*EA* 92)

You are you because your little dog knows you, but when your public knows you and does not want to pay for you and when your public knows you and does want to pay for you, you are not the same you. (*EA* 44–45)

IDLENESS

It is richly held
To be not all for it
Because
Idleness is no blessing. (*LO&P* 253)

IMAGINATION

One has to remember that about imagination, that is when the world gets dull when everybody does not know what they can or what they cannot really imagine. (*EA* 90)

INDIVIDUALITY

I don't envisage collectivism. There is no such animal, it is always individualism, sometimes the rest vote and sometimes they do not, and if they do they do and if they do not they do not. (*HWW* 53)

INDOLENCE

Nobody is particularly inclined to be industrious. (*UK* 110)

INTOLERANCE

We all begin well, for in our youth there is nothing we are more intolerant of than our sins writ large in others and we fight them fiercely in ourselves. . . . (*MOA* 3)

IOWANS

. . . you are brilliant and subtle if you come from Iowa and really strange and you live as you live and are always very well taken care of if you come from Iowa. (*EA* 224)

JEWS

The Modern Jew who has given up the faith of his fathers can reasonably and consistently believe in isolation. (*GSP* 161)
We can think and we know that we love our country so.
Can we believe that all Jews are these.
. . . Judaism should be a question of religion.
Don't talk about race. Race is disgusting if you don't love your country.
I don't want to go to Zion. (*PL* 94)
Jews do not like the country, yes thank you, christians do not all like the city. Yes and thank you. There are no differences between the city and the country and very likely every one can be daily daily and by that timely. (*NOTY* 237)

KNOWLEDGE

One cannot come back too often to the question what is knowledge and to the answer knowledge is what one knows. Knowledge is the thing you know and how can you know more than you do know. (*LIA* 11)

THE LANDSCAPE

You may have to make acquaintance with it, but it does not with you. . . . (*LIA* 122)

THE LOST GENERATION

It was this hotel [Pernollet] keeper who said what it is said I said that the war generation was a lost generation. And he said it in this way. He said that every man becomes civilized between the ages of eighteen and twenty-five. If he does not go through a civilizing experience at that time in his life he will not be a civilized man. And the men who went to the war at eighteen missed the period of civilizing, and they could never be civilized. They were a lost generation. Naturally if they are at war they do not have the influences of women of parents and of preparation. (*EA* 52)

LANGUAGE

Language as a real thing is not imitation either of sounds or colors or emotions it is an intellectual recreation and there is no possible doubt about it and it is going to go on being that as long as humanity is anything. (*LIA* 238)

LIARS

There are two kind of liars the kind that lie and the kind that don't lie the kind that lie are no good. (*NOTY* 165)

LITERATURE

. . . remarks are not literature. (*ABT* 270)

LOVE

It is very easy to love alone. (*FS3A* 49)

MARRIAGE

What is marriage, is marriage protection or religion, is marriage renunciation or abundance, is marriage a stepping-stone or an end. What is marriage. (*LO&P* 74)

MASTERPIECES

A master-piece certainly has nothing to do with identity because identity if it had an audience would not care to be a master-piece. (*GHA* 198)

Therefore a master-piece has essentially not to be necessary, it has to be that is it has to exist but it does not have to be necessary it is not in response to necessity as action is because the minute it is necessary it has in it no possibility of going on. (*WAM* 86)

MEN

Since there are no men in existence anywhere except here on this earth being men is not an easy thing to happen. (*PL* 69)

Men . . . are so conservative, so selfish, so boresome, and . . . they are so ugly, and . . . they are gullible, anybody can convince them. . . . (*LO&P* 60)

Men can not count, they do not know that two and two make four if women do not tell them so. (*LO&P* 73)

Drinkers think each other are amusing but that is only because they are both drunk. It is funny the two things most men are proudest of is the thing that any man can do and doing does in the same way, that is being drunk and being the father of their son. (*EA* 67)

MEN, AMERICAN

We talked about and that has always been a puzzle to me why American men think that success is everything when they know that eighty percent of them are not going to succeed more than to just keep going and why if they are not why do they not keep on being interested in the things that interested them when they were college men and why American men different from English men do not get more interesting as they get older. (*EA* 239)

MEN, MARRIED

There is no such thing as being good to your wife. (*PL* 43)

MEN, YOUNG

It does change the age that is young, once in Paris it was twenty-six, then it was twenty-two, then it was nineteen and now it is between thirty and forty. They tell about a new young man, how old is he you say and they say he is thirty. (*EA* 268)

There is a difference between twenty-nine and thirty. When you are twenty-nine it can be the beginning of everything. When you are thirty it can be the end of everything. (*MR* 83)

MONEY

When you earn money and spend money every day anybody can know the difference between a million and three. But when you vote money away there really is not any difference between a million and three. (*HWW* 106)

MUSIC

What is music. A passion for colonies not a love of country. (*PL* 36)

NAMES, PERSONAL

Name any name and then remember everybody you ever knew who bore that name. Are they all alike. I think so. (*FIA* 4)

NATURE

The phenomenon of nature is more splendid than the daily events of nature, certainly, so then the twentieth century is splendid. (*PIC* 43)

NATURE, HUMAN

Growing has no connection with audience.
Audience has no connection with identity.
Identity has no connection with the universe.
A universe has no connection with human nature. (*GHA* 157)

NOUNS (*See* Adjectives)

A noun has been the name of something for such a very long time. That is the reason that slang exists it is to change the nouns which have been names for so long. (*LIA* 214)
A noun is nature personified. . . . (*AFAM* xvi)

PARAGRAPHS (*See* Sentences)

There is no such thing as a natural sentence but there is such a thing as a natural paragraph and it must be found. (*AFAM* 364)
A paragraph is never finished therefore a paragraph is not natural. A paragraph is with the well acquainted. It languishes in mediocrity. (*AFAM* 372)
A resolution is a paragraph. (*AFAM* 373)

PATIENCE

I have declared that patience is never more than patient. I too have declared, that I who am not patient am patient. (*LO&P* 58)
If things do not take long it makes life too short. (*EA* 189)

PERFECTION

. . . If perfection is good more perfection is better. . . . (*PGU* 113)

PERIODS

Periods have a life of their own a necessity of their own a feeling of their own a time of their own. (*LIA* 218)

PHILOSOPHY

Philosophy tries to replace in the human mind what is not there that is time and beginning and so they always have to stop going on existing. There are consequently practically no master-pieces in philosophy. (*GHA* 194)

PIANO PLAYING

. . . you never want to use anything but white keys black keys are too harmonious and you never want to do a chord chords are too emotional, you want to use white keys and play two hands together but not bother which direction either hand takes not at all you want to make it like a design and always looking and you will have a good time. (*EA* 229)

PIGEONS

Pigeons on the grass alas.
Pigeons on the grass alas.
Short longer grass short longer longer shorter yellow grass Pigeons large pigeons on the shorter longer yellow grass alas pigeons on the grass. (*FS3A* 46)

POETRY

Poetry is concerned with using with abusing, with losing with wanting, with denying with avoiding with adoring with replacing the noun. It is doing that always doing that, doing that and doing nothing but that. Poetry is doing nothing but using losing refusing and pleasing and betraying and caressing nouns. That is what poetry does, that is what poetry has to do no matter what kind of poetry it is. And there are a great many kinds of poetry. (*LIA* 231)

Little bits of poetry.
Make a happy land
Landing.
When they see the land
Landing. (*SIM* 268)

Poetry consists in a rhyming dictionary and things seen. (*PL* 310)

PROGRESS

From the very nature of progress, all ages must be transitional. If they were not, the world would be at a stand-still and death would speedily ensue. It is one of the tamest of platitudes but it is always introduced by a flourish of trumpets. (*RAD* 122)

It is hard to go on when you are nearly there but near enough to hurry up to get there. (*TWR* 59)

PUBLICITY

There has always been a great passion for publicity in the world the greatest passion for publicity, and those who succeed best, who have the best instincts for publicity, do have a great tendency to be persecuted that is natural enough. . . . (*WIHS* 165)

QUESTION MARKS

The question mark is alright when it is all alone when it is used as a brand on cattle or when it could be used in decoration but connected with writing it is completely entirely completely uninteresting. . . . A question is a question, anybody can know that a question is a question and so why add to it the question mark when it is already there when the question is already there in the writing. (*LIA* 214–15)

QUESTIONS (*See* Answers)

RABBITS (*See* Hens)

READERS

An audience is pleasant if you have it, it is flattering and flattering is agreeable always, but if you have an audience the being an audience is their business, they are the audience you are the writer, let each attend to their own business. (*HWW* 55)

READING

. . . books are always complete to me completely books and I can always lose myself in practically any of them. (*PGU* 113)

REALITY

There is no real reality to a really imagined life any more. (*GHA* 74)

RELIGION

Religion is this. They act as in religion that is to say they neither wait nor stay away. Religion is best as it is. If they like it at all they like it all, not only more than once but often. (*FIA* 25)

REPETITION

Repeating then is in every one, in every one their being and their feeling and their way of realising everything and every one comes out of them in repeating. More and more then every one comes to be clear to some one. (*MOA* 284)

RETENTION

To retain means permission to find it more than convenient. (*AFAM* 22)

ROMANCE (*See* Adventure)

Romance is everything (UK ad)

ROSES

Rose is a rose is a rose is a rose. (*G&P* 187)

Do we suppose that all she knows is that a rose is a rose is a rose is a rose. (*O&P* 110)

. . . she would carve on the tree Rose is a Rose is a Rose is a Rose is a Rose until it went all the way around. (*TWR* 53)

A rose tree may be may be a rose tree may be a rosy rose tree if watered. (*A&B* 205)

Indeed a rose is a rose makes a pretty plate. . . . (*SIM* 213)

When I said.

A rose is a rose is a rose is a rose.

And then later made that into a ring I made poetry and what did I do I caressed completely caressed and addressed a noun. (*LIA* 231)

Civilisation begins with a rose. A rose is a rose is a rose is a rose. It continues with blooming and it fastens clearly upon excellent examples. (*AFAM* 262)

I determine myself that this is not a fancy that very really and presently I will establish rows and rows of roses.

A rose is a rose is a rose is a rose. (*AFAM* 242)

Lifting belly can please me because it is an occupation I enjoy.

Rose is a rose is a rose is a rose.

In print on top. (*BTV* 96)

Now listen! I'm no fool. I know that in daily life we don't go around saying "is a . . . is a . . . is a . . . " Yes, I'm no fool; but I think that in that line the rose is red for the first time in English poetry for a hundred years. (*FIA* vi)

SAINTS

A saint a real saint never does anything, a martyr does something but a really good saint does nothing. . . . Generally speaking anybody is more interesting doing nothing than doing something. (*EA* 109)

A saint is easily resisted. (*FS3A* 24)

SCULPTURE

Sculpture is made with two instruments and some supports and pretty air. (*NOTY* 246)

SENTENCES (*See* Paragraphs)

Taste has nothing to do with sentences. (*ABT* 268)

A Sentence is not emotional a paragraph is. (*HTW* 23)

A sentence is a hope of a paragraph. What is a paragraph that is easy. How can you know better if you say so. A sentence is never an answer. (*AFAM* 372)

SIGHING

All the world knows how to cry but not all the world knows how to sigh. Sighing is extra. (*MR* 1)

SISTERS

It is natural not to care about a sister certainly not when she is four years older and grinds her teeth at night. (*EA* 135)

STEIN, GERTRUDE

I think the reason I am important is that I know everything. (*HTW* 169)

I write to write we write too right.
I write to write. (*PL* 123)

Nobody knows what I am trying to do but I do and I know when I succeed.
. . . (*AFAM* xv)
I am writing for myself and strangers. (*MOA* 289)
There is every reason why they should all admire me greatly and tell of it just now to themselves and to each other. (*P&P* 140)

When they all listen to him I mean me, by him I mean me.
By him I mean me.
It is not necessary to have any meaning. . . . (*LO&P* 68–69)

. . . you haven't yet learned that I am at once impetuous and slow-minded. (*QED* 79)
Of course I am not logical, . . . logic is all foolishness. The whole duty of man consists in being reasonable and just. . . . I am reasonable because I know the difference between understanding and not understanding and I am just because I have no opinion about things I don't understand. (*QED* 56)
Anybody can like words of one syllable here and there but I like them anywhere. (*PL* 71)
When I write I write and when I talk I talk and the two are not one, . . . then the inside is not inside and the outside is not outside and I like the inside to be inside and the outside to be outside, it makes it more necessary to be one. (*EA* 264)
My writing is clear as mud, but mud settles and clear streams run on and disappear. . . . (*EA* 123)
Think of the Bible and Homer think of Shakespeare and think of me. (*GHA* 117)
Life is strife, I was a martyr all my life not to what I won but to what was done. (*LO&P* 88)

I will be well welcome when I come.
Because I am coming.
Certainly I come having come. (*SIM* 151)

Nobody is so rude
Not to remember Gertrude. (*A&B* 13)

SUCCESS

Success is the result achieved when nobody answers. (*A&B* 184)

TEMPERS

It is hard living down the tempers we are born with. (*MOA* 3)

UNEMPLOYMENT

Once unemployment is recognized as unemployment and organized as unemployment nobody starts to work. (*HWW* 109)

UNIVERSALITY

Supposing everyone lived at one time what would they say. They would observe that stringing string beans is universal. (*LCA* 21)

UNITED STATES

In the United States there is more space where nobody is than where anybody is. (*GHA* 53)

VERBS

It is wonderful the number of mistakes a verb can make and that is equally true of its adverb. . . .

Beside being able to be mistaken and to make mistakes verbs can change to look like themselves or to look like something else, they are, so to speak on the move and adverbs move with them and each of them find themselves not at all annoying but very often very much mistaken. (*LIA* 211–12)

WALKING (*See* Dancing)

If you are looking down while you are walking it is better to walk up hill the ground is nearer. (*MR* 84)

WAR (*See* Dancing)

War is more like a novel than it is like real life and that is its eternal fascination. It is a thing based on reality but invented, it is a dream made real, all the things that make a novel but not really life. (*PF* 38)

WISHES

If fishes were wishes the ocean would be all of our desire. (*AFAM* 230)

WOMEN

Ladies there is no neutral position for us to assume. (*LO&P* 70)

Once more I can climb about and remind you that a woman in this epoch does the important literary thinking. (*GHA* 220)

Why should a woman do the literary important literary thinking of this epoch. (*GHA* 224–25)

WRITERS

How is it that a certain number in any generation can read what is written but only one in any number of generations can write what is written. (*GHA* 152)

Writers only think they are interested in politics, they are not really, it gives them a chance to talk and writers like to talk but really no real writer is really interested in politics. (*HWW* 55)

WRITING

One of the pleasantest things those of us who write or paint do is to have the daily miracle. It does come. (*PF* 3)

Before one is successful that is before any one is ready to pay money for anything you do then you are certain that every word you have written is an important word to have written and that any word you have written is as important as any other word and you keep everything you have written with great care. (*EA* 39)

I like writing, it is so pleasant, to have the ink write it down on the paper as it goes on doing. . . . but I do not correct, I sometimes cut out a little not very often and not very much but correcting after all what is in your head comes down into your hand and if it has come down it can never come again no not again. (*EA* 311)

X

X is difficult, and X is not much use and it is kind of foolish that X should have been put into the alphabet, it almost makes it an elephant. (*A&B* 71)

YES

Yes, yes is for a very young man. . . . (*LO&P* 9)

ZERO

So Zero is a hero.

And why is Zero a hero.

Because if there was no Zero there would not be ten of them there would only be one. (*A&B* 85)

PART V

An Annotated Bibliography of Selected Criticism

This selective compilation concentrates almost entirely on books and published dissertations devoted exclusively to Gertrude Stein, although it does account for the work by five of her constant Constant Readers that has appeared in a wide range of publications: Donald Gallup,* William H. Gass, Robert Bartlett Haas,* Carl Van Vechten,* and Thornton Wilder.* Deliberately, it avoids works in which Gertrude Stein is the partial subject, since that list is sufficiently eclectic to give pause to many readers. She has been identified or otherwise invited to share close quarters—in an astonishing catalog of doctoral studies—with Sherwood Anderson,* W. H. Auden, Jane Austen, Djuna Barnes, Natalie Clifford Barney,* Samuel Beckett, Thomas Berger, Bertolt Brecht, Charles Dickens, William Faulkner, Ernest Hemingway,* Henry James, William James,* James Joyce, Franz Kafka, Wassily Kandinsky, Marianne Moore, Pablo Picasso,* Harold Pinter, Ezra Pound,* Marcel Proust, Alain Robbe-Grillet, George Santayana,* Jean Toomer, Mark Twain, Renée Vivien, Hugo Von Hofmannsthal, William Carlos Williams,* Virginia Woolf, and Louis Zukofsky. Her work has been categorized as structuralist, deconstructionist, semiotic, premodern, postmodern, abstract, concrete, and at least one sociologist appropriated it to teach existential concepts to counselor trainees and student personnel workers. This bibliography also ignores book reviews, essays, and articles in scholarly quarterlies, and memoirs in other publications. It does not account for musical versions of Stein's work nor for dramatizations and caricatures of her life and milieu—imaginary, synthetic, or fraudulent—of which there have now been too many, none of them entirely successful. These and attendant matters have been fully covered in the work of Ray Lewis White and Robert A. Wilson, covered hereinafter and recommended to supplement this selective list.

Bloom, Harold, ed. *Modern Critical Views: Gertrude Stein*. New York: Chelsea House, 1986.

> Bloom's sensitive introduction to this selection of critical essays, as well as chapters from a number of full-length studies of Stein's work, calls her the ''greatest master of dissociative rhetoric in modern writing'' (1). He begins with work by people represented elsewhere in this bibliography or among the biographical entries: Sherwood Anderson,* Katherine Anne Porter, Edmund Wilson,* William

Carlos Williams,* Thornton Wilder,* Donald Sutherland,* Allegra Stewart, B. L. Reid, Richard Bridgman, and Norman Weinstein, William Gass, and Marianne DeKoven. Also included are essays by Judith Saunders about *Paris France*;† Catherine Stimpson about feminist issues, both intellectual and physical; and Jayne Walker about Stein's first decade as a writer. It concludes with a useful chronology.

Bridgman, Richard. *Gertrude Stein in Pieces*. New York: Oxford University Press, 1970.

Like Donald Sutherland's* book, accounted for elsewhere in this bibliography, Bridgman's study is essentially a biography of her work, but unlike Sutherland's New Criticism, ruling out any reference to Stein's personal life, Bridgman reads each of her compositions through her personal life and, equally significantly, chronologically. Perhaps the most valuable assessment of Stein's achievement thus far published, it is luminously informative, completely nonpartisan, and crucial to any preliminary reading. If subsequent Stein scholarship has ranged more widely in focusing on sexual politics, psychobiographical implications, deconstructionist theory, feminism, or linguistic explication, in each of these approaches as contradiction to genre, it has done so in part because of Bridgman's skillful work.

Brinnin, John Malcolm. *The Third Rose: Gertrude Stein and Her World*. Boston: Little, Brown, 1959.

After an initial observation that time and closer reading have proven false—"If Gertrude Stein had never lived, sooner or later works very much like those she produced would have been written by someone else" (xiii)—Brinnin's discreet biography is a good introduction to Stein's life and milieu. Frequently, Brinnin's imperceptions lead him to dismiss some of the difficult texts. *Tender Buttons*,† for example, is a "resonant error" (137). The events of Stein's life are related in a sprightly manner, although Alice Toklas is downplayed at her own insistence. Brinnin quotes liberally from a variety of sources, but they are listed only by name and title in his acknowledgments, and the book is otherwise undocumented. Also, the book is blandly oblivious of specific dates.

Burnett, Avis. *Gertrude Stein*. New York: Atheneum, 1972.

" 'You're a stuffed shirt, Leo, and a grumpy one at that,' " Gertrude Stein tells her brother in a youthful, opening exchange in this hilariously bad novelized biography (3). Several chapters later, the reader encounters this unlikely invitation: " 'Get out your Spanish *mantilla*,' she called up the stairs to Alice's bedroom. 'I've just finished *The Making of Americans*† and we're going to Spain to celebrate' " (92). It goes along like that right up the deathbed scene: " 'What is the answer, Alice?' she asked. Tears streamed down Alice's face. 'I don't know, Lovey' " (178). Burnett may have intended her effort for juvenile readers, but that does not absolve her of the responsibility for several factual inaccuracies, non sequiturs, and dialogue as unbelievable as it is embarrassing.

Copeland, Carolyn Faunce. *Language & Time & Gertrude Stein*. Iowa City: University of Iowa Press, 1975.

The peculiar second ampersand in the title is exact and appropriate in Copeland's work, since she is concerned with Stein's relationship with language and time, not their manifestation in various works. The distinction is subtle but justified. Here, language is synonymous with the narrator's attitude. Through several representative works from different periods, Copeland traces Stein's progression from an objective point of view to a character's mask to a language that hides the narrator to, finally, a narrator reflecting a Bergsonian time. Time becomes synonymous with the élan vital arising from natural force and therefore unimpeded by space and movement other than its own. Copeland's claim that Stein's voice changed as her interests changed is sufficiently clear, if limited as a reading.

DeKoven, Marianne. *A Different Language: Gertrude Stein's Experimental Writing*. Madison: University of Wisconsin Press, 1983.

Reading Stein's work chronologically through its major periods, DeKoven establishes several "genres" that sensibly ignore conventional ones like poetry, fiction, and drama, although allowing for them as ancillary identifications. Strongly deconstructionist, partly feminist, the method examines the incoherence and unrestrictive play in the writing as essentially positive forces. "Insistence," "Lively Words," "Voices and Plays," "Melody," and "Landscape" are unique genres in Stein's writing that overcome conventional expectations of meaning, either literal or symbolic, and form identifiable through the writings of others. DeKoven's persuasive case—amply illustrated with close textual readings—is weakened only by her own "Insistence" not on "Lively Words" but sometimes on academic argot.

Doane, Janice. *Silence and Narrative; The Early Novels of Gertrude Stein*. Westport, Conn.: Greenwood Press, 1986.

The tone of the dissertation is not entirely absent from Doane's sensitive reading of *Fernhurst, Q.E.D., and Other Early Writings,*† *Three Lives,*† and *The Making of Americans.*† Focused fairly narrowly on Michel Foucault's contentions about the nature of silence as an integral part of communication, Doane reads Stein's own silences as a consciously thematic device through which women, or the feminine perspective, copes. In the early work, "silence is a very felt presence" (xiv), but in time it became "a mode of authority that deliberately challenges" a conventional patriarchal discourse (xxvi). Traditional "silence," Doane demonstrates, becomes verbalized as the narrator of *The Making of Americans* provides "moments of stasis, moments which halt the story" in which to clarify her own progress (123).

Dubnick, Randa. *The Structure of Obscurity: Gertrude Stein, Language, and Cubism.* Urbana and Chicago: University of Illinois Press, 1984.

Dubnick's "interdisciplinary study" deals "not only with Gertrude Stein but also with cubism, structuralism, and semiotics" (122), distinguishing between Stein's prose (a genuine cubism) that exaggerates syntax and minimizes vocabulary, and poetry (a synthetic one) that abbreviates syntax and extends vocabulary. Dubnick credits Stein with having anticipated *le nouveau roman,* absurdist theater, and structural linguistics. Despite evidence amassed by Richard Bridgman, Linda Simon, and others, Dubnick is resistant to readings in sexual code; while not denying them, she suggests that the obscurity results from Stein's attempts to understand the language. Dubnick is helpful in making persuasive connections between Stein's work and recent literary criticism.

Gallup,* Donald. "The Gertrude Stein Collection." *Yale University Library Gazette* XXII, 2 (October 1947), 21–32.

———. "A Book Is a Book." *The New Colophon* I (January 1948), 67–80.

———. "The Weaving of a Pattern: Marsden Hartley and Gertrude Stein." *Magazine of Art* XLI, 7 (November 1948), 256–61.

———. "Always Gertrude Stein." *Southwest Review* XXXIV, 3 (Summer 1949), 254–58.

———. "The Making of *The Making of Americans.*" *The New Colophon* III (1950), 54–74.

———. "Carl Van Vechten's Gertrude Stein." *Yale University Library Gazette* XXVII, 2 (October 1952), 77–86.

———, ed. *The Flowers of Friendship: Letters Written to Gertrude Stein.* New York: Alfred A. Knopf, 1953.

———. "Gertrude Stein and *The Atlantic.*" *Yale University Library Gazette* XXVIII, 3 (January 1954), 109–28.

———. Introduction to *Alphabets and Birthdays,*† vol. 7 of the Yale Edition of the Unpublished Writings of Gertrude Stein. New Haven: Yale University Press, 1957.

———. "Du Côté de Chez Stein." *The Book Collector* XIX, 2 (Summer 1970), 169–84.

———. "Introducing Gertrude Stein." *Widening Circle* I (Fall 1973), 6–10.

The Flowers of Friendship constitutes as good a public biography as Gertrude Stein is ever likely to receive. Culled with discretion and annotated, this modest selection of Stein's personal correspondence, now in the Collection of American Literature at Yale University, contains letters from everyone from William James* to some American GIs. Her early publishing struggles, her friendships, and her feuds are included. Dedicated to Alice Toklas "who was there when they came and who knows what they meant" ([v]), the collection is not entirely candid, but it serves as an excellent introduction to Gertrude Stein and her milieu, from her student days to La Belle Époque to the twenties of the Lost Generation, flanked by two wars, to her old age, always through the eyes of those who knew her. Gallup's other work on Stein's behalf is various: "A Book Is a Book," about *Three Lives,*† and "The Making of *The Making of Americans*"† trace the publishing vagaries of those two early titles. Three of the pieces edit Stein's letters, to Ellery Sedgwick,* to Marsden Hartley,* and to Gallup himself. Three are about the Stein collection at Yale, including much valuable biographical information about her friendship with Carl Van Vechten.* The last two are more personal, detailing some of Gallup's own associations with Gertrude Stein and Alice Toklas. His introduction to *Alphabets and Birthdays*† accounts for the composition and attempts at publication of the materials in that "cross section of Gertrude Stein's work" that "will perhaps serve for some readers as an introduction" to the other Yale volumes (xix).

Gass, William H. "Gertrude Stein: Her Escape from Protective Language" in *Fiction and the Figures of Life*. New York: Alfred A. Knopf, 1970, 79–96.

———. "Gertrude Stein and the Geography of the Sentence" in *The World within the Word*. New York: Alfred A. Knopf, 1978, 63–123.

———. " 'And' " in *Habitations of the Word*. New York: Simon & Schuster, 1985, 160–84.

———. "Thoroughly Modernist Intimacies." *Times Literary Supplement*, 7 November 1986, 12336–37.

William Gass has written no book about Gertrude Stein, but his less than two hundred pages about her work constitute a brilliant assessment of it. "Her Escape from Protective Language" first appeared in *Accent* in 1958; ostensibly a review of B. L. Reid's *Art by Subtraction* (included elsewhere in this bibliography), it is a rigorous defense of Stein's "intellectual reach" (96), assessing why she was first wrongly "admired by a few without judgment" and "now censured by many without reason" (80). The first and third sections of "The Geography of the Sentence" appeared in *The New York Review of Books* in 1973 and served as introduction to *The Geographical History of America*† that same year, placing Stein's early development in its historical context and tracing forward through luminous demonstrations the relationships between wordplay and repetition. In the essay's second section, Gass offers an explication of Stein's hermetic eroticism in *Tender Buttons*† with an unsettling—and, to some, embarrassing—clarity absent from the analyses of others who have approached this work's powerfully sexual descriptions disguised as wordplay. An abbreviated version of " 'And' " was published in *Harper's Magazine* in 1984, in Gass's unique and eccentric manner dissecting the use of that eponymous conjunction as a stylistic device. A single sentence from Stein's "Melanctha"—with "and" used six different ways—is his focal example. "Thoroughly Modernist Intimacies" is a review essay of Edward Burn's *Letters*† *of Gertrude Stein and Carl Van Vechten*, notable for its reasonable explanation of those sticky sobriquets, "Papa Woojums," "Baby Woojums," and "Mama Woojums."

Greenfield, Howard. *Gertrude Stein: A Biography*. New York: Crown, 1973.

A tipped-in erratum flag, correcting "a rose is a rose is a rose is a rose" to "Rose is a rose is a rose is a rose," portends only some of the trouble in this earnest but turgid and superficial account. Designed for a young audience of undetermined age, it is a factual summary of Stein's life and its major events. For adolescent readers, however, it is likely to prove a boring narrative of an essentially intellectual life; for mature readers, its generalizations and naive critical judgments are likely to prove unpersuasive. Lists of people's names lead to generalizations by association. *Tender Buttons*† is explained as "colloquial speech and a kind of singsong repetition" (41). Sometimes Greenfield is simply wrong, as in claiming that there was little critical response to *Tender Buttons*, when it was actually widely reviewed.

Haas,* Robert Bartlett. "Another Garland for Gertrude Stein" in *What Are Masterpieces*.† Los Angeles: Conference Press, 1940.

————. [Preface and Notes] in *A Primer for the Gradual Understanding of Gertrude Stein*.† Los Angeles: Black Sparrow Press, 1971.
————. "A Space of Time Filled with Moving" [and Notes] in *Reflection on the Atomic Bomb*.† Los Angeles: Black Sparrow Press, 1973.
————. "Gertrude Stein's 'Sense of the Immediate' " (and Notes] in *How Writing Is Written*.† Los Angeles: Black Sparrow Press, 1974.

Haas's introduction to *What Are Masterpieces* summarizes Stein's life and publications to 1940, musters her philosophical attitudes as an extension of those of William James,* and claims that she places "literature on a plane superior to philosophy and science" (22). His *Primer for the Gradual Understanding of Gertrude Stein* plays out "in miniature" an anthology to represent her major periods in chronological order on which he and Stein were working at the time of her death ([7]). It also contains an extended interview conducted six months before she died. Haas's two volumes of uncollected writings also are arranged in largely chronological order, and his notes clearly define—again, "in miniature"—Gertrude Stein's gradual progression.

Hobhouse, Janet. *Everybody Who Was Anybody*. New York: G. P. Putnam's Sons, 1975.

The *Library Journal* called this extravagantly illustrated biography "a rather plodding journey through over-familiar territory" (15 November 1975, 80). It is, further, murky in its chronology of Stein's compositions, defensive in its analyses, even cavalier and condescending. As an art critic, Hobhouse has difficulty in allowing Stein the same latitude with language she would allow an artist with paint. Wisely, she falls back on Stein's literary critics for her assessments; when she does venture her own—*Wars I Have Seen*,† for example, as the best of the biographical works—they are unsubstantiated. The book is a valuable visual record, however, with about one hundred photographs and other illustrations, some of them full-page reproductions in color of paintings in the Stein collection at one time or another.

Hoffman, Frederick J. *Gertrude Stein*. Minneapolis: University of Minnesota Press, 1961;

reprinted in *American Writers*, Leonard Unger, editor in chief. New York: Charles
Scribner's Sons, 1974.

In his useful monograph, first published before the ground swell of interest in
Stein, Hoffman contends that her creative work illuminated her critical theories
and, moreover, have their own integrity. Largely free of biographical readings,
his assessment of her work examines "an analysis of the mind in its precise
function of apprehending and experiencing objects" (28) through a carefully
chosen series of "substantial masterpieces" (45). In addition to obvious choices
of that time—*Three Lives*† as "intrinsically good" and *Four Saints in Three Acts*†
as "never truly separable from the variety of theoretical convictions from which
it emerged"—Hoffman cites *The Geographical History of America,*† *Paris
France,*† and *Ida*† as books "of unaffected wisdom" (45). His is a good preliminary introduction.

Hoffman, Michael J. *The Development of Abstractionism in the Writings of Gertrude
Stein*. Philadelphia: University of Pennsylvania Press, 1965.

———. *Gertrude Stein*. New York: Twayne, 1976.
———, ed. *Critical Essays on Gertrude Stein*. Boston: G. K. Hall, 1986.

In the published version of his earlier dissertation, Hoffman traces the chronological development of abstract elements in Stein's early work, from her Radcliffe
undergraduate manuscripts through her narratives, portraits, and what he calls
"still lifes" in *Tender Buttons*.† He allies her work with the nonliterary revolutions
of the same period in psychology and in cubist painting. It is a useful preliminary
study. Hoffman's Twayne biography builds on her earlier material and extends it
through her later work. In its economy, objectivity, and balance, it may be the
best general introduction to the Stein canon. Hoffman's collection of *Critical
Essays* is a mixed bag. It reprints much early criticism and preserves material
otherwise difficult to come by: a 1909 review of *Three Lives*† from the *Kansas
City Star*; W. H. Auden's review of *Ida*;† and chapters from books by Laura
Riding, Wyndham Lewis, Edmund Wilson,* and others. Among its later inclusions
are an early chapter of Neil Schmitz's *Huck and Alice*, about Stein's humor; and
substantial essays by James Breslin on *The Autobiography of Alice B. Toklas,*†
Elizabeth Fifer on *Useful Knowledge,*† and Catherine Stimpson's remarkable study
on "somagrams," lesbian confluences of body and language in which the body
is absorbed into the language. *Critical Essays* is a strong introduction to the corpus
of Stein's work despite its partisan stance. Simultaneously, it supports and contradicts William Gass's contention (also included) that her works lie "beside the
mass of modern literature like a straight line by a maze and give no hold to the
critic bent on explication" (80).

Katz, Leon. "The First Making of *The Making of Americans*: A Study Based on Gertrude
Stein's Notebooks and Early Versions of Her Novel (1902–08)," unpublished
dissertation, Columbia University, 1963.

————. Introduction to *Fernhurst, Q.E.D., and Other Early Writings*. New York: Liveright, 1971.

———— and Edward Burns. " 'They Walk in Light' Gertrude Stein and Pablo Picasso" in *Gertrude Stein on Picasso*. New York: Liveright, 1970.

Although Katz has never published his early investigation into Stein's working papers, charts, diagrams, and other organizing materials for *The Making of Americans*,† many Stein scholars have gratefully pillaged his pioneering efforts. Katz's painstaking examination of Stein's unpublished drafts has made possible a more exact chronology of her compositions and equally significantly, perhaps, an accounting for the subtle variations in styles as they evolved in her work during the first decade of her career as a writer. Katz's introduction to her early attempts at fiction is illuminating both biographically and critically. Liveright announced publication of Stein's notebooks for late 1974 or early 1975, with commentaries by Alice Toklas and annotations by Katz. They have not yet appeared in print.

Liston, Maureen R. *Gertrude Stein: An Annotated Critical Bibliography*. Kent, Ohio: Kent State University Press, 1979.

Readers requiring a more complete bibliography of secondary sources than this one will find a selection of dissertations and articles from scholarly publications similarly annotated in Liston's well-organized compilation. It is far from complete, however: several significant titles are ignored entirely; some lack critical reviews; some others that have undergone reprinting and, therefore, extensive reassessments on the basis of latter-day scholarship and readings through a variety of critical approaches, are represented only by initial and, therefore, sometimes bewildered responses. Liston's inclusion of abstracts for a number of doctoral studies, however, is of inestimable value, making them available under single cover for preliminary investigations by students.

Maubrey-Rose, Victoria. *The Anti-Representational Response: Gertrude Stein's "Lucy Church Amiably."* Uppsala, Sweden: Studia Anglistica Upsaliensia, 1979.

This hectoring study begins by postdating the composition of *Lucy Church Amiably*† by three years. It purports to consider Stein's 1927 novel "through certain semantic and linguistic aspects of feminist, schizophrastic, and avant-garde discourse taken from Marxist and post-structuralist literary criticism," according to its abstract ([2]). Identifying Stein's language with "phallogocentric discourse," it allies the events of her life in "anthropomorphic relationship" with the novel's heroine, both woman and church serving "as a metaphor for Gertrude Stein herself" ([2]). Having misdated the novel, Maubrey-Rose has also misdated Stein's acquiring the manoir at Bilignin as her summer home, errors unlikely to encourage a reader's confidence.

Mellow, James R. *Charmed Circle: Gertrude Stein & Company*. New York: Praeger, 1974.

In nearly five hundred pages, Mellow gathers together all the stories, true and apocryphal, to provide the only full-length account of Stein's life as both a writer and an art collector, as well as the broadest view of the cultural landscape in which she struggled and flourished, unembellished with either rancor or adulation. His straightforward narrative may lack much helpful attention to her hermetic works, but it makes up for that in documenting the world and the person from which they grew. As an art critic, Mellow is particularly informative about the early collecting, and he gives Leo Stein* more than his just due as his sister's aesthetic mentor. Moreover, readers ignorant of or indifferent to Gertrude Stein are likely to find the book genuinely satisfying simply as a life story.

Miller, Rosalind S. *Gertrude Stein: Form and Intelligibility*. New York: Exposition Press, 1949.

Miller announces in her preface to her less than a hundred-page essay about Stein's writings, more or less in chronological order as published, that it is "not a scholarly critique for the specialized student" ([ix]). Nevertheless, this first extended attempt to account for a fair representation of Stein's work is of some modest merit. Written at a time when little if any attention was paid Stein in the academic community, Miller's work is preliminary and tentative, settling too easily for "rhythmic prose" and "melodic flow of words" (95), but it is a fair enough introduction for the beginning reader. In the second half of this book, Miller has edited and annotated Stein's Radcliffe† college themes, written under William Vaughn Moody,* an invaluable source of information in approaching her early work.

Neuman, S. C. *Gertrude Stein: Autobiography and the Problem of Narration*. British Columbia, Canada: University of Victoria, 1979.

Shirley Neuman's monograph establishes the narrative voice in *The Autobiography of Alice B. Toklas*† as more than a clever imitation of the speech of its eponym. It is instead a "transition" to the narrative voice in the later autobiographical works from the distancing points of view that had preceded (23). The continuous present, or "beginning again and again" in *Three Lives*† and the early portraits, is employed in the autobiographies as well (25). Neuman's middle section, covering the lectures and *The Geographical History of America*† that came between autobiographies, contends "Stein's refusal to write out of a sense of her own identity results in one of the most individualistic and easily identifiable prose styles of the twentieth century" (44). Neuman is well reasoned, persuasive, and undeniable.

Neuman, Shirley, and Ira B. Nadel, eds. *Gertrude Stein and the Making of Literature*. New York: Macmillan, 1988.

Essays by eleven Stein scholars provide new approaches and perspectives on the full range of her work. Modernist and postmodernist theory and practice; explications of little-read works; and assessments of the process of composition from notebook to manuscript to printed page are included. Academics from ten universities in the United States and Canada are among the contributors, including the three essayists in the present volume. It concludes with three previously unpublished (in English) pieces by Gertrude Stein: "Realism in Novels," "American Language and Literature," and "A Poem about the End of the War." As in similar compilations, the writing is of uneven quality, but the wide variety in subject matter makes this a valuable addition to Stein criticism. It is not for the layman, however.

Rather, Lois. *Gertrude Stein and California*. Oakland, Calif.: Rather Press, 1974.

In the spate of Stein biographies during her centenary in 1974, Rather's modest account of Stein's youth in California and her brief return there in 1935 is unlikely to have received much attention. Handsomely hand-set, printed, and bound by Rather and her husband in an edition of 130 copies, the book sketches in Stein's life between and after her California experiences, but most of its well under a hundred pages stays close to home, calling on a variety of local records for support: city directories, newspaper articles, native reminiscences and memoirs, and Stein's mother's diary. Its close account of Stein's behavior and appearance during the lecture tour is valuable. Only some badly reproduced photographs mar this elegant little volume.

Reid, B. L. *Art by Subtraction: A Dissenting Opinion of Gertrude Stein*. Norman: University of Oklahoma Press, 1958.

Reid confesses at the outset that his "essay in decapitation" was born of "a gradual disenchantment" with Gertrude Stein's work (vii), but his two hundred pages are written in vitriol, and the disappointment he pretends to feel is unsuccessful in masking his anger at his own limitations. After accounting for her critics, taking comfort in her detractors, and dismissing her admirers—"too mild" (22), "shabby reasoning" (28)—Reid dissects book by book, dismissing them on moral or intellectual grounds. After *The Making of Americans*,† "she burrowed blindly, molewise, deeper into a cul-de-sac" (206), he contends, without "beauty," "instruction," or "passion, . . . mumbling to herself" (207). The book's major disappointment is its squandering of the author's obvious intelligence.

Rogers, W. G. *When This You See Remember Me: Gertrude Stein in Person*. New York: Rinehart, 1948.

———. *Gertrude Stein Is Gertrude Stein Is Gertrude Stein*. New York: Thomas Y. Crowell, 1973.

Rogers met Stein and Toklas when he was a soldier during World War I; they renewed acquaintance when *The Autobiography of Alice B. Toklas*† was published; he and his wife, writer Mildred Weston, entertained the visitors during the American lecture tour; subsequently the four of them made a "sentimental journey" (153) through France to retrace the route Rogers had taken with Stein and Toklas when they first met. These events are recounted with charm and affection in Rogers's memoir. Rogers makes some preliminary attempt as well to unravel the complexities of Stein's writings, and he laces the book with copious quotations from her to him. *When This You See Remember Me*—titled after one of Stein's favorite lines—also sketches in the rest of her biography. It is a good introduction to her. *Gertrude Stein Is Gertrude Stein Is Gertrude Stein* is part of a Women in America series designed, apparently, for high school students, but the tone is uneven. Rogers relates the major events in Stein's life, adding to his own firsthand knowledge with details from other published biographies, but there are no notes and no specified sources. He interrupts his own narrative to interject personal assessments that condescend to his readers, and some of the material is unlikely to hold the interest of young readers. The gossip, on the other hand, is always amusing. This is one of four "juveniles," or "books for younger readers," about Gertrude Stein. It is better than Burnett or Greenfield but no better than Wilson. Why any of them were written in the first place is a moot question.

Ryan, Betsy Alayne. *Gertrude Stein's Theatre of the Absolute*. Ann Arbor, Mich.: UMI Research, 1984.

After establishing the general aesthetic principles governing the corpus of Stein's work, Ryan applies it to her plays. Despite its brevity, this study is fairly comprehensive in considering virtually all of the compositions Stein labeled plays. From "What Happened. A Play" in 1913 through *The Mother of Us All*† in 1946, Ryan traces common traits to demonstrate that a work as immediately accessible as "Yes Is for a Very Young Man" and any number of Stein's most hermetic ones can demonstrate her aesthetic as they apply to her "theatre." Further, Ryan justifies Stein as a forerunner of the postabsurdist dramas of Samuel Beckett and Harold Pinter. Ryan's appendices account for a statistical account of the traits she identifies, a chronology of productions, and reviews, making this a valuable reference tool.

Simon, Linda, ed. *Gertrude Stein: A Composite Portrait*. New York: Avon Books, 1974.

———. *The Biography of Alice B. Toklas*. New York: Doubleday, 1977.

The advertising subtitle on Simon's "composite portrait" explains its contents: "Gertrude Stein as remembered well by some of her very famous friends." Simon's brief introduction is good enough to have been longer. The selections are drawn from various autobiographies, memoirs, and introductions to some of Stein's books by Fernande Olivier,* Alice Toklas, Ambroise Vollard,* Natalie Clifford Barney,* Carl Van Vechten* (her earliest extended criticism, long unavailable), Sylvia Beach,* Sherwood Anderson,* Ernest Hemingway,* Man Ray,* Jo Davidson,* Alvin Langdon Coburn,* Jacques Lipchitz,* Pavel Tchelitchew,* Francis Picabia,* Pablo Picasso,* Edith Sitwell,* Harold Acton,* Virgil Thomson,* Sir Francis Rose,* Bravig Imbs,* Canadian poet John Glassco, journalist

Samuel Putnam, and Thornton Wilder,* each prefaced with a cogent biographical sketch. Simon's full-length *Biography of Alice B. Toklas* is an excellent study, although she does not always seem to like her subject very much. Inevitably, Stein is given her just due, but the concentration is always on her companion, wry, acerbic, competent, and iron-willed. Toklas's early years are fully explored, and the account of her two decades of widowhood make a fascinating account of her discovering a life of her own despite her loneliness: her cookbooks, her memoirs, and her vast correspondence. As an aid to unlocking many of Stein's most hermetic texts, Simon supplies a chronology of passages that refer explicitly or implicitly to the Stein-Toklas courtship and fully sexual as well as intellectual marriage; her readings are always cogent and persuasive.

Sprigge, Elizabeth. *Gertrude Stein: Her Life and Work*. New York: Harper & Brothers, 1957.

Alice Toklas urged a friend to "desist from looking at" that "odious book," although she was "quite callous to its vulgarity," and to another friend she wrote of "La Sprigge—her hateful manuscript and her visit to defend herself and her vulgarities and insinuations" (*SOA* 337). Sprigge quotes liberally from her interviews with Toklas, who always resented any attention to her role in Stein's life. She might better have criticized Sprigge's earnest, plodding, partisan narrative. The factual record is complete, dates and events dutifully recorded, but as biography the book is lifeless; it is thorough but not very interesting, informative but uninvolving. Sprigge's interviews with Stein's contemporaries offer some fresh insights, however. It quotes liberally from published sources but offers no page references.

Steiner, Wendy. *Exact Resemblance to Exact Resemblance: The Literary Portraiture of Gertrude Stein*. New Haven: Yale University Press, 1978.

Steiner approaches Stein's portraits with a structuralist's eye to both representation and resemblance, seeing in her "self-conscious, programmatic work" a unique definition of twentieth-century modernism in both literature and painting (ix). This is a difficult book, closely argued and amply illustrated through semiotic explication; also, it is a necessary book for an serious student of Gertrude Stein's work. Steiner divides the portraits—as a genre in themselves—into three periods, accounting in detail for their evolution: the garrulously redundant pieces to 1913; the startling imagistic pieces to the mid-twenties; the verbal games and narrative play that followed. Stein's portraits require "indexical mimesis rather than description" (45), as Steiner's admirable work amply illustrates.

Steward, Samuel M. *Dear Sammy: Letters from Gertrude Stein and Alice B. Toklas*. Boston: Houghton Mifflin, 1977.

———. *Murder Is Murder Is Murder*. Boston: Alyson Publications, 1985.

Steward's "Memoir" preceding his edition of his letters from Stein and Toklas accounts for his acquaintance with them, first when he was a student, teacher, and beginning novelist; then, in detail, his two visits with them in Bilignin; finally, his more intimate association with Toklas after Stein's death. Based on careful notes he made throughout their friendship, the memoir is affectionate and warm, with memorable incidents and high good humor. Stein has a disconcerting way, however, of trying out vocally on Steward a remarkable number of opinions and pronouncements that later turned up—nearly verbatim—in her published work. The "Gertrude" and "Alice" serving as sleuths in Steward's mystery story, unencumbered by factual accuracy, are perhaps more believable in their fictional exaggerations than they are in his memoir.

Stewart, Allegra. *Gertrude Stein and the Present.* Cambridge: Harvard University Press, 1967.

Stewart's book concentrates on "the underlying experience of contemplation and creative dissociation" that determined Stein's metaphysics as well as her writing (vi). Focusing on *Tender Buttons*† and "Doctor Faustus Lights the Lights," Stewart assesses Stein's work on the basis of twentieth-century linguistic and psychological theories. These creative pieces read in view of a critical one like *The Geographical History of America*† demonstrate "a harmony between principle and application that cannot have evolved arbitrarily" (vi). Stewart reads *Tender Buttons* as a mandala for the mind, but her specific explications sometimes obfuscate rather than clarify; she reads "Doctor Faustus" through Jungian archetypes: Faust as protagonist, Faustus as ego, Doctor Faustus as persona, etcetera, a fascinating interpretation.

Sutherland, Donald. *Gertrude Stein: A Biography of Her Work.* New Haven: Yale University Press, 1951.

———. "Preface: The Turning Point," in *Stanzas in Meditation.* New Haven: Yale University Press, 1956.
———. "Gertrude Stein in the Twentieth Century," in *A Primer for the Gradual Understanding of Gertrude Stein.* Los Angeles: Black Sparrow Press, 1971.

Sutherland's superb example of the New Criticism in its decadence was the first serious examination of Stein's aims and achievements, examining the language and structure and intellectual content of her work as if Alice B. Toklas had never existed. She didn't even make his index. It is a remarkable study in twentieth-century aesthetics, predicated on Stein's extending philosophical and psychological principles through a variety of experiments, with some overlap: "naturalism," "the visible world," "plays," "melodrama and opera," "calligraphy," and "melody," "syntax," "history and legend" (205–8). From "The Elements" through abundant explication of individual titles to "Meditations," followed by a delightful mock interview based largely on quotations from Stein's writings, the book is brilliant. And bloodless. Sutherland's introduction to *Stanzas in Meditation* operates similarly. It argues that the work is "Her summit of innovation, this last

reach of her dialectic'' (v), influenced by the historical climate at the end of the
twenties, strongly influenced by thought rather than by spatial or temporal matters.
She keeps ''ideas in their primary life, that is, of making them events in a subjective
continuum of writing, of making them completely actual'' since the ideas in the
stanzas are about writing itself (xi). Sutherland's erudition is always dazzling, if
intimidating. ''Gertrude Stein and the Twentieth Century'' is an anecdotal essay
about ''the great predecessor,'' through ''a minutely tuned and perfected verbal
instrument, a radically philosophical intelligence applied to words and things alike
in their most vivid aspects'' (156).

Toklas, Alice B. *The Alice B. Toklas Cook Book*. New York: Harper & Brothers, 1954.

————. *What Is Remembered*. New York: Holt, Rinehart and Winston, 1963.

Toklas's running commentary between recipes offers a rewarding memoir of the
forty years she and Stein lived together: food they encountered in French homes
and through a seemingly endless stream of cooks; memorable and unmemorable
meals in restaurants on holidays in the French countryside and during the American
lecture tour, as well as their culinary survival during the occupation, all declared
in Toklas's primly acidulous manner already familiar to readers of Stein's imitation
of it in *The Autobiography of Alice B. Toklas*.† The recipes are often extravagant,
startling, original, even possible, including Carl Van Vechten's* garlic ice cream
and Brion Gysin's hashish fudge. Toklas's subsequent memoir, *What Is Remembered*, is often inaccurate, elliptical, and woefully lacking in substantive detail,
but its terse and pithy wit sustains it, and at least it tells the reader all that Toklas
cared to share. Autobiography by its nature tells only part of the truth anyway,
sometimes unconsciously. This decorous spinster disposes of her ''cherry-colored
corset'' by throwing it out the window of the train during her first trip to Italy
(48); next, on a holiday hike with Gertrude, she disposes of her ''silk combination
and stockings'' in the intense Italian heat (51); Stein had called her ''an old maid
mermaid'' during the previous winter, but ''by the time the buttercups were in
bloom, the old maid mermaid had gone into oblivion and I had been gathering
wild violets'' (44). Toklas's account of Stein's last words reversed the ''question''
and ''answer'' order she had recounted to friends several years before.

Van Vechten, Carl. ''Cubist of Letters Writes a New Book,'' *The New York Times*, 24
    February 1913.

————. ''How to Read Gertrude Stein,'' *Trend* 8 (August 1914), 553–57.
————. Introduction to *Three Lives*,† New York: Modern Library, 1933.
————. Introduction to *Four Saints in Three Acts*.† New York: Random House, 1934.
————. ''How I Listen to *Four Saints in Three Acts*'' in *Four Saints in Three Acts*
    [souvenir program]. New York: Aaronson & Cooper, 1934.
————. ''Gertrude Stein'' in *We Moderns*. New York: Gotham Book Mart, 1939.
————. ''A Stein Song'' in *Selected Writings of Gertrude Stein*.† New York: Random
    House, 1946.
————. ''Pigeons and Roses Pass, Alas!'' *New York Post*, 9 December 1946.

———. " 'How Many Acts Are There in It' " in *Last Operas and Plays.*† New York: Rinehart, 1949.

———. "A Few Notes À Propos of a *'Little' Novel of Thank You.*" Introduction to *A Novel of Thank You*, vol. 8 of the Yale Edition of the Unpublished Writings of Gertrude Stein. New Haven: Yale University Press, 1958.

In addition to the foregoing entries, Van Vechten wrote several book reviews, catalog and dust jacket blurbs, and program notes of minor consequence. His various writings about Stein were always appreciative and impressionistic rather than objective or critical. The first two are significant because of their early date: the *New York Times* article, declaring that Stein had apparently "forgotten how to write," preceded everything but a few reviews of *Three Lives* circa 1910; his *Trend* article was surely the first extended attempt to assess her aims, even though he flails in hyperbole. His introduction to the reissue of *Three Lives* traces its printing history and offers a personality sketch, settling for pronouncements about the book—"a masterpiece" (x)—rather than any significant commentary. His essays about *Four Saints in Three Acts* explain its genesis and preparations for its first production, and urge the audience to respond to it as a collaborative spectacle rather than judge it by other works. After Stein's death, Van Vechten served as her literary executor, editing *Last Operas and Plays* with an introduction commenting on the selections, and the eight volumes in the Yale edition of her unpublished writings, for the last of which he supplied the introduction. "A Stein Song," introducing his edition of her *Selected Writings*, musters the opinions of various reputable critics, and he prepared helpful headnotes for individual titles. His obituary for her, "Pigeons and Roses Pass, Alas!"—a title for which he bore no responsibility—is a deeply moving tribute.

Walker, Jayne. *The Making of a Modernist: Gertrude Stein from Three Lives to Tender Buttons*. Amherst: University of Massachusetts Press, 1984.

Having found language inadequate for detailing human experience, Gertrude Stein moved from linguistic realism to subjectively obscure description in her early work, according to this modest study, as concise as it is persuasive. Working directly with Stein's early notebooks—particularly those devoted to the portraits— Walker deliberately avoids the writer's later observations about her alliances with art, psychology, and philosophy, in favor of a closer examination of the literary work in and of itself. Walker demonstrates Stein's early natural progression between circa 1905 and circa 1912 as a serious engagement rather than some game-playing pastime in the tortured locutions of the interim writings. Walker's bibliographical endnotes are valuable, as are her careful if conservative readings.

Weinstein, Norman. *Gertrude Stein and the Literature of the Modern Consciousness*. New York: Frederick Ungar, 1970.

Weinstein places Gertrude Stein's work in the context of modern experimental writing, concentrating on her major titles, *Three Lives*,† *The Making of Americans*,† *Tender Buttons*,† *Four Saints in Three Acts*,† and *Stanzas in Meditation*.†

He does not ignore her unique idiosyncrasies, but he does read her through contemporary theories of language. Despite too many false references, misquotations, and cheerful generalities, Weinstein's enthusiasm for his subject has a sufficiently tonic effect to persuade others, perhaps, of Stein's long-reaching influence and even similarities to other modernists. A section titled "Documents and Correspondences" is especially interesting in comparing linguistic relationships. Weinstein's cavalier logic is unlikely to strengthen his case, however.

White, Ray Lewis. *Gertrude Stein and Alice B. Toklas: A Reference Guide*. Boston: G. K. Hall, 1984.

In this exhaustive compilation, White has prepared a chronology of virtually everything ever written about Stein and Toklas, not only full-length biographical and critical studies, but essays and articles in scholarly quarterlies and commercial periodicals. Further, he has included books about various literary subjects or about other writers in which sections are devoted to Stein and Toklas. This is no mere listing, however. Every entry has been annotated either with White's own commentary or with a brief quotation from the work to indicate its scope and application. Further, it is cross-referenced to account for those Ph.D. dissertations that came into subsequent print, summarizing or quoting from their abstracts.

Wilder, Thornton. Introduction to *Narration*.† Chicago: University of Chicago Press, 1935.

———. Introduction to *The Geographical History of America*.† New York: Random House, 1936.
———. Introduction to *Four in America*.† New Haven: Yale University Press, 1947.
———. *The Journals of Thornton Wilder*, ed. Donald Gallup.* New Haven: Yale University Press, 1985.

Perhaps Stein's most sensitive critic and intellectual champion, Wilder left in these four brief entries a valuable guide to her work. The tentative introduction to *Narration*, "models of artistic form" (v), recognizes the value of individual words in their "terrifying exactness" (vi) long in advance of other readers. For *The Geographical History of America* he distinguishes between the metaphysician and the artist in this difficult work and defends its humor as well as its eccentricities. Ten years later, for *Four in America*, Wilder supplied a warm and rewarding defense of her work. Beginning with Stein's own explanation of "Rose is a rose is a rose is a rose" from a question-and-answer period at the University of Chicago, Wilder assesses *Four in America* in the context of her other writings, particularly the "Henry James" section, to explain the broad intentions of her career. His conclusions are persuasive: her "fundamental occupation . . . was not the work of art but the shaping of a theory of knowledge, a theory of time, and a theory of the passions" (x). Wilder's posthumously edited journals spill over with references to Gertrude Stein and strongly suggest that she shared with classics the strongest influence on his own aesthetics. One observation repeats itself variously: "As Gertrude Stein said: 'The difficulty of thinking is that you must hold so many things in your head at the same time' '' (256). Further, he includes several of her conversational asides, notably: "Before you write it must be in your head almost in words, but if it is already in words in your head, it will come out dead" (45).

Wilson, Ellen. *They Named Me Gertrude Stein*. New York: Farrar Straus, 1973.

Another in the quartet of biographies for young readers, all issued around the time of the Stein centenary, Wilson's effort is no worse than the others and surely an improvement over two of them. It suffers from some of Burnett's embarrassing, invented dialogue, but it is largely unfictionalized. Gossipy and chatty, it weaves in several episodes from Stein's own fiction as Stein's own experiences—Martha Hershland and her umbrella in *The Making of Americans*,† for example—and sensibly, since it was designed as a juvenile, it concentrates on Stein's early years. Indeed, Alice Toklas doesn't even put in an appearance until two-thirds of its brief 120 pages have passed. Hastily then, World War I, the Lost Generation, the lecture tour, the occupation, and most of Stein's published books skim right by.

Wilson, Robert A. *Gertrude Stein: A Bibliography*. New York: Phoenix Bookshop, 1974.

Building on the Donald Gallup*–Robert Bartlett Haas* *Catalogue of Published and Unpublished Writings of Gertrude Stein* (Yale, 1941) and Julian Sawyer's* fully descriptive *Gertrude Stein: A Bibliography* (Arrow, 1940), Robert A. Wilson's exhaustive compilation not only expands them but—now that the full corpus of Stein's work has been brought into print—supersedes them. Every published title, in all its incarnations and variations, is fully described: books, pamphlets, contributions to books and periodicals, translations, musical settings, recordings, ephemera and miscellanea, a section devoted to Alice Toklas's published work, a selective secondary bibliography, and even a book attributed to Gertrude Stein. Wilson's work is an invaluable contribution to Stein scholarship.

PART VI

Works Consulted and Cited

Abrams, M. S., et al., eds. *Norton Anthology of English Literature*, vol. 2. New York: Norton, 1974.

Acton, Sir Harold. *Memoirs of an Aesthete*. London: Hamish Hamilton, 1984.

Adams, Robert M. *The Land and Literature of England*. New York: Norton, 1983.

Anderson, Margaret. *The Fiery Fountains*. New York: Hermitage, 1951.

———. *My Thirty Years' War*. New York: Covici Friede, 1930.

Anderson, Ruth E., ed. *Contemporary American Composers, A Biographical Dictionary*, 2nd ed. Boston: G. K. Hall, 1982.

Ashbery, John. "The Impossible." *Poetry* 90 (July 1957), 251–52.

Auden, W. H. *The Dyer's Hand*. New York: Random House, 1962.

Baker's Biographical Dictionary of Musicians, rev. Nicholas Slonimsby. New York: Macmillan, 1984.

Beach, Sylvia. *Shakespeare and Company*. New York: Harcourt Brace, 1959.

Benét, William Rose. *The Reader's Encyclopedia*. New York: Crowell, 1965.

Benstock, Shari. *Women of the Left Bank, Paris 1900–1940*. Austin: University of Texas Press, 1986.

Berenson, Bernard. *A Bernard Berenson Treasury*. New York: Simon and Schuster, 1962.

Berkley, Miriam. "The Way It Was: James Laughlin and New Directions." *Publishers Weekly*, 22 November 1985, 24–29.

Berners, Gerald Lord. *First Childhood and Far from the Madding War*. New York: Oxford University Press, 1983.

Birkenhead, Sheila. *Peace in Piccadilly*. New York: Reynal and Hitchcock, 1958.

Block, Haskell M., and Robert G. Shedd, eds. *Masters of Modern Drama*. New York: Random House, 1962.

Bloom, Harold, ed. *Modern Critical Views: Gertrude Stein*. New York: Chelsea House, 1986.

Bordman, Gerald Martin, ed. *Oxford Companion to the American Theatre*. New York: Oxford University Press, 1984.

Bowen, E. "The Last Great Aristotelian." *Time*, 4 May 1987, 84–85.

———. "A Philosopher for Everyman." *Time*, 6 May 1985, 68.

Bridgman, Richard. *Gertrude Stein in Pieces*. New York: Oxford University Press, 1970.

Brinnin, John Malcolm. *The Third Rose*. Boston: Little, Brown, 1959.

Brooks, Richard, ed. *A Critical Bibliography of French Literature*. Syracuse: Syracuse University Press, 1951.

Brown, Bob. *1450–1950*. New York: Jargon, 1959.

Brown, Milton W. *The Story of the Armory Show*. New York: Graphic Society, 1963.

Bruccoli, Matthew J., and Margaret M. Duggan, eds. *Correspondence of F. Scott Fitzgerald*. New York: Random House, 1980.

Burbank, Rex. *Thornton Wilder*. Boston: Twayne, 1978.

Burke, W. J. and Will D. Howe, eds. *American Authors and Books*. New York: Crown, 1972.

Burns, Edward, ed. *The Letters of Gertrude Stein and Carl Van Vechten, 1913–1946*. 2 vols. New York: Columbia University Press, 1986.

———. *Staying on Alone: Letters of Alice B. Toklas*. New York: Liveright, 1973.

Butcher, Fanny. *Many Lives, One Love*. New York: Harper & Row, 1972.

Cambridge History of American Literature. New York: Macmillan, 1945.

Campbell, Lawrence. "Georges Hugnet at Zabriski." *Art in America*, November 1984, 162–63.

Cargill, Oscar. *Intellectual America*. New York: Macmillan, 1941.

Cerf, Bennett. *At Random: Reminiscences*. New York: Random House, 1971.

Chatterton, Wayne. *Alexander Woollcott*. Boston: Twayne, 1978.

Columbia Dictionary of Modern European Literature. New York: Columbia University Press, 1947.

Contemporary Authors: A Bio-Bibliographical Guide to Current Writers. vols. 61–64. Detroit: Gale, 1967–1980.

Craven, Wayne. *Sculpture in America*. New York: Crowell, 1968.

Current Biography. New York: Wilson, 1940–1980.

Danziger, Joseph, ed. *Beaton*. New York: Viking, 1980.

DeKoven, Marianne. *A Different Language: Gertrude Stein's Experimental Writing*. Madison: University of Wisconsin Press, 1983.

Derrida, Jacques. *Of Grammatology*, trans. Gayatri Chakravorty Spivak. Baltimore: Johns Hopkins University Press, 1974.

Dictionary of American Biography. New York: Scribners, 1928–1981.

Dictionary of Literary Biography 4, 5, 7, 9, 34, 36, 43. Detroit: Gale, 1978–1986.

Dydo, Ulla E. "How to Read Gertrude Stein: The Manuscript of 'Stanzas in Meditation.' " *Text: Transactions of the Society for Textual Scholarship* 1 (1981), 217–303.

———. "*Stanzas in Meditation*: The Other Autobiography." *Chicago Review* 35 (Winter 1985), 4–32.

———. "To Have the Winning Language: Texts and Contexts of Gertrude Stein." *Coming to Light: American Women Poets in the Twentieth Century*, ed. Diane Middlebrook and Marilyn Yalom. Ann Arbor: University of Michigan Press, 1985.

Edstrom, David. *The Testament of Caliban*. New York: Funk & Wagnalls, 1937.

Emanuel, Muriel, et al., eds., *Contemporary Artists*. New York: St. Martin's Press, 1983.

Everett, Patricia. "*Mabel Dodge: The Salon Years, 1912–1917*. New York: Barbara Mathes Gallery, 1985.

Fahlman, Betsy. *Pennsylvania Modern, Charles Demuth of Lancaster*. Philadelphia: Philadelphia Museum of Art, 1983.

Fanning, Michael. *France and Sherwood Anderson*. Baton Rouge: Louisiana State University Press, 1976.

Farnham, Emily. *Charles Demuth: Behind a Laughing Mask*. Norman: University of Oklahoma Press, 1971.

Fitch, Noel Reiley. *Sylvia Beach and the Lost Generation*. New York: Norton, 1983.

Ford, Hugh. *Published in Paris*. New York: Macmillan, 1975.

Four Americans in Paris. New York: Museum of Modern Art, 1970.

Frank, Waldo, et al., eds. *America and Alfred Stieglitz, A Collective Portrait*. New York: Literary Guild, 1934.

Froula, Christine. ''When Eve Reads Milton: Undoing the Canonical Economy.'' *Canons*, ed. Robert von Hallberg. Chicago: University of Chicago Press, 1983.

Galanes, Philip. ''Gertrude Stein: Letters to a Friend.'' *Paris Review* 100 (Summer-Fall 1986), 359–78.

Gallup, Donald, ed. *The Flowers of Friendship: Letters Written to Gertrude Stein*. New York: Knopf, 1953.

―――. ''Du Côté de Chez Stein.'' *Book Collector* 19 (Summer 1970), 169–84.

―――. ''Gertrude Stein and the *Atlantic*.'' *Yale University Library Gazette* 28 (January 1954), 109–28.

Gass, William H. Introduction to *The Geographical History of America* by Gertrude Stein. New York: Vintage, 1973.

―――. ''Thoroughly Modernist Intimacies.'' *The Times Literary Supplement*, 7 November 1986, 1236–37.

Gilman, Lawrence. *Orchestral Music: An Armchair Guide*. New York: Oxford University Press, 1951.

Glendinning, Victoria. *Edith Sitwell: A Unicorn among Lions*. New York: Knopf, 1981.

Glueck, Grace. ''Putting Rousseau in Perspective.'' *The New York Times Magazine*, 17 February 1985, 48.

Gregory, Horace, and Marya Zaturensky. *A History of American Poetry 1900–1940*. New York: Harcourt Brace, 1946.

Grosser, Maurice. *Painting in Public*. New York: Knopf, 1948.

Haas, Robert Bartlett, ed. *How Writing Is Written*. Vol. 2 of The Previously Uncollected Writings of Gertrude Stein. Los Angeles: Black Sparrow Press, 1973.

―――. *A Primer for the Gradual Understanding of Gertrude Stein*. Los Angeles: Black Sparrow Press, 1971.

―――. *Reflection on the Atomic Bomb*. Vol. 1 of The Previously Uncollected Writings of Gertrude Stein. Los Angeles: Black Sparrow Press, 1973.

Haas, Robert Bartlett, and Donald Clifford Gallup, compilers. *A Catalogue of the Published and Unpublished Writings of Gertrude Stein*. New Haven: Yale University Library, 1941.

Hall, Larry. ''A Van Vechten Pose.'' *Glasgow Newsletter* 17 (October 1982), 5–16; 18 (March 1983), 5–15.

Hanson, Harry. *Midwest Portraits*. New York: Harcourt Brace, 1923.

Hapgood, Hutchins. *A Victorian in the Modern World*. New York: Harcourt Brace, 1939.

Hart, James D. *Oxford Companion to American Literature*. New York: Oxford University Press, 1965.

Hart-Davis, Rupert, ed. *The Letters of Oscar Wilde*. New York: Harcourt Brace, 1962.

Hartley, Marsden. *Adventures in the Arts*. New York: Hacker, 1972.

Harvey, Sir Paul, and J. E. Heseltine, eds. *Oxford Companion to French Literature*. Oxford: Clarendon Press, 1959.

Haskell, Barbara. *Marsden Hartley*. New York: Whitney Museum of Art, 1980.

Hejinian, Lyn. "Two Stein Talks: Language and Realism, Grammar and Landscape." *Temblor* 3 (1986), 128–39.

Hemingway, Ernest. *A Moveable Feast*. New York: Scribner's, 1964.

Hobhouse, Janet. *Everybody Who Was Anybody*. New York: Putnam, 1975.

Hoffman, Frederick J. *The Little Magazine. A History and a Bibliography*. Princeton, N.J.: Princeton University Press, 1947.

Hollis, Cornwall [pseud. Donald Evans]. *The Art of Donald Evans*, privately printed, circa 1916.

Hoover, Kathleen, and John Cage. *Virgil Thomson: His Life and Music*. New York: Thomas Yoseloff, 1954.

Hunter, Samuel, ed. *Oxford Companion to Twentieth Century Art*. New York: Oxford University Press, 1981.

Imbs, Bravig. *Confessions of Another Young Man*. New York: Henkle-Yewdale, 1936.

James, Edward T., Janet T. James, and Paul S. Boyer, eds. *Notable American Women*. Cambridge, Mass.: Belknap Press, 1971.

Johnson, Una E. *Ambroise Vollard, Editeur*. New York: Museum of Modern Art, 1977.

Joyce, James. *A Portrait of the Artist as a Young Man*. Hammondsworth: Penguin, 1976.

Kamber, Gerald. *Max Jacob and the Poetics of Cubism*. Baltimore: Johns Hopkins University Press, 1971.

Katz, Leon. "The First Making of *The Making of Americans*: A Study Based on Gertude Stein's Notebooks and Early Versions of Her Novel (1902–08)." Unpublished dissertation, Columbia University, 1963.

Kellner, Bruce. *Carl Van Vechten and the Irreverent Decades*. Norman: University of Oklahoma Press, 1968.

———. *Friends and Mentors*. Richmond, Va.: University of Richmond Press, 1979.

———. "The Origin of The Origin of the Sonnets from the Patagonian by Carl Van Vechten." *Hartwick Review* 3 (Spring 1967), 50–56.

———, ed. *The Harlem Renaissance: A Historical Dictionary for the Era*. Westport, Conn.: Greenwood Press, 1984.

———. *Letters of Carl Van Vechten*. New Haven: Yale University Press, 1987.

Kenner, Hugh. *A Homemade World: The American Modernist Writers*. New York: Morrow, 1975.

Kirstein, Lincoln. *The Sculpture of Elie Nadelman*. New York: Museum of Modern Art, 1948.

Knoll, Robert E., ed. *McAlmon and the Lost Generation*. Lincoln: University of Nebraska Press, 1962.

Kostelanetz, Richard, ed. *The Yale Gertrude Stein*. New Haven: Yale University Press, 1980.

Kreymborg, Alfred. *Our Singing Strength*. New York: Coward McCann, 1929.

———. *Troubadour*. New York: Boni and Liveright, 1925.

Lehman, John. *A Nest of Tigers*. Boston: Little, Brown, 1968.

Leider, Emily. "A Tale of Two Gertrudes." *San Francisco Examiner & Chronicle*, 30 November 1980, 70–73.

Leinbaugh, Harold P., and John D. Campbell. *The Men of Company K: The Autobiography of a World War II Rifle Company*. New York: Morrow, 1985.

Levy, Harriet Lane. *920 O'Farrell Street*. New York: Doubleday, 1947.

————. "A Supper in Montmartre." *Bancroftiana* 91 (April 1986), 1–3.

Lewis, Wyndham. *Time and the Western Man*. New York: Harcourt Brace, 1928.

Lipchitz, Jacques. *My Life in Sculpture*. New York: Viking, 1972.

Loeb, Harold. *The Way It Was*. New York: Criterion, 1959.

Lowe, Sue Davidson. *Stieglitz; A Memoir/Biography*. New York: Farrar Straus & Giroux, 1983.

Loy, Mina. *The Last Lunar Baedeker*, ed. Roger Conover. New York: Jargon, 1982.

Luhan, Mabel Dodge. *European Experiences*. New York: Harcourt Brace, 1935.

————. *Movers and Shakers*. New York: Harcourt Brace, 1936.

McAlmon, Robert, and Kay Boyle. *Being Geniuses Together*. New York: Doubleday, 1968.

McBride, Henry. *The Flow of Art*, ed. Daniel Catton Rich. New York: Atheneum, 1975.

McDonald, Edgar. "Hunter Stagg." *Glasgow Newsletter* 15 (October 1981), 2–15.

Mackworth, Cecily. *Guillaume Apollinaire and the Cubist Life*. New York: Horizon, 1963.

McMillan, Dougald. *Transition 1927–38; The History of a Literary Era*. New York: Braziller, 1976.

Mainiero, Linda, ed. *American Women Writers*. New York: Ungar, 1979.

Mariani, Paul L. *William Carlos Williams; A New World Naked*. New York: McGraw-Hill, 1981.

Martin, John. "Isadora Duncan and the Basic Dance." *Isadora Duncan*, ed. Paul Magriel. New York: Holt, 1947.

Mellow, James R. *Charmed Circle: Gertrude Stein & Company*. New York: Praeger, 1974; Avon, 1975.

————. *Charmed Circle: Gertrude Stein and Company*. New York: Avon, 1975.

————. *Invented Lives: F. Scott and Zelda Fitzgerald*. Boston: Houghton Mifflin, 1984.

Metken, Günther. *Realismus: Zwischen Revolution und Reaktion 1919–1939*. Munich: Prestal Verlag, 1981.

Middlebrook, Diane, and Marilyn Yalom, eds. *Coming to Light: American Women Poets in the Twentieth Century*. Ann Arbor: University of Michigan Press, 1985.

Meyers, Bernard, ed. *McGraw-Hill Dictionary of Art*. New York: McGraw-Hill, 1969.

The New York Times, 1913–1958.

Osborne, Harold, ed. *Oxford Companion to Twentieth Century Art*. Oxford: Clarendon Press, 1981.

Padgette, Paul. "Sculpture Became Her Language," *Lost Generation Journal*, Fall 1975, 20–23.

————, ed. *Dance Photography of Carl Van Vechten*. New York: Schirmer, 1981.

Pearson, John. *The Sitwells; A Family Biography*. New York: Harcourt Brace, 1978.

Peterson, Elmer. *Tristan Tzara, Dada and Surrational Theorist*. New Brunswick; N.J.: Rutgers University Press, 1971.

Petteys, Chris. *An International Dictionary of Women Artists Before 1900*. Boston: G. K. Hall, 1982.

Phaidon Dictionary of Twentieth Century Art. New York: Phaidon, 1973.

Popkin, Debra, and Michael Popkin. *Modern French Literature*. New York: Ungar, 1971.

Pound, Ezra. *Selected Poems*. New York: New Directions, 1957.

Praeger, F. A. *Praeger Encyclopedia of Art*. New York: Praeger, 1971.

————. *Praeger Picture Encyclopedia of Art*. New York: Praeger, 1958.

Quinn, Arthur Hobson, ed. *Representative American Plays*. New York: Century, 1925.

Reader's Encyclopedia of American Literature. New York: Crowell, 1962.

Reid, B. L. *Art by Subtraction: A Dissenting Opinion of Gertrude Stein*. Norman: University of Oklahoma Press, 1958.

Riba-Rovira. New York: Passedoit Gallery, 1955.

Riding, Laura. *Contemporaries and Snobs*. London: Cape, 1928.

Rockwell, John. "Virgil Thomson's 'Saints' Goes Marching On." *The New York Times*, 9 November 1986, 2:1–2.

Rogers, W. G. *When This You See Remember Me; Gertrude Stein in Person*. New York: Rinehart, 1948.

————. *Wise Men Fish Here*. New York: Harcourt Brace, 1965.

Rose, B. "Art of Value." *Vogue*, March 1983, 372–75.

Rose, Sir Francis. *Saying Life*. London: Cassell, 1961.

Rosenshine, Annette. "Life's Not a Paragraph" (unpublished autobiography). Berkeley: Bancroft Library, University of California, circa 1960–1965.

Rubin, William, ed. *Picasso, a Retrospective*. New York: Museum of Modern Art, 1980.

Rudnick, Lois Palken. *Mabel Dodge Luhan: New Woman, New Worlds*. Albuquerque: University of New Mexico Press, 1984.

Russell, John, ed. *The World of Matisse*. New York: Time Life, 1969.

Sawyer, Julian. *Gertrude Stein: A Bibliography*. New York: Arrow, 1940.

Sedgwick, Ellery. *The Happy Profession*. Boston: Atlantic/Little, Brown, 1946.

Seligman, Edwin R. A., and Alvin Johnson, eds. *Encyclopedia of the Social Sciences*. New York: Macmillan, 1935.

Seymour-Smith, Martin. *Who's Who in Twentieth Century Literature*. New York: McGraw-Hill, 1976.

Sharrar, Jack Frederick. "Avery Hopwood, American Playwright," unpublished dissertation. University of Utah, 1984.

Shattuck, Roger. *The Banquet Years*. New York: Random House, 1968.

Sicherman, Barbara et al., eds. *Notable American Women: The Modern Period*. Cambridge, Mass: Belknap Press, 1980.

Simon, Linda. *The Biography of Alice B. Toklas*. New York: Doubleday, 1977.

————, ed. *Gertrude Stein: A Composite Portrait*. New York: Avon, 1974.

Sitwell, Edith. *Taken Care Of*. New York: Atheneum, 1965.

Sitwell, Osbert. *Left Hand, Right Hand*. Boston: Atlantic-Little Brown, 1945.

Sprigge, Elizabeth. *Gertrude Stein: Her Life and Work*. New York: Harper, 1957.

Steegmuller, Francis. *Apollinaire, Poet among the Painters*. New York: Farrar Straus, 1963.

Stein, Bobbie. "One for the Books." *People*, 26 January 1987, 90.

Stein, Gertrude. [For an alphabetical listing of all of Gertrude Stein's published books as well as relevant ephemera, with full publication information—all of which have been both cited and consulted for this volume—the reader is referred to Part I, Ex Libris section.]

Stein, Leo. *The ABC of Aesthetics*. New York: Boni & Liveright, 1927.

————. *Appreciation: Painting, Poetry and Prose*. New York: Crown, 1947.

————. *Journey into the Self: Being the Letters, Papers & Journals of Leo Stein*, ed. Edmund Fuller. New York: Crown, 1950.

Steiner, Wendy. *Exact Resemblance to Exact Resemblance: The Literary Portraiture of Gertrude Stein*. New Haven: Yale University Press, 1978.

Steloff, Frances. "In Touch with Genius." *Journal of Modern Literature* 4 (April 1975), 749–883.

———. "The Making of an American Visit: Gertrude Stein." *Confrontation* 8 (Spring 1974), 9–18.

Sterne, Maurice. *Shadow and Light*. New York: Harcourt Brace, 1965.

Steward, Samuel M. *Dear Sammy: Letters from Gertrude Stein and Alice B. Toklas*. Boston: Houghton Mifflin, 1977.

Stewart, Allegra. *Gertrude Stein and the Present*. Cambridge: Harvard University Press, 1967.

Sutherland, Donald. *Gertrude Stein: A Biography of Her Work*. New Haven: Yale University Press, 1951.

Talvart, Hector, and Joseph Place, eds. *Bibliographie des auteurs modernes de langue française*. Paris: Editions de la Chronique, 1937.

"Testimony against Gertrude Stein." *transition* supplement, February 1935.

Thomson, Virgil. *Virgil Thomson*. New York: Knopf, 1966.

Thrall, William Flint, and Addison Hibbard. *A Handbook to Literature*. New York: Odyssey, 1963.

Time, 1944–1987.

Toklas, Alice B. *The Alice B. Toklas Cook Book*. New York: Harper, 1954.

———. *What Is Remembered*. New York: Holt, Rinehart and Winston, 1963.

Trent, William P., et al., eds. *Cambridge History of American Literature*. New York: Putnam, 1947.

Tyler, Parker. *Florine Stettheimer: A Life in Art*. New York: Farrar Straus, 1963.

Van Vechten, Carl. "An Artist Cook." *The Reviewer* 3 (October 1922), 637.

———. *Excavations*. New York: Knopf, 1926.

———. *The Merry Go Round*. New York: Knopf, 1918.

———. "More Laurels for our Gertrude." *Gertrude Stein Catalogue 1964*. New York: Gotham Book Mart, 1964.

———. *Peter Whiffle: His Life and Works*. New York: Knopf, 1922.

———. *Red*. New York: Knopf, 1925.

———, ed. *Selected Writings of Gertrude Stein*. New York: Random House, 1946; Modern Library, 1962; Vintage, 1972.

Verplank, Laura. Letter to Margaret Woodbridge, 24 February 1987.

Vinson, James, ed. *American Writers since 1900*. London: St. James Press, 1983.

———. *Great Writers of the English Language*. London: St. James Press, 1981.

Vollard, Ambroise. *Recollections of a Picture Dealer*. Boston: Little, Brown, 1978.

Vollmer, Hans, ed. *Allgemeines Lexikon der Bildenden Kunstler des XX Jahrhunderts*. Leipzig: Seeman, 1956.

Walsh, George, et al., eds. *Contemporary Photographers*. New York: St. Martin's Press, 1982.

Warfel, Harry R. *American Novelists of Today*. New York: American Book, 1951.

White, Ray Lewis. *Gertrude Stein and Alice B. Toklas; A Reference Guide*. Boston: G K. Hall, 1984.

———, ed. *Sherwood Anderson/Gertrude Stein: Correspondence and Personal Essays*. Chapel Hill: University of North Carolina Press, 1972.

Who's Who 1973. London: Black, 1974.

Who's Who in America, Chicago: Marquis, 1930–1981.

Who Was Who in America. New York: Marquis, 1943–1968.

Who Was Who. London: Black, 1981.

Who Was Who among North American Authors, 1921–1939. Detroit: Gale, 1976.

Who Was Who in American Art. Madison, Conn.: Soundview, 1984.

Wickes, George. *The Amazon of Letters: The Life and Loves of Natalie Clifford Barney*. New York: Putnam, 1976.

Wilde, Oscar. *The Letters of Oscar Wilde*, Rupert Hart-Davis, ed. New York: Harcourt Brace, 1962.

Wilder, Thornton. *Journals*, ed. Donald Gallup. New Haven: Yale University Press, 1985.

———. "Introduction" to *Four in America* by Gertrude Stein. New Haven: Yale University Press, 1947.

Wilson, Edmund. *Axel's Castle*. New York: Scribner's, 1959.

———. *The Shores of Light*. New York: Farrar Straus & Young, 1952.

Wilson, Robert A. *Gertrude Stein: A Bibliography of Her Work*. New York: Phoenix Bookshop, 1974.

Windham, Donald. *Tanaquil*. New York: Holt, Rinehart & Winston, 1977.

Woollcott, Alexander. *The Portable Woollcott*. New York: Viking, 1946.

Wright, Richard. *Black Boy*. Cleveland: World, 1950.

INDEX

Page numbers in bold-face indicate the location of a main entry; page numbers in italic indicate substantive quotations from Gertrude Stein's writings.

NOTES ON CONTRIBUTORS

BRUCE KELLNER is Professor of English at Millersville University in Pennsylvania. Among his books are *Letters of Carl Van Vechten* (1987), *The Harlem Renaissance: A Historical Dictionary for the Era* (1984), and *Carl Van Vechten and the Irreverent Decades* (1968). He has written articles and essays on many other early modern literary figures and movements, including Gertrude Stein and her circle.

WILLIAM ALFRED. See "Friends and Enememies," page 140.

SHIRLEY ANDERS won the Devins Award in 1986 for her book of poems, *The Bus Home*, and she has published a Palamon Press chapbook of her work. She has been Visiting Writer in Residence at the University of North Carolina, at Greensboro, and taught composition and poetry at Guilford College there. She is now teaching at Lawrenceville University in Wisconsin.

MARIANNE DeKOVEN is the author of *A Different Language: Gertrude Stein's Experimental Writing* (1983). She teaches in the English Department at Rutgers University. She has published articles—some about Gertrude Stein's work—in several scholarly journals and collections, and presently she is writing a book about gender and modernism.

ULLA DYDO has taught at Vassar College, Brooklyn College, and currently at Bronx Community College of the City University of New York. She has published many papers about Gertrude Stein's work, and she is completing a book about the 1923–1932 decade when Stein began systematically to examine her own writing. Her study is based entirely on manuscripts and other archival materials heretofore unexamined.

LINDLEY WILLIAMS HUBBELL. See "Friends and Enemies," page 206.

MINA LOY. See "Friends and Enemies," page 219.

VASSAR MILLER has published several volumes of her poetry, including *Struggling to Swim on Concrete* (1984) and *If I Could Sleep Deeply Enough* (1974), and she has edited *Despite This Flesh* (1985), an anthology of literature about people with handicaps. One of her earlier collections, *Wage War on Silence* (1961), was nominated for the Pulitzer Prize. She has taught creative writing at St. John's Academy in Houston, Texas.

PRISCILLA OPPENHEIMER is a freelance writer and lecturer in Lancaster, Pennsylvania. Her poetry has been published in *The Christian Science Monitor*, and she was a contributor to *The Harlem Renaissance: A Historical Dictionary for the Era* (1984).

PAUL PADGETTE has been a bookseller in San Francisco for over twenty years. Earlier he worked as an editor and writer for several trade journals. He edited Carl Van Vechten's *Dance Writings* (1974) and *Dance Photography* (1981). As a bibliophile he collects writers from the twenties, including Gertrude Stein.

MARJORIE PERLOFF has written books on W. B. Yeats, Robert Lowell, and Frank O'Hara, as well as *The Futurist Movement: Avant-Garde, Avant-Guerre, and the Language of Rupture* (1986), *The Dance of the Intellect: Studies of the Poetry of the Pound Tradition* (1985), and *The Poetics of Interdeterminancy: Rimbaud to Cage* (1981). She is Professor of English and Comparative Literature at Stanford University.

TOM SMITH is Professor English at Castleton State College in Vermont and author of four volumes of poems including *Mummer's Echo* (1988), *Traffic* (1984), and *Singing in the Middle Ages* (1982). His work has appeared in a number of literary quarterlies since 1959 when as a college student he wrote his poem about Gertrude Stein.

SARAH WHITE has published poetry in *The Massachusetts Review* and prose in *The Village Voice*, and elsewhere as well. She has written libretti for two operas by John Carbon and is at work on a third. She is Associate Professor of French and Italian at Franklin and Marshall College in Lancaster, Pennsylvania.

MARGARET WOODBRIDGE is Associate Professor Emerita of English at Millersville University in Pennsylvania where she taught courses in Chaucer, Irish literature, and drama. She is now a freelance writer and lecturer and has published articles on Charles Demuth and his family.